VATICAN COUNCIL II

For my friends and co-workers
Kathleen O'Connor,
Michael Glazier
and Harry Costello

THE BASIC SIXTEEN DOCUMENTS

VATICAN COUNCIL II

CONSTITUTIONS
DECREES
DECLARATIONS

A Completely Revised Translation
in Inclusive Language

GENERAL EDITOR

AUSTIN FLANNERY, O.P.

 COSTELLO PUBLISHING COMPANY
Northport, New York

DOMINICAN PUBLICATIONS
Dublin, Ireland

Nihil Obstat: Rev. Francis J. Schneider, J.C.D.
Censor librorum
September 6th, 1995

Imprimatur: Most Reverend John R. McGann, D.D.
Bishop of Rockville Centre
November 7th, 1995

Vatican Collection
The Basic Volume

VATICAN COUNCIL II
THE BASIC SIXTEEN DOCUMENTS

First printing, April 1996

Library of Congress Catalog Card Number: 96-83820

International Standard Book Number: 0-918344-37-9 (Costello)
1-871552-53-2 (Dominican)

Printed in the United States of America

Costello Publishing Company, Inc.   Dominican Publications
P.O. Box 9   42 Parnell Square
Northport, New York 11768   Dublin 1, Ireland

Table of Contents

Latin Titles of Council Documents

Each council document has two Latin titles. One of these is made up of the first two or three words of the document's Latin original, the other being its descriptive title — eg *Constitutio Dogmatica de Ecclesia:* The Dogmatic Constitution on the Church. English authors usually use the English version of a document's descriptive title, or a shortened version of it. However, "The Pastoral Constitution on the Church in the Modern World" is frequently given the title *Gaudium et spes*, the first words of the Latin original, as is "The Decree on the Up-to-date Renewal of Religious Life" *(Perfectae caritatis).* "The Dogmatic Constitution on the Church," however, is sometimes referred to as *Lumen gentium*, sometimes as *De Ecclesia.*

Ad gentes divinitus: Decree on the Church's Missionary Activity.

Apostolicam actuositatem: Decree on the Apostolate of the Laity.

Christus Dominus: Decree on the Pastoral Office of Bishops in the Church.

Constitutio de Sacra Liturgia, Constitution on the Sacred Liturgy: see *Sacrosanctum Concilium.*

Constitutio Dogmatica de Divina Revelatione, Dogmatic Constitution on Divine Revelation: see *Dei verbum.*

Constitutio Dogmatica de Ecclesia, Dogmatic Constitution on the Church: see *Lumen gentium.*

Constitutio Pastoralis de Ecclesia in Mundo huius Temporis, Pastoral Constitution on the Church in the Modern World: see *Gaudium et spes.*

Declaratio de Ecclesiae Habitudine ad Religiones Non-Christianas, Declaration on the Relation of the Church to non-Christian Religions: see *Nostra aetate.*

Declaratio de Educatione Christiana, Decree on Christian Education: see *Gravissimum educationis.*

Declaratio de Libertate Religiosa, Declaration on Religious Liberty: see *Dignitatis humanae.*

Decretum de Accomodata Renovatione Vitae Religiosae, Decree on the Up-do-date Renewal of Religious Life: see *Perfectae caritatis.*

Decretum de Activitate Missionali Ecclesiae, Decree on the Church's Missionary Activity: see *Ad gentes divinitus.*

Decretum de Apostolatu Laicorum, Decree on the Apostolate of Lay People: see *Apostolicam actuositatem.*

Decretum de Ecclesiis Orientalibus Catholicis, Decree on the Catholic Eastern Churches: see *Orientalium Ecclesiarum.*

Decretum de Instrumentis Communicationis Socialis, Decree on the Mass Media: see *Inter mirifica.*

Decretum de Oecumenismo, Decree on Ecumenism: see *Unitatis redintegratio.*

Decretum de Pastorali Episcoporum Munere in Ecclesia, Decree on the Pastoral Office of Bishops in the Church: see *Christus Dominus.*

Decretum de Presbyterorum Ministerio et Vita, Decree on the Ministry and Life of Priests: see *Presbyterorum ordinis.*

Dei verbum: Dogmatic Constitution on Divine Revelation.

Dignitatis humanae: Declaration on Religious Liberty.

Gaudium et spes: Pastoral Constitution on the Church in the Modern World.

Gravissimum educationis: Declaration on Christian Education.

Inter mirifica: Decree on the Mass Media.

Lumen gentium: Dogmatic Constitution on the Church.

Nostra aetate: Declaration on the Church's Relations with non-christian religions.

Optatam totius: Decree on the Training of Priests.

Orientalium Ecclesiarum: Decree on the Catholic Eastern Churches.

Perfectae caritatis: Decree on the Up-to-date Renewal of Religious Life.

Presbyterorum ordinis: Decree on the Life and Ministry of Priests.

Sacrosanctum Concilium: Constitution on the Sacred Liturgy.

Unitatis redintegratio: Decree on Ecumenism.

Abbreviations

AA   *Apostolicam actuositatem:* Decree on the Apostolate of the Laity.

AAS   *Acta Apostolicae Sedis:* the Vatican gazette, carries the original text (mostly Latin) of the more important official Vatican documents.

Abbott   *The Documents of Vatican II,* edited by Walter Abbott, New York and London, 1966.

AGD   *Ad gentes divinitus:* Decree on the Church's Missionary Activity.

ASS   *Acta Sanctae Sedis:* the name of the Vatican gazette (see AAS) up to 1 January, 1909.

CChr   *Corpus Christianorum,* Turnhout, 1953-.

CD   *Christus Dominus:* Decree on the Pastoral Office of Bishops in the Church.

CT   *Concilium Tridentinum. Diariorum, actorum, epistularum, tractatuum nova collectio,* ed. Goerresian Society, Freiburg, 1901-.

CIC   *Codex Juris Canonici,* Rome, 1917.

CSEL   *Corpus Scriptorum Ecclesiasticorum Latinorum,* Vienna, 1866-.

Denz.   H. Denzinger and A. Schönmetzer, *Enchiridion Symbolorum, definitionum et declarationum de rebus fidei et morum,* Barcelona and Freiburg, 1965.

DH   *Dignitatis humanae:* Declaration on Religious Liberty.

DV   *Dei verbum:* Dogmatic Constitution on Divine Revelation.

Funk   F. X. Funk, *Patres Apostolici,* two volumes, Tübingen, 1901.

GCS   *Die Griechischen Christlichen Schriftseller der ersten Jahrhunderte,* Leipzig and Berlin, 1897-.

GE   *Gravissimum educationis:* Declaration on Christian Education.

GS	*Gaudium et spes:* Pastoral Constitution on the Church in the Modern World.
IM	*Inter mirifica:* Decree on the Media of Communication.
LG	*Lumen gentium:* Dogmatic Constitution on the Church.
Mansi	J. D. Mansi, *Sacrorum conciliorum nova et amplissima collectio* L. Petit and J. B. Martin, 60 volumes, 1899-1927.
NA	*Nostra aetate:* Declaration on the Church's Relations with non-christian religions.
OE	*Orientalium ecclesiarum:* Decree on the Catholic Eastern Churches.
OT	*Optatam totius:* Decree on the Training of Priests.
PC	*Perfectae caritatis:* Decree on the Up-to-date Renewal of Religious Life.
PG	J. P. Migne, editor, *Patrologia Graeca,* 161 volumes, Paris, 1857-66.
PL	J. P. Migne, editor, Patrologia Latina, 217 volumes and 4 volumes of indices, Paris, 1878-90.
PO	*Presbyterorum ordinis:* Decree on the Life and Ministry of Priests.
SC	*Sacrosanctum concilium:* Constitution on the Sacred Liturgy.
SCh	H. de Lubac and J. Danielou, editors, *Sources Chrétiennes,* Paris, 1942-.
Tanner	Decrees of the Ecumenical Councils, volume II, Trent and Vatican II, edited by Norman Tanner, SJ, London and Washington, 1990.
UR	*Unitatis redintegratio:* Decree on Ecumenism.
Vatican Collection	Volume I, *Vatican II: Conciliar and Post-Conciliar Documents,* edited by Austin Flannery, OP, Dublin, Northport, Collegeville, Chicago and Grand Rapids.
Vorgrimler	*Commentary on the Documents of Vatican II,* edited by Herbert Vorgrimler, 5 volumes, London, 1967.

Introduction

The first session of Vatican Council II was held in Saint Peter's basilica, Rome, on 11 October, 1962. It was attended by some 2,450 churchmen, out of a total of 2,908 who were entitled to attend. Some bishops were too old or too infirm to attend, and the majority of bishops in Communist countries were refused permission to travel, though restrictions were somewhat eased for subsequent sessions.

The other christian churches had been invited to send "observers", who would be free to attend all sessions, but not to speak or to vote. Thirty-five observers from other christian churches attended the first session and their numbers increased in subsequent sessions.

The work of the council was spread over four years, about ten weeks being devoted to it in the autumn months of 1962, 1963, 1964 and 1965, with a great deal of work being done each year in the intervening periods by the various conciliar commissions.

1995 marked the thirtieth anniversary of the closing of the Vatican council. It seemed an appropriate time to publish this volume devoted exclusively to the sixteen conciliar texts. In fact, the suggestion that I publish the sixteen council documents on their own was first put to me a few years ago by Father Richard McCullen, CM, who was then Superior General of the Vincentians.

When we published the sixteen conciliar texts twenty years ago, in 1975, they were accompanied by many other official Vatican texts, rightly entitled "postconciliar" texts, since so many of them spelled out the manner in which a number of the conciliar texts were to be implemented.

We will continue to publish that first volume, which has already gone through several editions: *Vatican II: Conciliar and Post-conciliar Documents*, and also its companion volume, Vatican II: *More Post Conciliar Documents*. They are, respectively, volumes 1 and 2 in the series "Vatican Collection". Two other volumes (at least) are in preparation. The first of these (volume three in the series "Vatican Collection") will contain all major papal documents from the time of John XXIII and not already included in the first two volumes, while the second will carry on from where volume three of Vatican Collection leaves off.

The translation of the text of the Vatican documents in the present volume differs from that in the previous publication in two respects. It has been very considerably revised and, in places, corrected. It is also, to a very large extent, in inclusive language.

I say 'to a very large extent', because we have used inclusive language in passages about men and women, but not however in passages about God, except where the use of the masculine pronoun was easily avoidable.

Concern about exclusive language has grown very much since Vatican II, a concern now shared by many men as well as women. My co-workers and I have done our best to render the documents in inclusive language, on the horizontal level, as it were. This is sometimes done by translating *homines*, for example, as "men and women", *filii*, as "sons and daughters", *fratres*, as "brothers and sisters". Naturally, one does this only where it is clear that the text has women in mind, as well as men. This is the case in the majority of passages and in fact there are many passages where it would be heretical to deny that they apply to women too, as with the phrase in the second paragraph of the Dogmatic Constitution on the Church: "The eternal Father ... chose to raise up men to share in his divine life. "To add"and women" after the word "men" in that phrase is not to change its meaning but to put it beyond dispute.

A similar procedure was adopted where, for example, the Latin original uses the word *homo* in the collective sense, this is usually rendered as "men and women". To sum up: wherever a document clearly means both women and men, while using words such as man and mankind, laymen, sons, brothers, fraternal, we have used words which make the document's meaning clear.

We have done our best to make the translation as accurate as possible, but I know from experience that mistakes can occur. *Quod potest deficere, aliquando deficit.* Readers who detect erroneous or debatable renderings would render a service if they bring them to my attention — address below.

However, it has to be accepted that there will be no pleasing everybody, for the simple reason that there are words and phrases — less important words and phrases — which, quite legitimately, can be rendered in different ways.

The following is a phrase from the *Church in the Modern World* (no 36): *"per oblivionem Dei ipsa creatura obscuratur."* In this volume, it is rendered: "once God is forgotten, the creature itself is left in darkness." Our other edition has: "once God is forgotten, the creature is lost sight of as well." Tanner has "if God is ignored, the creature is impoverished." An Italian version has *"l'oblio di Dio priva di luce la creatura stessa:* forgetfulness of God deprives the creature itself of light." A French version has *"l'oubli de Dieu rend opaque la créature elle-même:* forgetfulness of God renders the creature itself opaque."

The official text of the council documents is in:

*Sacrosanctum Oecumenicum Concilium Vaticanum II:
Constitutiones, Decreta, Declarationes,* Vatican, 1966. Of
other English translation there is that contained in
the excellent *Decrees of the Ecumenical Councils:* volume II (Trent-Vatican II), edited by Norman P. Tanner,
SJ, (Latin and English on facing pages), London and
Washington, 1990 and (the first in the field) *The
Documents of Vatican II,* edited by Walter Abbott, New
York and London, 1966.

I have compared notes with both Tanner and
Abbott, with the French version *Concile Oecuménique
Vatican II: Constitutions, Décrets, Déclarations, Messages,* Paris, 1967, and with the Italian in *Enchiridion
Vaticanum,* volume 1, *Documenti Ufficiali del Concilio
Vaticano II: 1962-1965.* Both versions carry the Latin
original as well.

For a short account of the proceedings at Vatican II,
see my "Vatican Council II", in *The Modern Catholic
Encyclopedia,* Collegeville and Dublin, 1994.

AUSTIN FLANNERY, OP
42 Parnell Square
Dublin 1, Ireland.

DOGMATIC CONSTITUTION ON THE CHURCH

Lumen Gentium
21 November, 1964

Chapter I[a]

THE MYSTERY OF THE CHURCH

1. Christ is the light of the nations and consequently this holy synod, gathered together in the holy Spirit, ardently desires to bring to all humanity that light of Christ which is resplendent on the face of the church, by proclaiming his Gospel to every creature (see Mk 16:15). Since the church, in Christ, is a sacrament—a sign and instrument, that is, of communion with God and of the unity of the entire human race — it here proposes, for the benefit of the faithful and of the entire world, to describe more clearly, and in the tradition laid down by earlier council, its own nature and universal mission. The present situation lends greater urgency to this duty of the church, so that all people, who nowadays are drawn ever more closely together by social, technical and cultural bonds, may achieve full unity in Christ.

2. The eternal Father, in accordance with the utterly free and mysterious design of his wisdom and goodness, created the entire universe. He chose to raise up men and women to share in his own divine life; and when they had fallen in Adam, he did not

abandon them, but at all times offered them the
means of salvation, bestowed in consideration of
Christ, the Redeemer, "who is the image of the invisible God, the firstborn of all creation" (Col 1:15). All
those chosen, the Father "foreknew" before time began "and also predestined to become conformed to
the image of his Son that he should be the firstborn
of a large family" (Rom 8:29). He determined to call
together in the holy church those who believe in
Christ. Already prefigured at the beginning of the
world, this church was prepared in marvellous fashion in the history of the people of Israel and in the
ancient alliance.[1] Established in this last age of the
world, and made manifest in the outpouring of the
Spirit, it will be brought to glorious completion at the
end of time. At that moment, as the Fathers put it, all
the just from the time of Adam, "from Abel, the just
one, to the last of the elect"[2] will be gathered together with the Father in the universal church.

3. The Son, accordingly, came, sent by the Father,
who before the foundation of the world chose us and
predestined us in him to be his adopted sons and
daughters. For it is in him that it pleased the Father to
restore all things (see Eph 1: 4-5 and 10). To carry out
the will of the Father, Christ inaugurated the kingdom
of heaven on earth and revealed his mystery to us; by
his obedience he brought about the redemption. The
church—that is, the kingdom of Christ already present in mystery — grows visibly in the world through
the power of God. The origin and growth of the
church are symbolized by the blood and water which
issued from the open side of the crucified Jesus (see
Jn 19:34), and were foretold in the words of the Lord
referring to his death on the cross: "And I, if I be lifted
up from the earth, will draw all people to myself" (Jn
12:32; Greek text). As often as the sacrifice of the cross
by which "Christ our Pasch is sacrificed" (1 Cor 5:7) is

celebrated on the altar, the work of our redemption is carried out. Likewise, in the sacrament of the Eucharistic bread, the unity of believers, who form one body in Christ (see 1 Cor 10:17), is both expressed and achieved. All are called to this union with Christ, who is the light of the world, from whom we come, through whom we live, and towards whom we direct our lives.

4. When the work which the Father gave the Son to do on earth (see Jn 17:4) was completed, the holy Spirit was sent on the day of Pentecost to sanctify the church continually and so that believers might have access to the Father through Christ in the one Spirit (see Eph 2:18). This is the Spirit of life, the fountain of water springing up to eternal life (see Jn 4:14; 7:38-39), through whom the Father gives life to human beings dead in sin, until the day when, in Christ, he raises to life their mortal bodies (see Rom 8:10-11). The Spirit dwells in the church and in the hearts of the faithful, as in a temple (see 1 Cor 3:16; 6:19), prays and bears witness in them that they are his adopted children (see Gal 4:6; Rom 8:15-16 and 26). He guides the church in the way of all truth (see Jn 16:13) and, uniting it in fellowship and ministry, bestows upon it different hierarchic and charismatic gifts, and in this way directs it and adorns it with his fruits (see Eph 4 11-12; 1 Cor 12:4; Gal 5:22). By the power of the Gospel he rejuvenates the church, constantly renewing it and leading it to perfect union with its spouse.[3] For the Spirit and the Bride both say to Jesus, the Lord, Come! (see Apoc 22:17). Hence the universal church is seen to be "a people made one by the unity of the Father, the Son and the holy Spirit."[4]

5. The mystery of the holy church is already brought to light in the manner of its foundation. For the Lord Jesus inaugurated his church by preaching the good news of the coming of the kingdom of God,

promised over the ages in the scriptures: "The time is fulfilled, and the kingdom of God is at hand" (Mk 1:15; see Mt 4:17). This kingdom shines out before humanity in the words, the works and the presence of Christ. The word of the Lord is compared to a seed which is sown in a field (see Mk 4:14); those who hear the word with faith and form part of the little flock of Christ (see Lk 12:32) have received the kingdom itself. Then, by its own power the seed sprouts and grows until the harvest (see Mk 4:26-29). The miracles of Jesus also demonstrate that the kingdom has already come on earth: "If I cast out devils by the finger of God, then the kingdom of God has come upon you" (Lk 11:20; see Mt 12:28). But principally the kingdom is revealed in the person of Christ himself, Son of God and Son of Man, who came "to serve and to give his life as a ransom for many" (Mk 10:45).

When Jesus, having died on the cross for humanity, rose again from the dead, he appeared as Lord, Christ, and priest established for ever (see Acts 2:36; Heb 5:6; 7:17-21), and he poured out on his disciples the Spirit promised by the Father (see Acts 2:23). Henceforward the church, equipped with the gifts of its founder and faithfully observing his precepts of charity, humility and self-denial, receives the mission of proclaiming and establishing among all peoples the kingdom of Christ and of God, and is, on earth, the seed and the beginning of that kingdom. While it slowly grows to maturity, the church longs for the completed kingdom and, with all its strength, hopes and desires to be united in glory with its king.

6. In the Old Testament symbols are often used to convey the revelation of the kingdom and similarly the inner nature of the church is now made known to us in various images. Taken either from pastoral life, agriculture, construction work, or from family life and betrothal, these images are prepared in the books of

the prophets.

The church is, accordingly, a *sheepfold,* the sole and necessary entrance to which is Christ (see Jn 10:1-10). It is also a flock, of which God foretold that he would himself be the shepherd (see Is 40:11; Ez 34:11 ff.), and whose sheep, although watched over by human shepherds, are nevertheless at all times led and brought to pasture by Christ himself, the Good Shepherd and prince of shepherds (see Jn 10:11; 1 Pet 5:4), who gave his life for his sheep (see Jn 10:11-15).

The church is God's *farm* or field (see 1 Cor 3:9). In this field the ancient olive tree grows whose holy root were the patriarchs and in which the reconciliation of Jews and Gentiles has been achieved and will continue to be achieved (see Rom 11:13-16). The church has been planted by the heavenly farmer as a choice vineyard (see Mt 21:33-43 and parallels; Is 5:1 ff.). The true vine is Christ who gives life and fruitfulness to the branches, that is, to us, who through the church abide in Christ without whom we can do nothing (see Jn 15:1-5).

Often, too, the church is called God's *building* (see 1 Cor 3:9). The Lord compared himself to the stone which the builders rejected, but which was made into the cornerstone (see Mt 21:42 and parallels; Acts 4:11; 1 Pet 2:7; Ps 117:22). On this foundation the church is built by the apostles (see 1 Cor 3:11) and from this it receives stability and cohesion. This edifice is given various names: the house of God (see 1 Tim 3:15) in which his family lives; the household of God in the Spirit (see Eph 2:19-22); "the dwelling-place of God among mortals" (Apoc 21:3); and, especially, the holy *temple.* This temple, represented in sanctuaries built of stone, is praised by the Fathers and is rightly compared in the liturgy to the holy city, the new Jerusalem.[5] As living stones we here on earth are built into it (see 1 Pet 2:5). It is this holy city which John contemplates as it comes down out of heaven from God when the world is made anew, "prepared like a bride adorned for her husband" (Apoc 21:1 f.).

Moreover, the church which is called "that Jerusalem which is above" and "our mother" (Gal 4:26; see Apoc 12:17), is described as the spotless *spouse* of the spotless lamb (Apoc 19:7; 21:2 and 9; 22:17), whom Christ "loved . . . and for whom he delivered himself up that he might sanctify her" (Eph 5:26). It is the church which he unites to himself by an unbreakable alliance, and which he constantly "nourishes and cherishes" (Eph 5:29). It is the church which, once purified, he willed to be joined to himself, subject in love and fidelity (see Eph 5:24), and which, finally, he filled with heavenly gifts for all eternity, in order that we may know the love of God and of Christ for us, a love which surpasses all understanding (see Eph 3:19). While on earth it journeys in a foreign land away from the Lord (see 2 Cor 5:6), the church sees itself as an exile. It seeks and is concerned about those things which are above, where Christ is seated at the right hand of God, where the life of the church is hidden with Christ in God until it appears in glory with its Spouse (see Col 3:1-4).

7. In the human nature united to himself, the son of God, by overcoming death through his own death and resurrection, redeemed humanity and changed it into a new creation (see Gal 6:15; 2 Cor 5:17). For by communicating his Spirit, Christ mystically constitutes as his body his brothers and sisters who are called together from every nation.

In this body the life of Christ is communicated to those who believe and who, through the sacraments, are united in a hidden and real way to Christ in his passion and glorification.[6] Through Baptism we are formed in the likeness of Christ: "For in one Spirit we were all baptized into one body" (1 Cor 12:13). In this sacred rite our union with Christ's death and resurrection is symbolized and effected: "For we were buried with him by Baptism into death"; and if "we have been united with him in the likeness of his death, we shall be so in the likeness of his resurrection also" (Rom 6:4-5). Really sharing in the body of the Lord in the breaking of the Eucharistic bread, we are taken up into communion with him and with one another. "Because the bread is one, we, though many, are one body, all of us who partake of the one bread" (1 Cor 10:17). In this way all of us are made members of his body (see 1 Cor 12:27), "individually members one of another" (Rom 12:5).

As all the members of the human body, though they are many, form one body, so also do the faithful in Christ (see 1 Cor 12:12). A diversity of members and functions is engaged in the building up of Christ's body, too. There is only one Spirit who, out of his own richness and the needs of the ministries, gives his various gifts for the welfare of the church (see 1 Cor 12:1-11). Among these gifts the primacy belongs to the grace of the apostles to whose authority the Spirit subjects even those who are endowed with charisms (see 1 Cor 14). The same Spirit who of himself is the principle of unity in the body, by his own power and by the interior cohesion of the members produces and stimulates love among the faithful. From this it follows that if one member suffers in any way, all the members suffer, and if one member is honored, all the members together rejoice (see 1 Cor 12:26).

The head of this body is Christ. He is the image of the invisible God and in him all things came into being. He is before all creatures and in him all things hold together. He is the head of the body which is the church. He is the beginning, the firstborn from the dead, that in all things he might hold the primacy (see

Col 1:15-18). By the magnitude of his power he rules heaven and earth, and with his all-surpassing perfection and activity he fills the whole body with the riches of his glory (see Eph 1:18-23).[7]

All the members must be formed in his likeness, until Christ is formed in them (see Gal 4:19). For this reason we, who have been made like to him, who have died with him and risen with him, are taken up into the mysteries of his life, until we reign together with him (see Phil 3:21; 2 Tim 2:11; Eph 2:6; Col 2:12, etc.). On earth, still as pilgrims in a strange land, following in trial and in oppression the paths he trod, we are associated with his sufferings as the body with its head, suffering with him, that with him we may be glorified (see Rom 8:17).

From him "the whole body, supplied and built up by joints and ligaments, attains a growth that is of God" (Col 2:19). He constantly makes available in his body, which is the church, gifts of ministries through which, by his power, we provide each other with the helps needed for salvation so that, doing the truth in love, we may in all things grow into him who is our head (see Eph 4:11-16, Greek.).

In order that we might be unceasingly renewed in him (see Eph 4:23), he has shared with us his Spirit who, being one and the same in head and members, gives life to, unifies and moves the whole body. Consequently, his work could be compared by the Fathers of the church to the function that the principle of life, the soul, fulfills in the human body.[8]

Christ loves the church as his bride, making himself the model of a man loving his wife as his own body (see Eph 5:25-28); the church, in its turn, is subject to its head (Eph 5:23-24). "Because in him dwells all the fullness of the Godhead bodily" (Col 2:9), he fills the church, which is his body and his fullness, with his divine gifts (see Eph 1:22-23) so that it may increase and attain to all the fullness of God (see Eph 3:19).

8. The one mediator, Christ, established and constantly sustains here on earth his holy church, the community of faith, hope and charity, as a visible structure[9] through which he communicates truth and grace to everyone. But, the society equipped with hierarchical structures and the mystical body of Christ, the visible society and the spiritual community, the earthly church and the church endowed with heavenly riches, are not to be thought of as two realities. On the contrary, they form one complex reality comprising a human and a divine element.[10] For this reason the church is compared, in no mean analogy, to the mystery of the incarnate Word. As the assumed nature, inseparably united to him, serves the divine Word as a living instrument of salvation, so, in somewhat similar fashion, does the social structure of the church serve the Spirit of Christ who vivifies it, in the building up of the body (see Eph 4:16).[11]

This is the unique church of Christ which in the Creed we profess to be one, holy, catholic and apostolic[12] which our Saviour, after his resurrection, entrusted to Peter's pastoral care (Jn 21:17), commissioning him and the other apostles to extend and rule it (see Mt 28:18, etc.), and which he raised up for all ages as the pillar and mainstay of the truth (see 1 Tim 3:15). This church, constituted and organized as a society in the present world, subsists in the Catholic Church, which is governed by the successor of Peter and by the bishops in communion with him.[13] Nevertheless, many elements of sanctification and of truth are found outside its visible confines. Since these are gifts belonging to the church of Christ, they are forces impelling towards catholic unity.

Just as Christ carried out the work of redemption in poverty and oppression, so the church is called to follow the same path if it is to communicate the fruits of salvation to humanity. Christ Jesus, "though he was by nature God . . . emptied himself, taking the nature of a slave" (Phil 2:6-7), and "being rich, became poor" (2 Cor 8:9) for our sake. Likewise, the church, although it needs human resources to carry out its mission, is not set up to seek earthly glory, but to proclaim, and this by its own example, humility and self-denial. Christ was sent by the Father "to bring good news to the poor . . . to heal the broken hearted" (Lk 4:18), "to seek and to save what was lost" (Lk 19:10). Similarly, the church encompasses with its love all those who are afflicted by human infirmity and it recognizes in those who are poor and who suffer, the likeness of its poor and suffering founder. It does all in its power to relieve their need and in them it endeavours to serve Christ, who, "holy, innocent and undefiled" (see Heb 7:26) knew nothing of sin (see 2 Cor 5:21), but came only to expiate the sins of the people (see Heb 2:17). The church, however, clasping sinners to its bosom, at once holy and always in need of purification, follows constantly the path of penance and renewal.

The church, "like a stranger in a foreign land, presses forward amid the persecutions of the world and the consolations of God,"[14] announcing the cross and death of the Lord until he comes (see 1 Cor 11:26). But by the power of the risen Lord it is given strength to overcome, in patience and in love, its sorrows and its difficulties, both those that are from within and those that are from without, so that it may reveal in the world, faithfully, although with shadows, the mystery of its Lord until, in the end, it shall be manifested in full light.

a. This chapter was translated by the late Colman O'Neill, OP, University of Fribourg, Switzerland. It was revised for this edition by Henry Peel, OP, Dublin and AF.

1. See St Cyprian, Epist. 64, 4: PL 3, 1017, CSEL (Hartel) III B,

p. 720; St Hilary of Poitiers, *In Mt.* 23, 6: PL 9, 1047. St Augustine, *passim;* St Cyril of Alexandria, *Glaph. in Gen.* 2, 10: PG 69, llO A.

2. St Gregory the Great, *Hom. In Evang.* 19, 1: PL 76; 1154 B. See St Augustine, *Serm.* 341, 9, 11: PL 39, 1499 f. St John Damascene, *Adv. Iconocl.* 11: PG 96, 1357.

3. See St Irenaeus, *Adv. Haer.* III, 24, 1: PG 7, 966 B; Harvey 2, 131, ed. Sagnard, SC p. 398.

4. St Cyprian, *De Orat. Dom.* 23: PL 4, 553; Hartel III A, p. 285; St Augustine, *Serm.* 71, 20, 33: PL 38, 463 f. St John Damascene, *Adv. Iconocl.* 12: PG 96 1358 D.

5. See *Origen, In Mt.,* 16, 21: PG 13, 1443 C; Tertullian, *Adv. Marc.* 3, 7: PL 2, 357 C: CSEL, 47, 3, p. 386. For liturgical documents see *Sacramentarium Gregorianum:* PL 78, 160 B; or C. Mohlberg, *Liber Sacramentorum Romanae Ecclesiae,* Rome, 1960, p. 111, XC: "God who prepare for yourself an eternal habitation from the assembly of the saints. . .". The hymn *Urbs Jerusalem beata* in the monastic breviary and the hymn *Coelestis Urbs Jerusalem* in the Roman breviary.

6. See St Thomas Aquinas, *Summa Theologiae,* III q. 62, a 5 ad 1.

7. See Pius XII, Encyclical, *Mystici Corporis,* 29 June 1943: AAS 35 (1943), p. 208.

8. See Leo XIII, Encyclical, *Divinum Illud,* 9 May 1897: ASS 29 (1896-97), p. 650. Pius XII, Encyclical, *Mystici Corporis, loc. cit.,* pp. 219-220: Denz. 2288 (3808). St Augustine, *Serm.* 268, 2: PL 38, 1232, and elsewhere. St John Chrysostom, *In Eph.,* Homily 9, 3: PG. 62, 72. Didymus of Alex., *Trin.* 2, 1: PG 39, 449 f. St Thomas Aquinas, *In Col.,* 1, 18, lect. 5; ed. Marietti, II, no. 46:"Just as one body is formed by the unity of the soul, so is the church by the unity of the Spirit. . ."

9. See Leo XIII, Encyclical *Sapientiae Christianae,* 10 Jan. 1890: ASS 22 (1889-90) p. 392. Idem Encyclical *Satis Cognitum,* 29 June 1896: ASS 28 (1895-96) pp. 710 and 724 ff. Pius XII, Encyclical *Mystici Corporis,* loc. cit., pp. 199-200.

10. See Pius XII, Encyclical *Mystici Corporis,* loc cit., p. 221 ff.; Idem, Encyclical *Humani Generis* 12 August 1950, AAS 42 (1950), p. 571.

11. See Leo XIII, Encyclical *Satis Cognitum,* loc. cit., p. 713.

12. See *Apostles' Creed:* Denz. 6-9 (10-13); *Nicene-Const. Creed:* Denz. 86 (150), compare *Tridentine profession of faith:* Denz. 994 and 999 (1862 and 1868).

13. It is called:"Holy (Catholic Apostolic) Roman church"in the *Tridentine profession of faith,* loc. cit., and in Vatican Council I, Dogmatic Constitution on the Catholic Faith, *Dei Filius:* Denz. 1782 (3001).

14. St Augustine. *De Civ. Dei,* XVIII, 51, 2: PL 41, 614.

Chapter II[a]

THE PEOPLE OF GOD

9. At all times and in every nation, anyone who fears God and does what is right has been acceptable to him (see Acts 10:35). He has, however, willed to make women and men holy and to save them, not as individuals without any bond between them, but rather to make them into a people who might acknowledge him and serve him in holiness. He therefore chose the people of Israel to be his own people and established a covenant with them. He instructed them gradually, making both himself and his intentions known in the course of their history, and made them holy for himself. All these things, however, happened as a preparation and figure of that new and perfect covenant which was to be ratified in Christ, and of the fuller revelation which was to be given through the Word of God made flesh. "Behold the days are coming, says the Lord, when I will make a new covenant with the house of Israel and the house of Judah . . . I will put my law within them, and I will write it upon their hearts, and they shall be my people . . . For they shall all know me from the least of them to the greatest, says the Lord" (Jer 31:31-34). Christ instituted this new covenant, the new covenant in his blood (see 1 Cor 11:25); he called a people together made up of Jews and Gentiles which would be one, not according to the flesh, but in the Spirit, and it would be the new people of God. For those who believe in Christ, who are reborn, not from a corruptible but from an incorruptible seed, through the word of the living God (see 1 Pet 1:23), not from flesh, but from water and the holy Spirit (see Jn 3:5-6), are finally established as "a chosen race, a royal priesthood, a holy nation, a people for his possession

... who in times past were not a people, but now are the people of God" (1 Pet 2:9-10).

That messianic people has as its head Christ, "who was delivered up for our sins and rose again for our justification" (Rom 4:25), and now, having acquired the name which is above all names, reigns gloriously in heaven. This people possesses the dignity and freedom of the daughters and sons of God, in whose hearts the holy Spirit dwells as in a temple. Its law is the new commandment to love as Christ loved us (see Jn 13:34). Its destiny is the kingdom of God which has been begun by God himself on earth and which must be further extended until it is brought to perfection by him at the end of time when Christ our life (see Col 3:4), will appear and "creation itself also will be delivered from its slavery to corruption into the freedom of the glory of the sons and daughters of God" (Rom 8:21). Consequently, this messianic people, although it does not, in fact, include everybody, and at times may seem to be a little flock, is, however, a most certain seed of unity, hope and salvation for the whole human race. Established by Christ as a communion of life, love and truth, it is taken up by him also as the instrument for the salvation of all; as the light of the world and the salt of the earth (see Mt 5:13-16) it is sent forth into the whole world.

Just as the people of Israel in the flesh, who wandered in the desert, were already called the church of God (see 2 Esd 13:1; Num 20:4; Deut 23:1 ff.), so too, the new Israel, which advances in this present era in search of a future and permanent city (see Heb 13:14), is also called the church of Christ (see Mt 16:18). It is Christ indeed who had purchased it with his own blood (see Acts 20:28); he has filled it with his Spirit; he has provided it with organs suited to its visible and social unity. All those, who in faith look towards Jesus, the author of salvation and the source of unity and peace, God has gathered together and established as the church, that it may be for each and everyone the visible sacrament of this saving unity.[1] In order to extend to all regions of the earth, it enters into human history, though it transcends at once all times and all boundaries between peoples. Advancing through trials and tribulations, the church is strengthened by God's grace, promised to it by the Lord so that it may not waver, through the weakness of the flesh, from perfect fidelity, but remain the worthy bride of the Lord, ceaselessly renewing itself through the action of the holy Spirit until, through the cross, it may arrive at that light which knows no setting.

10. Christ the Lord, high priest taken from the midst of humanity (see Heb 5:1-5), made the new people "a kingdom of priests to his God and Father" (Apoc 1:6; see 5:9-10). The baptized, by regeneration and the anointing of the holy Spirit, are consecrated as a spiritual house and a holy priesthood, that through all their christian activities they may offer spiritual sacrifices and proclaim the marvels of him who has called them out of darkness into his wonderful light (see 1 Pet 2:4-10). Therefore, all the disciples of Christ, persevering in prayer and praising God (see Acts 2:42-47), should present themselves as a sacrifice, living, holy and pleasing to God (see Rom 12:1). They should everywhere on earth bear witness to Christ and give an answer to everyone who asks a reason for their hope of eternal life (see 1 Pet 3:15).

Though they differ essentially and not only in degree, the common priesthood of the faithful and the ministerial or hierarchical priesthood are none the less interrelated; each in its own way shares in the one priesthood of Christ.[2] The ministerial priest, by the sacred power that he has, forms and governs the priestly people; in the person of Christ he brings about the Eucharistic sacrifice and offers it to God in the name of all the people. The faithful indeed, by virtue of their royal priesthood, share in the offering of the Eucharist.[3] They exercise that priesthood, too, by the reception of the sacraments, by prayer and thanksgiving, by the witness of a holy life, self-denial and active charity.

11. The sacred character and organic structure of the priestly community are brought into being through the sacraments and the virtues. Incorporated into the church by Baptism, the faithful are appointed by their baptismal character to christian religious worship; reborn as sons and daughters of God, they must profess publicly the faith they have received from God through the church.[4] By the sacrament of Confirmation they are more perfectly bound to the church and are endowed with the special strength of the holy Spirit. Hence, as true witnesses of Christ, they are more strictly obliged both to spread and to defend the faith by word and deed.[5]

Taking part in the Eucharistic sacrifice, the source and summit of the christian life, they offer the divine victim to God and themselves along with him.[6] And so it is that, both in the offering and in holy Communion, in their separate ways, though not of course indiscriminately, all have their own part to play in the liturgical action. Then, strengthened by the body of Christ in the Eucharistic communion, they manifest in a concrete way that unity of the people of God which this most holy sacrament aptly signifies and admirably realizes.

Those who approach the sacrament of Penance obtain pardon through God's mercy for the offense committed against him, and are, at the same time, reconciled with the church which they have wounded by their sins and which by charity, by example and by prayer labors for their conversion. By the sacred Anointing of the Sick and the prayer of the priests, the whole church commends those who are ill to the suffering and glorified Lord that he may give them relief and save them (see Jas 5:14-16). And indeed, it exhorts them to contribute to the good of the people of God by freely uniting themselves to the passion and death of Christ (see Rom 8:17; Col 1:24; 2 Tim 2:11-12; 1 Pet 4:13). Those among the faithful who have received holy Orders are appointed to nourish the church with the word and grace of God in the name of Christ. Finally, in virtue of the sacrament of Matrimony by which they signify and share in (see Eph 5:32) the mystery of the unity and fruitful love between Christ and the church, christian married couples help one another to attain holiness in their married life and in accepting and educating their children. Hence in their state and rank in life they have their own gifts within the people of God (see 1 Cor 7:7).[7] From their union comes the family in which new citizens of human society are born and, by the grace of the holy Spirit in Baptism, these are made children of God so that the people of God may be perpetuated throughout the centuries. In what might be regarded as the domestic church, the parents are to be the first preachers of the faith for their children by word and example. They must foster the vocation which is proper to each child, taking special care if it be a sacred vocation.

Strengthened by so many and such great means of salvation, all the faithful, whatever their condition or state are called by the Lord — each in his or her own way — to that perfect holiness by which the Father himself is perfect.

12. The holy people of God shares also in Christ's prophetic office: it spreads abroad a living witness to him, especially by a life of faith and love and by offering to God a sacrifice of praise, the fruit of lips confessing his name (see Heb 13:15). The whole body of the faithful who have received an anointing which

comes from the holy one (see 1 Jn 2:20 and 27) cannot be mistaken in belief. It shows this characteristic through the entire people's supernatural sense of the faith, when, "from the bishops to the last of the faithful,"[8] it manifests a universal consensus in matters of faith and morals. By this sense of the faith, aroused and sustained by the Spirit of truth, the people of God, guided by the sacred magisterium which it faithfully obeys, receives not the word of human beings, but truly the word of God (see 1 Th 2:13), "the faith once for all delivered to the saints" (Jude 3). The people unfailingly adheres to this faith, penetrates it more deeply through right judgment, and applies it more fully in daily life.

Moreover, it is not only through the sacraments and the ministries that the holy Spirit makes the people holy, leads them and enriches them with his virtues. Allotting his gifts "at will to each individual" (1 Cor 12:11), he also distributes special graces among the faithful of every rank. By these gifts, he makes them fit and ready to undertake various tasks and offices for the renewal and building up of the church, as it is written, "the manifestation of the Spirit is given to everyone for profit" (1 Cor 12:7). Whether these charisms be very remarkable or more simple and widely diffused, they are to be received with thanksgiving and consolation since they are primarily suited to and useful for the needs of the church. Extraordinary gifts are not to be rashly desired, nor from them are the fruits of apostolic labors to be presumptuously expected. Those who have charge over the church should judge the genuineness and orderly use of these gifts, and it is especially their office not indeed to extinguish the Spirit, but to test all things and hold fast to what is good (see 1 Th 5:12 and 19-21).

13. All women and men are called to belong to the new people of God. This people therefore, whilst

remaining one and unique, is to be spread throughout the whole world and to all ages in order that the design of God's will may be fulfilled: he made human nature one in the beginning and has decreed that all his children who were scattered should be finally gathered together as one (see John 11:52). It was for this purpose that God sent his Son, whom he appointed heir of all things (see Heb 1:2), that he might be teacher, king and priest of all, the head of the new and universal people of God's sons and daughters. This, too, is why God sent the Spirit of his Son, the Lord and giver of life, who for the church and for each and every believer is the principle of their union and unity in the teaching of the apostles and communion, in the breaking of bread and prayer (see Acts 2:42 Greek).

The one people of God is accordingly present in all the nations of the earth, and takes its citizens from all nations, for a kingdom which is not earthly in character but heavenly. All the faithful scattered throughout the world are in communion with each other in the holy Spirit so that"he who dwells in Rome knows the Indians to be his members."[9] Since the kingdom of Christ is not of this world (see Jn 18:36), in establishing this kingdom the church or people of God does not detract from anyone's temporal well-being. Rather it fosters and takes to itself, in so far as they are good, people's abilities, resources and customs. In so taking them to itself it purifies, strengthens and elevates them. The church, indeed, is mindful that it must gather in along with that King to whom the nations were given for an inheritance (see Ps 2:8) and to whose city they bring gifts and offerings (see Ps 71 [72]: 10; Is 60:4-7; Apoc 21:24). The universality which adorns the people of God is a gift from the Lord himself whereby the catholic church ceaselessly and effectively strives to recapitulate the whole of humanity and all its riches under Christ the Head in the unity of his Spirit.[10]

In virtue of this catholicity, each part contributes its own gifts to other parts and to the entire church, so that the whole and each of the parts are strengthened by the common sharing of all things and by the common effort to achieve fullness in unity. Hence, it is that the people of God is not only an assembly of different peoples, but in itself is made up of various ranks. This diversity among its members is either by reason of their duties — some exercise the sacred ministry for the good of their brothers and sisters; or it is due to their condition and manner of life, since many enter the religious state and, in tending to sanctity by the narrower way, stimulate their brothers and sisters by their example. Again, there are, legitimately, in the ecclesial communion particular churches which retain their own traditions, without prejudice to the Chair of Peter which presides over the entire assembly of charity,[11] and protects their legitimate variety while at the same time taking care that these differences do not diminish unity, but rather contribute to it. Finally, between all the various parts of the church there is a bond of intimate communion whereby spiritual riches, apostolic workers and temporal resources are shared. For the members of the people of God are called upon to share their goods, and the words of the apostle apply also to each of the churches, "according to the gift that each has received, administer it to one another as good stewards of the manifold grace of God" (1 Pet 4:10).

All are called to this catholic unity of the people of God which prefigures and promotes universal peace. And to it belong, or are related in different ways: the catholic faithful, others who believe in Christ, and finally all of humankind, called by God's grace to salvation.

14. This holy council, first of all, turns its attention to the catholic faithful. Relying on scripture and tradition, it teaches that this pilgrim church is required for salvation. Present to us in his body which is the church, Christ alone is mediator and the way of salvation. He expressly asserted the necessity of faith and Baptism (see Mk 16:16; Jn 3:5) and thereby affirmed at the same time the necessity of the church, which people enter through Baptism as through a door. Therefore, those could not be saved who refuse either to enter the church, or to remain in it, while knowing that it was founded by God through Christ as required for salvation.

Fully incorporated into the society of the church are those who, possessing the Spirit of Christ, accept its entire structure and all the means of salvation established within it and who in its visible structure are united with Christ, who rules it through the Supreme Pontiff and the bishops, by the bonds of profession of faith, the sacraments, ecclesiastical government, and communion. A person who does not persevere in charity, however, is not saved, even though incorporated into the church. Such people remain indeed in the bosom of the church, but only "bodily" not "in their hearts."[12] All daughters and sons of the church should nevertheless remember that their exalted status is not to be ascribed to their own merits, but to the special grace of Christ. If they fail to respond in thought, word and deed to that grace, not only will they not be saved, they will be the more severely judged.[13]

Catechumens who, moved by the holy Spirit, explicitly desire to be incorporated into the church, are by that very wish made part of it and with love and solicitude mother church already embraces them as her own.

15. The church has many reasons for knowing that

it is joined to the baptized who are honored by the name of Christian, but do not profess the faith in its entirety or have not preserved unity of communion under the successor of Peter.[14] For there are many who hold sacred scripture in honor as a rule of faith and of life, who display a sincere religious zeal, who lovingly believe in God the Father Almighty and in Christ, the Son of God and the Saviour.[15] They are sealed by Baptism which unites them to Christ and they recognize and accept other sacraments in their own churches or ecclesiastical communities. Many of them possess the episcopate, celebrate the holy Eucharist and cultivate devotion to the Virgin Mother of God.[16] There is furthermore a communion in prayer and other spiritual benefits. Indeed, there is a true union in the holy Spirit for, by his gifts and graces, his sanctifying power is active in them also and he has strengthened some of them even to the shedding of their blood. And so the Spirit stirs up desires and actions in all of Christ's disciples in order that all may be peacefully united, as Christ ordained, in one flock under one shepherd.[17] Mother church never ceases to pray, hope and work that this may be achieved, and she exhorts her children to purification and renewal so that the sign of Christ may shine more brightly over the face of the church.

16. Finally, those who have not yet accepted the Gospel are related to the people of God in various ways.[18] There is, first, that people to whom the covenants and promises were made, and from whom Christ was born in the flesh (see Rom 9:4-5), a people in virtue of their election beloved for the sake of the fathers, for God never regret his gifts or his call (see Rom 11:28-29). But the plan of salvation also includes those who acknowledge the Creator, first among whom are the Moslems: they profess to hold the faith of Abraham, and together with us they adore the one,

merciful God, who will judge humanity on the last day. Nor is God remote from those who in shadows and images seek the unknown God, since he gives to everyone life and breath and all things (see Acts 17:25-28) and since the Saviour wills everyone to be saved (see 1 Tim 2:4). Those who, through no fault of their own, do not know the Gospel of Christ or his church, but who nevertheless seek God with a sincere heart, and, moved by grace, try in their actions to do his will as they know it through the dictates of their conscience—these too may attain eternal salvation.[19] Nor will divine providence deny the assistance necessary for salvation to those who, without any fault of theirs, have not yet arrived at an explicit knowledge of God, and who, not without grace, strive to lead a good life. Whatever of good or truth is found amongst them is considered by the church to be a preparation for the Gospel[20] and given by him who enlightens all men and women that they may at length have life. But very often, deceived by the Evil One, people have lost their way in their thinking, have exchanged the truth of God for a lie and served the creature rather than the Creator (see Rom 1:21 and 25). Or else, living and dying in this world without God, they are exposed to ultimate despair. This is why, to procure the glory of God and the salvation of all of these people, the church, mindful of the Lord's command, "preach the Gospel to every creature" (Mk 16:15) takes great care to encourage the missions.

17. As he had been sent by the Father, the Son himself sent the apostles (see Jn 20:21) saying, "Go therefore and make disciples of all nations, baptizing them in the name of the Father, and of the Son, and of the holy Spirit, teaching them to observe all that I have commanded you; and see, I am with you all days even to the end of the world" (Mt 28:19-20). The church has received from the apostles Christ's solemn

command to proclaim the truth which saves, and it must carry it to the very ends of the earth (see Acts 1:8). Therefore, it makes the words of the apostle its own,"Woe to me if I do not preach the Gospel"(1 Cor 9:16), and accordingly never ceases to send preachers of the Gospel until such time as the infant churches are fully established, and they can themselves continue the work of evangelization. For the church is driven by the holy Spirit to play its part in bringing to completion the plan of God, who has constituted Christ as the source of salvation for the whole world. By its proclamation of the Gospel, it draws its hearers to faith and the profession of faith, it prepares them for Baptism, snatches them from servitude to error, and incorporates them into Christ so that by love they may grow to full maturity in him. The effect of its activity is that whatever good is found sown in people's hearts and minds, or in the rites and customs of peoples, is not only saved from destruction, but is purified, raised up, and perfected for the glory of God, the confusion of the devil, and the happiness of humanity. All disciples of Christ are obliged to spread the faith to the best of their ability[21] However, while anyone can baptise those who believe, it is for the priests to complete the building up of the body by the Eucharistic sacrifice, thus fulfilling the words of God spoken by the prophet,"From the rising of the sun to its setting my name is great among the nations. And in every place there is a sacrifice, and there is offered to my name a clean offering" (Mal 1:11).[22] Thus the church both prays and works so that the fullness of the whole world may move into the people of God, the body of the Lord and the temple of the holy Spirit, and that in Christ, the head of all things, all honor and glory may be rendered to the Creator, the Father of the universe.

a. This chapter has been translated by Christopher O'Donnell, O.Carm., Milltown Institute of Theology and Philosophy, Dublin and he also revised it for this edition.

1. See St Cyprian, *Epist.* 69, 6: PL 3, 1142 B; Hartel 3 B, p. 754: "the inseparable sacrament of unity."

2. See Pius XII, Allocution. *Magnificate Dominum,* 2 Nov. 1954: AAS 46 (1954) p. 669. Encyclical *Mediator Dei,* 20 Nov. 1947: AAS 39 (1947) p. 555.

3. See Pius XI, Encyclical *Miserentissimus Redemptor,* 8 May 1928: AAS 20 (1928) p. 171 f.; Pius XII, Allocution. *Vous nous avez,* 22 Sept. 1956: AAS 48 (1956) p. 714.

4. See St Thomas Aquinas, *Summa Theologiae,* III, q. 63, a. 2.

5. See St Cyril of Jerusalem, *Catech.* 17, de Spiritu Sancto, II, 35-37: PG 33, 1009-1012. Nicholas Cabasilas, *De Vita in Christo,* bk. III, de utilitate chrismatis: PG 150, 569-580. St Thomas Aquinas, *Summa Theologiae,* III, q. 65, a. 3 and q. 72, a 1 and 5.

6. See Pius XII, Encyclical *Mediator Dei,* 20 Nov., 1947: AAS 39 (1947), especially p. 552 f.

7. 1 Cor 7:7:"All have their own gifts from God, one of this sort, another of the other." See St Augustine *De Dono Persev.,* 14, 37: PL 45, 1015 f."It is not only continence which is a gift of God, so also is the chastity of married people."

8. See St Augustine, *De Praed. Sanct.* 14, 27: PL 44, 980.

9. See St John Chrysostom, *In Io.* Homily 65, 1: PG 59, 361.

10. See St Irenaeus, *Adv. Haer.* III, 16, 6; III, 22, 1-3; PG 7, 925 C-926 A and 955 C-958 A; Harvey 2, 87 f. and 120-123; Sagnard, ed. S.Ch., pp. 290-292 and 372 ff.

11. See St Ignatius Martyr, *Ad Rom.*, Preface: ed. Funk, 1, p. 252.

12. See St Augustine, *Bapt. c. Donat.* V. 28, 39: PL 43, 197: "It is clear that when we speak of "inside" and "outside" the church we should have the heart in mind, not the body." See *ibid.*, III, 19, 26: col. 152; V. 18, 24: col. 189; *In Io.* Treatise 61, 2: PL 35,1800, and often elsewhere.

13. See Lk 12:48:"From everyone to whom much is given much will be required." See also Mt 5: 19-20; 7:21-22; 25:41-46; Jas 2: 14.

14. See Leo XIII, Encyclical *Praeclara gratulationis,* 20 June 1894: ASS 26 (1893-94) p. 707.

15. See Leo XIII, Encyclical *Satis cognitum,* 29 June 1896: ASS 28 (1895-96) p. 738. Encyclical *Caritatis studium,* 25 July 1898: ASS 31 (1898-99) p. 11. Pius XII, Radio Message *Nell' alba,* 24 Dec. 1941: AAS 34 (1942) p. 21.

16. See Pius XI, Encyclical *Rerum Orientalium,* 8 Sept. 1928: AAS 20 (1928) p. 287. Pius XII, Encyclical *Orientalis Ecclesiae,* 9 April 1944: AAS 36 (1944) p. 137.

17. See Instruction of the Holy Office, 20 Dec. 1949: AAS 42 (1950) p. 142.

18. See St Thomas Aquinas, *Summa Theologiae*, III, q. 8, a. 3, to 1.

19. See Letter of the Sacred Cong. of the Holy Office to the Archbishop of Boston: Denz. 3869-72.

20. See Eusebius of Caesarea, *Praeparatio Evangelica*, I, I: PG 21, 28 AB.

21. See Benedict XV, Encyclical *Maximum illud:* AAS 11 (1919) p. 440, especially p. 451 ff. Pius XI, Encyclical *Rerum Ecclesia*: AAS 18 (1926) pp. 68-69. Pius XII, Encyclical *Fidei Donum*, 21 April 1957: AAS 49 (1957) pp. 236-237.

22. See *Didache*, 14: ed. Funk, 1, p. 32. St Justin, *Dial.* 41: PG 6, 564. St Irenaeus, *Adv. Haer.* IV, 17, 5; PG 7, 1023; Harvey, 2, p. 199 f. Council of Trent, Session 22, ch. 1: Denz. 939 (1742).

Chapter III^a

THE CHURCH IS HIERARCHICAL

18. In order to ensure that the people of God would have pastors and would enjoy continual growth, Christ the Lord set up in his church a variety of offices whose aim is the good of the whole body. Ministers, invested with a sacred power, are at the service of their brothers and sisters, so that all who belong to the people of God and therefore enjoy true christian dignity may attain to salvation through their free, combined and well-ordered efforts in pursuit of a common goal.

This holy synod, following in the steps of the first Vatican Council, with it teaches and declares that Jesus Christ, the eternal pastor, established the holy church by sending the apostles as he himself had been sent by the Father (see Jn 20:21). He willed that their successors, the bishops, should be the shepherds in his church until the end of the world. In order that the episcopate itself, however, might be one and undivided he placed blessed Peter over the other apostles, and in him he set up a lasting and visible source and foundation of the unity both of faith and of communion.[1] This teaching on the institution, the permanence, the nature and the force of the sacred primacy of the Roman Pontiff and his infallible teaching office, the sacred synod proposes anew to be firmly believed by all the faithful. Further, continuing with this same undertaking, it intends to profess before all and to declare the teaching on bishops, successors of the apostles, who together with Peter's successor, the Vicar of Christ[2] and the visible head of the whole church, govern the house of the living God.

19. The Lord Jesus, having prayed at length to the Father, called to himself those whom he wanted and appointed twelve to be with him, whom he might send to preach the kingdom of God (see Mk 3:13-19; Mt 10:1-42). These apostles (see Lk 6:13) he established as a college or permanent assembly, at the head of which he placed Peter, chosen from their number (see Jn 21:15-17). He sent them first to the children of Israel and then to all peoples (see Rom 1:16), so that, sharing in his power, they might make all peoples his disciples and sanctify and govern them (see Mt 28:16-20; Mk 16:15; Lk 24:45-48; Jn 20:21-23), thus propagating the church, being its ministers and pastors, under the guidance of the Lord, all days until the end of the world (see Mt 28:20). They were fully confirmed in this mission on the day of Pentecost (see Acts 2:1-36) according to the promise of the Lord: "You shall receive power when the holy Spirit descends upon you; and you shall be my witnesses both in Jerusalem and in all Judea and Samaria, and to the remotest part of the earth" (Acts 1:8). By preaching the Gospel everywhere (see Mk 16:20), which, thanks to the influence of the holy Spirit, was accepted by those who heard it, the apostles gather together the universal church, which the Lord

founded upon the apostles and built upon blessed
Peter their leader, the chief corner-stone being Christ
Jesus himself (see Apoc 21:14; Mt 16:18; Eph 2:20).[3]

20. This divine mission, which was committed by
Christ to the apostles, is destined to last until the end
of the world (see Mt 28:20), since the Gospel which
they were obliged to hand on is the principle of all of
the Church's life for all time. For that very reason the
apostles were careful to appoint successors in this
hierarchically constituted society.

Not only did they have various helpers in their
ministry,[4] but, to ensure the continuation after their
death of the mission entrusted to them they gave, by
will and testament as it were, their immediate collaborators the task of completing and consolidating the
work they had begun,[5] urging them to tend to the
whole flock, in which the holy Spirit had appointed
them to tend the church of God (see Acts 20:28). They
accordingly designated such men and ruled that on
their death other approved men should take over
their ministry.[6] Among the various ministries which
have been exercised in the church from the earliest
times the chief one, according to tradition, is that performed by those who, having been appointed to the
episcopate through an unbroken succession going
back to the beginning,[7] are transmitters of the apostolic seed.[8] Thus, according to the testimony of St
Irenaeus, the apostolic tradition is manifested[9] and
preserved[10] throughout the world by those whom the
apostles made bishops and by their successors down
to our own time.

The bishops, therefore, with priests and deacons as
helpers,[11] took on the ministry to the community, presiding in God's place over the flock[12] of which they are
the pastors, as teachers of doctrine, priests for sacred
worship and ministers of government.[13] Just as the
office which the Lord confided to Peter personally, as

first of the apostles, is permanent, intended to be transmitted to his successors, so too is the office which the apostles received as pastors of the church, a task destined to be exercised without interruption by the sacred order of bishops.[14] The sacred synod consequently teaches that the bishops have by divine institution taken the place of the apostles as pastors of the church[15] in such wise that whoever hears them hears Christ and whoever rejects them rejects Christ and him who sent Christ (see Lk 10:16).[16]

21. In the person of the bishops, then, assisted by the priests, the Lord Jesus Christ, supreme high priest, is present in the midst of believers. Seated at the right hand of God the Father, he is not absent from the assembly of his pontiffs;[17] indeed, it is primarily through their signal service that he preaches the word of God to all peoples and administers unceasingly to believers the sacraments of faith; thanks to their paternal role (see 1 Cor 4:15) he incorporates, by a supernatural rebirth, new members into his body; finally, through their wisdom and prudence he directs and guides the people of the New Testament on their journey towards eternal happiness. Chosen to shepherd the Lord's flock, these pastors are servants of Christ and dispensers of the mysteries of God (see 1 Cor 4:1), to whom is entrusted the duty of affirming the Gospel of the grace of God (see Rom 15:16; Acts 20:24), and the glorious service of the Spirit and of justice (see 2 Cor 3: 8-9).

In order to fulfil such exalted functions, the apostles were endowed by Christ with a special outpouring of the holy Spirit coming upon them (see Acts 1:8; 2:4; Jn 20:22- 23), and, by the imposition of hands (see 1 Tim 4:14; 2 Tim 1:6-7) they passed on to their collaborators the gift of the Spirit, which is transmitted down to our day through episcopal consecration.[18] The holy synod teaches, moreover, that the fullness of the sacrament of Orders is conferred by episcopal consecration, and both in the liturgical tradition of the church and in the language of the Fathers of the church it is called the high priesthood, the summit of the sacred ministry.[19] Episcopal consecration confers, together with the office of sanctifying, the offices also of teaching and ruling, which, however, of their very nature can be exercised only in hierarchical communion with the head and members of the college. Tradition, which is expressed especially in the liturgical rites and in the customs of both the eastern and western church, makes it abundantly clear that, through the imposition of hands and the words of consecration, the grace of the holy Spirit is given,[20] and a sacred character is impressed[21] in such a way that bishops, eminently and visibly, take the place of Christ himself, teacher, shepherd and priest, and act in his person.[22] It is for bishops to admit newly elected members into the episcopal body by means of the sacrament of Orders.

22. Just as, in accordance with the Lord's decree, St Peter and the other apostles constitute one apostolic college, so in like fashion the Roman Pontiff, Peter's successor, and the bishops, the successors of the apostles, are joined together. Indeed, the collegiate character and structure of the episcopal order is clearly shown by the very ancient discipline whereby the bishops installed throughout the whole world lived in communion with one another and with the Roman Pontiff in a bond of unity, charity and peace;[23] it is also shown in the holding of councils[24] in order to reach agreement on questions of major importance,[25] a balanced decision being made possible thanks to the number of those giving counsel.[26] It is made abundantly clear by the ecumenical council which have been held over the centuries. Indeed, it is clearly indicated in the custom, dating from very early times, of

summoning a number of bishops to take part in the
elevation of one newly elected to the highest sacerdo-
tal office. A person is made a member of the episcopal body in virtue of the sacramental consecration
and by hierarchical communion with the head and
members of the college.

The college or body of bishops has no authority,
however, other than the authority which it is
acknowledged to have in union with the Roman Pontiff, Peter's successor, as its head, his primatial authority over everyone, pastors or faithful, remaining intact.
For the Roman Pontiff, by reason of his office as Vicar
of Christ and as pastor of the entire church, has full,
supreme and universal power over the whole church,
a power which he can always exercise freely. The
order of bishops is the successor to the college of the
apostles in their role as teachers and pastors, and in it
the apostolic college is perpetuated. Together with its
head, the Supreme Pontiff, and never apart from him,
it is the subject of supreme and full authority over the
universal church;[27] but this power cannot be exercised
without the consent of the Roman Pontiff. The Lord
made Simon alone the rock and the holder of the
keys of the church (see Mt 16:18-19), and constituted
him shepherd of his entire flock (see Jn 21:15 ff.). It is
clear, however, that the office of binding and loosing
which was given to Peter (Mt 16:19), was also given to
the college of the apostles united to its head (Mt
18:18; 28:16-20).[28] This college, in so far as it is composed of many members, is the expression of the variety and universality of the people of God; and of the
unity of the flock of Christ, in so far as it is assembled
under one head. In it the bishops, while faithfully
upholding the primacy and pre-eminence of their
head, exercise their own proper authority for the good
of their faithful, indeed even for the good of the
whole church, the organic structure and harmony of

which are strengthened by the continued influence of the holy Spirit. The supreme authority over the whole church, which this college possesses, is exercised in a solemn way in an ecumenical council. There never is an ecumenical council which is not confirmed or at least accepted as such by Peter's successor.

And it is the prerogative of the Roman Pontiff to convoke such council, to preside over them and to confirm them.[29] This same collegiate power can be exercised in union with the pope by the bishops residing in different parts of the world, provided the head of the college summon them to collegiate action, or at least approve or freely accept the corporate action of the unassembled bishops, so that a truly collegiate act may result.

23. Collegiate unity is also apparent in the mutual relations of individual bishops to particular dioceses and to the universal church. The Roman Pontiff, as the successor of Peter, is the perpetual and visible source and foundation of the unity both of the bishops and of the whole company of the faithful.[30] Individual bishops are the visible source and foundation of unity in their own particular churches,[31] which are modelled on the universal church; it is in and from these that the one and unique catholic church exists.[32] And for that reason each bishop represents his own church, whereas all of them together with the pope represent the whole church in a bond of peace, love and unity.

Individual bishops, in so far as they are set over particular churches, exercise their pastoral office over the portion of the people of God assigned to them, not over other churches nor over the church universal. But as members of the episcopal college and legitimate successors of the apostles, by Christ's arrangement and decree,[33] each is bound to be solicitous for the entire church; such solicitude, even though it is not exercised by an act of jurisdiction, is very much to the advantage of the universal church. All the bishops, in fact, have the obligation to foster and safeguard the unity of the faith and to uphold the discipline which is common to the whole church; they are obliged to instruct the faithful in a love of the whole mystical body of Christ and, in a special way, of the poor, the suffering, and those who are undergoing persecution for the sake of justice (see Mt 5:10); finally, they have the duty to promote the kind of active apostolate which is common to the whole church, especially in order that the faith may increase and the light of truth may rise in its fullness on everyone. Besides, it is a fact of experience that, in governing their own churches properly as parts of the universal church, they contribute effectively to the welfare of the whole mystical body, which is also a body of churches.[34]

The task of proclaiming the Gospel to the entire world belongs to the body of pastors, to whom, as a group, Christ gave a general injunction and imposed a general obligation, to which Pope Celestine called the attention of the Fathers of the Council of Ephesus.[35] Individual bishops, therefore, provided it does not impede the fulfilment of their own particular obligations, are obliged to collaborate with one another and with Peter's successor, to whom, in a special way, the noble task of propagating the christian name was entrusted.[36] Thus, they should help the missions by every means in their power, supplying both harvest workers and also spiritual and material aids, either directly and personally themselves, or by arousing the fervent cooperation of the faithful. Lastly, following the venerable example of antiquity, bishops should gladly extend their fraternal assistance, in the fellowship of an all-pervading charity, to other churches, especially to neighboring ones and to those most in need of help.

It has come about through divine providence that, in the course of time, different churches set up in various places by the apostles and their successors joined together in a multiplicity of organically united groups which, while safeguarding the unity of the faith and the unique divine structure of the universal church, have their own discipline, enjoy their own liturgical usage and inherit a theological and spiritual patrimony. Some of these, notably the ancient patriarchal churches, as matrices of the faith, gave birth to other daughter-churches, as it were, and down to our own days they are linked with these by bonds of a more intimate charity, in what pertains to the sacramental life and in a mutual respect for rights and obligations.[37] This multiplicity of local churches, unified in a common effort, shows all the more resplendently the catholicity of the undivided church. In like fashion, the episcopal conferences at the present time are in a position to contribute in many and fruitful ways to the concrete realization of the collegiate spirit.

24. The bishops, in as much as they are the successors of the apostles, receive from the Lord, to whom all power is given in heaven and on earth, the mission of teaching all peoples, and of preaching the Gospel to every creature, so that all may attain salvation through faith, Baptism and the observance of the commandments (see Mt 28:18-20; Mk 16:15-16; Acts 26:17 f.). For the carrying out of this mission Christ the Lord promised the holy Spirit to the apostles and sent him from heaven on the day of Pentecost, so that through his power they might be witnesses to him in the remotest parts of the earth, before nations and peoples and kings (see Acts 1:8; 2:1 ff.; 9:15). That office, however, which the Lord committed to the pastors of his people, truly is a service, which is called very expressively in sacred scripture a *diakonia* or ministry (see Acts 1:17 and 25; 21:19; Rom 11:13; 1

Tim 1:12).

The canonical mission of bishops, on the other hand, can be given by legitimate customs that have not been revoked by the supreme and universal authority of the church, or by laws made or acknowledged by the same authority, or directly by Peter's successor himself. Should he object or refuse the apostolic communion, the bishops cannot be admitted to office.[38]

25. Among the more important duties of bishops, that of preaching the Gospel has pride of place.[39] For the bishops are heralds of the faith, who draw new disciples to Christ; they are authentic teachers, that is, teachers endowed with the authority of Christ, who preach to the people assigned to them the faith which is to be believed and applied in practice; and under the light of the holy Spirit they cause that faith to radiate, drawing from the storehouse of revelation new things and old (see Mt 13:52); they make it bear fruit and they vigilantly ward off whatever errors threaten their flock (see 2 Tim 4:14). Bishops[39a] who teach in communion with the Roman Pontiff are to be respected by all as witnesses of divine and catholic truth; the faithful, for their part, should concur with their bishop's judgment, made in the name of Christ, in matters of faith and morals, and adhere to it with a religious docility of spirit. This religious docility of the will and intellect must be extended, in a special way, to the authentic teaching authority of the Roman Pontiff, even when he does not speak *ex cathedra*, in such wise, indeed, that his supreme teaching authority be acknowledged with respect, and that one sincerely adhere to decisions made by him conformably with his manifest mind and intention, which is made known principally either by the character of the documents in question, or by the frequency with which a certain doctrine is proposed, or by the manner in

which the doctrine is formulated.

Although individual bishops do not enjoy the prerogative of infallibility, they do, however, proclaim infallibly the doctrine of Christ[40] when, even though dispersed throughout the world but maintaining among themselves and with Peter's successor the bond of communion, in authoritatively teaching matters to do with faith and morals, they are in agreement that a particular teaching is to be held definitively. This is still more clearly the case when, assembled in an ecumenical council, they are, for the universal church, teachers of and judges in matters of faith and morals, whose definitions must be adhered to with the obedience of faith.[41]

This infallibility, however, with which the divine redeemer wished to endow his church in defining doctrine pertaining to faith and morals, extends just as far as the deposit of revelation, which must be religiously guarded and faithfully expounded. The Roman Pontiff, head of the college of bishops, enjoys this infallibility in virtue of his office, when, as supreme pastor and teacher of all the faithful — who confirms his brothers and sisters in the faith (see Lk 22: 32) — he proclaims in a definitive act a doctrine pertaining to faith or morals.[42] For that reason, his definitions are rightly said to be irreformable by their very nature and not by reason of the consent of the church, in as much as they were made with the assistance of the holy Spirit promised to him in blessed Peter; and as a consequence they are not in need of the approval of others, and do not admit of appeal to any other tribunal. For in such a case, the Roman Pontiff does not deliver a pronouncement as a private person, but rather does he expound and defend the teaching of the catholic faith as the supreme teacher of the universal church, in whom, as an individual, the charism of infallibility of the church itself is pres-

ent.[43] The infallibility promised to the church is also
present in the body of bishops when, together with
Peter's successor, they exercise the supreme teaching
office. The assent of the church can never be lacking
to such definitions on account of the same holy
Spirit's influence, through which Christ's whole flock
is maintained in the unity of the faith and makes
progress in it.[44]

Furthermore, when the Roman Pontiff, or the body
of bishops together with him, define a doctrine, they
do so in conformity with revelation itself, by which all
are bound to abide and to which they are obliged to
conform; and this revelation is transmitted in its
entirety either in written form or in oral tradition
through the legitimate succession of bishops and
above all through the care of the Roman Pontiff himself; and through the light of the Spirit of truth it is
scrupulously preserved in the church and unerringly
explained.[45] The Roman Pontiff and the bishops, in
virtue of their office and because of the seriousness of
the matter, are assiduous in examining this revelation
by every suitable means and in expressing it properly;[46] they do not, however, admit any new public revelation as pertaining to the divine deposit of faith.[47]

26. The bishop, invested with the fullness of the
sacrament of Orders, is "the steward of the grace of
the supreme priesthood,"[48] above all in the Eucharist,
which he himself offers, or ensures that it is offered,[49]
and by which the church continues to live and grow.
This church of Christ is really present in all legitimately organized local groups of the faithful which,
united with their pastors, are also called churches in
the New Testament.[50] For these are in fact, in their
own localities, the new people called by God, in the
holy Spirit and with full conviction (see 1 Thess I :5).
In them the faithful are gathered together by the
preaching of the Gospel of Christ, and the mystery of

the Lord's Supper is celebrated "so that, by means of the flesh and blood of the Lord the whole brotherhood and sisterhood of the body may be welded together."[51] In any community of the altar, under the sacred ministry of the bishop,[52] a manifest symbol is to be seen of that charity and "unity of the mystical body, without which there can be no salvation."[53] In these communities, though they may often be small and poor, or dispersed, Christ is present through whose power and influence the one, holy, catholic and apostolic church is constituted.[54] For "the sharing in the body and blood of Christ has no other effect than to accomplish our transformation into that which we receive."[55]

Moreover, every lawful celebration of the Eucharist is regulated by the bishop, to whom is confided the duty of presenting to the divine majesty the worship of the christian religion and of ordering it in accordance with the Lord's injunctions and the church's regulations, as further defined for the diocese by his particular decision.

Thus, by praying and working for the people, the bishops apportion, in many different forms and without stint, what flows abundantly from Christ's holiness. By the ministry of the word, they impart to those who believe the power of God for their salvation (see Rom 1:16), and through the sacraments, the regular and fruitful distribution of which they regulate by their authority,[56] they sanctify the faithful. They control the conferring of Baptism, through which a sharing in the priesthood of Christ is granted. They are the original ministers of Confirmation; it is they who confer sacred Orders and regulate the discipline of Penance. They diligently encourage and instruct their flocks to play their part, in a spirit of faith and reverence, in the liturgy and above all in the holy sacrifice of the Mass. Finally, by the example of their way of life they should exercise a powerful influence for good on those over whom they are placed, by abstaining from all wrongdoing in their conduct, and doing their utmost, with the help of the Lord, to make their conduct even more admirable, so that together with the flock entrusted to them, they may attain eternal life.[57]

27. The bishops, as vicars and legates of Christ govern by their counsels, persuasion and example the particular churches assigned to them,[58] and also by the authority and sacred power which they exercise exclusively for the spiritual development of their flock in truth and holiness, keeping in mind that the greater must become like the lesser, and the leader as the servant (see Lk 22:26-27). This power, which they exercise personally in the name of Christ, is proper, ordinary and immediate, although its exercise is ultimately controlled by the supreme authority of the church and can be confined within certain limits should the usefulness of the church and the faithful require this. In virtue of this power bishops have a sacred right and a duty before the Lord of legislating for and of passing judgment on their subjects, as well as of regulating everything that concerns the good order of divine worship and of the apostolate.

The pastoral charge, that is, the permanent and daily care of their sheep, is entrusted to them fully; nor are they to be regarded as vicars of the Roman Pontiff; for they exercise a power which they possess in their own right and are most truly said to be at the head of the people whom they govern.[59] Consequently their authority, far from being damaged by the supreme and universal power, is in fact defended, upheld and strengthened by it,[60] since the holy Spirit preserves unfailingly that form of government which was set up by Christ the Lord in his church.

Sent as he is by the Father to govern his family, a bishop should keep before his eyes the example of the

Good Shepherd, who came not to be served but to serve (see Mt 20:28; Mk 10:45) and to lay down his life for his sheep (see Jn 10:11). Taken from among human beings and subject to weakness himself, he can sympathise with those who are ignorant and erring (see Heb 5:1-2). He should not refuse to listen to his subjects whose welfare he promotes as of his very own children and whom he urges to collaborate readily with him. Destined to render an account for their souls to God (see Heb 13:17), by prayer, preaching and all good works of charity he should be solicitous both for their welfare and also for that of those who do not yet belong to the one flock, all of whom he should regard as entrusted to him in the Lord. Since, like St Paul, he is in duty bound to everyone, he should be eager to preach the Gospel to all (see Rom 1:14-15), and to spur his faithful on to apostolic and missionary activity. As to the faithful, they should be closely attached to the bishop as the church is to Jesus Christ, and as Jesus Christ is to the Father, so that all things may conspire towards harmonious unity,[61] and bring forth abundant fruit to the glory of God (see 2 Cor 4:15).

28. Christ, whom the Father sanctified and sent into the world (see Jn 10:36), has, through his apostles, made their successors the bishops[62] sharers in his consecration and mission; and these, in their turn, duly entrusted in varying degrees various members of the church with the office of their ministry. Thus the divinely instituted ecclesiastical ministry is exercised in different degrees by those who even from ancient times have been called bishops, priests and deacons.[63] While they do not have the supreme degree of the pontifical office and depend on the bishops for the exercise of their power, priests are for all that associated with them by reason of their priestly dignity.[64] By virtue of the sacrament of Orders,[65] they are conse-

crated in the image of Christ, the supreme and eternal priest (see Heb 5:1-10; 7:24; 9:11-28), to preach the Gospel and shepherd the faithful as well as to celebrate divine worship as true priests of the New Testament.[66] On the level of their own ministry sharing in the unique office of Christ, the mediator (see 1 Tim 2:5), they announce to everyone the word of God. However, it is above all in the Eucharistic worship or assembly of the faithful that they exercise their sacred functions. Then, acting in the person of Christ[67] and proclaiming his mystery, they unite the prayers of the faithful to the sacrifice of Christ their head, and in the sacrifice of the Mass they make present again and apply, until the coming of the Lord (see 1 Cor 11:26), the unique sacrifice of the New Testament, Christ offering himself once for all an unblemished victim to the Father (see Heb 9:11-28).[68] For the faithful who are repentant or are ill they exercise to the fullest degree a ministry of reconciliation and comfort, while they carry the needs and supplications of the faithful to God the Father (see Heb 5:1-4). Exercising, within the limits of the authority which is theirs, the office of Christ, the Shepherd and Head,[69] they assemble the family of God as brothers and sisters animated by the spirit of unity,[70] and through Christ in the Spirit they lead them to God the Father. In the midst of the flock they adore him in spirit and in truth (see Jn 4:24). In short, they labor in preaching and instruction (see 1 Tim 5:17), firmly adhering to what they have read and meditated in the law of God, teaching what they have believed, and putting into practice what they have preached.[71]

The priests, prudent cooperators of the episcopal college[72] and its support and instrument, called to the service of the people of God, constitute, together with their bishop, one presbyterate,[73] though dedicated to a variety of duties. In each local assembly of the faithful they make the bishop present, in a sense, and they are associated with him in trust and generosity; for their part they take upon themselves his duties and solicitude and carry them out in their daily work for the faithful. Priests who, under the authority of the bishop, sanctify and govern that portion of the Lord's flock assigned to them render the universal church visible in their locality and contribute effectively towards building up the whole body of Christ (see Eph 4:12). And ever anxious for the good of the children of God they should be eager to lend their efforts not only to the pastoral work of the whole diocese but also of the whole church. By reason of this sharing in the priesthood and mission, priests should see in the bishop a true father and obey him with all respect. The bishop, for his part, should treat the priests, his helpers, as his sons and friends, just as Christ calls his disciples no longer servants but friends (see Jn 15:15). All priests, then, whether diocesan or religious, by reason of the sacrament of Orders and of the ministry are associated with the body of bishops and, according to their vocation and the grace that is given them they work for the good of the whole church.

In virtue of their sacred ordination and of their common mission, all priests are united together by bonds of intimate brotherhood. This should manifest itself in mutual help, spiritual or temporal, pastoral or personal, spontaneously and freely given in reunions and togetherness in life, work and charity.

As their fathers in Christ, they should care for the faithful whom they have begotten spiritually by Baptism and instruction (see 1 Cor 4:15; 1 Pet 1:23). Having gladly become examples for their flock (see 1 Pet 5:3), they should preside over and serve their local community in such a way that it may deserve to be called by the name which is given to the one people of God in its entirety, that is to say, the church of God (see 1 Cor 1:2; 2 Cor 1:1, and passim). They should be mindful that by their daily conduct and solicitude they should show the face of a truly priestly and pastoral ministry to believers and unbelievers alike, to Catholics and non-Catholics: that they are bound to bear witness before all people to truth and life, and as good shepherds seek after those too (see Lk 15:4-7) who, having been baptised in the Catholic Church, have given up the practice of the sacraments, or even fallen away from the faith.

Since the human race today is tending more and more towards civil, economic and social unity, it is all the more necessary that priests should unite their efforts and combine their resources under the leadership of the bishops and the Supreme Pontiff and thus eliminate division and dissension in every shape or form, so that all humanity may be led into the unity of the family of God.

29. At a lower level of the hierarchy are to be found deacons, who receive the imposition of hands "not for the priesthood, but for the ministry."[74] For, strengthened by sacramental grace, they are dedicated to the people of God, in communion with the bishop and his presbyterate, in the service of the liturgy, of the word and of charity. It is a deacon's task, as authorized by the competent authority, to administer Baptism solemnly, to reserve and distribute the Eucharist, to assist at and to bless marriages in the name of the church, to take Viaticum to the dying, to read the sacred scripture to the faithful, to instruct and exhort the people, to preside over the worship and the prayer of the faithful, to administer sacramentals, and to officiate at funeral and burial services. Dedicated to works of charity and functions of administration, deacons should recall the admonition of St Polycarp: "Let them be merciful, and zealous, and let them walk according to the truth of the Lord, who became the

servant of all."[75]

Since, however, the laws and customs of the Latin church in force today in many areas render it difficult to fulfil these functions, which are so extremely necessary for the life of the church, it will be possible in the future to restore the diaconate as a proper and permanent rank of the hierarchy. But it pertains to the competent local episcopal conferences, of one kind or another, with the approval of the Supreme Pontiff, to decide whether and where it is opportune that such deacons be appointed. Should the Roman Pontiff think fit, it will be possible to confer this diaconal order even upon married men, provided they be of more mature age, and also on suitable young men, for whom, however, the law of celibacy must remain in force.

a. This chapter was translated by the late Cornelius Williams, OP, University of Fribourg, Switzerland and has been revised by Henry Peel, OP, Dublin.

1. See Vatican Council I, Dogmatic Constitution on the Church, *Pastor aeternus:* Denz. 1821 (3050 f.).

2. See Council of Florence, *Decretum pro Graecis:* Denz. 694 (1307) and Vatican Council I, ibid.: Denz. 1826 (3059).

3. See St Gregory, Liber *sacramentorum Praef. in natali St Mathiae et St Thomae:* PL 78, 51 and 152; see Cod. Vat. lat. 3548, f. 18. St Hilary, *In Ps.* 67, 10: PL 9, 450, CSEL 22 p. 286. St Jerome, *Adv. Iovin.* 1, 26: PL 23, 247 A. St Augustine, *in Ps.* 86, 4: PL 37, 1103. St Gregory the Great, *Mor.* in *Iob,* XXVIII, V: PL 76, 455-456. Primasius, *Comm.* in *Apoc.,* V: PL 68, 924 BC. Paschasius Radb., *In Mt* bk. 8, ch. 16: PL 120, 561 C. See Leo XIII, *Et sane,* 17 Dec. 1888: ASS 21 (1888) p. 321.

4. See Acts 6:2-6;11:30; 13:1;14:23; 20:17;1 Th 5:12-13; Phil 1:1; Col 4:11 and passim.

5. See Acts 20:25:27; 2 Tim 4:6 f.; in conjunction with 1 Tim 5:22; 2 Tim 2:2; Tit 1:5; Clement of Rome, *Ad Cor.* 44, 3: ed. Funk, I, p. 156.

6. St Clement of Rome, *Ad Cor* 44, 2: ed. Funk, I, p. 154 f.

7. See Tertullian, *Praescr. Haer.* 32: PL 2, 52 f.

8. See Tertullian, *Praescr. Haer.* 32: PL 2, 52 f. St Ignatius, Martyr, passim.

9. See St Irenaeus, *Adv Haer.* III, 3, 1: PG 7, 848 A: Harvey 2, 8; Sagnard, p. 100 f.:"manifestated".

10. See St Irenaeus, Adv Haer. III, 2, 2: PG 7, 847: Harvey 2, 7; Sagnard, p. 100: "is safeguarded," see ibid. IV, 26, 2; col. 1053; Harvey 2, 236, and IV, 33, 8: col. 1077; Harvey 2, 262.

11. See St Ignatius, Martyr, *Philad.*, Praef.: ed. Funk, I, p. 264.

12. See St Ignatius, Martyr, *Philad.*, 1, 1; *Magn.* 6, 1: ed. Funk, 264 and 234.

13. St Clement of Rome, loc cit., 42, 3-4; 44, 3-4; 57,1-2: ed. Funk, I, 152, 156, 171. f. St Ignatius, Martyr, *Philad.* 2; *Smyrn.* 8, *Magn.* 3; *Trall.* 7: ed Funk, I, p. 265 f.; 282; 232; 246 f. etc.; St Justin, *Apol.*, 1, 65: PG 6, 428; St Cyprian, *Epist.*, passim.

14. See Leo XIII, Encyclical *Satis cognitum*, 29 June 1896: ASS 28 (1895-1896) p. 732.

15. See Council of Trent, Decree on the Sacrament of Order, ch. 4: Denz. 960 (1768); Vatican Council I, Dogmatic Constitution on the Church of Christ, *Pastor Aeternus* ch. 3: Denz 1828 (3061). Pius XII, Encyclical *Mystici Corporis*, 29 June 1943; AAS 35 (1943) pp. 209 and 212. *Code of Canon Law*, C.329 §1.

16. See Leo XIII, Letter, *Et Sane*, 17 Dec. 1888: ASS 21 (1888) p. 321 f.

17. See St Leo Martyr, Sermon 5, 3: PL 54, 154.

18. Council of Trent, Session 23, ch. 3 quotes the words of 2 Tim 1:6-7 to show that in Orders we have a true sacrament: Denz. 959 (1766)

19. In *Trad. Apost.* 3, ed. Botte, *S.Chr,* pp. 27-30, the "primacy of priesthood" is attributed to the bishop. See *Sacramentarium Leonianum*, ed. C. Mohlberg, *Sacramentarium Veronense*, Rome, 1955, p. 119: "to the ministry of the high priesthood . . . Make the height of your mystery complete in your priests" . . . Idem., *Liber Sacramentorum Romanae Ecclesiae,* Rome, 1960, pp. 121-122: "Grant them the episcopal throne, Lord, to rule your church and all the people." See PL 78, 224.

20. *Trad Apost.* 2, ed. Botte, p. 27.

21. Council of Trent, Session 23, ch. 4, teaches that the sacrament of Orders imprints an indelible character: Denz. 960 (1767). See John XXIII, Allocution *Jubilate Deo*, 8 May 1960: AAS 52 (1960) p. 466. Paul VI homily in Vatican, 20 Oct. 1963, AAS 55 (1963), p. 1014.

22. St Cyprian, *Epist.* 63, 14: PL 4, 386; Hartel, IIIB, p. 713: "The priest truly acts in the place of Christ." St John Chrysostom, *In 2 Tim* homily 2, 4: PG 62, 612: The priest is the "symbol" of Christ. St Ambrose, In Ps. 38, 25-26: PL 14, 1051-52: CSEL 64, 203-204. Ambrosiaster, *In I Tim* 5, 19: PL 17, 479 C and *In Eph* 4:11-12: PL 17, 387 C. Theodore of Mopsuestia, *Hom. Catech.*, XV, 21 and 24: ed. Tonneau, pp. 497 and 503. Hesychius of Jerusalem, *In Lev*, bk 2, 9, 23: PG. 93, 894 B.

23. See Eusebius, *Hist. Eccl.*, V, 24, 10: GCS. II, 1, p. 495: ed. Bardy, *Sources Chr.* II, p. 69. Dionysius, in Eusebius, ibid. VII, 5, 2: GCS. II,

2, p. 638 f.; Bardy, II, p. 168 f.

24. See concerning the ancient council, Eusebius, *Hist. Eccl.*, V, 23-24: GCS. II, 1, p. 488 ff.; Bardy, II, p. 66 ff. and passim. Council of Nicaea, 1, can 5: *Conc. Oec. Decr.* p. 7.

25. Tertullian, *De Jeiunio,* 13: PL 2, 972 B; CSEL 20, p. 292, lines 13-16.

26. St Cyprian, *Epist.* 56, 3: Hartel, III B, p. 650; Bayard, p. 154.

27. See Zinelli's *Relatio* on Vatican Council I: Mansi 52, 1109 C.

28. See Vatican Council I, Schema of the Dogmatic Constitution II, *de Ecclesia Christi*, ch. 4: Mansi 53, 310. See Kleutgen's *Relatio* on the reformed schema: Mansi 53, 321 B-322 B and Zinelli's *Declaratio:* Mansi 52, 1110 A. See also St Leo the Great, Sermon 4. 3: PL 54, 151 A.

29. See Code of Canon Law, canons 222 and 227.

30. See Vatican Council I, Dogmatic Constitution *Pastor aeternus:* Denz. 1821 (3050 f.).

31. See St Cyprian, Letter. 66, 8: Hartel, III, 2, p. 733: "The bishop in the church and the church in the bishop."

32. See St Cyprian, *Epist.* 55, 24: Hartel, p. 624, line 13: "One church throughout the world divided into many members." *Epist.* 36, 4: Hartel, p. 575, lines 20-21.

33. Pius XII, Encyclical *Fidei Donum,* 21 April 1957: AAS 49 (1957) p. 237.

34. See St Hilary of Poit., *In Ps.* 14, 3: PL 9, 206; CSEL 22, p. 86. St Gregory the Great, *Moral.* IV, 7, 12: PL 75, 643 C. Pseudo Basil, *In Is.* 15, 296: PG 30, 637 C.

35. St Celestine, *Epist.* 18, 1-2, to the Council of Ephesus: PL 50, 505 AB; Schwartz, *Acta Conc.* Oec. I, 1, 1, p. 22. See Benedict XV, Apostolic Letter *Maximum illud:* AAS 11 (1919) p. 440. Pius XI Encyclical *Rerum Ecclesiae,* 28 Feb. 1926: AAS 18 (1926) p. 69. Pius XII, Encyclical *Fidei Donum,* loc. cit.

36. Leo XIII, Encyclical *Grande munus,* 30 Sept. 1880: ASS 13 (1880) p. 145. See Code of Canon Law, canon 1327; canon 1350 par. 2.

37. On the rights of patriarchal Sees, see Council of Nicaea, canon 6 concerning Alexandria and Antioch, canon 7 concerning Jerusalem: *Conc. Oec. Decr.*, p. 8 Lateran Council IV in the year 1215, Constitution V: *De dignitate Patriarcharum:* ibid. p. 212. Council of Ferrara-Florence: ibid. p. 504.

38. Code of Canon Law for the Oriental church, canons 216-314: on patriarchs; canons 324-339: on greater archbishops; canons 362-391: on other dignitaries; in particular, canon. 238 par. 3; 216; 240; 251 and 255: on the nomination of bishops by the patriarch.

39. See Council of Trent, *Decree. de reform.*, session 5, ch. 2; n. 9, and session 24, canon 4.

39a. The Latin original of the remainder of this paragraph reads as follows: *Episcopi in communione cum Romano pontifice docentes ab*

omnibus tamquam divinae et catholicae veritatis testes venerandi sunt;
fideles autem in sui episcopi sententiam de fide et moribus nomine
Christi prolatam concurrere, eique religioso animo adhaerere debent.
Hoc vero religiosum voluntatis et intellectus obsequium singulari ratione
praestandum est Romani pontificis authentico magisterio etiam cum non
ex cathedra loquitur; ita nempe ut magisterium eius supremum rever-
enter agnoscatur, et sententiis ab eo prolatis sincere adhaereatur, juxta
mentem et voluntatem manifestatam ipsius, quae se prodit praecipue
sive indole documentorum, sive ex frequenti propositione eiusdem doc-
trinae, sive ex dicendi ratione.

40. See Vatican Council I, Dogmatic Constitution *Dei Filius*, 3:
Denz. 1792 (3011). See the note added to schema I *de Eccl.* (taken
from St Rob. Bellarmine): Mansi 51, 579 C; also the revised schema
of Constitution II *de Ecclesia Christi*, with Kleutgen's commentary:
Mansi 53, 313 AB. Pius IX, Letter *Tuas libenter*: Denz. 1683 (2879).

41. Code of Canon Law, canons 1322-1323.

42. See Vatican Council I, Dogmatic Constitution, *Pastor aeter-*
nus:, 4 Denz 1839 (3074).

43. See Gasser's explanation of Vatican Council I: Mansi 52, 1213
AC. [In previous editions this phrase had been translated "in whom
the Church's charism of infallibility is present in a singular way."—
Latin: *in quo charisma infallibilitatis ipsius ecclesiae singulariter inest.*
The word "singular" is not helpful, being apt to be read as "pre-eminent", whereas the meaning is that the charism is given to the Pope
as an individual. However, the word "individual" may need some
clarification, hence the footnote reference Mgr Gasser (relator for
the schema of 1870), who states that infallibility is not given to the
Pope in his personal, private capacity, but in his capacity as Pope,
"as a public person, as head of the church in his relations with the
church universal" (our own translation). Editor.]

44. Gasser, ibid: Mansi 1214 A.

45. Gasser, ibid.: Mansi 1215 CD, 1216-1217 A.

46. Gasser, ibid.: Mansi 1213.

47. Vatican Council I, Dogmatic Constitution *Pastor aeternus*, 4:
Denz. 1836 (3070).

48. Prayer of episcopal consecration in the Byzantine rite:
Euchologion to mega, Rome, 1873, p. 139.

49. See St Ignatius, Martyr, *Smyrn.* 8, 1: ed. Funk, I, p. 282.

50. See Acts 8:1; 14:22-23; 20:17 and *passim*.

51. Mozarabic prayer: PL 96, 759 B.

52. See St Ignatius, Martyr, *Smyrn.* 8, 1: ed. Funk, I, p. 282.

53. St Thomas Aquinas, *Summa Theologiae*, III, q. 73, a. 3.

54. See St Augustine, C. *Faustum*, 12, 20: PL 42, 265; *Serm.* 57, 7:
PL 38, 389, etc.

55. St Leo the Great, *Serm.* 63, 7: PL 54, 357 C.

56. *Traditio Apostolica* of Hippolytus, 2-3: ed. Botte, pp. 26-30.

57. See the text of the *Examination* at the beginning of the con-

secration of bishops, and the Prayer at the end of the Mass of the same consecration, after the *Te Deum.*

58. Benedict XIV, Brief. *Romana Ecclesia,* 5 Oct. 1752 par. 1: *Bullarium Benedicti XIV,* t. IV, Rome, 1758, 21: "A bishop bears the likeness of Christ, it is his office that he is performing." Pius XII, Encyclical *Mystici Corporis,* loc. cit., p. 211: "Each of them feeds and rules in the name of Christ the flocks assigned to him."

59. Leo XIII, Encyclical *Satis cognitum,* 29 June 1896: ASS 28 (1895-1896) p. 732: Idem. Letter *Officio sanctissimo,* 22 Dec. 1887: ASS 20 (1887) p. 264. Pius IX, Apost. Letter to bishops of Germany 12 March 1875 and Consistorial Allocution, 15 March 1875. Denz. 3112-3117, only in recent editions.

60. Vatican Council I, Dogm. Const. *Pastor aeternus,* 3: Denz. 1828 (3061). See Zinelli's *Relatio:* Mansi 52, 1114 D.

61. See St Ignatius, Martyr, *Ad Ephes.* 5, 1: ed. Funk, 1, p. 216.

62. See St Ignatius, Martyr, *Ad Ephes.* 6, 1: ed. Funk I, p. 218.

63. See Council of Trent, Session 23, On the sacrament of Order, ch. 2: Denz. 958 (1765), and canon 6: Denz. 966 (1776).

64. See Innocent 1, *Epist. ad Decentium:* PL 20, 554 A; Mansi 3, 1029; Denz. 98 (215): "Presbyters, although they are *priests* of the second rank, do not possess the *high degree* of the pontificate." St Cyprian, *Epist.* 61, 3: ed. Hartel, p. 696.

65. See Council of Trent, loc. cit., Denz. 956a-968 (1763-1778), and specifically canon 7: Denz. 967 (1777). Pius XII, Apostolic Constitution *Sacramentum ordinis:* Denz. 2301 (3857-61).

66. See Innocent I, loc. cit. St Gregory Naz., *Apol.* II, 22: PG 35, 432 B. Pseudo Dionysius, *Eccl. Hier.,* 1, 2: PG 3, 372 D.

67. See Council of Trent. Session 22: Denz. 940 (1743). Pius XII, Encyclical *Mediator Dei,* 20 Nov. 1947: AAS 39 (1947) p. 553; Denz. 2300 (3850).

68. See Council of Trent, Session 22: Denz. 938 (1739-40). Vatican Council II, Const. *De Sacra Liturgia,* no. 7 and no. 47.

69. See Pius XII, Encyclical *Mediator Dei,* loc. cit., under no. 67.

70. See St Cyprian, *Epist.* 11, 3: PL 4, 242 B; Hartel, II, 2, p. 497.

71. Ordination of priests, at the clothing with the vestments.

72. Ordination of priests, the Preface.

73. See St Ignatius, Martyr, *Philad.* 4: ed. Funk, I, p. 266. St Cornelius I in St Cyprian, *Epist.* 48, 2: Hartel, III, 2, p. 610.

74. *Constitutions of the Egyptian Church,* III, 2: ed. Funk, *Didascalia,* II, p. 103, *Statuta Eccl. Ant.* 37-41: Mansi 3, 954.

75. St Polycarp, *Ad Phil.* 5, 2: ed. Funk, I, p. 300: It is said that Christ "became the servant of all". See *Didache,* 15, I: ibid. p. 32. St Ignatius, Martyr, *Trall.* 2, 3: ibid., p. 242. *Constitutiones Apostolorum* 8, 28, 4: ed. Funk, Didascalia, I, p. 530.

Chapter IVª

THE LAITY

30. Having described the functions of the hierarchy, the holy council is pleased to turn its attention to the state of those Christians who are called the laity. Everything that has been said of the people of God is addressed equally to laity, religious and clergy. Certain matters refer especially to the laity, both men and women, however, because of their situation and mission and these must be examined in greater depth, owing to the special circumstances of our time. The sacred pastors, indeed, know well how much the laity contribute to the well-being of the whole church. For they know that they were not established by Christ to undertake by themselves the entire saving mission of the church to the world. They appreciate, rather, that it is their exalted task to shepherd the faithful and at the same time acknowledge their ministries and charisms so that all in their separate ways, but of one mind, may cooperate in the common task. For it is necessary that all "doing the truth in love, must grow up in all things in him who is the head, Christ, from whom the whole body, joined and knit together by every ligament with which it is supplied, as each part is working properly, promotes the body's growth in building itself up in love" (Eph 4:15-16).

31. The term laity is here understood to mean all the faithful except those in holy Orders and those who belong to a religious state approved by the church: all the faithful, that is, who by Baptism are incorporated into Christ, are constituted the people of God, who have been made sharers in their own way in the priestly, prophetic and kingly office of Christ and play their part in carrying out the mission of the whole christian people in the church and in the

world.

To be secular is the special characteristic of the laity. Although people in holy Orders may sometimes be engaged in secular activities, or even practice a secular profession, yet by reason of their particular vocation they are principally and expressly ordained to the sacred ministry, while religious bear outstanding and striking witness that the world cannot be transfigured and offered to God without the spirit of the beatitudes. It is the special vocation of the laity to seek the kingdom of God by engaging in temporal affairs and directing them according to God's will. They live in the world, in each and every one of the world's occupations and callings and in the ordinary circumstances of social and family life which, as it were, form the context of their existence. There they are called by God to contribute to the sanctification of the world from within, like leaven, in the spirit to the Gospel, by fulfilling their own particular duties. Thus, especially by the witness of their life, resplendent in faith, hope and charity they manifest Christ to others. It is their special task to illuminate and order all temporal matters in which they are closely involved in such a way that these are always carried out and develop in Christ's way and to the praise of the Creator and Redeemer.

32. By divine institution, the holy church is directed and governed with a wonderful diversity. "For just as in one body we have many members, yet all the members have not the same function, so we the many, are one body in Christ, but individually members one of another" (Rom 12:4-5).

The chosen people of God is, therefore, one: "one Lord, one faith, one Baptism" (Eph 4:5); there is a common dignity of members deriving from their rebirth in Christ, a common grace as sons and daughters, a common vocation to perfection, one salvation, one hope and undivided charity. In Christ and in the church there is, then, no inequality arising from race or nationality, social condition or sex, for "there is neither Jew nor Greek; there is neither slave nor freeman; there is neither male nor female. For you are all one in Christ Jesus" (Gal 3: 28 Greek; see Col 3 :11).

In the church not everyone walks along the same path, yet all are called to holiness and have obtained an equal privilege of faith through the justice of God (see 2 Pet 1:1). Although by Christ's will some are appointed teachers, dispensers of the mysteries and pastors for the others, yet all the faithful enjoy a true equality with regard to the dignity and the activity which they share in the building up of the body of Christ. The distinction which the Lord has made between the sacred ministers and the rest of the people of God implies union, for the pastors and the other faithful are joined together by a close relationship. The pastors of the church, following the example of the Lord, should minister to each other and to the rest of the faithful; the latter should eagerly collaborate with the pastors and teachers. And so, amid their variety all bear witness to the wonderful unity in the body of Christ: this very diversity of graces, of ministries and of works gathers the children of God into one, for "all these things are the work of the one and the same Spirit" (1 Cor 12:11).

As the laity by divine condescension have as their brother Christ who, though Lord of all, came not to be served but to serve (see Mt 20:28), they also have as brothers those who have been placed in the sacred ministry and who by Christ's authority, through teaching, sanctifying and ruling so nourish the family of God that the new commandment of love may be fulfilled by all. As St Augustine puts it so very well: "When I am frightened by what I am to you, then I am consoled by what I am with you. To you I am the bishop, with you I am a Christian. The first is an office, the second a grace; the first a danger, the second salvation."[1]

33. Gathered together in the people of God and established in the one body of Christ under one head, the laity, whoever they are, are called as living members to apply to the building up of the church and to its continual sanctification all the powers which they have received from the goodness of the Creator and from the grace of the Redeemer.

The apostolate of the laity is a sharing in the church's saving mission. Through Baptism and Confirmation all are appointed to this apostolate by the Lord himself. Moreover, by the sacraments, and especially by the sacred Eucharist, that love of God and humanity which is the soul of the entire apostolate is communicated and nourished. The laity, however, are given this special vocation: to make the church present and fruitful in those places and circumstances where it is only through them that it can become the salt of the earth.[2] Thus, all lay people, through the gifts which they have received, are at once the witnesses and the living instruments of the mission of the church itself "according to the measure of Christ's gift" (Eph 4:7).

Besides this apostolate which belongs to absolutely every Christian, the laity can be called in different ways to more immediate cooperation in the apostolate of the hierarchy,[3] like those men and women who helped the apostle Paul in the Gospel, working hard in the Lord (see Phil 4-3; Rom 16:3 ff.). They may, moreover, be appointed by the hierarchy to certain ecclesiastical offices which have a spiritual aim.

All the laity, then, have the exalted duty of working for the ever greater extension of the divine plan of salvation to all people of every time and every place. Every opportunity should therefore be given them to share zealously in the salvific work of the church according to their ability and the needs of the times.

34. Since he wishes to continue his witness and his service through the laity also, the supreme and eternal priest, Christ Jesus, gives them life through his Spirit and ceaselessly impels them to accomplish every good and perfect work.

To them, whom he intimately joins to his life and mission, he also gives a share in his priestly office of offering spiritual worship for the glory of the Father and the salvation of humanity. Hence the laity, dedicated as they are to Christ and anointed by the holy Spirit, are marvellously called and prepared so that ever richer fruits of the Spirit may be produced in them. For all their works, if accomplished in the Spirit, become spiritual sacrifices acceptable to God through Jesus Christ: their prayers and apostolic undertakings, family and married life, daily work, relaxation of mind and body, even the hardships of life if patiently borne (see Pet 2:5). In the celebration of the Eucharist, these are offered to the Father in all piety along with the body of the Lord. And so, worshipping everywhere by their holy actions, the laity consecrate the world itself to God.

35. Christ is the great prophet who proclaimed the kingdom of the Father both by the testimony of his life and by the power of his word. Until the full manifestation of his glory, he fulfils this prophetic office, not only through the hierarchy who teach in his name and by his power, but also through the laity. He accordingly both establishes them as witnesses and provides them with an appreciation of the faith (*sensus fidei*) and the grace of the word (see Acts 2:17-18; Apoc 19:10) so that the power of the Gospel may shine out in daily family and social life. They show themselves to be the children of the promise if, strong in faith and hope, they make the most of the present

time (Eph 5:16; Col 4:5), and with patience await the future glory (see Rom 8:25). Let them not hide this hope then in the depths of their hearts, but rather express it through the structure of their secular lives in continual conversion and in wrestling "against the world rulers of this darkness, against the spiritual forces of iniquity" (Eph 6:12).

As the sacraments of the New Law, which nourish the life and the apostolate of the faithful, prefigure the new heaven and the new earth (see Apoc 21:1), so too the laity become powerful heralds of the faith in things to be hoped for (see Heb 11:1) if they unhesitatingly join the profession of faith to the life of faith. This evangelization — that is, the proclamation of Christ by word and the witness of their lives — acquires a special character and a particular effectiveness because it is accomplished in the ordinary circumstances of the world.

The state of life that is sanctified by a special sacrament, namely, married and family life, has a special value in this prophetic office. Where the christian religion pervades the whole structure of life, constantly and increasingly transforming it, there is both the practice and an outstanding school of the lay apostolate. In it the married partners have their own proper vocation: they must be witnesses of their faith and love of Christ to each another and to their children. The christian family proclaims aloud both the virtues of the kingdom of God here and now and the hope of the blessed life hereafter. Hence, by example and by their testimony, they convict the world of sin and enlighten those who seek the truth.

Therefore, even when occupied with temporal affairs, the laity can and must be involved in the precious work of evangelizing the world. When there is a shortage of sacred ministers or when government persecution prevents their functioning, some lay people make up for this by performing some sacred functions to the best of their ability; others, more numerous, are engaged full time in apostolic work. Nevertheless, it is the duty of all lay people to cooperate in spreading and building up the kingdom of Christ. The laity, consequently, have the duty to work hard to acquire a deeper knowledge of revealed truth and earnestly to pray to God for the gift of wisdom.

36. Christ, obedient to the point of death and because of this exalted by the Father (see Phil 2:8-9), has entered into the glory of his kingdom. All things are subjected to him until he subjects himself and all created things to the Father, so that God may be all in all (see 1 Cor 15:27-28). He communicated this power to the disciples that they too may be established in royal liberty and, by a holy life of self-denial, overcome the reign of sin in themselves (see Rom 6:12), and indeed that by serving Christ in others they may through humility and patience bring their sisters and brothers to that King to serve whom is to reign. The Lord desires that his kingdom be spread by the lay faithful also: the kingdom of truth and life, the kingdom of holiness and grace, the kingdom of justice, love and peace.[4] In this kingdom, creation itself will be set free from the slavery of corruption and will obtain the glorious freedom of the children of God (see Rom 8:21). Clearly, a great promise, a great commandment is given to the disciples: "all things are yours, you are Christ's, and Christ is God's" (1 Cor 3:23).

The faithful must, then, acknowledge the inner nature and the value of the whole of creation and its orientation to the praise of God. They help one another, even through their secular activity, to achieve greater holiness of life, so that the world may be filled with the spirit of Christ and may the more effectively attain its destiny in justice, in love and in peace. The laity enjoy the principal role in the universal fulfillment of this task. Therefore, by their competence in secular disciplines and by their activity which grace elevates from within, let them do all in their power to ensure that through human labor, technical skill and civil culture the goods of creation may be developed for the benefit of everyone without exception, according to the plan of the creator and the light of his word, that these goods may be more equitably distributed among all men and women and may make their own contribution to universal progress in human and christian liberty. Thus, through the members of the church, Christ will increasingly illuminate the whole of human society with his saving light.

Moreover, let the laity band together to remedy those secular institutions and conditions which are an inducement to sin, so that they may be brought into line with the rules of justice, favoring rather than hindering the practice of virtue. By so doing they will imbue culture and human works with a moral value. In this way the field of the world is better prepared for the seed of the divine word and the doors of the church are opened more widely to allow the message of peace to enter the world.

Because of the very economy of salvation the faithful should learn to distinguish carefully between the rights and duties which they have as members of the church and those which fall to them as members of human society. They are to do their best to ensure that the two work together harmoniously, remembering that in all temporal matters they are to be guided by a christian conscience, since not even in temporal business may any human activity be withdrawn from God's dominion. It is especially important nowadays that both this distinction and this harmony should be clearly evident in the conduct of the faithful, in order that the mission of the church may match more fully the special circumstances of the world today. But just as it must be recognized that the earthly city, rightly concerned with secular affairs, is governed by its own principles, so also must the evil doctrine be rejected which seeks to build society without any reference to religion and which attacks and eliminates the religious liberty of its citizens.[5]

37. Like all the faithful, the laity have the right to receive abundant help from their pastors out of the church's spiritual treasury, especially the word of God and the sacraments.[6] The laity should disclose their needs and desires to the pastors with that liberty and confidence which befits children of God and brothers and sisters in Christ. To the extent of their knowledge, competence or authority the laity are entitled, and indeed sometimes duty-bound, to express their opinion on matters which concern the good of the church.[7] Should the occasion arise this should be done through the institutions established by the church for that purpose and always with truth, courage and prudence and with reverence and charity towards those who, by reason of their office, represent the person of Christ.

Like all the faithful, the laity should promptly accept in christian obedience what is decided by the pastors who, as teachers and rulers of the church, represent Christ. In this they will follow Christ's example who, by his obedience to the point of death, opened the blessed way of the liberty of the children of God to all of humanity. Nor should they fail to commend to God in their prayers those who have been placed over them, who indeed keep watch as having to render an account of our souls, that they may do this with joy and not with grief (see Heb 13:17).

The sacred pastors, however, should recognize and promote the dignity and responsibility of the laity in the church. They should willingly use their prudent advice and confidently assign offices to them in the service of the church, leaving them freedom and scope for activity. Indeed, they should encourage them to take on work on their own initiative. They should with paternal love consider attentively in Christ initial moves, suggestions and desires proposed by the laity.[8] Moreover the pastors must respect and recognize the liberty which belongs to all in the earthly city.

Many benefits for the church are to be expected from this familiar relationship between the laity and the pastors. The laity's sense of their own responsibility is strengthened, their zeal is encouraged, they are more ready to add their strengths to the work of their pastors. The pastors, helped by the experience of the laity, are enabled to judge more clearly and more appropriately in spiritual and in temporal matters. Strengthened by all its members, the church can thus more effectively fulfil its mission for the life of the world.

38. Each individual lay person must be a witness before the world to the resurrection and life of the Lord Jesus, and a sign of the living God. All together, and each one to the best of his or her ability, must nourish the world with spiritual fruits (see Gal 5:22). They must diffuse in the world the spirit which animates the poor, the meek and the peace-makers whom the Lord in the Gospel proclaimed blessed (see Mt 5:3-9). In a word: "what the soul is in the body, let Christians be in the world."[9]

a. This chapter was translated by Christopher O'Donnell, O.Carm., Milltown Institute of Theology and Philosophy, Dublin and he also revised it for this edition.

1. St Augustine, *Serm.* 340, 1 PL 38, 1483.

2. See Pius XI, Encyclical *Quadragesimo anno*, 15 May 1931: AAS 23 (1931) p. 221 f. Pius XII, Allocution *De Quelle consolation*, 14 Oct. 1951: AAS 43 (1951) p. 790 f.

3. See Pius XII, Allocution. *Six ans sont écoulé*, 5 Oct. 1957: AAS 49 (1957) p. 927.

4. From the Preface of the Feast of Christ the King.

5. See Leo XIII, Encyclical *Immortale Dei*, 1 Nov. 1885: ASS 18 (1885) p 166 ff. Idem. Encyclical *Sapientiae Christianae*, 10 Jan. 1890: ASS 22 (1889-1890) p. 397 ff. Pius XII, Allocution. *Alla vostra filiale*, 23 March 1958: AAS 50 (1958) p. 220: "the legitimate and healthy lay nature of the state".

6. Code of Canon Law, canon 682.

7. See Pius XII, Allocution. *De quelle Consolation*, loc. cit., p. 789: "In decisive battles it is often from the front that the best initiatives come." Idem, Allocution. *L'importance de la presse catholique*, 17 Feb. 1950: AAS 42 (1950) p. 256.

8. See 1 Th 5:19 and 1 Jn. 4:1.

9. Letter to Diognetus 6: ed. Funk, I, p. 400. See St John Chrysostom, *In Matt.* Homily 46 (47), 2: PG 58, 478, on the leaven in the dough.

Chapter V^a

THE UNIVERSAL CALL TO HOLINESS

39. The church, whose mystery is set forth by this sacred synod, is held, as a matter of faith, to be unfailingly holy. This is because Christ, the Son of God, who with the Father and the Spirit is hailed as "alone holy,"[1] loved the church as his Bride, giving himself up for it so as to sanctify it (see Eph 5:25-26); he joined it to himself as his body and endowed it with the gift of the holy Spirit for the glory of God. Therefore, all in the church, whether they belong to the hierarchy or are cared for by it, are called to holiness, according to the apostle's saying: "For this is the will of God, your sanctification" (1 Th 4:3; see Eph 1:4). This holiness of the church is shown constantly in the fruits of grace which the Spirit produces in the faithful and so it must be; it is expressed in many ways by the individuals who, each in their own state of life, tend to the

perfection of charity, and are thus a source of edification for others; it appears in a way especially suited to
it in the practice of those counsels which are usually
called evangelical. This practice of the counsels
prompted by the holy Spirit, undertaken by many
Christians whether privately or in a form or state
sanctioned by the church, provides in the world, as it
should, a striking witness and example of that holiness.

40. The Lord Jesus, divine teacher and model of all
perfection, preached holiness of life, which he both
initiates and brings to perfection, to each and every
one of his disciples no matter what their condition of
life: "You, therefore, must be perfect, as your heavenly
Father is perfect" (Mt 5:4-8).[2] For he sent the holy
Spirit to all to move them interiorly to love God with
their whole heart, with their whole soul, with their
whole understanding and with their whole strength
(see Mk 12:30), and to love one another as Christ
loved them (see Jn 13:34; 15:12). The followers of
Christ, called by God not for what they had done but
by his design and grace, and justified in the Lord
Jesus, have been made sons and daughters of God by
the Baptism of faith and partakers of the divine
nature, and so are truly sanctified. They must therefore hold on to and perfect in their lives that holiness
which they have received from God. They are told by
the apostle to live "as is fitting among saints" (Eph
5:3), and, "as God's chosen ones, holy and beloved, to
show compassion, kindness, lowliness, meekness,
and patience" (Col 3:12), to have the fruits of the
Spirit for their sanctification (see Gal 5:22; Rom 6:22).
But since we all offend in many ways (see Jas 3:2), we
constantly need God's mercy and must pray every
day: "And forgive us our debts" (Mt 6:12).[3]

It is therefore quite clear that all Christians in
whatever state or walk in life are called to the fullness

of christian life and to the perfection of charity,[4] and
this holiness is conducive to a more human way of
living even in society here on earth. In order to reach
this perfection the faithful should use the strength
dealt out to them by Christ's gift, so that, following in
his footsteps and conformed to his image, doing the
will of God in everything, they may wholeheartedly
devote themselves to the glory of God and to the service of their neighbor. Thus the holiness of the people
of God will grow in fruitful abundance, as is clearly
shown in the history of the church by the lives of so
many saints.

41. The forms and tasks of life are many but there
is one holiness, which is cultivated by all who are led
by God's Spirit and, obeying the Father's voice and
adoring God the Father in spirit and in truth, follow
Christ, poor and humble in carrying his cross, that
they may deserve to be sharers in his glory. All, however, according to their own gifts and duties must
steadfastly advance along the way of a living faith,
which arouses hope and works through love.

In the first place, the shepherds of Christ's flock, in
the image of the high and eternal priest, shepherd
and bishop of our souls, should carry out their ministry with holiness and zeal, with humility and courage; thus fulfilled, this ministry will also be for them
an outstanding means of sanctification. Called to the
fullness of the priesthood, they are endowed with a
sacramental grace, so that by prayer, sacrifice and
preaching, and through every form of episcopal care
and service, they may fulfil the perfect duty of pastoral
love.[5] They should not be afraid to lay down their lives
for their sheep and, having become examples for their
flock (see 1 Pet 5:3), they must help the church, also
by their own example, to grow daily in holiness.

Priests, who form the spiritual crown of the bishop,[6] share as do the order of bishops in the grace of

office through Christ the eternal and only Mediator. They should grow in the love of God and of their neighbor by the daily performance of their duty, should keep the bond of priestly communion, should abound in every spiritual good and give to all a living witness to God,[7] imitating those priests who over the centuries left behind them an outstanding example of holiness, often in humble and hidden service and whose praise lives on in God's church. They have the duty to pray and offer sacrifice for their own people and for the entire people of God, conscious of what they are doing and imitating what they touch with their hands.[8] Far from being held back by their apostolic labors, perils and hardships, they should rise through them to greater holiness, nourishing and fostering their action with an overflowing contemplation, for the encouragement of the entire church of God. Let all priests, especially those who by special title of ordination are called diocesan priests, remember that their loyal union and generous cooperation with their bishop greatly helps their sanctification.

Ministers of lesser rank also share in a special way in the mission and grace of the high priest; first among them are deacons who, as servants of the mysteries of Christ and of the church,[9] should keep themselves free from every vice, should please God and give a good example to all in everything (see 1 Tim 3: 8-10 and 12-13). Clerics, called by the Lord and set aside for his service, should prepare themselves for their ministerial duties under the pastors' watchful care; they are bound to keep their minds and hearts in harmony with so high a calling, persevering in prayer, fervent in love, thinking about whatever is true, just and of good repute, doing everything for the glory and honor of God. Then there are those lay persons chosen by God who are called by the bishop to give themselves fully to apostolic works and who labour very fruitfully in the Lord's field.[10]

Christian married couples and parents, following their own way, should with faithful love support one another in grace all through life. They should train their children, lovingly welcomed from God, in christian doctrine and evangelical virtues. Because in this way they present to all an example of unfailing and generous love, they build up the community of charity and stand as witnesses to and cooperators in the fruitfulness of mother church, as a sign of and a share in that love with which Christ loved his bride and gave himself for her.[11] In a different way, a similar example is given by widows, widowers and single people, who can also greatly contribute to the holiness and activity of the church. And as for those who are engaged in work which is frequently fatiguing, their human activity should enrich them personally, enabling them to help their fellow-citizens, to promote the betterment of all of human society and of creation; enabling them indeed to imitate, by their active charity, Christ who worked as a carpenter and works constantly with the Father for everyone's salvation. Thus, rejoicing in hope and bearing one another's burdens, they should rise through their everyday work itself to a higher sanctity which is truly apostolic.

In a special way also, those who are weighed down by poverty, infirmity, sickness and other hardships, or who suffer persecution for the sake of justice, should realize that they are united to Christ, who suffers for the salvation of the world. In the Gospel the Lord called those people blessed and after they have "suffered for a little while, the God of all grace, who has called us to his eternal glory in Christ Jesus, will himself restore, establish, strengthen and settle" them (1 Pet 5:10)

Accordingly, all Christians, in the conditions, duties

and circumstances of their lives and through all these, will grow constantly in holiness if they receive all things with faith from the hand of the heavenly Father and cooperate with the divine will, making manifest in their ordinary work the love with which God has loved the world.

42. "God is love, and they who abide in love abide in God, and God abides in them" (1 Jn 4:16). God has poured out his love in our hearts through the holy Spirit who has been given to us (see Rom 5:5); therefore the first and most necessary gift is charity, by which we love God above all things and our neighbor because of him. But if charity is to grow and like a good seed produce fruit in the soul, all of the faithful must willingly hear the word of God and carry out his will by what they do, with the help of his grace; they must frequently partake of the sacraments, especially the Eucharist, and take part in the liturgy; they must constantly apply themselves to prayer, self-denial, active sisterly and brotherly service and the practice of all the virtues. This is because love, as the bond of perfection and fullness of the law (see Col 3:14; Rom 13:10), directs and gives meaning to all the means of sanctification and leads them to their goal.[12] Hence the true disciples of Christ are noted both for love of God and love of their neighbor.

Since Jesus, the Son of God, showed his love by laying down his life for us, no one has greater love than they who lay down their lives for him and for their sisters and brothers (see 1 Jn 3:16, Jn 15:13). Some Christians have been called from the beginning, and will always be called, to give this greatest testimony of love to everyone, especially to persecutors. Martyrdom makes the disciples like their master, who willingly accepted death for the salvation of the world, and through it they are made like him by the shedding of blood. Therefore, the church considers it the highest gift and supreme test of love. And while it is given to few, all however must be prepared to confess Christ before humanity and to follow him along the way of the cross amid the persecutions which the church never lacks.

Likewise the church's holiness is fostered in a special way by the manifold counsels whose observance the Lord proposes to his disciples in the Gospel.[13] Outstanding among these counsels is that precious gift of divine grace given to some by the Father (see Mt 19:11; 1 Cor 7:7) to devote themselves to God alone more easily with an undivided heart (see 1 Cor 7: 32-34) in virginity or celibacy.[14] This perfect continence for the sake of the kingdom of heaven has always been held in high esteem by the church as a sign and stimulus of love, and as a singular source of spiritual fertility in the world.

The church bears in mind too the apostle's admonition when calling the faithful to charity and exhorting them to share the sentiment of Christ Jesus who "emptied himself, taking the form of a servant ... and became obedient unto death" (Phil 2:7-8) and for our sake "became poor, though he was rich" (2 Cor 8:9). Since the disciples must always imitate this love and humility of Christ and bear witness to it, mother church rejoices that it has within itself many men and women who follow more closely the Saviour's self-emptying and show it forth more clearly, by undertaking poverty with the freedom of God's sons and daughters and by renouncing their own will. They subject themselves to another person for the love of God, thus going beyond what is of precept in the matter of perfection, so as to become more like the obedient Christ.[15]

Therefore all the faithful are invited and obliged to try to achieve holiness and the perfection of their own state of life. Accordingly, all of them must ensure that they keep emotions under proper control, lest they be hindered in their pursuit of perfect love by the use of worldly goods and by an attachment to riches which is contrary to the spirit of evangelical poverty, following the apostle's advice: Let those who use this world not fix their abode in it, for the form of this world is passing away (see 1 Cor 7:31, Greek text).[16]

a. This chapter was translated by Joseph M. de Torre. Revised for this edition by AF.

1. The Roman Missal, *Gloria in excelsis.* See Lk 1:35; Mk 1:24; Jn 6:69 (the holy one of God); Acts 3:14; 4:27 and 30; Heb 7:26; 1 Jn 2:20; Apoc 3:7.

2. See Origen, *Comm. Rom.* 7, 7: PG 14, 1122 B.; Ps.-Macarius, *De Oratione,* 11: PG 34, 861 AB; St Thomas Aquinas, *Summa Theologiae* II-II, q. 184, a. 3.

3. See St Augustine, *Retract.* II, 18: PL 32, 637 f.; Pius XII, Encyclical *Mystici Corporis,* 29 June 1943: AAS 35 (1943) p. 225.

4. See Pius XI Encyclical *Rerum Omnium,* 26 Jan 1923: AAS 15 (1923) p. 50 and 59-60; Idem, Encyclical *Casti Connubii,* 31 Dec. 1930: AAS 22 (1930) p. 548; Pius XII, Apostolic Constitution *Provida Mater,* 2 Feb. 1947: AAS 39 (1947) p. 117; Idem, Address *Annus sacer,* 8 Dec. 1950: AAS 43 (1951) pp. 27-28; Idem, Address *Nel darvi,* 1 July 1956: AAS 48 (1956) p. 574 f.

5. See St Thomas Aquinas, *Summa Theologiae* II-II, q. 184, a. 5 and 6; Idem, *De perf. vitae spir.,* ch. 18; Origen, *In Is.* Homily 6, 1: PG 13, 239.

6. See St Ignatius Martyr, *Magn.* 13, 1: ed. Funk, 1, p. 241.

7. See St Pius X, Exhortation *Haerent animo,* 4 Aug. 1908: ASS 41 (1908) p. 560 f.; Code of Canon Law, canon 124; Pius XI, Encyclical *Ad catholici sacerdotii,* 20 Dec. 1935: AAS 28 (1936) p. 22.

8. See Ordination of priests, introductory exhortation.

9. See St Ignatius Martyr, *Trall.,* 2, 3: ed. Funk, I, p. 244.

10. See Pius XII, Address *Sous la maternelle protection,* 9 Dec. 1957: AAS 50 (1958) p. 36.

11. Pius XI, Encyclical *Casti Connubii,* 31 Dec. 1930: AAS 22 (1930) p. 548 f.; St John Chrysostom, *In Ephes.* Homily 20, 2: PG 62, 136 ff.

12. See St Augustine, *Enchir.* 121, 32: PL 40, 288; St Thomas Aquinas, *Summa Theologiae,* II-II, q. 184, a. 1; Pius XII, Apostolic Exhortation *Menti Nostrae,* 23 Sept. 1950: AAS 42 (1950) p. 660.

13. On the counsels in general see Origen, *Comm. Rom.* X, 14: PG 14, 1275 B; St Augustine, *De S. Virginitate,* 15, 15: PL 40, 403; St Thomas Aquinas, *Summa Theologiae,* I-II, q. 100, a 2 c (end); II-II, q. 44, a 4 to 3.

14. On the excellence of holy Virginity see Tertullian, *Exhort. Cast.* 10: PL 2, 925 C; St Cyprian, *Hab. Virg.* 3 and 22: PL 4, 443 B and 461 A f.; St Athanasius (?), *De Virg.*: PG 28, 252 ff.; St John Chrysostom, De Virg.: PG 48, 533 ff.

15. On spiritual poverty see Mt 5:3 and 19:21; Mk 10:21; Lk 18:22; on obedience: Christ's example is presented in Jn 4:34 and 6:38; Phil 2:8-10; Heb 10:5-7. Texts of Fathers and founders of orders are abundant.

16. On the effective practice of the counsels which is not imposed on everyone see St John Chrysostom, *In Mt.* Homily 7, 7: PG 57, 81 f.; St Ambrose, *De Viduis*, 4, 23- PL 16, 241 f.

Chapter VI^a

RELIGIOUS

43. The teaching and example of Christ provide the foundation of the evangelical counsels of chaste self-dedication to God, of poverty and of obedience. The Apostles and Fathers of the church commend them as do its doctors and pastors. Thus they constitute a divine gift which it has received from its Lord and which by his grace it always cherishes.

Under the guidance of the holy Spirit, church authority has been at pains to explain the counsels, to regulate their practice and also to establish stable forms of living deriving from them. The result has been that a wonderful and wide-spreading tree has sprung up in the field of the Lord from the God-given seed, branching out into various forms of religious life lived in solitude or in community. A variety of religious families has grown up in which resources are multiplied for the spiritual progress of their members and for the good of the whole body of Christ.[1]

These families provide their members with many helps — greater stability in their way of life; sound teaching on striving after perfection; the bond of communion in the army of Christ; the strengthening of their freedom by obedience. Thus they are enabled to live securely, and to maintain faithfully, the religious life which they profess and, rejoicing in spirit, to advance in the way of love.[2]

This state of life, from the point of view of the divine and hierarchical nature of the church, is not to be seen as a middle way between the clerical and lay states of life. Rather it should be seen as a way of life to which some Christians are called by God, both from the clergy and the laity, so that they may enjoy a special gift of grace in the life of the church and may contribute, each in their own way, to its saving mission.[3]

44. Christians who embrace this way of life bind themselves to the practice of the three evangelical counsels by vows or other sacred ties of a similar nature. Dedicating themselves wholly to God their supreme love, they are committed in a new and special way to serving and honoring him. True, as baptised Christians they are dead to sin and consecrated to God; but in order to draw still more abundant fruit from the grace of their Baptism they make profession of the evangelical counsels in the church. They do this in order to be freed from hindrances that could hold them back from loving God ardently and worshipping him wholeheartedly and in order to be consecrated more closely to his service.[4] The bonds by which they dedicate themselves show forth the indissoluble bond of union that exists between Christ and his bride the church. Accordingly, the more stable and firm these bonds are, the more perfect will be their religious consecration.

Since the evangelical counsels, by reason of the

charity to which they lead,[5] unite those who follow them in a special way to the church and its mystery, the spiritual life of these persons must be dedicated to the good of the whole church also. Hence they have the duty, in accordance with their capacities and in keeping with their particular vocation, whether it be by prayer or by active labor as well, to work for the implanting and development of the kingdom of Christ in souls and for spreading it to all parts of the world. It is for this reason that the church upholds and fosters the distinctive character of the different religious institutes.

Therefore the profession of the evangelical counsels acts as a sign that can and should effectively inspire all the members of the church to fulfil indefatigably the duties of their christian vocation. The people of God has here no lasting city but looks to that which is to come. This being so, the religious state, which gives its followers greater freedom from earthly cares, also reveals with greater clarity to all believers the heavenly blessings that are already present in this world. Furthermore it bears witness to the new and eternal life won for us by Christ's redemption and foretells the future resurrection and the glory of the heavenly kingdom. Again, the religious state offers a closer imitation and an abiding representation in the church of the way of life that the Son of God made his own when he came into the world to do the will of the Father and which he put before the disciples who followed him. Finally, this state shows forth in a special way the transcendence of the kingdom of God over all earthly things and its sovereign demands, bringing home to all humankind the incomparable grandeur of the power of Christ in his lordship and the infinite might of the holy Spirit which works so marvellously in the church.

The state of life, then, which is constituted by the

profession of the evangelical counsels, while not belonging to the hierarchical structure of the church, belongs absolutely to its life and holiness.

45. Since it is the task of the church's hierarchy to feed the people of God and to lead them to the richest pastures (see Ezek 34:14), it is for it to regulate by wise laws the practice of the evangelical counsels whereby the perfect love of God and neighbor is fostered in a unique way.[6] It is the hierarchy too, in docile response to the promptings of the holy Spirit, that receives the religious rules presented to it by outstanding men and women, puts them into better order and gives them official approval. Moreover it uses its supervisory and protective authority to ensure that religious institutes established far and wide for the building up of the body of Christ shall develop and flourish according to the spirit of their founders.

With a view to providing more effectively for the needs of the whole of the Lord's flock and for the sake of the general good, any religious institute and its individual members can be exempted by the Supreme Pontiff, as primate of the universal church, from the jurisdiction of local bishops and be made subject to him alone.[7] In the same way they can be left or entrusted to the appropriate patriarchal authorities. Religious themselves, however, in fulfilling the duty to the church which is inherent in their particular form of life must show respect and obedience to bishops in accordance with canon law, both because these exercise pastoral authority in their respective churches and because this is necessary for unity and harmony in apostolic work.[8]

Besides giving legal sanction to religious life and thus raising it to the dignity of a canonical state, the church also gives liturgical expression to the fact that it is a state consecrated to God. It, itself, in virtue of its God-given authority, receives the vows of those who make profession, implores the divine aid and grace for them in its public prayer, commends them to God and bestows a spiritual blessing on them, joining their self-offering to the eucharistic sacrifice.

46. Let religious see to it that through them the church may truly and ever more clearly show forth Christ to believers and unbelievers alike — Christ in contemplation on the mountain, or proclaiming the kingdom of God to the crowds, or healing the sick and maimed and converting sinners to a good life, or blessing children and doing good to all, always in obedience to the will of the Father who sent him.[9]

At the same time, let all bear in mind that while the profession of the evangelical counsels involves the renunciation of goods that are unquestionably to be highly valued, it does not stand in the way of the true development of the human person but rather by its very nature is supremely conducive to that process. For the counsels, when willingly embraced in accordance with each one's personal vocation, contribute in no small measure to the purification of the heart and to spiritual freedom. They continually urge one to more fervent charity and above all they have the power to conform the christian person to the kind of virginal and poor life that Christ the Lord chose for himself and which his virgin mother also embraced. This is confirmed by the example of the many holy founders of religious institutes.

Let no one think either that their consecration alienates religious from humanity or renders them useless to human society. Even though sometimes they have no direct contact with their contemporaries, still in a deeper way they have their fellow men and women present with them in the heart of Christ and cooperate with them spiritually, so that the building up of the earthly city may always have its foundation in the Lord and have him as its goal: otherwise those who build it may have labored in vain.[10]

For this reason, then, this holy council gives its support and praise to men and women, brothers and sisters, who in monasteries or in schools and hospitals or in missions adorn the bride of Christ by the steadfast and humble fidelity of their consecration and give generous service of the most varied kinds to all manner of people.

47. Let all therefore who have been called to the profession of the counsels make every effort to persevere and excel still more in the vocation to which God has called them, for the increase of the holiness of the church, to the greater glory of the one and undivided Trinity, which in Christ and through Christ is the source and origin of all holiness.

a. This chapter was translated by Father Sean O'Riordan CSSR, Alphonsianum, Rome, and he also revised it for this edition.

1. See Rosweyde, *Vitae Patrum,* Antwerp, 1628 Apophtegmata Patrum: PG 65; Palladius, *Historia Lausiaca:* PG 34, 995 ff., ed. C. Butler, Cambridge, 1898 (1904); Pius XI, Apostolic Constitution *Umbratilem,* 8 July 1924 (AAS 16 (1924), pp. 386-387. Pius XII, Allocution *Nous sommes heureux,* 11 April 1958: AAS 50 (1958), p. 283.

2. Paul VI, Allocution *Magno gaudio,* 23 May 1964: AAS 56 (1964) p. 566.

3. See Code of Canon Law, canons 487 and 488, 4°; Pius XII, Allocution *Annus sacer,* 8 December 1950: AAS 43 (1951) p 27 f.; Pius XII, Apostolic Constitution *Provida Mater,* 2 Feb. 1947: AAS 39 (1947), p. 120 ff.)

4. See Paul VI, loc. cit. p. 567.

5. See St Thomas Aquinas, *Summa Theologiae* II-II, q. 184, a. 3 and q. 188, a. 2. St Bonaventure, Opusc. X1, *Apologia Pauperum,* ch. 3, 3: ed. Opera, Quaracchi, vol. 8, 1898, p. 245 a.

6. See Vatican Council I, schema *De Ecclesia Christi,* ch. XV and note 48: Mansi 51, 549 f. and 619 f.; Leo XIII, Letter *Au Milieu des consolations,* 23 December 1900: ASS 33 (1900-1901), p. 361; Pius XII, Apostolic Constitution *Provida Mater,* loc. cit., p. 114 f.

7. See Leo XIII, Constitution *Romanos Pontifices,* 8 May 1881: ASS 13 (1880-1881), p. 483); Pius XII, Allocution *Annus sacer,* 8 December 1950: AAS 43 (1951), p. 28 f..

8. See Pius XII, Allocution *Annus sacer,* loc. cit., p. 28; Pius XII, Apostolic Constitution *Sedes Sapientiae,* 31 May 1956: AAS 48

(1956), p. 355; Paul VI, Allocution *Magno gaudio*, 23 May, 1964: AAS 56 (1964) pp. 570-571.

9. See Pius XII, Encyclical *Mystici Corporis*, 29 June 1943: AAS 35 (1943), p. 214 f.

10. See Pius XII, Allocution *Annus sacer*, loc. cit., p. 30; Allocution *Sous la maternelle protection*, 9 December 1957: AAS 50 (1958) p 39 f.

Chapter VII^a

THE PILGRIM CHURCH

48. The church, to which we are all called in Christ Jesus, and in which by the grace of God we attain holiness, will receive its perfection only in the glory of heaven, when the time for the renewal of all things will have come (Acts 3:21). At that time, together with the human race, the universe itself, which is closely related to humanity and which through it attains its destiny, will be perfectly established in Christ (see Eph 1:10; Col 1:20; 2 Pet 3:10-13).

Christ when he was lifted up from the earth drew all humanity to himself (see Jn 12:32 Greek text). Rising from the dead (see Rom 6:9) he sent his life-giving Spirit upon his disciples and through him set up his body which is the church as the universal sacrament of salvation. Sitting at the right hand of the Father he is continually active in the world in order to lead people to the church and through it to join them more closely to himself; by nourishing them with his own body and Blood, he makes them sharers in his glorious life. The promised and hoped for restoration, therefore, has already begun in Christ. It is carried forward in the sending of the holy Spirit and through him continues in the church in which, through faith, we learn the meaning of our earthly life while, as we hope for the benefits which are to come, we bring to its conclusion the task allotted to us in the world by the Father, and so work out our salvation (see Phil 2:12).

Already the final age of the world is with us (see 1 Cor 10:11) and the renewal of the world is irrevocably under way; it is even now anticipated in a certain real way, for the church on earth is endowed already with a sanctity that is true though imperfect. However, until the arrival of the new heavens and the new earth in which justice dwells (see 2 Pet 3:13) the pilgrim church, in its sacraments and institutions, which belong to this present age, carries the mark of this world which will pass, and it takes its place among the creatures which groan and until now suffer the pains of childbirth and await the revelation of the children of God (see Rom 8:19-22).

United therefore with Christ in the church and marked with the holy Spirit "who is the guarantee of our inheritance" (Eph 1:14) we are truly called children of God, as indeed we are (see 1 Jn 3:1), though we have not yet appeared with Christ in glory (see Col 3:4), in which we will be like God, for we will see him as he is (see 1 Jn 3:2). "While we are at home in the body we are away from the Lord" (2 Cor 5:6) and having the firstfruits of the Spirit we groan inwardly (see Rom 8:23) and we desire to be with Christ (see Phil 1:23). That same charity urges us to live more for him who died for us and who rose again (see 2 Cor 5:15). We make it our aim, then, to please the Lord in all things (see 2 Cor 5:9) and we put on the armor of God that we may be able to stand against the wiles of the devil and resist in the evil day (see Eph 6:11-13). Since we know neither the day nor the hour, we should follow the advice of the Lord and watch con-

stantly so that, when the single course of our earthly
life is completed (see Heb 9:27), we may merit to
enter with him into the marriage feast and be numbered among the blessed (see Mt 25:31-46) and not,
like the wicked and slothful servants (see Mt 25:26),
be ordered to depart into the eternal fire (see Mt
25:41), into the outer darkness where there will be
"weeping and gnashing of teeth" (Mt 22:13 and
25:30). Before we reign with Christ in glory we must
all appear "before the judgment seat of Christ, so that
each one may receive good or evil, according to what
each has done in the body" (2 Cor 5:10), and at the
end of the world "they will come forth, those who
have done good, to the resurrection of life, and those
who have done evil, to the resurrection of judgment"
(Jn 5:29; see Mt 25:46). We reckon then that "the sufferings of this present time are not worth comparing
with the glory that is to be revealed to us" (Rom 8:18;
see 2 Tim 2:11-12), and strong in faith we look for "the
blessed hope, the appearing of the glory of our great
God and Savior Jesus Christ" (Tit 2:13) "who will
change our lowly body to be like his glorious body"
(Phil 3:21) and who will come "to be glorified in his
saints, and to be marvelled at in all who have believed" (2 Th 1:10).

49. When the Lord will come in glory, and all his
angels with him (see Mt 25:31), death will be no more
and all things will be subject to him (see 1 Cor 15:26-
27). But at the present time some of his disciples are
pilgrims on earth, others have died and are being
purified, while still others are in glory, contemplating
"in full light, God himself triune and one, exactly as
he is." All of us, however, in varying degrees and in
different ways share in the same love of God and our
neighbor, and we all sing the same hymn of glory to
our God. All, indeed, who are of Christ and who have
his Spirit form one church and in Christ are joined

together (Eph 4:16). So it is that the union of the way-
farers with the brothers and sisters who sleep in the
peace of Christ is in no way interrupted; but on the
contrary, according to the constant faith of the church,
this union is reinforced by an exchange of spiritual
goods.[2] Being more closely united to Christ, those
who dwell in heaven consolidate the holiness of the
whole church, add to the nobility of the worship that
the church offers to God here on earth, and in many
ways help in a greater building up of the church (see
1 Cor 12:12-27).[3] Once received into their heavenly
home and being present to the Lord (see 2 Cor 5:8),
through him and with him and in him they do not
cease to intercede with the Father for us,[4] as they
proffer the merits which they acquired on earth
through the one mediator between God and humanity, Christ Jesus (see 1 Tim 2:5), serving God in all
things and completing in their flesh what is lacking in
Christ's sufferings for the sake of his body, which is
the church (see Col 1:24).[5] So by their familial concern
is our weakness greatly helped.

50. In full consciousness of this communion of the
whole mystical body of Jesus Christ, the church in its
pilgrim members, from the very earliest days of the
christian religion, has honored with great respect the
memory of the dead;[6] and, because "it is a holy and a
wholesome thought to pray for the dead that they
may be loosed from their sins" (2 Mac 12:46) it offers
its prayers for them. The church has always believed
that the apostles and Christ's martyrs, who gave the
supreme witness of faith and charity by the shedding
of their blood, are closely united with us in Christ; it
has always venerated them, together with the Blessed
Virgin Mary and the holy angels, with a special love,[7]
and has asked piously for the help of their intercession. Soon there were added to these others who had
chosen to imitate more closely the virginity and pov-

erty of Christ,[8] and still others whom the outstanding practice of the christian virtues[9] and the wonderful graces of God recommended to the pious devotion and imitation of the faithful.[10]

When we look on the lives of those women and men who have faithfully followed Christ we are inspired anew to seek the city which is to come (see Heb 13:14 and 11:10), while at the same time we are taught about the safest path by which, through a changing world and in keeping with each one's state of life and condition, we will be able to arrive at perfect union with Christ, which is holiness.[11] In the lives of those companions of ours in the human condition who are more perfectly transformed into the image of Christ (see 2 Cor 3:18) God shows, vividly, to humanity his presence and his face. He speaks to us in them and offers us a sign of his kingdom,[12] to which we are powerfully attracted, so great a cloud of witnesses are we given (see Heb 12:1) and such an affirmation of the truth of the Gospel.

It is not only by reason of their example that we cherish the memory of those in heaven; we seek, rather, that by the practice of fraternal and sororal charity the union of the whole church in the Spirit may be strengthened (see Eph 4:1-6). Exactly as christian communion among pilgrims brings us closer to Christ, so our communion with the saints joins us to Christ, from whom as from its fountain and head flow all grace and life of the people of God itself.[13] It is most fitting, therefore, that we love those friends and coheirs of Jesus Christ who are also our sisters and brothers and outstanding benefactors, and that we give due thanks to God for them,[14] "humbly invoking them, and having recourse to their prayers, their aid and help in obtaining from God through his Son, Jesus Christ, Our Lord, our only Redeemer and Savior, the benefits we need."[15] Every authentic witness of love, indeed, offered by us to those who are in heaven tends towards and terminates in Christ, "the crown of all the saints,"[16] and through him in God who is wonderful in his saints and is glorified in them.[17]

It is especially in the sacred liturgy that our union with the heavenly church is best realized; in the liturgy, the power of the holy Spirit acts on us through sacramental signs; there we celebrate, rejoicing together, the praise of the divine majesty,[18] and all who have been redeemed by the blood of Christ from every tribe and tongue and people and nation (see Apoc 5:9), gathered together into one church glorify, in one common song of praise, the one and triune God. When, then, we celebrate the eucharistic sacrifice we are most closely united to the worship of the heavenly church; when in one communion we honor and remember the glorious Mary ever virgin, St Joseph, the holy apostles and martyrs and all the saints.[19]

51. This sacred council accepts loyally the venerable faith of our ancestors in the living communion which exists between us and our sisters and brothers who are in the glory of heaven or who are yet being purified after their death; and it reiterates the decrees of the Second Council of Nicea,[20] the Council of Florence,[21] and the Council of Trent.[22] At the same time, in keeping with its pastoral preoccupations, this council urges all concerned to remove or correct any abuses, excesses or defects which may have crept in here or there, and so restore all things that Christ and God be more fully praised. Let them teach the faithful, therefore, that the authentic cult of the saints does not consist so much in a multiplicity of external acts, but rather in a more intense practice of our love, whereby, for our own greater good and that of the church, we seek from the saints "example in their way

of life, a sharing in their communion, and the help of their intercession."[23] On the other hand, let the faithful be taught that our relationship with the saints in heaven, provided that it is understood in the full light of faith, in no way diminishes the worship of adoration given to God the Father, through Christ, in the Spirit; on the contrary, it greatly enriches it.[24]

For if we continue to love one another and to join in praising the most holy Trinity—all of us who are children of God and form one family in Christ (see Heb 3:6) — we will be faithful to the deepest vocation of the church and will share in a foretaste of the liturgy of perfect glory.[25] At the hour when Christ will appear, when the glorious resurrection of the dead will occur, the glory of God will light up the heavenly city, and the Lamb will be its lamp (see Apoc 21:23). Then the whole church of the saints in the supreme happiness of charity will adore God and "the Lamb who was slain" (Apoc 5:12), proclaiming with one voice: "To him who sits upon the throne and to the Lamb be blessing and honor and glory and might for ever and ever" (Apoc 5:13-14).

a. This chapter was translated by Father Thomas McInerney, OP, St Mary's, Tallaght, and he and AF revised it for this edition.

1. Council of Florence, Decree for the Greeks, Denz. 693 (1305).

2. Besides older documents against any kind of invocation of spirits, from the time of Alexander IV (27 Sept. 1258), see Encyclical of the Holy Office, De magnetismi abusu, 4 Aug. 1856: ASS (1865) pp. 177-178, Denz. 1653-1654 (2823-2825); reply of the Holy Office, 24 April 1917: AAS 9 (1917) p. 268, Denz. 2182 (3642).

3. A synthesis of this pauline doctrine may be seen in: Pius XII, Encyclical Mystici Corporis: AAS 35 (1943) p. 200, and passim.

4. See for example, St Augustine, Enarr. in Ps. 85, 24: PL 37, 1099. St Jerome, Liber contra Vigilantium, 6: PL 23, 344. St Thomas Aquinas, In 4m Sent., d. 45, q. 3, a 2. St Bonaventure In 4m Sent., d. 45, a 3, 2; etc.

5. See Pius XII, Encyclical Mystici Corporis: AAS 35 (1943) p. 245.

6. See many inscriptions in the Roman catacombs.

7. See Gelasius I, Decretal De Libris Recipiendis, 3: PL 59, 160, Denz. 165 (353).

8. St Methodius, *Symposium*, V11, 3: GCS (Bonwetsch), p. 74.

9. See Benedict XV, *Decretum approbationis virtutum in Causa beatifications et canonizationis Servi Dei Joannis Nepomuceni Neumann:* AAS 14 (1922) p. 23. Many allocutions of Pius XI on the saints: *Inviti all'eroismo, Discorsi e Radiomessaggi,* t. I-III, Rome 1941-1942, *passim;* Pius XII, *Discorsi e Radiomessaggi,* t. 10, 1949, pp. 37-43.

10. See Pius XII, Encyclical *Mediator Dei:* AAS 39 (1947) p. 581.

11. See Heb 13:7; Eccl 44-50; Heb 11:3-40. See also Pius XII, Encyclical *Mediator Dei:* AAS 39 (1947) pp. 582-583).

12. See Vatican Council I, Dogmatic Constitution on the Catholic Faith, *Dei Filiius,* ch. 3, Denz. 1794 (3013)

13. See Pius XII, Encyclical *Mystici Corporis:* AAS 35 (1943) p. 216.

14. On the question of gratitude to the saints, see E. Diehl, *Inscriptiones latinae christianae veteres,* I, Berlin, 1925, nos. 2008, 2382 and *passim.*

15. Council of Trent, session 25, *De invocatione . . . Sanctorum,* Denz. 984 (1821).

16. Roman Breviary, Invitatory for the feast of All Saints.

17. See, for example, 2 Th 1:10.

18. Vatican Council II, Constitution On the Sacred Liturgy, ch. 5, n. 104.

19. See Canon of the Roman Mass.

20. See Second Council of Nicaea, session. VII, Denz. 302 (600).

21. See Council of Florence, Decree for the Greeks, Denz. 693 (1304).

22. See Council of Trent, Session 25, On the invocation, veneration and relics of saints and on sacred images, Denz. 984-988 (1821-1824); Session 25, Decree on Purgatory, Denz. 983 (1820); Session 6, Decree on justification, canon 30, Denz. 840 (1580).

23. The Mass, Preface of saints, granted to some dioceses

24. See St Peter Canisius, *Catechismus Maior seu Summa Doctrinae christianae,* ch. III (ed. crit. F. Streicher), Part I, pp. 15-16, n. 44 and pp. 100-101, n. 49.

25. See Vatican Council II, Constitution on the Sacred Liturgy, ch. 1, no. 8.

Chapter VIII[a]

OUR LADY

I. Introduction

52. Wishing in his supreme goodness and wisdom to effect the redemption of the world, "when the fullness of time came, God sent his Son, born of a woman . . . that we might be adopted as sons and daughters" (Gal 4:4). "For us and for our salvation he came down from heaven: by the power of the holy Spirit he was born of the Virgin Mary."[1] This divine mystery of salvation is revealed to us and continues in the church, which the Lord established as his body. Joined to Christ their head and in communion with all his saints, the faithful must reverence the memory "first of all of the glorious ever Virgin Mary, Mother of God and of our Lord Jesus Christ."[2]

53. The Virgin Mary, who at the message of the angel received the Word of God in her heart and in her body and brought forth life to the world, is acknowledged and honored as truly the mother of God and of the Redeemer. Redeemed, in a more exalted fashion, by reason of the merits of her Son and united to him by a close and indissoluble tie, she is endowed with the high office and dignity of being the mother of the Son of God, and therefore she is also the beloved daughter of the Father and the temple of the holy Spirit. Because of this gift of sublime grace she far surpasses all creatures, both in heaven and on earth. But, being of the race of Adam, she is at the same time also united to all those who are to be saved; indeed, "she is clearly the mother of the members of Christ . . . since she has by her charity joined in bringing about the birth of believers in the church, who are members of its head."[3] Therefore she is

hailed as pre-eminent and as a wholly unique member of the church, and as its exemplar and outstanding model in faith and charity. The catholic church taught by the holy Spirit, honors her with filial affection and devotion as a most beloved mother.

54. Therefore this sacred synod, while expounding the doctrine on the church, in which the divine Redeemer brings about our salvation, intends to set forth diligently both the role of the Blessed Virgin in the mystery of the Incarnate Word and in the mystical body, and the duties of the redeemed towards the Mother of God, who is mother of Christ and mother of humanity, and especially of those who believe. It does not, however, intend to give a complete doctrine on Mary, nor does it wish to decide those questions which the work of theologians has not yet fully clarified. Those opinions therefore may be lawfully retained which are freely propounded in catholic schools concerning her, who occupies a place in the church which is the highest after Christ and also closest to us.[4]

II. The Role of the Blessed Virgin in the Plan of Salvation

55. The sacred writings of the Old and New Testaments, as well as venerable tradition, show the role of the mother of the Saviour in the plan of salvation in an ever clearer light and call our attention to it. The books of the Old Testament describe the history of salvation, by which the coming of Christ into the world was slowly prepared. The earliest documents, as they are read in the church and are understood in the light of further and full revelation, bring the figure of a woman, mother of the Redeemer, into a gradually clearer light. Considered in this light, she is already

prophetically foreshadowed in the promise of victory over the serpent which was given to our first parents after their fall into sin (see Gen 3:15). Likewise, she is the virgin who shall conceive and bear a son, whose name shall be called Emmanuel (see Is 7:14; compare Mic 5:2-3; Mt 1:22-23). She stands out among the poor and humble of the Lord, who confidently hope for and receive salvation from him. After a long period of waiting for the promise, the times are fulfilled in her, the exalted Daughter of Sion and the new plan of salvation is established, when the Son of God has taken human nature from her, that he might in the mysteries of his flesh free humanity from sin.

56. The Father of mercies willed that the Incarnation should be preceded by assent on the part of the predestined mother, so that just as a woman had a share in bringing about death, so also a woman should contribute to life. This is pre-eminently true of the Mother of Jesus, who gave to the world the life that renews all things, and who was enriched by God with gifts appropriate to such a role. It is no wonder then that it was customary for the holy Fathers to refer to the mother of God as all holy and free from every stain of sin, as though fashioned by the holy Spirit and formed as a new creature.[5] Enriched from the first instant of her conception with the splendor of an entirely unique holiness, the virgin from Nazareth is hailed by the heralding angel, by divine command, as "full of grace" (see Lk 1:28), and to the heavenly messenger she replies: "Behold the handmaid of the Lord, be it done to me according to your word" (Lk 1:38). Thus the daughter of Adam, Mary, consenting to the word of God, became the Mother of Jesus. Committing herself whole-heartedly to God's saving will and impeded by no sin, she devoted herself totally, as a handmaid of the Lord, to the person and work of her Son, under and with him, serving the mystery

of redemption, by the grace of Almighty God. Rightly, therefore, the holy Fathers see Mary not merely as a passive instrument in the hands of God, but as freely cooperating in the work of human salvation through faith and obedience. For, as St Irenaeus says, she "being obedient, became the cause of salvation for herself and for the whole human race."[6] Hence not a few of the early Fathers freely assert with him in their preaching:"the knot of Eve's disobedience was untied by Mary's obedience: what the virgin Eve bound through her disbelief, Mary loosened by her faith."[7] Comparing Mary with Eve, they call her "Mother of the living,"[8] and frequently claim:"death through Eve, life through Mary."[9]

57. This union of the mother with the Son in the work of salvation is made manifest from the time of Christ's virginal conception up to his death; first when Mary, setting out in haste to visit Elizabeth, was proclaimed blessed by her because of her belief in the promise of salvation, and the precursor leaped with joy in the womb of his mother (see Lk 1:41-45); then also at the birth of Our Lord, who did not diminish his mother's virginal integrity but consecrated it.[10] The Mother of God joyfully showed her firstborn Son to the shepherds and the Magi. When she presented him to the Lord in the temple, making the offering of the poor, she heard Simeon foretelling at the same time that her Son would be a sign of contradiction and that a sword would pierce the mother's soul, that the intimate thoughts of many hearts would be revealed (see Lk 2:34-35); when the child Jesus was lost and they had searched for him sorrowing, his parents found him in the temple, engaged in his Father's business, and they did not understand the words of their Son. His mother, however, kept all these things to be pondered in her heart (see Lk 2:41-51).

58. In the public life of Jesus, Mary appears prominently; at the very beginning when at the marriage feast of Cana, moved with pity, she brought about by her intercession the beginning of miracles of Jesus the Messiah (see Jn 2:1-11). In the course of her Son's preaching she accepted the words whereby, in extolling a kingdom beyond the concerns and ties of flesh and blood, he declared blessed those who heard and kept the word of God (see Mk 3:35; Lk 11:27-27) as she was faithfully doing (see Lk 2:19; 51). Thus the blessed Virgin advanced in her pilgrimage of faith, and faithfully persevered in her union with her Son until she stood at the cross, in keeping with the divine plan (see Jn 19:25), suffering deeply with her only begotten Son, associating herself with his sacrifice in her mother's heart, and lovingly consenting to the immolation of this victim who was born of her. Finally, she was given by the same Christ Jesus dying on the cross as a mother to his disciple, with these words: "Woman, this is your Son" (Jn 19:26-27).[11]

59. But since it had pleased God not to manifest solemnly the mystery of the salvation of the human race before he would pour forth the Spirit promised by Christ, we see the apostles before the day of Pentecost "persevering with one mind in prayer with the women and Mary the Mother of Jesus, and with his brothers" (Acts 1:14), and we also see Mary by her prayers imploring the gift of the Spirit, who had already overshadowed her at the Annunciation. Finally the immaculate Virgin preserved free from all stain of original sin,[12] was taken up body and soul into heavenly glory,[13] when her earthly life was over, and exalted by the Lord as Queen over all things, that she might be the more fully conformed to her Son, the Lord of lords, (see Apoc 19:16) and conqueror of sin and death.[14]

III. The Blessed Virgin and the Church

60. In the words of the apostle there is but one mediator: "for there is but one God and one mediator between God and humankind, the man Christ Jesus, who gave himself a redemption for all" (1 Tim 2:5-6). But Mary's function as mother of humankind in no way obscures or diminishes this unique mediation of Christ, but rather shows its power. All the Blessed Virgin's salutary influence on men and women originates not in any inner necessity but in the disposition of God. It flows forth from the superabundance of the merits of Christ, rests on his mediation, depends entirely on it and draws all its power from it. It does not hinder in any way the immediate union of the faithful with Christ but on the contrary fosters it.

61. The predestination of the Blessed Virgin as Mother of God was associated with the incarnation of the divine word: in the designs of divine Providence she was the gracious mother of the divine Redeemer here on earth, and above all others and in a singular way the generous associate and humble handmaid of the Lord. She conceived, gave birth to, and nourished Christ, she presented him to the Father in the temple, shared his sufferings as he died on the cross. Thus, in a very special way she cooperated by her obedience, faith, hope and burning charity in the work of the Savior in restoring supernatural life to souls. For this reason she is a mother to us in the order of grace.

62. This motherhood of Mary in the order of grace continues without interruption from the consent which she loyally gave at the Annunciation and which she sustained without wavering beneath the cross, until the eternal consummation of all the elect. Taken up to heaven, she did not lay aside this saving office but by her manifold intercession continues to procure for us the gifts of eternal salvation.[15] By her motherly

love she cares for her Son's sisters and brothers who still journey on earth surrounded by dangers and difficulties, until they are led into their blessed home. Therefore the blessed Virgin is invoked in the church under the titles of advocate, helper, benefactress, and mediatrix.[16] This, however, is understood in such a way that it neither takes away anything from, nor adds anything to, the dignity and efficacy of Christ the one Mediator.[17]

No creature could ever be counted along with the Incarnate Word and Redeemer; but just as the priesthood of Christ is shared in various ways both by his ministers and the faithful, and as the one goodness of God is radiated in different ways among his creatures, so also the unique mediation of the Redeemer does not exclude but rather gives rise to a manifold cooperation which is but a sharing in one source.

The church does not hesitate to profess this subordinate role of Mary, which it constantly experiences and recommends to the heartfelt attention of the faithful, so that encouraged by this maternal help they may the more closely adhere to the Mediator and Redeemer.

63. By reason of the gift and role of her divine motherhood, by which she is united with her Son, the Redeemer, and with her unique graces and functions, the Blessed Virgin is also intimately united to the church. As St Ambrose taught, the Mother of God is a type of the church in the order of faith, charity, and perfect union with Christ.[18] For in the mystery of the church, which is itself rightly called mother and virgin, the Blessed Virgin stands out in eminent and singular fashion as exemplar both of virgin and mother.[19] Through her faith and obedience she gave birth on earth to the very Son of the Father, without sexual intercourse but by the overshadowing of the holy Spirit, in the manner of a new Eve who placed her

faith, not in the serpent of old but in God's messenger without wavering in doubt. The Son whom she brought forth is he whom God placed as the first born among many children (see Rom 8:29), that is, the faithful, in whose generation and formation she cooperates with a mother's love.

64. The church contemplating her hidden sanctity, imitating her charity and faithfully fulfilling the Father's will, by receiving the word of God in faith becomes herself a mother. By preaching and Baptism she brings forth daughters and sons, who are conceived by the holy Spirit and born of God, to a new and immortal life. The church is a virgin, who keeps in its entirety and purity the faith she pledged to her spouse. Imitating the mother of her Lord, and by the power of the holy Spirit, she keeps intact faith, firm hope and sincere charity.[20]

65. But while in the most Blessed Virgin the church has already reached that perfection whereby she exists without spot or wrinkle (see Eph 5:27), the faithful still strive to conquer sin and grow in holiness. And so they turn their eyes to Mary who shines out to the whole community of the elect as the model of virtues. Devoutly meditating on her and contemplating her in the light of the Word made man, the church reverently penetrates more deeply into the great mystery of the Incarnation and becomes more and more like its spouse. Having entered deeply into the history of salvation, Mary, in a way, unites in her person and re-echoes the most important doctrines of the faith: and when she is the subject of preaching and honor she prompts the faithful to come to her Son, to his sacrifice and to the love of the Father. Seeking after the glory of Christ, the church becomes more like its lofty exemplar, and continually progresses in faith, hope and charity, seeking and doing the will of God in all things. The church, therefore, in

its apostolic work also, rightly looks to her who gave birth to Christ, who was thus conceived by the holy Spirit and born of a virgin, in order that through the church he could be born and increase in the hearts of the faithful. In her life the Virgin was a model of that motherly love with which all who join in the church's apostolic mission for the regeneration of humanity should be animated.

IV. The Cult of the Blessed Virgin in the Church

66. Mary has by grace been exalted above all angels and humanity to a place after her Son, as the most holy mother of God who was involved in the mysteries of Christ: she is rightly honored with a special cult by the church. From the earliest times the Blessed Virgin has been honored with the title of "mother of God", under whose protection the faithful take refuge together in prayer in all their perils and needs.[21] Accordingly, especially after the Council of Ephesus, the cult of the people of God for Mary developed marvellously in veneration and love, in invocation and imitation, according to her own prophetic words: "all generations will call me blessed, because he that is mighty has done great things to me" (Lk 1:48).

This cult, as it has always existed in the church, while it is totally extraordinary, it yet differs essentially from the cult of adoration which is offered equally to the Incarnate Word and to the Father and the holy Spirit, and is most favorable to this adoration.[21a] The various forms of piety towards the Mother of God which, within the limits of sound and orthodox doctrine, the church has approved for various times and places according to the character and temperament of the faithful, ensure that while the mother is honored, the Son through whom all things have their being (see Col 1:15-16) and in whom it has pleased the

Father that "all fullness should dwell" (Col 1:19) is rightly known, loved and glorified and his commandments are observed.

67. The sacred synod expressly teaches this catholic doctrine and at the same time urges all the sons and daughters of the church to foster generously the cult, especially the liturgical cult, of the Blessed Virgin, and to hold in high regard the practices and exercises of devotion towards her recommended by the teaching authority of the church in the course of centuries, and religiously to observe those decrees laid down in the past regarding the cult of images of Christ, the Blessed Virgin and the saints.[22] But it strongly urges theologians and preachers of the word of God to be careful to refrain as much from all false exaggeration as from too summary an attitude in considering the special dignity of the Mother of God.[23] Following the study of sacred scripture, the Fathers, the doctors and the liturgy of the church, and under the guidance of the church's magisterium, let them rightly illustrate the offices and privileges of the Blessed Virgin which always refer to Christ, the source of all truth, sanctity, and devotion. Let them carefully refrain from whatever might by word or deed lead the separated sisters and brothers or any others whatsoever into error about the true doctrine of the church. Let the faithful remember moreover that true devotion consists neither in sterile or transitory feeling, nor in an empty credulity, but proceeds from true faith, by which we are led to recognize the excellence of the Mother of God, and we are moved to a filial love towards our mother and to the imitation of her virtues.

V. Mary, Sign of True Hope and Comfort for the Pilgrim People of God

68. In the meantime the Mother of Jesus in the

glory which she possesses in body and soul in heaven is the image and beginning of the church as it is to be perfected in the world to come. Likewise, she shines forth on earth, until the day of the Lord shall come (see 2 Pet 3:10), a sign of certain hope and comfort to the pilgrim people of God.

69. It gives great joy and comfort to this sacred synod that among the separated brothers and sisters too there are those who give due honor to the Mother of Our Lord and Saviour, especially among the eastern Christians, who with devout mind and fervent impulse reverence the Mother of God, ever virgin.[24] Let all Christians pour forth urgent supplications to the Mother of God and of humanity that she, who aided the beginnings of the church by her prayers, may now, exalted as she is above all the angels and saints, intercede before her Son in the communion of all the saints, until all families of people, whether they are honored with the title of christian or whether they still do not know the Saviour, may be happily gathered together in peace and harmony into one people of God, for the glory of the most holy and undivided Trinity.

a. The chapter was translated by the late Hilda Graef, Oxford, and was revised for this edition by Christopher O'Donnell, OCarm., Milltown Park, Dublin, and AF.

1. Creed of the Roman mass: Symbol of Constantinople: Mansi 3, 566. See Council of Ephesus: Mansi. 4, 1130 (also Mansi 2, 665 and 4, 1071); Council of Chalcedon: Mansi. 7, 111-116; Council of Constantinople II: Mansi 9, 375-396.

2. Canon of the Roman Mass.

3. St Augustine, *De S. Virginitate*, 6: PL 40, 399.

4. See Paul VI, Allocution to the Council, 4 December 1963: AAS 56 (1964), p. 37.

5. See Germanus of Constantinople, *Hom. in Annunt. Deiparae:* PG 98, 328 A; *In Dorm.* 2: PG 98, 357. Anastasius of Antioch, *Serm. 2 de Annunt.* 2: PG 89, 1377 AB; *Serm.* 3. 2: PG 89 1388 C. St Andrew of Crete, *Can. in B.V. Nat.*, 4: PG 97, 1321 B; *In B.V. Nat.* 1: PG. 97, 812 A; *Hom. in Dorm.* 1: PG 97 1068 C. St Sophronius, *Or. 2 in Annunt.* 18: PG 87 (3), 3237 BD.

6. St Irenaeus, *Adv. Haer.* III, 22, 4: PG 7, 959 A, Harvey, 2, 123.

7. St Irenaeus, *ibid.:* Harvey 2, 124.

8. St Epiphanius, *Haer.* 78, 18: PG 42, 728 CD-729 AB.

9. St Jerome, *Epist.* 22, 21: PL 22, 408. See St Augustine, *Serm.* 51, 2, 3: PL 38, 335; *Serm.* 232, 2: PL 38 1108. St Cyril of Jerusalem, *Catech.* 12, 15: PG 33, 741 AB. St John Chrysostom, *In Ps* 44, 7: PG 55,193. St John Damascene, *Hom. 2 in dorm.* B.M.V., 3: PG 96, 728.

10. See Council of Lateran in 649, Can. 3: Mansi 10,1151. St Leo the Great, *Epist. ad Flav.:* PL 54, 759. Council of Chalcedon: Mansi 7, 462. St Ambrose, *De instit. virg.:* PL 16, 320.

11. See Pius XII, Encyclical *Mystici Corporis,* 29 June 1943: AAS 35 (1943), pp. 247-248.

12. See Pius IX, Bull *Ineffabilis,* 8 Dec. 1854: Acta Pii IX, 1, 1, p. 616; Denz. 1641 (2803).

13. See Pius XII, Const. Apost. *Munificentissimus* 1 Nov. 1950: AAS 42 (1950): Denz. 2333 (3903). See St John Damascene, *Enc. in dorm. Dei Genitricis, Hom.* 2 and 3: PG 96, 721-761, esp. col. 728 B. St Germanus of Constantinople In *S. Dei gen. dorm. Serm.* 1: PG 98 (6), 340-348; *Serm.* 3: PG 98 (6) 361. St Modestus of Jerusalem, *In dorm. SS. Deiparae:* PG 86 (2), 3277-3312.

14. See Pius XII, Encyclical *Ad coeli Reginam,* 11 Oct. 1954: AAS 46 (1954), pp. 633-636: Denz. 3913 ff. See St Andrew of Crete, *Hom. 3 in dorm. SS Deiparae:* PG 97, 1089-1109. St John Damascene, *De fide orth,* IV, 14: PG 94, 1153-1161.

15. See Kleutgen, corrected text *De mysterio verbi incarnati* ch IV: Mansi 53, 290. See St Andrew of Crete, *In nat. Mariae, Serm.* 4: PG 97, 865A. St Germanus of Constantinople, *In ann. Deiparae:* PG 98, 321 BC. *In dorm. Deiparae* III: PG 98 361 D. St John Damascene *In dorm B.V.M., Hom.* 1, 8: PG 96, 712 BC-713 A.

16. See Leo XIII, Encyclical *Adjutricem populi,* 5 Sept. 1895: ASS 15 (1895-1896), p. 303. St Pius X, Encyclical *Ad diem illum,* 2 Feb. 1904 Acta 1, p. 154: Denz. 1978 a (3370). Pius XI, Encyclical *Miserentissimus* 8 May 1928: AAS 20 (1928), p. 178. Pius XII, Radio Message 13 May 1946: AAS 38 (1946), p. 266.

17. St Ambrose, *Epist.* 63: PL 16 1218

18. Ambrose, *Expos.* Lc. II, 7: PL 15, l555

19. See Pseudo Peter Damien, *Serm.* 63: PL 144, 861 AB. Geoffrey (de Breteuil) of St Victor, *In nat. B. M.,* MS. Paris, Mazarine, 1002, fol. 109 r Gerhoh of Reichersberg, *De gloria et honore Filii hominis* 10: PL 194, 1105 AB.

20. St Ambrose, *Expos. in Lc.* 2, 7 and 10, 24-25: PL 15, 1555 and 1810. St Augustine, *In Io. Tr.* 13. 12: PL 35, 1499. See *Serm.* 191, 2, 3: PL 38, 1010, etc. See also Ven. Bede, *In Lc. Expos,* 1, ch. 2: PL 92, 330. Isaac of Stella, *Serm.* 31: PL 194,1863 A.

21. See Roman Breviary, antiphon "*Sub tuum praesidium*: We fly to your protection", first vespers of the little office of the Blessed Virgin Mary.

21a. The Latin reads: *Qui cultus, prout in ecclesia semper exstitit, singularis omnino quamquam est, essentialiter differt a cultu adorationis, qui Verbo incarnato aeque ac Patri et Spiritui sancto exhibetur, eidemque potissimum favet.* The word *singularis* could also be rendered "pre-eminent", or "very special" (Tanner) or, simply, "singular", except that "singular" can be read as meaning "unique" [Editor].

22. Council of Nicea II A.D. 787: Mansi 13, 378-379; Denz. 302 (600-601). Council of Trent, Session 25: Mansi 33, 171-172.

23. See Pius XII, Radio message, 24 Oct. 1954: AAS 46 (1954), p. 679, Encyclical *Ad coeli Reginam*, 11 Oct. 1954. AAS 46 (1954), p. 637.

24. See Pius XI, Encyclical *Ecclesiam Dei*, 12 Nov. 1923: AAS 15 (1923), p. 581; Pius XII, Encyclical *Fulgens corona*, 8 Sept. 1953: AAS 45 (1953), pp. 590-591.

THE EXPLANATORY NOTE
Announcement Made by the Secretary General of the Council at the One Hundred and Twenty-Third General Congregation 16 November, 1964

A query has been made as to what is the theological qualification to be attached to the teaching put forward in the schema *The Church,* on which a vote is to be taken. The doctrinal commission has replied to this query in appraising the amendments proposed to the third chapter of the draft of the document, *The church:*

As is self-evident, the conciliar text is to be interpreted in accordance with the general rules which are known to all.

On this occasion the doctrinal commission referred to its Declaration of 6 March, 1964, which we reproduce here:

Taking into account conciliar practice and the pastoral purpose of the present council, the sacred synod defined as binding on the church only those matters of faith and morals which it has expressly put forward as such. Whatever else it proposes as the teaching of the supreme magisterium of the church is to be acknowledged and accepted by each and every member of the faithful according to the mind of the council which is clear from the subject matter and its formulation, following the norms of theological interpretation.

The following explanatory note prefixed to the amendments of chapter three of the schema *The church* is given to the Fathers, and it is according to the mind and sense of this note that the teaching contained in chapter three is to be explained and understood.

PRELIMINARY EXPLANATORY NOTE

The commission has decided to preface its assessment of the amendments with the following general observations.

1. The word *College* is not taken in the *strictly juridical* sense, that is as a group of equals who transfer their powers to their chairperson, but as a permanent body whose form and authority is to be ascertained from revelation. For this reason, it is explicitly said about the twelve apostles in the reply to amendment 12 that Our Lord constituted them "as a college or *permanent group*" (see amendment 53, c). In the same way the words *Order* or *body* are used at other times for the college of bishops. The parallel between Peter and the apostles on the one hand and the Pope and the bishops on the other does not imply the transmission of the extraordinary power of the apostles to their successors, nor obviously does it imply *equality* between the head and members of the college, but only a *proportion* between the two relationships: Peter — apostles and pope — bishops. And therefore the commission decided to write in Art. 22 not "in the same manner" *(eadem ratione)* but "in like manner" *(pari ratione)*.

2. A man becomes a *member* of the college through episcopal consecration and hierarchical communion with the head of the college and its members (see art. 22, end of par. 1).

It is the unmistakable teaching of tradition, including liturgical tradition, that an *ontological* share in the *sacred* functions is given by consecration. The word *function* is deliberately used in preference to powers which can have the sense of power *ordered to action*. A *canonical* or *juridical determination* through hierarchical authority is required for such power ordered to action. A determination of this kind can come about through appointment to a particular office or the assignment of subjects, and is conferred according to norms approved by the supreme authority. The need for a further norm follows from the nature of the case, because it is a question of functions to be discharged by *more than one subject*, who work together in the hierarchy of functions intended by Christ. "Communion" of this kind was in fact a feature abiding in the varying circumstances *of the life* of the church through the ages, before it was endorsed and codified *by law*.

For this reason, it is expressly stated that *hierarchical* communion with the head and members is required. The idea of *communion* was highly valued in the early church, as indeed it is today especially in the East. It is not to be understood as some vague sort of *goodwill*, but as *something organic* which calls for a juridical structure as well as being enkindled by charity. The commission, therefore, agreed, almost unanimously, on the wording "in *hierarchical* communion" (see amendment 40 and the statements about canonical mission in art. 24).

The documents of recent Popes dealing with episcopal jurisdiction are to be interpreted as referring to this necessary determination of powers.

3. There is no such thing as the college without its head: it is *"The subject of supreme and entire power* over the whole church."This much must be acknowledged lest the fullness of the Pope's power be jeopardized. The idea of college necessarily and at all times involves a head and *in the college the head preserves intact his function as Vicar of Christ and pastor of the universal church.* In other words, it is not a distinction between the Roman Pontiff and the bishops taken together but between the Roman Pontiff by himself and the Roman Pontiff along with the bishops. The Pope alone, in fact, being *head* of the college, is qualified to perform certain actions in which the bishops have no competence whatsoever, for example, the convocation and direction of the college, approval of the norms of its activity, and so on (see amendment 81). It is for the Pope, to whom the care of the whole flock of Christ has been entrusted, to decide the best manner of implementing this care, either personal or collegiate, in order to meet the changing needs of the church in the course of time. The Roman Pontiff undertakes the regulation, encouragement, and approval of the exercise of collegiality as he sees fit.

4. The Pope, as supreme pastor of the church, may exercise his power at any time, as he sees fit, by reason of the demands of his office. But as the church's tradition attests, the college, although it is always in existence, is not for that reason continually engaged in *strictly* collegiate activity. In other words it is not always "in full activity" *(in actu pleno)*; in fact it is only occasionally that it engages in strictly collegiate activity and that only *with the consent of the head (nonnisi consentiente capite).* The phrase *with the consent of the head* is used in order to exclude the impression of *dependence* on something *external:* but the word "consent" entails *communion* between head and members and calls for this *action* which is exclusive to the head. The point is expressly stated in art. 22, par. 2 and it is explained at the end of the same article. The negative formulation "only with" *(nonnisi)* covers all cases: consequently it is evident that the norms approved by the supreme authority must always be observed (see amendment 84).

Clearly it is the *connection* of bishops *with their head* that is in question throughout and not the activity of bishops *independently* of the Pope. In a case like that, in default of the Pope's action, the bishops cannot act as a college, for this is obvious from the idea of "college"itself. This hierarchical communion of all bishops with the Pope is unmistakably hallowed by tradition.

N.B.—The ontologico-sacramental function, which must be distinguished from the juridico-canonical aspect, *cannot* be discharged without hierarchical communion. It was decided in the commission not to enter into questions of *liceity* and *validity*, which are to be left to theologians, particularly in regard to the power exercised *de facto* among separated eastern Christians, about which there are divergent opinions.

a. The following was published as an appendix to the official Latin version of the Constitution on the Church.

DOGMATIC CONSTITUTION ON DIVINE REVELATION[a]

Dei Verbum
18 November, 1965

Prologue

1. Hearing the word of God reverently and proclaiming it confidently, this holy synod makes its own the words of St John: "We proclaim to you the eternal life which was with the Father and was made manifest to us — that which we have seen and heard we proclaim also to you, so that you may have fellowship with us; and our fellowship is with the Father and with his Son Jesus Christ" (l Jn 1:2-3). Following, then, in the steps of the councils of Trent and Vatican I, this synod wishes to set forth the authentic teaching on divine revelation and its transmission. For it wants the whole world to hear the summons to salvation, so that through hearing it may believe, through belief it may hope, through hope it may come to love.[1]

Chapter I

DIVINE REVELATION ITSELF

2. It pleased God, in his goodness and wisdom, to reveal himself and to make known the mystery of his will (see Eph 1:9), which was that people can draw near to the Father, through Christ, the Word made

flesh, in the holy Spirit, and thus become sharers in the divine nature (see Eph 2:18; 2 Pet 1:4). By this revelation, then, the invisible God (see Col 1:15; 1 Tim 1:17), from the fullness of his love, addresses men and women as his friends (see Ex 33:11; Jn 15; 14-15), and lives among them (see Bar 3:38), in order to invite and receive them into his own company. The pattern of this revelation unfolds through deeds and words which are intrinsically connected: the works performed by God in the history of salvation show forth and confirm the doctrine and realities signified by the words; the words, for their part, proclaim the works, and bring to light the mystery they contain. The most intimate truth thus revealed about God and human salvation shines forth for us in Christ, who is himself both the mediator and the sum total of revelation.[2]

3. God, who creates and conserves all things by his Word (see Jn 1:3), provides constant evidence of himself in created realities (see Rom 1:19-20). Furthermore, wishing to open up the way to heavenly salvation, he manifested himself to our first parents from the very beginning. After the fall, he buoyed them up with the hope of salvation, by promising redemption (see Gen 3:15); and he has never ceased to take care of the human race, in order to give eternal life to all those who seek salvation by persevering in doing good (see Rom 2:6-7). In his own time, God called Abraham and made him into a great nation (see Gen 12:2). After the era of the patriarchs, he taught this nation, through Moses and the prophets, to recognize him as the only living and true God, as a provident Father and just judge. He taught them, too, to look for the promised Saviour. And so, throughout the ages, he prepared the way for the Gospel.

4. After God had spoken many times and in various ways through the prophets, "in these last days he has spoken to us by a Son" (Heb 1:1-2). For he sent his

Son, the eternal Word who enlightens all humankind, to live among them and to tell them about the inner life of God. Hence, Jesus Christ, sent as "a man being men and women",[3] "speaks the words of God" (Jn 3:34), and accomplishes the saving work which the Father gave him to do (see Jn 5:36; 17:4). As a result, he himself — to see whom is to see the Father (see Jn 14:9) — completed and perfected revelation and confirmed it with divine guarantees. Everything to do with his presence and his manifestation of himself was involved in achieving this: his words and works, signs and miracles, but above all his death and glorious resurrection from the dead, and finally his sending of the Spirit of truth. He revealed that God was with us, to deliver us from the darkness of sin and death, and to raise us up to eternal life.

The christian dispensation, therefore, since it is the new and definitive covenant, will never pass away; and no new public revelation is to be expected before the glorious manifestation of our Lord, Jesus Christ (see 1 Tim 6:14 and Tit 2:13).

5. "The obedience of faith" (see Rom 16:26; compare Rom 1:5; 2 Cor 10:5-6) must be our response to God who reveals. By faith one freely commits oneself entirely to God, making "the full submission of intellect and will to God who reveals",[4] and willingly assenting to the revelation given by God. For this faith to be accorded we need the grace of God, anticipating it and assisting it, as well as the interior helps of the holy Spirit, who moves the heart and converts it to God, and opens the eyes of the mind and "makes it easy for all to accept and believe the truth".[5] The same holy Spirit constantly perfects faith by his gifts, so that revelation may be more and more deeply understood.

6. By divine revelation God wished to manifest and communicate both himself and the eternal decrees of his will concerning the salvation of humankind. He

wished, in other words, "to share with us divine benefits which entirely surpass the powers of the human mind to understand".[6]

The holy synod professes that "God, the first principle and last end of all things, can be known with certainty from the created world, by the natural light of human reason" (see Rom 1:20). It teaches that it is to his revelation that we must attribute the fact "that those things, which in themselves are not beyond the grasp of human reason, can, in the present condition of the human race, be known by all with ease, with firm certainty, and without the contamination of error".[7]

a. Prologue and Chapters 1, 2, 6 translated by Liam Walsh, OP, chapters 3, 4, 5 by Wilfred Harrington, OP, who have revised their respective chapters for this edition. Further revision was done by AF.

1. St Augustine, *De Catechizandis rudibus*, 4, 8: PL 40, 316.

2. See Mt 11:27; Jn 1:14 and 17; 14:6; 17:1-3; 2 Cor 3:16 and 4:6; Eph 1:3-14.

3. *Letter to Diognetus*, 7, 4: Funk, *Patres Apostolici*, I, p. 403.

4. Vatican Council I, Dogmatic Constitution on the Catholic Faith, *Dei Filius*, ch. 3: Denz. 1789 (3008).

5. Council of Orange II, canon 7: Denz. 180 (377). Vatican Council I, loc. cit.: Denz. 1791 (3010).

6. Vatican Council I, Dogmatic Constitution on the Catholic Faith, *Dei Filius*, ch. 2: Denz. 1786 (3005).

7. Ibid.: Denz. 1785 and 1786 (3004 and 3005).

Chapter II

THE TRANSMISSION OF DIVINE REVELATION

7. God graciously arranged that what he had once revealed for the salvation of all peoples should last for

ever in its entirety and be transmitted to all generations. Therefore, Christ the Lord, in whom the entire
revelation of the most high God is summed up (see 2
Cor 1:20; 3:16-4:6), having fulfilled in his own person
and promulgated with his own lips the Gospel promised beforehand by the prophets, commanded the
apostles to preach it to everyone as the source of all
saving truth and moral law, communicating God's
gifts to them.[1] This was faithfully done: it was done by
the apostles who handed on, by oral preaching, by
their example, by their dispositions, what they themselves had received — whether from the lips of
Christ, from his way of life and his works, or by coming to know it through the prompting of the holy
Spirit; it was done by those apostles and others associated with them who, under the inspiration of the
same holy Spirit, committed the message of salvation
to writing.[2]

In order that the full and living Gospel might
always be preserved in the church the apostles left
bishops as their successors. They gave them "their
own position of teaching authority."[3] This sacred tradition, then, and the sacred scripture of both Testaments, are like a mirror, in which the church, during
its pilgrim journey here on earth, contemplates God,
from whom it receives everything, until such time as
it is brought to see him face to face as he really is (see
Jn 3:2).

8. Thus, the apostolic preaching, which is expressed
in a special way in the inspired books, was to be preserved in a continuous line of succession until the end
of time. Hence the apostles, in handing on what they
themselves had received, warn the faithful to maintain the traditions which they had learned either by
word of mouth or by letter (see 2 Th 2:15), and to fight
for the faith that had been handed on to them once
and for all (see Jude 3).[4] What was handed on by the

apostles comprises everything that serves to make the people of God live their lives in holiness and increase their faith. In this way the church, in its doctrine, life and worship, perpetuates and transmits to every generation all that it itself is, all that it believes.

The tradition that comes from the apostles makes progress in the church, with the help of the holy Spirit.[5] There is a growth in insight into the realities and words that are being passed on. This comes about through the contemplation and study of believers who ponder these things in their hearts (see Lk 2:19 and 51). It comes from the intimate sense of spiritual realities which they experience. And it comes from the preaching of those who, on succeeding to the office of bishop, have received the sure charism of truth. Thus, as the centuries go by, the church is always advancing towards the plenitude of divine truth, until eventually the words of God are fulfilled in it.

The sayings of the church Fathers are a witness to the life-giving presence of this tradition, showing how its riches are poured out in the practice and life of the believing and praying church. By means of the same tradition, the full canon of the sacred books is known to the church and the holy scriptures themselves are more thoroughly understood and constantly made effective in the church. Thus God, who spoke in the past, continues to converse with the spouse of his beloved Son. And the holy Spirit, through whom the living voice of the Gospel rings out in the church — and through it in the world — leads believers to the full truth and makes the word of Christ dwell in them in all its richness (see Col 3:16).

9. Sacred tradition and sacred scripture, then, are bound closely together, and communicate one with the other. Flowing from the same divine well-spring, both of them merge, in a sense, and move towards the same goal. Sacred scripture is the utterance of

God put down as it is in writing under the inspiration of the holy Spirit. And tradition transmits in its entirety the word of God which has been entrusted to the apostles by Christ the Lord and the holy Spirit; it transmits it to the successors of the apostles so that, enlightened by the Spirit of truth, they may faithfully preserve, expound and disseminate it by their preaching. Thus it is that the church does not draw its certainty about all revealed truths from the holy scriptures alone. Hence, both scripture and tradition must be accepted and honored with equal devotion and reverence.[6]

10. Tradition and scripture make up a single sacred deposit of the word of God, which is entrusted to the church. By adhering to it the entire holy people, united to its pastors, remains always faithful to the teaching of the apostles, to the communion of life, to the breaking of bread and the prayers (see Acts 2:42 Greek). So, in maintaining, practicing and professing the faith that has been handed on there is a unique interplay between the bishops and the faithful.[7]

But the task of giving an authentic interpretation of the word of God, whether in its written form or in the form of tradition,[8] has been entrusted to the living teaching office of the church alone.[9] Its authority in this matter is exercised in the name of Jesus Christ. This magisterium is not superior to the word of God, but is rather its servant. It teaches only what has been handed on to it. At the divine command and with the help of the holy Spirit, it listens to this devoutly, guards it reverently and expounds it faithfully. All that it proposes for belief as being divinely revealed it draws from this sole deposit of faith.

It is clear, therefore, that, in the supremely wise arrangement of God, sacred tradition, sacred scripture and the magisterium of the church are so connected and associated that one of them cannot stand without the others. Working together, each in its own way under the action of the one holy Spirit, they all contribute effectively to the salvation of souls.

1. See Mt 28:19-20 and Mk 16:15. Council of Trent, Decree *On the Canonical Scriptures:* Denz. 783 (1501).

2. See Council of Trent, loc. cit.; Vatican Council I, Dogmatic Constitution on the Catholic Faith, *Dei Filius,* ch. 2: Denz. 1787 (3006).

3. St Irenaeus, *Adv. Haer.,* III, 3,1: PG 7, 848; Harvey, 2, p. 9.

4. See Council of Nicea II: Denz. 303 (602). Council of Constantinople IV, Session X, can. 1: Denz. 336 (650-652).

5. See First Vatican Council, Dogmatic Constitution on the Catholic Faith, *Dei Filius,* ch. 4: Denz. 1800 (3020).

6. See Council of Trent, Decree *On the Canonical Scriptures:* Denz. 783 (1501).

7. See Pius XII, Apost. Const. *Munificentissimus Deus,* 1 Nov. 1950: AAS 42 (1950), p.756, taken along with the words of St Cyprian, *Epist.* 66, 8: CSEL, III, 2, 733: "The church is the people united to its priests, the flock adhering to its shepherd."

8. See Vatican Council I, Dogmatic Constitution on the Catholic Faith, *Dei Filius,* ch. 3: Denz. 1972 (3011).

9. See Pius XII, Encyclical *Humani Generis,* 12 Aug. 1950: AAS 42 (1950) 568-569: Denz. 2314 (3886).

Chapter III

SACRED SCRIPTURE: ITS DIVINE INSPIRATION AND ITS INTERPRETATION

11. Those things revealed by God which are contained and presented in the text of sacred scripture have been written under the inspiration of the holy Spirit. For holy mother church, relying on the faith of the apostolic age, accepts as sacred and canonical the books of the Old and the New Testaments, whole and entire, with all their parts, on the grounds that, written under the inspiration of the holy Spirit (see Jn 20:31; 2 Tim 3:16; 2 Pet 1:19-21; 3:15-16), they have

God as their author, and have been handed on as such to the church itself.[1] To compose the sacred books, God chose certain men who, all the while he employed them in this task, made full use of their powers and faculties[2] so that, though he acted in them and by them,[3] it was as true authors that they consigned to writing whatever he wanted written, and no more.[4]

Since, therefore, all that the inspired authors, or sacred writers, affirm should be regarded as affirmed by the holy Spirit, we must acknowledge that the books of scripture, firmly, faithfully and without error, teach that truth which God, for the sake of our salvation, wished to see confided to the sacred scriptures.[5] Thus "all scripture is inspired by God, and is useful for teaching, for reproof, for correction and for training in righteousness, so that everyone who belongs to God may be proficient, equipped for every good work" (2 Tim 3:16-17, Greek text).

12. Seeing that, in sacred scripture, God speaks through human beings in human fashion,[6] it follows that the interpreters of sacred scripture, if they are to ascertain what God has wished to communicate to us, should carefully search out the meaning which the sacred writers really had in mind, that meaning which God had thought well to manifest through the medium of their words.

In determining the intention of the sacred writers, attention must be paid, among other things, to *literary genres*.

The fact is that truth is differently presented and expressed in the various types of historical writing, in prophetical and poetical texts, and in other forms of literary expression. Hence the exegete must look for that meaning which the sacred writers, in given situations and granted the circumstances of their time and culture, intended to express and did in fact express, through the medium of a contemporary literary form.[7] Rightly to understand what the sacred authors wanted to affirm in their work, due attention must be paid both to the customary and characteristic patterns of perception, speech and narrative which prevailed in their time, and to the conventions which people then observed in their dealings with one another.[8]

But since sacred scripture must be read and interpreted with its divine authorship in mind,[9] no less attention must be devoted to the content and unity of the whole of scripture, taking into account the tradition of the entire church and the analogy of faith, if we are to derive their true meaning from the sacred texts. It is the task of exegetes to work, according to these rules, towards a better understanding and explanation of the meaning of sacred scripture in order that their research may help the church's judgment to mature. For, of course, all that has been said about the manner of interpreting scripture is ultimately subject to the judgment of the church which exercises the divinely conferred commission and ministry of watching over and interpreting the word of God.[10]

13. Hence, in sacred scripture, without prejudice to God's truth and holiness, the marvellous "condescension" of eternal wisdom is plain to be seen, "that we may come to know the ineffable loving-kindness of God and see for ourselves the thought and care he has given to accommodating his language to our nature".[11] Indeed the words of God, expressed in human language, are in every way like human speech, just as the Word of the eternal Father, when he took on himself the weak flesh of human beings, became like them.

1. See Vatican Council I, Dogmatic Constitution on the Catholic Faith, *Dei Filius*, ch. 2: Denz. 1787 (3006). Pontifical biblical commission, Decree 18 June 1915: Denz. 2180 (3629); EB 420. Holy Office, *Letter*, 22 Dec. 1923: EB 499.

2. See Pius XII, Encyclical *Divino Afflante Spiritu*, 30 Sept. 1943: AAS 35 (1943), p. 314; EB 556.

3. *In* and *through* human beings: see Heb 1:1 and 4:7 *(in)*; 2 Kg. 23:2; Mt 1:22 and *passim* (through); Vatican Council I, Scheme on catholic doctrine, note 9: Collectio Lacensis, VII, 522.

4. Leo XIII, Encyclical *Providentissimus Deus*, 18 Nov. 1893: Denz. 1952 (3293); EB 125.

5. See St Augustine, *De Gen.ad Litt.*, 2, 9, 20: PL 34, 270-271; *Epistola 82*, 3: PL 33, 277; CSEL 34, 2, p. 354. St Thomas Aquinas, *De Veritate*, q. 12, a 2, C. Council of Trent, Session IV, On the canonical scriptures: Denz. 783 (1501) Leo XIII, Encyclical *Providentissimus Deus*: EB 121, 124, 126-127. Pius XII, Encyclical *Divino Afflante:* EB 539.

6. St Augustine, *De Civitate Dei*, XVII, 6, 2: PL 41, 537: CSEL 40, 2, 228.

7. St Augustine, *De Doctrina Christiana*, III, 18, 26; PL 34, 75-76.

8. Pius XII, loc. cit.: Denz. 2294 (3829-3830); EB 557-562.

9. See Benedict XV, Encyclical *Spiritus Paraclitus*, 15 Sept. 1920: EB 469. St Jerome, *In Gal 5*, 19-21: PL 26, 417 A.

10. See Vatican Council I, Dogmatic Constitution on the Catholic Faith, *Dei Filius*, c. 2: Denz. 1788 (3007).

11. St John Chrysostom, *In Gen 3*, 8 (homily 17, 1): PG 53, 134. *Attemperatio* corresponds to the Greek *synkatabasis*.

Chapter IV

THE OLD TESTAMENT

14. In his great love God intended the salvation of the entire human race. In preparation for this, in a special undertaking, he chose for himself a people to whom he would entrust his promises. By his covenant with Abraham (see Gen 15:18) and, through Moses, with the race of Israel (see Ex 24:8), he acquired a people for himself, and to them he revealed himself in words and deeds as the one, true, living God. It was his strategy that Israel might learn by experience God's ways with humanity and by listening to the voice of God speaking to them through the prophets

might gradually understand his ways more fully and more clearly, and make them more widely known among the nations (see Ps 21:28-29; 95:1-3; Is 2:14; Jer 3:17). The plan of salvation, foretold, recounted and explained by the sacred authors, appears as the true word of God in the books of the Old Testament, which is why these books, divinely inspired, retain a lasting value: "For whatever was written in former days was written for our instruction, so that by steadfastness and by the encouragement of the scriptures we might have hope" (Rom 15:4).

15. The primary objective of the plan and lay-out of the Old Testament was that it should prepare for and declare in prophecy the coming of Christ, universal redeemer, and of the messianic kingdom (see Lk 24:44; Jn 5:39; 1 Pet 1:10), and should indicate it by means of various foreshadowing signs and symbols (see 1 Cor 10:11). For in the context of the human situation before the era of salvation established by Christ, the books of the Old Testament provide an understanding of God and humanity and make clear to all how a just and merciful God deals with humankind. These books, even though they contain matters which are imperfect and provisional, nevertheless contain authentic divine teaching.[1] Christians should accept with reverence these writings, which express a lively sense of God, which are a storehouse of sublime teaching on God and of sound wisdom on human life, as well as a wonderful treasury of prayers; in them, too, the mystery of our salvation is implicitly present.

16. God, the inspirer and author of the books of both Testaments, in his wisdom has so brought it about that the New should be hidden in the Old and that the Old should be made manifest in the New.[2] For, although Christ founded the New Covenant in his blood (see Lk 22:20; 1 Cor 11:25), nevertheless the

books of the Old Testament, all of them given a place in the preaching of the Gospel,[3] attain and display their full meaning in the New Testament (see Mt 5: 17: Lk 24-27; Rom 16:25-26: 2 Cor 3:14-16) and, in their turn, shed light on it and explain it.

1. Pius XI, Encyclical *Mit brennender Sorge,* 14 March 1937: AAS 29 (1937), p. 151.
2. St *Augustine, Quaest. in Hept.* 2, 73: PL 34, 623.
3. St Irenaeus, *Adv. Haer.,* III, 21, 3: PG 7, 950 (= 25, 1) Harvey 2, p. 115. St Cyril of Jerusalem, *Catech.* 4, 35: PG 33, 497. Theodore of Mopsuestia, *In Soph* 1, 4-6: PG 66, 452D-453A.

Chapter V

THE NEW TESTAMENT

17. The word of God, which to everyone who has faith contains God's saving power (see Rom 1:16), is set forth and marvellously displays its power in the writings of the New Testament. For when the time had fully come (see Gal 4:4), the Word became flesh and dwelt among us, full of grace and truth (see Jn 1:14). Christ established on earth the kingdom of God, revealed his Father and himself by deeds and words and by his death, resurrection and glorious ascension, as well as by sending the holy Spirit, completed his work. Lifted up from the earth he draws all people to himself (see Jn 10:32, Greek text), for he alone has the words of eternal life (see Jn 6:68). This mystery was not made known to other generations as it has now been revealed to his holy apostles and prophets by the holy Spirit (see Eph 3:4-6, Greek text), that they might preach the Gospel, foster faith in Jesus Christ and the Lord, and bring together the

church. The writings of the New Testament stand as a perpetual and divine witness to these realities.

18. It is common knowledge that among all the inspired writings, including those of the New Testament, the Gospels have a special place, and rightly so, because they are our principal source for the life and teaching of the incarnate Word, our Saviour.

The church has always and everywhere maintained, and continues to maintain, the apostolic origin of the four Gospels. The apostles preached, as Christ had charged them to do, and then, under the inspiration of the holy Spirit, they and others of the apostolic age handed on to us in writing the same message they had preached, the foundation of our faith: the fourfold Gospel, according to Matthew, Mark, Luke and John.[1]

19. Holy mother church has firmly and with absolute constancy maintained and continues to maintain, that these four Gospels, whose historicity it unhesitatingly affirms, faithfully hand on what Jesus, the Son of God, while he lived among men and women, really did and taught for their eternal salvation, until the day when he was taken up (see Acts 1:1-2). For, after the ascension of the Lord, the apostles handed on to their hearers what he had said and done, but with that fuller understanding which they, instructed by the glorious events of Christ and enlightened by the Spirit of truth,[2] now enjoyed.[3] The sacred authors, in writing the four Gospels, selected certain of the many elements which had been handed on, either orally or in written form; others they synthesized or explained with an eye to the situation of the churches. They retained the preaching style, but always in such a fashion that they have told us the authentic truth about Jesus.[4] Whether they relied on their own memory and recollections or on the testi-

mony of those who"from the beginning were eyewitnesses and ministers of the word," their purpose in writing was that we might know the"truth"concerning the things of which we have been informed (see Lk 1:2-4).

20. Besides the four Gospels, the New Testament also contains the letters of St Paul and other apostolic writings composed under the inspiration of the holy Spirit. In accordance with God's wise design these writings firmly establish those matters which concern Christ the Lord, formulate more precisely his authentic teaching, preach the saving power of Christ's divine work and foretell its glorious consummation.

For the Lord Jesus was with his apostles as he had promised (see Mt 28:20) and he had sent to them the Spirit, the Counsellor, who would guide them into all the truth (see Jn 16: 13).

1. See St Irenaeus, *Adv. Haer.*, III, 11, 8: PG 7, 885; ed. Sagnard, p. 194
2. See Jn 14:26; 16:13.
3. Jn 2:22; 12-16; see 14:26; 16:12-13; 7:39.
4. See The Instruction *Sacra Mater Ecclesia* of the Pontifical Biblical Commission: AAS 56 (1964), p. 715.

Chapter VI

SACRED SCRIPTURE IN THE LIFE OF THE CHURCH

21. The church has always venerated the divine scriptures as it has venerated the Body of the Lord, in that it never ceases, above all in the sacred liturgy, to partake of the bread of life and to offer it to the faithful from the one table of the word of God and the

Body of Christ. It has always regarded and continues to regard the scriptures, taken together with sacred tradition, as the supreme rule of its faith. For, since they are inspired by God and committed to writing once and for all time, they present God's own word in an unalterable form, and they make the voice of the holy Spirit sound again and again in the words of the prophets and apostles. It follows that all the preaching of the church, as indeed the entire christian religion, should be nourished and ruled by sacred scripture. In the sacred books the Father who is in heaven comes lovingly to meet his children, and talks with them. And such is the force and power of the word of God that it is the church's support and strength, imparting robustness to the faith of its daughters and sons and providing food for their souls. It is a pure and unfailing fount of spiritual life. It is eminently true of holy scripture that: "The word of God is living and active" (Heb 4:12), and "is able to build you up and to give you the inheritance among all those who are sanctified" (Acts 20:32; see 1 Th 2:13).

22. Access to sacred scripture ought to be widely available to the christian faithful. For this reason the church, from the very beginning, made its own the ancient translation of the Old Testament called the Septuagint; it honors also the other eastern translations, and the Latin translations, especially that known as the Vulgate. But since the word of God must be readily available at all times, the church, with motherly concern, sees to it that suitable and correct translations are made into various languages, especially from the original texts of the sacred books. If, when the opportunity presents itself and the authorities of the church agree, these translations are made jointly with churches separated from us, they can then be used by all Christians.

23. Taught by the holy Spirit, the spouse of the

incarnate Word, which is the church, strives to reach an increasingly more profound understanding of the sacred scriptures, in order to nourish its children with God's words. For this reason also it duly encourages the study of the Fathers, both eastern and western, and of the sacred liturgies. Catholic exegetes and other workers in the field of sacred theology should work diligently together and under the watchful eye of the sacred magisterium. Using appropriate techniques they should together set about examining and explaining the sacred texts in such a way that as many as possible of those who are ministers of God's word may be able to dispense fruitfully the nourishment of the scriptures to the people of God. This nourishment enlightens the mind, strengthens the will and fires the hearts of men and women with the love of God.[1] The holy synod encourages those members of the church who are engaged in biblical studies constantly to renew their efforts, in order to carry on, with complete dedication and in accordance with the mind of the church,[2] the work they have so happily begun.

24. Sacred theology relies on the written word of God, taken together with sacred tradition, as its permanent foundation. By this word it is powerfully strengthened and constantly rejuvenated, as it searches out, under the light of faith, all the truth stored up in the mystery of Christ. The sacred scriptures contain the word of God, and, because they are inspired, they truly are the word of God; therefore, the study of the sacred page should be the very soul of sacred theology.[3] The ministry of the word, too — pastoral preaching, catechetics and all forms of christian instruction, among which the liturgical homily should hold pride of place — gains healthy nourishment and holy vitality from the word of scripture.

25. Therefore, all clerics, particularly priests of Christ and others who, as deacons or catechists, are

officially engaged in the ministry of the word, should immerse themselves in the scriptures by constant spiritual reading and diligent study. For it must not happen that any of them become "empty preachers of the word of God to others, not being hearers of the word in their own hearts",[4] when they ought to be sharing the boundless riches of the divine word with the faithful committed to their care, especially in the sacred liturgy. Likewise. the holy synod forcefully and specifically exhorts all the christian faithful, especially those who live the religious life, to learn "the surpassing knowledge of Jesus Christ" (Phil 3:8) by frequent reading of the divine scriptures. "Ignorance of the scriptures is ignorance of Christ".[5] Therefore, let them go gladly to the sacred text itself, whether in the sacred liturgy, which is full of the divine words, or in devout reading, or in such suitable exercises and various other helps which, with the approval and guidance of the pastors of the church, are happily spreading everywhere in our day. Let them remember, however, that prayer should accompany the reading of sacred scripture, so that it becomes a dialogue between God and the human reader. For, "we speak to him when we pray; we listen to him when we read the divine oracles".[6]

It is the duty of bishops, "with whom the apostolic doctrine resides"[7] suitably to instruct the faithful entrusted to them in the correct use of the divine books, especially the New Testament and in particular the Gospels. This is done by translations of the sacred texts which are equipped with necessary and really adequate explanations. Thus, the children of the church can familiarize themselves safely and profitably with the sacred scriptures, and become steeped in their spirit.

Moreover, editions of sacred scripture, provided with suitable notes, should be prepared for the use even of non-Christians, and adapted to their circumstances. These should be prudently circulated, either by pastors of souls, or by Christians of any walk of life.

26. So may it come that, by the reading and study of the sacred books "the word of God may speed on and triumph" (2 Th 3:1) and the treasure of revelation entrusted to the church may more and more fill people's hearts. Just as from constant attendance at the eucharistic mystery the life of the church draws increase, so a new impulse of spiritual life may be expected from increased veneration of the word of God, which "stands forever" (Is 40:8; see 1 Pet 1:23-25).

1. See Pius XII, Encyclical *Divino Afflante:* EB 551, 553, 567. Pontifical biblical commission, *Instructio de S. Scriptura in Clericorum Seminariis et Religiosorum Collegiis recte docenda,* 13 May 1950: AAS 42 (1950), pp 495-505.

2. See Pius XII, ibid.: EB 569.

3. See Leo XIII Encyclical *Providentissimus Deus:* EB 114; Benedict XV, Encyclical *Spiritus Paraclitus:* EB 483.

4. St Augustine *Serm.* 179: PL 38, 966.

5. St Jerome, *Comm. in Is,* Prol.: PL 24, 17. See Benedict XV, Encyclical *Spiritus Paraclitus:* B 475-480; Pius XII, Encyclical *Divino Afflante:* EB 544.

6. St Ambrose, *De Officiis. ministrorum* I, 20, 88: PL 16, 50.

7. St Irenaeus, Adv. Haer. IV, 32, 1: PG 7, 1071; (=49, 2) Harvey, 2, p. 255.

THE CONSTITUTION ON THE SACRED LITURGY[a]

Sacrosanctum Concilium

4 December, 1963

Introduction

1. The sacred council has set out to impart an ever-increasing vigor to the Christian lives of the faithful; to adapt more closely to the needs of our age those institutions which are subject to change; to encourage whatever can promote the union of all who believe in Christ; to strengthen whatever serves to call all of humanity into the church's fold. Accordingly it sees particularly cogent reasons for undertaking the reform and promotion of the liturgy.

2. For the liturgy, through which "the work of our redemption takes place,"[1] especially in the divine sacrifice of the Eucharist, is supremely effective in enabling the faithful to express in their lives and portray to others the mystery of Christ and the real nature of the true church. For the church is both human and divine, visible but endowed with invisible realities, zealous in action and dedicated to contemplation, present in the world, yet a migrant, so constituted that in it the human is directed toward and subordinated to the divine, the visible to the invisible, action to contemplation, and this present world to that city yet to come, the object of our quest (see Heb 13:14). The liturgy daily builds up those who are in the

church, making of them a holy temple of the Lord, a dwelling-place for God in the Spirit (see Eph 2:21-22), to the mature measure of the fullness of Christ (see Eph 4:13). At the same time it marvellously enhances their power to preach Christ and thus show the church to those who are outside as a sign lifted up among the nations (see Is 11:12), a sign under which the scattered children of God may be gathered together (see Jn 11:52) until there is one fold and one shepherd (see Jn 10:16).

3. That is why the sacred council judges that the following principles concerning the renewal and advancement of the liturgy should be called to mind, and that practical norms should be established.

Among these principles and norms there are some which can and should be applied both to the Roman rite and also to all the other rites. The practical norms which follow, however, should be taken as applying only to the Roman rite, except for those which of their nature affect other rites as well.

4. Finally, in faithful obedience to tradition, the sacred council declares that the church holds all lawfully recognized rites to be of equal legal force and dignity; that it wishes to preserve them in the future and to foster them in every way. The council also desires that, where necessary, the rites be revised carefully in the light of sound tradition, and that they be given new vigor to meet present-day circumstances and needs.

Chapter I

GENERAL PRINCIPLES FOR THE RESTORATION AND PROGRESS OF THE SACRED LITURGY

I. The Nature of the Sacred Liturgy and Its Importance in the Life of the Church

5. God who "wills that all be saved and come to the knowledge of the truth" (1 Tim 2:4), "who in many times and various ways spoke of old to our ancestors through the prophets" (Heb 1:1), when the fullness of time had come, sent his Son, the Word made flesh, anointed by the Holy Spirit, to preach the Gospel to the poor, to soothe the broken hearted (see Is 61:1; Lk 4:18), to be a bodily and spiritual physician,[2] the mediator between God and humanity (see 1 Tim 2:5). For his humanity united with the person of the Word was the instrument of our salvation. Therefore, in Christ "our reconciliation was perfectly achieved and the fullness of divine worship was given to us."[3]

This work of human redemption and perfect glorification of God, foreshadowed by the wonders which God performed among the people of the Old Testament, Christ the Lord completed principally in the paschal mystery of his blessed passion, resurrection from the dead, and glorious ascension, whereby "dying, he destroyed our death and rising, restored our life."[4] For it was from the side of Christ as he slept the sleep of death upon the cross that there came forth the wondrous sacrament of the whole church.[5]

6. Just as Christ was sent by the Father so also he sent the apostles, filled with the Holy Spirit. This he did so that they might preach the Gospel to every creature (see Mk 16:15) and proclaim that the Son of God by his death and resurrection had freed us from

the power of Satan (see Acts 26:18) and from death, and brought us into the Kingdom of his Father. But he also willed that the work of salvation which they preached they should enact through the sacrifice and sacraments around which the entire liturgical life revolves. Thus by Baptism men and women are implanted in the paschal mystery of Christ; they die with him, are buried with him, and rise with him (see Rom 6:4; Eph 2:6; Col 3:1; 2 Tim 2:11). They receive the spirit of adoption as sons and daughters "in which we cry, Abba, Father" (Rom 8:15) and thus become true adorers such as the Father seeks (see Jn 4:23). Similarly, as often as they eat the Supper of the Lord they proclaim the death of the Lord until he comes (see 1 Cor 11:26). That was why on the very day of Pentecost when the church appeared before the world those "who received the word" of Peter "were baptized." And "they continued steadfastly in the teaching of the apostles and in the communion of the breaking of bread and in prayers ... praising God and being in favor with all the people" (Acts 2:41-42, 47). From that time onward the church has never failed to come together to celebrate the paschal mystery, reading those things "which were in all the scriptures concerning him" (Lk 24:27), celebrating the Eucharist in which "the victory and triumph of his death are again made present,"[6] and at the same time "giving thanks to God for his inexpressible gift" (2 Cor 9:15) in Christ Jesus, "in praise of his glory" (Eph 1:12) through the power of the Holy Spirit.

7. To accomplish so great a work Christ is always present in his church, especially in liturgical celebrations. He is present in the sacrifice of the Mass both in the person of his minister, "the same now offering, through the ministry of priests, who formerly offered himself on the cross,"[7] and most of all in the eucharistic species. By his power he is present in the sacra-

ments so that when anybody baptizes it is really Christ himself who baptizes.[8] He is present in his word since it is he himself who speaks when the holy scriptures are read in church. Lastly, he is present when the church prays and sings, for he has promised "where two or three are gathered together in my name there am I in the midst of them" (Mt 18:20).

Christ, indeed, always associates the church with himself in this great work in which God is perfectly glorified and men and women are sanctified. The church is his beloved bride who calls to its Lord, and through him offers worship to the eternal Father.

The liturgy, then, is rightly seen as an exercise of the priestly office of Jesus Christ. In the liturgy the sanctification of women and men is given expression in symbols perceptible by the senses and is carried out in ways appropriate to each of them. In it, complete and definitive public worship is performed by the mystical body of Jesus Christ, that is, by the Head and his members.

From this it follows that every liturgical celebration, because it is an action of Christ the priest and of his body, which is the church, is a preeminently sacred action. No other action of the church equals its effectiveness by the same title nor to the same degree.[8a]

8. In the earthly liturgy we take part in a foretaste of that heavenly liturgy which is celebrated in the holy city of Jerusalem toward which we journey as pilgrims, where Christ is sitting at the right hand of God, minister of the sanctuary and of the true tabernacle (see Apoc 21:2; Col 3:1; Heb 8:2). With all the hosts of heaven we sing a hymn of glory to the Lord; venerating the memory of the saints, we hope to share their company; we eagerly await the Saviour, Our Lord Jesus Christ, until he our life shall appear and we too will appear with him in glory (Phil 3:20; Col 3:4).

9. The sacred liturgy is not the church's only activity. Before people can come to the liturgy they must be called to faith and to conversion. "How then are they to call upon him in whom they have not believed? And how are they to believe in him of whom they have not heard? And how are they to hear without a preacher? And how are they to preach unless they be sent?" (Rom 10: 14-15).

Therefore the church proclaims the message of salvation to those who do not believe, so that all may know the one true God and Jesus Christ whom he has sent and may change their ways, doing penance (see Jn 17:3; Lk 24:47; Acts 2:38). To believers, too, the church must ever preach faith and repentance; it must prepare them for the sacraments, teach them to observe all that Christ has commanded (see Mt 28:20), and encourage them to engage in all the works of charity, piety and the apostolate, thus making it clear that Christ's faithful, though not of this world, are to be the light of the world and are to give glory to the Father in the midst of the people.

10. Nevertheless, the liturgy is the summit toward which the activity of the church is directed; it is also the source from which all its power flows. For the goal of apostolic endeavor is that all who are made children of God by faith and Baptism should come together to praise God in the midst of his church, to take part in the sacrifice and to eat the Lord's Supper.

The liturgy, in its turn, moves the faithful filled with "the paschal sacraments" to be "one in their commitment to you";[9] it prays that "they hold fast in their lives to what they have grasped by their faith."[10] The renewal in the Eucharist of the covenant between them and the Lord draws the faithful and sets them aflame with Christ's compelling love. From the liturgy, therefore, and especially from the Eucharist, grace is poured forth upon us as from a fountain, and our sanctification in Christ and the glorification of God to which all other activities of the church are directed, as toward their end, are achieved with maximum effectiveness.

11. But in order that the liturgy may be able to produce its full effects it is necessary that the faithful come to it with proper dispositions, that their minds be attuned to their voices, and that they cooperate with heavenly grace lest they receive it in vain (see 2 Cor 6:1). Pastors of souls must, therefore, realize that, when the liturgy is celebrated, their obligation goes further than simply ensuring that the laws governing valid and lawful celebration are observed. They must also ensure that the faithful take part fully aware of what they are doing, actively engaged in the rite and enriched by it.

12. The spiritual life, however, is not limited solely to participation in the liturgy. Christians are indeed called to pray with others, but they must also enter into their rooms to pray to their Father in secret (see Mt 6:6); furthermore, according to the teaching of the apostle, they must pray without ceasing (see 1 Th 5 17). We also learn from the same apostle that we must always carry around in our bodies the dying of Jesus, so that the life too of Jesus may be made manifest in our mortal flesh (see 2 Cor 4:10-11). That is why we beg the Lord in the sacrifice of the Mass that "receiving the offering of the spiritual victim" he may fashion us for himself "as an eternal gift."[11]

13. The Christian people's devotions, provided they conform to the laws and norms of the church, are to be highly recommended, especially when they are authorized by the Apostolic See.

Devotions authorized by bishops in particular churches according to lawfully approved customs or books are also held in special esteem.

But such devotions should be so drawn up that

they harmonize with the liturgical seasons, accord
with the sacred liturgy, are in some way derived from
it, and lead the people to it, since in fact the liturgy by
its very nature is far superior to any of them.

II. The Promotion of Liturgical Formation and Active Participation

14. It is very much the wish of the church that all
the faithful should be led to take that full, conscious,
and active part in liturgical celebrations which is demanded by the very nature of the liturgy, and to
which the Christian people, "a chosen race, a royal
priesthood, a holy nation, a redeemed people" (1 Pet
2:9, 4-5) have a right and to which they are bound by
reason of their Baptism.

In the restoration and development of the sacred
liturgy the full and active participation by all the people is the paramount concern, for it is the primary, indeed the indispensable source from which the faithful are to derive the true Christian spirit. Therefore, in
all their apostolic activity, pastors of souls should
energetically set about achieving it through the requisite formation.

Yet there is no hope of achieving this unless pastors
of souls, in the first place, themselves become fully
imbued with the spirit and power of the liturgy and
attain competence in it. Thus it is absolutely essential,
first of all, that steps be taken to ensure the liturgical
training of the clergy. For that reason the sacred council has decided on the following enactments:

15. Professors who are appointed to teach liturgy in
seminaries, religious houses of studies, and theological faculties, must be properly trained for their work
in institutes specifically designed for this purpose.

16. Sacred liturgy is to be ranked among the compulsory and major courses in seminaries and religious

houses of studies. In theological faculties it is to be one of the principal courses. It is to be taught under its theological, historical, spiritual, pastoral, and juridical aspects. In addition, those who teach other subjects, especially dogmatic theology, sacred scripture, spiritual and pastoral theology, should — while accepting the intrinsic demands of their own disciplines — expound the mystery of Christ and the history of salvation in a manner that will make clear the connection between their subjects and the liturgy, and the unity of all priestly training.

17. The spiritual formation of clerical students in seminaries and religious houses should be given a liturgical orientation. For this they will need a proper initiation, enabling them to understand the sacred rites and participate in them wholeheartedly. They will also need to celebrate the sacred mysteries and popular devotions which are imbued with the spirit of the sacred liturgy. Likewise, they must learn to observe the liturgical laws so that life in seminaries and religious institutes may be thoroughly influenced by the liturgical spirit.

18. Priests, both secular and religious, who are already working in the Lord's vineyard, are to be helped in every way that is appropriate to acquire a deepening understanding of what they are about when they perform sacred rites, to live the liturgical life and to share it with the faithful entrusted to their care.

19. With diligence and patience pastors of souls should see to the liturgical instruction of the faithful and their active participation, internal and external, in the liturgy, taking into account their age, condition, way of life and standard of religious culture. By so doing, pastors will be fulfilling one of the chief duties of a faithful dispenser of the mysteries of God, and in this matter they must lead their flock not only by

word but also by example.

20. Transmission of the sacred rites by radio and television, especially the Mass, should be done with delicacy and dignity. A suitable person, appointed by the bishops, should direct it and have the responsibility for it.

III. The Reform of the Sacred Liturgy

21. It is the wish of the church to undertake a careful general reform of the liturgy in order that the Christian people may be more certain to derive an abundance of graces from it. For the liturgy is made up of unchangeable elements divinely instituted, and of elements subject to change. These latter not only may be changed but ought to be changed with the passage of time, if they have suffered from the intrusion of anything out of harmony with the inner nature of the liturgy or have become less suitable. In this renewal, both texts and rites should be ordered so as to express more clearly the holy things which they signify. The christian people, as far as is possible, should be able to understand them easily and take part in them in a celebration which is full, active and the community's own.

Therefore, the sacred council establishes the following general norms:

A. General Norms

22. (1) Regulation of the sacred liturgy depends solely on the authority of the church, that is, on the apostolic see, and, in accordance with law, on the bishop.

(2) In virtue of the power conferred on them by law, the regulation of the liturgy within certain defined limits belongs also to various kinds of group-

ings of bishops, legitimately established, with competence in given territories.

(3) Therefore no other person whatsoever, not even a priest, may add, remove, or change anything in the liturgy on their own authority.

23. In order that sound tradition be retained, and yet the way remain open to legitimate progress, a careful investigation—theological, historical, and pastoral—should always, first of all, be made into each section of the liturgy which is to be revised. Furthermore the general laws governing the structure and meaning of the liturgy must be taken into account, as well as the experience derived from recent liturgical reforms and from the concessions granted in various places. Finally, there must be no innovations unless the good of the church genuinely and certainly requires them, and care must be taken that any new forms adopted should in some way grow organically from forms already existing.

As far as possible, notable differences between the rites used in neighboring regions should be avoided

24. Sacred scripture is of the greatest importance in the celebration of the liturgy. For from it are drawn the lessons which are read and which are explained in the homily; from it too come the psalms which are sung. It is from scripture that the petitions, prayers and hymns draw their inspiration and their force, and that actions and signs derive their meaning. Hence, in order to achieve the restoration, progress, and adaptation of the sacred liturgy it is essential to promote that warm and lively appreciation of sacred scripture to which the venerable tradition of eastern and western rites gives testimony.

25. The liturgical books are to be revised as soon as possible. Experts are to be employed on this task, and bishops from various parts of the world are to be consulted.

B. Norms Drawn from the Hierarchic and Communal Nature of the Liturgy

26. Liturgical services are not private functions but are celebrations of the church which is "the sacrament of unity," namely, the holy people united and organized under their bishops.[12]

Therefore, liturgical services have to do with the whole body, the church. They make it visible and have effects on it. But they also touch individual members of the church in different ways, depending on ranks, roles and levels of participation.

27. It must be emphasized that rites which are meant to be celebrated in common, with the faithful present and actively participating, should as far as possible be celebrated in that way rather than by an individual and quasi-privately.

This applies with special force to the celebration of Mass (even though every Mass has of itself a public and social character) and to the administration of the sacraments.

28. All taking part in liturgical celebrations, whether ministers or members of the congregation, should do all that pertains to them, and no more, taking into account the rite and the liturgical norms.

29. Servers, readers, commentators, and members of the choir also exercise a genuine liturgical ministry. They ought, therefore, to carry out their functions with the sincere piety and decorum which is appropriate to so exalted a ministry and which God's people rightly expect.

Consequently, they must all be deeply imbued with the spirit of the liturgy, each in their own measure, and they must be trained to perform their functions in a correct and orderly manner.

30. To develop active participation, the people should be encouraged to take part by means of acclamations, responses, psalms, antiphons, hymns, as

well as by actions, gestures and bodily attitudes. And at the proper time a reverent silence should be observed.

31. It is important that when the liturgical books are being revised the rubrics should indicate the people's parts.

32. In the liturgy, apart from the distinctions arising from liturgical function or sacred Orders and apart from the honors due to civil authorities in accordance with liturgical law, no special preference is to be accorded any private persons or classes of persons whether in the ceremonies or by external display.

C. Norms Based on the Educative and Pastoral Nature of the Liturgy

33. Although the sacred liturgy is principally the worship of the divine majesty it likewise contains much instruction for the faithful.[13] For in the liturgy God speaks to his people, Christ is still proclaiming his gospel, and the people respond to God both in song and in prayer.

Moreover, the prayers addressed to God by the priest who, in the person of Christ, presides over the assembly, are said in the name of the entire holy people and of all present. And the visible signs which the sacred liturgy uses to signify invisible divine things have been chosen by Christ or by the church. Thus not only when things are read "which were written for our instruction" (Rom 15:4), but also when the church prays or sings or acts, the faith of those taking part is nourished, and their minds are raised to God so that they may offer him their spiritual homage and receive his grace more abundantly.

Therefore in the revision of the liturgy the following general norms should be observed:

34. The rites should radiate a noble simplicity. They should be short, clear, and free from useless repeti-

tion. They should be within the people's powers of comprehension, and normally should not require much explanation.

35. So that the intimate connection between rite and words may be apparent in the liturgy:

(1) In liturgical celebrations, a more ample, more varied, and more suitable selection of readings from sacred scripture should be restored.

(2) The most suitable place for a sermon ought to be indicated in the rubrics, for the sermon is part of the liturgical action whenever the rite permits one. The ministry of preaching should be carried out properly and with the greatest care. The primary source of the sermon, moreover, should be scripture and liturgy, for in them is found the proclamation of God's wonderful works in the history of salvation, the mystery of Christ ever made present and active in us, especially in the celebration of the liturgy.

(3) Instruction which is more explicitly liturgical should also be given in every way possible. If necessary, short directives to be spoken by the priest or competent minister should be provided within the rites themselves. But they should be given only at suitable moments and in prescribed words or their equivalent.

(4) Sacred celebration of the word of God is to be encouraged, especially on the vigils of the more solemn feasts, on some weekdays of Advent and Lent, and on Sundays and holydays, especially in places where no priest is available. In that case, a deacon or some other person authorized by the bishop should preside over the celebration.

36. (1) The use of the Latin language, except when a particular law prescribes otherwise, is to be preserved in the Latin rites.

(2) But since the use of the vernacular, whether in the Mass, the administration of the sacraments, or in

other parts of the liturgy, may frequently be of great advantage to the people, a wider use may be made of it, especially in readings, directives and in some prayers and chants. Regulations governing this will be given separately in subsequent chapters.

(3) These norms being observed, it is for the competent territorial ecclesiastical authority mentioned in article 22:2, to decide whether, and to what extent, the vernacular language is to be used. Its decrees have to be approved, that is confirmed, by the Apostolic See. Where circumstances warrant it, it is to consult with bishops of neighboring regions which have the same language.

(4) Translations from the Latin for use in the liturgy must be approved by the competent territorial ecclesiastical authority already mentioned.

D. Norms for Adapting the Liturgy to the Temperament and Traditions of Peoples

37. Even in the liturgy the church does not wish to impose a rigid uniformity in matters which do not affect the faith or the well-being of the entire community. Rather does it cultivate and foster the qualities and talents of the various races and nations. Anything in people's way of life which is not indissolubly bound up with superstition and error the church studies with sympathy, and, if possible, preserves intact. It sometimes even admits such things into the liturgy itself, provided they harmonize with its true and authentic spirit.

38. Provided that the substantial unity of the Roman rite is preserved, provision shall be made, when revising the liturgical books, for legitimate variations and adaptations to different groups, regions and peoples, especially in mission countries. This should be borne in mind when drawing up the rites and rubrics.

39. Within the limits set by the standard editions of the liturgical books it shall be for the competent territorial ecclesiastical authority mentioned in article 22: 2 to specify adaptations, especially as regards the administration of the sacraments, sacramentals, processions, liturgical language, sacred music and the arts — in keeping, however, with the fundamental norms laid down in this Constitution.

40. In some places and circumstances, however, an even more radical adaptation of the liturgy is needed, and this entails greater difficulties. For this reason: (1) The competent territorial ecclesiastical authority mentioned in article 22:2 must, in this matter, carefully and prudently consider which elements from the traditions and cultures of individual peoples might appropriately be admitted into divine worship. Adaptations which are considered useful or necessary should then be submitted to the Apostolic See, to be introduced with its consent. (2) To ensure that adaptations may be made with the requisite care, the Apostolic See will, if needs be, grant permission to this same territorial ecclesiastical authority to permit and to direct the necessary preliminary experiments over a determined period of time among certain groups suitable for the purpose. (3) Because liturgical laws usually involve special difficulties with respect to adaptation, especially in mission lands, people who are experts in the matters in question must be employed when they are being formulated.

E. Promotion of the Liturgical Life
in Diocese and Parish

41. The bishop is to be considered the high priest of his flock from whom the life of his people in Christ is in some way derived and on whom it in some way depends.

Therefore, all should hold in the greatest esteem

the liturgical life of the diocese centered around the bishop, especially in his cathedral church. They must be convinced that the principal manifestation of the church consists in the full, active participation of all God's holy people in the same liturgical celebrations, especially in the same Eucharist, in one prayer, at one altar, at which the bishop presides, surrounded by his college of priests and by his ministers.[14]

42. Since it is impossible for the bishop in his church always and everywhere to preside over the whole flock, he must of necessity establish groupings of the faithful. Parishes, each set up locally under a pastor who takes the place of the bishop, are the most important of these, for in some way they represent the visible church established throughout the world.

Therefore the liturgical life of the parish and its relation to the bishop must be developed in the spirit and practice of the laity and clergy. Efforts must also be made to encourage a sense of community within the parish, above all in the common celebration of Sunday Mass.

F. Promotion of Pastoral Liturgical Action

43. Enthusiasm for the promotion and restoration of the sacred liturgy is rightly held to be a sign of the providential dispositions of God in our time, and as a movement of the holy Spirit in his church. It is today a distinguishing mark of the life of the church, and, indeed, of the whole tenor of contemporary religious thought and action.

Therefore, so that this pastoral liturgical action may become still more vigorous in the church the holy council decrees:

44. It is desirable that the competent territorial ecclesiastical authority mentioned in article 22:2 set up a liturgical commission to be assisted by experts in liturgical science, music, sacred art and pastoral prac-

tice. As far as possible the commission should be aided by some kind of institute for pastoral liturgy, consisting of people who are outstanding in their grasp of these matters, not excluding lay people, if circumstances so demand. It will be the task of this commission, under the direction of the above-mentioned competent territorial ecclesiastical authority, to regulate pastoral liturgical action throughout the territory, and to promote studies and necessary experiments whenever there is a question of adaptations to be proposed to the Holy See.

45. For the same reason every diocese is to have a liturgical commission, to develop the liturgical apostolate under the direction of the bishop.

Sometimes it may be convenient for several dioceses to combine their resources by forming one single commission for the development of the liturgical enterprise.

46. In addition to the commission on sacred liturgy, every diocese, as far as possible, should have commissions for sacred music and sacred art.

It is necessary that these three commissions work closely together. Indeed it will often be best for the three of them to join forces in one commission.

Chapter II

THE SACRED MYSTERY OF THE EUCHARIST

47. At the last supper, on the night he was betrayed, our Savior instituted the eucharistic sacrifice of his body and blood. This he did in order to perpetuate the sacrifice of the cross throughout the ages until he should come again, and so to entrust to his beloved

spouse, the church, a memorial of his death and resurrection: a sacrament of love, a sign of unity, a bond
of charity,[15] "a paschal banquet in which Christ is
received, the mind is filled with grace, and a pledge of
future glory is given to us."[16]

48. The church, therefore, spares no effort in trying
to ensure that, when present at this mystery of faith,
Christian believers should not be there as strangers or
silent spectators. On the contrary, having a good
grasp of it through the rites and prayers, they should
take part in the sacred action, actively, fully aware,
and devoutly. They should be formed by God's word,
and be nourished at the table of the Lord's Body. They
should give thanks to God. Offering the immaculate
victim, not only through the hands of the priest but
also together with him, they should learn to offer
themselves. Through Christ, the Mediator,[17] they
should be drawn day by day into ever more perfect
union with God and each other, so that finally God
may be all in all.

49. For this reason and having in mind Masses celebrated with the faithful assisting, especially on
Sundays and holydays of obligation, the holy council
has made the following regulations so that the sacrifice of the Mass, even through the way its rites are
designed, may achieve full pastoral effectiveness.

50. The rite of the Mass is to be revised in such a
way that the intrinsic nature and purpose of its several parts, as well as the connection between them, may
be more clearly shown, and that devout and active
participation by the faithful may be more easily
achieved.

To this end, the rites are to be simplified, due care
being taken to preserve their substance. Duplications
made with the passage of time are to be omitted, as
are less useful additions. Other parts which were lost
through the vicissitudes of history are to be restored

according to the ancient tradition of the holy Fathers, as may seem appropriate or necessary.

51. The treasures of the bible are to be opened up more lavishly so that a richer fare may be provided for the faithful at the table of God's word. In this way the more significant part of the sacred scriptures will be read to the people over a fixed number of years.

52. By means of the homily, the mysteries of the faith and the guiding principles of the christian life are expounded from the sacred text during the course of the liturgical year. The homily is strongly recommended since it forms part of the liturgy itself. In fact, at those Masses which are celebrated on Sundays and holydays of obligation, with the people assisting, it should not be omitted except for a serious reason.

53. The "common prayer" or "prayer of the faithful" is to be restored after the gospel and homily, especially on Sundays and holydays of obligation. By this prayer in which the people are to take part, intercession will be made for the church, for the civil authorities, for those oppressed by various needs, for all humankind, and for the salvation of the entire world (see 1 Tim 2:1-2).

54. A suitable place may be allotted to the vernacular in Masses which are celebrated with the people, especially in the readings and "the common prayer," and also, as local conditions may warrant, in those parts which pertain to the people, according to the rules laid down in article 36 of this constitution.

Nevertheless care must be taken to ensure that the faithful may also be able to say or sing together in Latin those parts of the ordinary of the Mass which pertain to them.

Wherever a more extended use of the vernacular in the Mass seems desirable, the regulation laid down in article 40 of this constitution is to be observed.

55. The more perfect form of participation in the

Mass whereby the faithful, after the priest's communion, receive the Lord's body from the same sacrifice, is warmly recommended.

The dogmatic principles about communion of the faithful which were laid down by the Council of Trent are confirmed,[18] yet communion under both kinds may be granted when the bishops think fit, not only to clerics and religious but also to the laity, in cases to be determined by the Apostolic See. Examples could be: the newly ordained in the Mass of their ordination; the newly professed in the Mass of their religious profession; the newly baptized in the Mass which follows their Baptism.

56. The two parts which in a sense go to make up the Mass, viz. the liturgy of the word and the eucharistic liturgy, are so closely connected with each other that they form but one single act of worship. Accordingly this sacred synod strongly urges pastors of souls that, when instructing the faithful, they take care to teach them to take part in the entire Mass, especially on Sundays and holydays of obligation.

57. §1. Concelebration, which is an appropriate way of manifesting the unity of the priesthood, has remained in use to this day in the church both in the east and in the west. The council has therefore decided to extend permission for concelebration to the following occasions:

1. (a) Holy Thursday, at the Mass of the chrism and the evening Mass;

(b) Masses during councils, bishops' conferences and synods;

(c) the Mass for the blessing of an abbot;

2. In addition, with the permission of the Ordinary, with whom rests the decision as to whether concelebration is appropriate:

(a) at conventual Mass, and at the principal Mass in churches, when the needs of the faithful do not require that all the priests available should celebrate individually;

(b) at Mass celebrated at any kind of meeting of priests, secular or religious.

§2. 1. It is for the bishop, however, to regulate the discipline of concelebration in his diocese.

2. Every priest shall always retain his right to celebrate Mass individually, though not at the same time in the same church as a concelebrated Mass nor on Holy Thursdays.

58. A new rite for concelebration is to be drawn up and inserted into the Pontifical and into the Roman Missal.

Chapter III

THE OTHER SACRAMENTS AND THE SACRAMENTALS

59. The purpose of the sacraments is to sanctify people, to build up the body of Christ, and, finally, to worship God. Because they are signs they also belong in the realm of instruction. They not only presuppose faith, but by words and objects they also nourish, strengthen, and express it. That is why they are called sacraments of faith. They do, indeed, confer grace, but, in addition, the very act of celebrating them is most effective in making people ready to receive this grace to their profit, to worship God duly, and to practise charity.

It is, therefore, of the greatest importance that the faithful should easily understand the symbolism of the sacraments and should eagerly frequent those sacraments which were instituted to nourish the Christian life.

60. The church has, moreover, instituted sacramentals. These are sacred signs by which, somewhat after the manner of the sacraments, effects of a spiritual nature, especially, are symbolised and are obtained through the church's intercession. By them, people are made ready to receive the much greater effect of the sacraments, and various occasions in life are rendered holy.

61. Thus, for well-disposed members of the faithful, the liturgy of the sacraments and sacramentals sanctifies almost every event of their lives with the divine grace which flows from the paschal mystery of the passion, death and resurrection of Christ. From this source all sacraments and sacramentals draw their power. There is scarcely any proper use of material things which cannot thus be directed toward people's sanctification and the praise of God.

62. With the passage of time, however, certain features have crept into the rites of the sacraments and sacramentals which have made their nature and purpose less clear to the people of today. Hence some changes are necessary to adapt them to present-day needs. For that reason the sacred council decrees as follows concerning their revision.

63. Because the use of the vernacular in the administration of the sacraments and sacramentals can often be of very great help to the people, this use is to be extended according to the following norms:

(a) In the administration of the sacraments and sacramentals the vernacular may be used according to what is laid down in article 36.

(b) The competent territorial ecclesiastical authority designated in article 22:2 of this constitution should forthwith prepare, in accordance with the new edition of the Roman Ritual, local rituals adapted as regards language and otherwise to the needs of the different regions. When this procedure has been duly confirmed by the Apostolic See, these rituals are to be followed in the regions in question. But in drawing up those rituals or particular collections of rites, the instructions prefixed to the individual rites in the Roman Ritual, whether they be pastoral and rubrical or whether they have a special social import, shall not be omitted.

64. The catechumenate for adults, divided into several distinct steps, is to be restored and brought into use at the discretion of the local Ordinary. By this means, the time of the catechumenate, which is destined for the requisite formation, may be sanctified by sacred rites to be celebrated at successive stages.

65. In mission countries, in addition to what is found in the christian tradition, those elements of initiation may be admitted which are already in use among every people, insofar as they can be adapted to the Christian ritual in accordance with articles 37-40 of this constitution.

66. Both rites for the Baptism of adults are to be revised, not only the simpler rite but also, taking into consideration the restored catechumenate, the more solemn rite. A special Mass "For the conferring of Baptism" is to be inserted into the Roman Missal.

67. The rite for the Baptism of infants is to be revised. The revision should take into account the fact that those to be baptized are babies. The roles of parents and godparents, and also their duties, should be brought out more clearly in the rite itself.

68. The baptismal rite should contain variants, to be used at the discretion of the local Ordinary, when a large number is to be baptized. Likewise a shorter rite is to be drawn up, especially for mission countries, which may be used by catechists when neither priest nor deacon is available and, when there is danger of

death, by the faithful in general.

69. In place of what is known as the "Rite for making up for what was omitted in the Baptism of an infant" a new rite is to be drawn up. This rite should indicate more fittingly and clearly that the infant baptized by the short rite has already been received into the church.

Likewise, a new rite is to be drawn up for converts who have already been validly baptized. It should indicate that they are now admitted to communion with the church.

70. Baptismal water, outside of paschal time, may be blessed within the rite of Baptism itself by an approved shorter formula.

71. The rite of confirmation is to be revised also so that the intimate connection of this sacrament with the whole of Christian initiation may be shown more clearly. For this reason it is appropriate that the renewal of baptismal promises should precede the reception of this sacrament.

Confirmation may be administered during Mass, when possible. For administration outside Mass, a formula should be drawn up to serve as an introduction.

72. The rite and formulas of Penance are to be revised so that they more clearly express both the nature and effect of the sacrament.

73. "Extreme Unction", which may also and more fittingly be called "Anointing of the Sick," is not a sacrament intended only for those who are at the point of death. Hence, it is certain that as soon as any of the faithful begins to be in danger of death from sickness or old age, this is already a suitable time for them to receive this sacrament.

74. In addition to the separate rites for anointing of the sick and for Viaticum, a continuous rite must be prepared in which sick people are anointed after they

have made their confession and before they receive Viaticum.

75. The number of the anointings should be whatever suits the occasion, and the prayers which belong to the rite of anointing are to be revised so as to correspond to the varying conditions of the sick people who receive the sacrament.

76. Both the ceremonies and texts of the ordination rites are to be revised. The addresses given by the bishop at the beginning of each ordination or consecration may be in the vernacular.

In the consecration of a bishop the laying on of hands may be done by all the bishops present.

77. The marriage rite now found in the Roman Ritual is to be revised and enriched so that it will more clearly symbolise the grace of the sacrament and will emphasize the spouses' duties.

"If any regions use other praiseworthy customs and ceremonies" when celebrating the sacrament of Matrimony "the holy synod very much hopes that they will be retained in their entirety."[19]

Moreover, an ecclesiastical authority having the territorial competence described in article 22:2 of this constitution is free to draw up its own rite suited to its people and region, according to the provisions of article 63, but on the express condition that the priest assisting at the marriage ask for and obtain the consent of the contracting parties.

78. Matrimony is normally to be celebrated during Mass, after the reading of the gospel and the homily and before "the prayer of the faithful." The prayer over the bride, duly amended to remind both spouses of their equal obligation of mutual fidelity, may be said in the vernacular.

But if the sacrament of Matrimony is celebrated outside Mass, the epistle and gospel from the nuptial Mass are to be read at the beginning of the rite, and the blessing should always be given to the couple.

79. The sacramentals are to be revised, account being taken of the primary principle of enabling the faithful to participate actively, easily and with awareness of what is happening. The needs of our times must also be considered. When rituals are being revised as laid down in article 63, new sacramentals may also be added as necessity requires.

Reserved blessings should be very few, and they should be reserved only to bishops or ordinaries.

Provision should be made for the administration of some sacramentals, at least in special circumstances and at the discretion of the Ordinary, by qualified lay persons.

80. The rite of the consecration of virgins contained in the Roman Pontifical is to be subjected to review.

Moreover, a rite of religious profession and renewal of vows is to be drawn up which will have greater uniformity, sobriety, and dignity. Except where there is a particular law to the contrary, this rite should be adopted by those who make their profession or renewal of vows during Mass.

It is recommended that religious profession be made during Mass.

81. Funeral rites should express more clearly the paschal character of Christian death, and should correspond more closely to the circumstances and traditions found in various regions. This also applies to the liturgical color to be used.

82. The rite for the burial of infants is to be revised, and a special Mass for the occasion should be provided.

Chapter IV

THE DIVINE OFFICE

83. Jesus Christ, high priest of the new and eternal covenant, taking human nature, introduced into this earthly exile that hymn which is sung throughout all ages in the realms above. He joins the entire community of humankind to himself, associating it with himself in singing his divine song of praise.

For it is through his church itself that he continues this priestly work. The church, by celebrating the Eucharist and in other ways, especially the celebration of the divine office, is ceaselessly engaged in praising the Lord and interceding for the salvation of the entire world.

84. The Divine Office, in keeping with ancient christian tradition, is so devised that the whole course of the day and night is consecrated by the praise of God. Therefore, when this wonderful song of praise is correctly celebrated by priests and others deputed for this purpose by the church's ordinance, or by the faithful praying together with a priest in an approved form, then it is truly the voice of the bride herself addressed to her bridegroom. And what is more, it is the prayer which Christ himself together with his body addresses to the Father.

85. Hence, all who take part in the divine office are not only performing a duty of the church, they are also sharing in what is the greatest honor for Christ's bride; for by offering these praises to God they are standing before God's throne in the name of the church, their mother.

86. Priests who are engaged in the sacred pastoral ministry will pray the praises of the hours more fervently the more conscious they are that they need to heed St Paul's exhortation, "Pray without ceasing" (1

Th 5:17). For only the Lord, who said, "Without me you can do nothing" (Jn 15:5), can make their work effective and fruitful. That is why the apostles when instituting deacons said, "We will devote ourselves to prayer and to the ministry of the word" (Acts 6:4).

87. In order that, in present circumstances, the Divine Office may be better and more perfectly carried out, whether by priests or by other members of the church, the sacred council, continuing the restoration so happily begun by the Apostolic See, decrees as follows concerning the office of the Roman rite:

88. Since the purpose of the office is to sanctify the day, the traditional sequence of the hours is to be restored so that, as far as possible, they may again become also in fact what they have been in name.[19a] At the same time account must be taken of the conditions of modern life especially as they affect those engaged in apostolic work.

89. Therefore, in the revision of the office these norms are to be observed:

(a) By the venerable tradition of the universal church, Lauds as morning prayer, and Vespers as evening prayer, are the two hinges on which the daily office turns. They must be considered the chief hours and are to be celebrated as such.

(b) Compline is to be drawn up so as suitably to mark the close of the day.

(c) The hour called Matins, although it should retain the character of nocturnal prayer when recited in choir, should be so adapted that it may be recited at any hour of the day, and it should be made up of fewer psalms and longer readings.

(d) The hour of Prime is to be suppressed.

(e) In choir the minor hours of Terce, Sext, and None are to be retained. Outside of choir it is permissible to select one of the three most suited to the time of the day.

90. The Divine Office, as the public prayer of the church, is a source of piety and of nourishment for personal prayer. For this reason, priests and all others who take part in the divine office are earnestly exhorted in the Lord to attune their minds to their voices when praying it. The better to achieve this, they should take steps to improve their understanding of the liturgy and of the bible, especially of the psalms. When the Roman office is being revised, its venerable centuries-old treasures are to be so adapted that those to whom it is handed on may profit from it more fully and more easily.

91. So that it may be possible in practice to adhere to the scheme for the hours proposed in article 89, the psalms are no longer to be distributed over one week but over a longer period of time.

The task of revising the psalter, which has been successfully begun, is to be finished as soon as possible. It should take the style of christian Latin into account, the liturgical use of the psalms—including the singing of the psalms—and the entire tradition of the Latin church.

92. As regards the readings, the following points are to be observed:

(a) Readings from sacred scripture are to be so arranged that the riches of the divine word may be more easily and more fully accessible;

(b) there is to be a better selection of readings from the works of the Fathers, Doctors, and ecclesiastical writers;

(c) the accounts of the martyrdoms or lives of the saints are to be made historically accurate.

93. Hymns are to be restored to their original form, as far as may be desirable. Whatever smacks of mythology or accords ill with christian piety is to be removed or changed. Also, as is judged appropriate, other selections are to be made from the treasury of

hymns.

94. So that the day may be truly sanctified and that the hours themselves may be recited with spiritual benefit, it is important that each canonical hour be recited as closely as possible to the time of day for which it is intended.

95. Communities obliged to choral office are bound to celebrate the office in choir every day in addition to the conventual Mass. In particular:

(a) orders of canons, monks, and nuns, and of other regulars bound by law or their constitutions to choral office are bound to the entire office;

(b) cathedral or collegiate chapters are bound to recite those parts of the office imposed on them by general or particular law;

(c) all members of the above communities who are in major Orders or who are solemnly professed, except for lay brothers, are bound to recite individually those canonical hours which they do not recite in choir.

96. Clerics not bound to office in choir, but who are in major Orders, are bound to pray the entire office every day, either in common or individually, as laid down in article 89.

97. The rubrics shall determine when it is appropriate to substitute a liturgical service for the divine office.

In particular cases, and for adequate reasons, ordinaries may dispense their subjects, wholly or in part, from the obligation of reciting the Divine Office, or they may change it to another obligation.

98. Members of any institute dedicated to acquiring perfection who in virtue of their constitutions recite parts of the divine office, are thereby praying the public prayer of the church.

The same can be said of those who, under their constitutions, recite any little office, provided it is drawn up after the pattern of the divine office, and is duly approved.

99. Since the Divine Office is the voice of the church, of the whole mystical body, publicly praising God, it is recommended that clerics who are not obliged to attend office in choir, especially priests who live together or who assemble for any purpose, should pray at least some part of the Divine Office in common.

All who pray the Divine Office, whether in choir or in common, should fulfill the task entrusted to them as perfectly as possible. This refers not only to the internal devotion of mind but also to the external manner of celebration. It is, moreover, fitting that whenever possible the office, both in choir and in common, be sung.

100. Pastors should see to it that the principal hours, especially Vespers, are celebrated in common in church on Sundays and on the more solemn feasts. The laity, too, are encouraged to recite the divine office, either with the priests, or among themselves, or even individually.

101. (1) In accordance with the age-old tradition of the Latin rite, the Latin language is to be retained by clerics in the divine office. But in individual cases the Ordinary has the power to grant the use of a vernacular translation to those clerics for whom the use of Latin constitutes a grave obstacle to their praying the office properly. The vernacular version, however, must be one that is drawn up in accordance with the provisions of article 36.

(2) The competent superior has the power to grant the use of the vernacular for the Divine Office, even in choir, to nuns, to religious men who are not clerics and to women religious. The vernacular version, however, must be one that is approved.

(3) Any cleric bound to the Divine Office fulfils his

obligation if he prays the office in the vernacular together with a group of the faithful or with those mentioned in par. 2, above, provided that the text used has
been approved.

Chapter V

THE LITURGICAL YEAR

102. The church believes that its nature requires it
to celebrate the saving work of the divine Bridegroom
by devoutly calling it to mind on certain days
throughout the year. Every week, on the day which it
has called the Lord's Day, it commemorates the
Lord's resurrection. It also celebrates it once every
year, together with his blessed passion, at Easter, that
most solemn of all feasts.

In the course of the year, moreover, it unfolds the
whole mystery of Christ from the incarnation and
nativity to the ascension, to Pentecost and the expectation of the blessed hope of the coming of the Lord.

Thus recalling the mysteries of the redemption, it
opens up to the faithful the riches of the Lord's powers and merits, so that these are in some way made
present at all times; the faithful lay hold of them and
are filled with saving grace.

103. In celebrating this annual cycle of the mysteries of Christ, the church honors the blessed Mary,
Mother of God, with a special love. She is inseparably
linked with her Son's saving work. In her the church
admires and exalts the most excellent fruit of the
redemption, and joyfully contemplates, as in a fault-
less image, the goal it anticipates and desires for all its
members.

104. The church has also included memorial days of the martyrs and other saints in the annual cycle. Raised up to perfection by the manifold grace of God and already in possession of eternal salvation, they sing God's perfect praise in heaven and pray for us. By celebrating the days on which they died, the church proclaims the paschal mystery in the saints who have suffered and have been glorified with Christ. It proposes them to the faithful as models who draw all people to the Father through Christ, and through their merits it begs for God's favor.

105. Finally, in the various seasons of the year and in keeping with its traditional discipline, the church completes the formation of the faithful by means of pious practices for soul and body, by instruction, prayer, and works of penance and mercy.

Accordingly, the sacred council has decided to decree as follows:

106. By a tradition handed down from the apostles, which took its origin from the very day of Christ's resurrection, the church celebrates the paschal mystery every eighth day,[19b] which day is appropriately called the Lord's day or Sunday. For on this day Christ's faithful are bound to come together so that, by hearing the word of God and taking part in the Eucharist, they may commemorate the suffering, resurrection, and glory of the Lord Jesus, giving thanks to God who "has given us a new birth into a living hope through the resurrection of Jesus Christ from the dead" (1 Pet 1:3). The Lord's Day is the original feast day, and it should be presented to the faithful and taught to them so that it may become in fact a day of rejoicing and of freedom from work. Other celebrations, unless they be truly of the greatest importance, shall not have precedence over Sunday, which is the foundation and kernel of the entire liturgical year.

107. The liturgical year is to be revised so that the

traditional customs and discipline of the sacred seasons shall be preserved or restored in line with the conditions of modern times. Their specific character is to be retained so that they duly nourish the piety of the faithful as they celebrate the mysteries of the christian redemption and, above all, the paschal mystery. If certain adaptations are necessary because of local conditions, they are to be made in accordance with the provisions of articles 39 and 40.

108. The minds of the faithful should be directed primarily toward the feasts of the Lord whereby the mysteries of salvation are celebrated throughout the year. For this reason, the Proper of the Seasons must be given due preference over the feasts of the saints so that the entire cycle of the mysteries of salvation may be suitably recalled.

109. The two elements which are especially characteristic of Lent—the recalling of Baptism or the preparation for it, and Penance — should be given greater emphasis in the liturgy and in liturgical catechesis. It is by means of them that the church prepares the faithful for the celebration of Easter, while they listen more attentively to God's word and devote more time to prayer. Accordingly:

(a) more use is to be made of the baptismal features which are part of the Lenten liturgy; some features which had formed part of an earlier tradition are to be restored as may seem advisable;

(b) the same may be said of the penitential elements. Further, as well as pointing out the social consequences of sin, the catechesis must impress on the minds of the faithful the distinctive character of penance as a detestation of sin because it is an offence against God. The role of the church in penitential practices is not to be omitted, and the need to pray for sinners should be emphasized.

110. During Lent penance should be not only

internal and individual but also external and social. The practice of penance should be encouraged in ways suited to the present day, to different regions, and to individual circumstances. It should be recommended by the authorities mentioned in article 22.

But the paschal fast must be kept sacrosanct. It should be celebrated everywhere on Good Friday, and where possible should be prolonged through Holy Saturday so that the faithful may attain the joys of Easter Sunday with uplifted and receptive minds.

111. The saints have been traditionally honored in the church, and their authentic relics and images held in veneration. For the feasts of the saints proclaim the wonderful works of Christ in his servants and offer to the faithful fitting examples for their imitation.

Lest the feasts of the saints take precedence over the feasts which commemorate the actual mysteries of salvation, the celebration of many of them should be consigned to particular churches, nations, or religious families. Only those should be extended to the universal church which commemorate saints of truly universal importance.

Chapter VI

SACRED MUSIC

112. The musical tradition of the universal church is a treasure of inestimable value, greater even than that of any other art. The main reason for this pre-eminence is that, as a combination of sacred music and words, it forms a necessary or integral part of the solemn liturgy.

Sacred scripture, indeed, has praised sacred song (see Eph 5:19; Col 3:16). So have the Fathers of the church and the Roman pontiffs who in more recent times, led by St Pius X, have explained more precisely the ministerial function of sacred music in the service of the Lord.

Therefore sacred music is to be considered the more holy, the more closely connected it is with the liturgical action, whether making prayer more pleasing, promoting unity of minds, or conferring greater solemnity on the sacred rites. The church, indeed, approves of all forms of true art which have the requisite qualities, and admits them into divine worship.

Accordingly, the sacred council, keeping to the norms and precepts of ecclesiastical tradition and discipline and having regard to the purpose of sacred music, which is the glory of God and the sanctification of the faithful, decrees as follows:

113. Liturgical worship takes on a more dignified character when the rites are celebrated solemnly in song, with sacred ministers taking part and with the active participation of the people.

As regards the language to be used, the provisions of article 36 are to be observed; for the Mass, article 54; for the sacraments, article 63; for the Divine Office, article 101.

114. The treasury of sacred music is to be preserved and cultivated with great care. Choirs must be diligently developed, especially in cathedral churches. Bishops and other pastors of souls must do their best to ensure that whenever a liturgical service is to be accompanied by chant, the whole body of the faithful may be able to take that active part which is rightly theirs, as laid down in articles 28 and 30.

115. Much emphasis should be placed on the teaching of music and on musical activity in seminaries, in the novitiates and houses of studies of religious

of both sexes, and also in other Catholic institutions and schools. To impart this instruction teachers are to be carefully trained and put in charge of the teaching of sacred music.

It is desirable also that higher institutes of sacred music be established whenever possible.

Musicians and singers, especially boys, must also be given a genuine liturgical training.

116. The church recognizes Gregorian chant as especially native to the Roman liturgy. Therefore, other things being equal, it should be given pride of place in liturgical services.

Other kinds of sacred music, especially polyphony, are by no means excluded from liturgical celebrations so long as they accord with the spirit of the liturgical action as laid down in article 30.

117. The standard edition of the books of Gregorian chant is to be completed. In addition a more critical edition is to be prepared of those books already published since the restoration by St Pius X.

It is desirable also that an edition be prepared containing simpler melodies for use in smaller churches.

118. Religious singing by the faithful is to be skilfully encouraged so that in devotional exercises[19c] as well as in liturgical services the voices of the faithful may be heard, in conformity with the norms and requirements of the rubrics.

119. In some places, in mission lands especially, there are people who have their own musical tradition, and this plays an important part in their religious and social life. For this reason their music should be held in due esteem and should be given a suitable role, not only in forming their religious sense but also in adapting worship to their native genius, as indicated in articles 39 and 40.

Therefore, in the musical training of missionaries, special care should be taken to ensure that they will be capable of encouraging the traditional music of those peoples both in the schools and in sacred services, as far as may be practicable.

120. The pipe organ is to be held in high esteem in the Latin church, for it is the traditional musical instrument, the sound of which can add a wonderful splendor to the church's ceremonies and can most effectively elevate people's spirits to God and things above.

Other instruments may also be used in divine worship, at the discretion and with the consent of the competent territorial authority as laid down in articles 22 § 2, 37 and 40, provided they are suitable, or can be made suitable, for sacred use, that they accord with the dignity of the sacred building, and that they truly contribute to the edification of the faithful.

121. Composers, animated by the christian spirit, should accept that it is part of their vocation to cultivate sacred music and increase its store of treasures.

Let them produce compositions which have the qualities proper to genuine sacred music, and which can be sung not only by large choirs but also by smaller choirs, and which make possible the active participation of the whole congregation.

The texts intended to be sung must always be in conformity with catholic doctrine. Indeed, they should be drawn chiefly from the sacred scripture and from liturgical sources.

Chapter VII

SACRED ART AND FURNISHINGS

122. The fine arts are rightly classed among the noblest activities of human genius; this is especially true of religious art and of its highest achievement, sacred art. Of their nature the arts are directed toward expressing in some way the infinite beauty of God in works made by human hands. They are dedicated to God, they praise him and extend his glory to the extent that their only purpose is to turn people's spirits devoutly toward God.

For that reason the church has always been a friend of the fine arts, has ever sought their noble ministry and has trained artists. Its chief purpose has been to ensure that all things set apart for use in divine worship should be worthy, becoming, and beautiful, signs and symbols of things supernatural. In fact the church has, with good reason, always seen itself as an arbiter of the arts, deciding which of the works of artists are consistent with faith, piety and the traditional laws of religion, and are to be considered suitable for sacred use.

The church has been particularly careful to ensure that sacred furnishings should be dignified and beautiful and thus contribute to the decorum of worship. It has admitted changes in material, style, or ornamentation prompted by the progress of artistic technique with the passage of time. The fathers have therefore decided to issue the following decrees on these matters:

123. The church has not adopted any particular style of art as its own, but guided by people's temperaments and circumstances, and the needs of the various rites, it has admitted styles from every period. Thus in the course of the centuries it has brought into

existence a treasury of art which must be very carefully preserved. The art of our own times from every race
and country should also be given free scope in the
church, provided it bring to the task the reverence and
honor due to the sacred buildings and rites. Thus it is
enabled to join its voice to that wonderful chorus of
praise sung by the great masters in past ages of
catholic faith.

124. Ordinaries are to take care that in encouraging
and favoring truly sacred art, they should look for
noble beauty rather than sumptuous display. The
same principle applies also to sacred vestments and
ornaments.

Bishops should be careful to ensure that works of
art which are repugnant to faith, morals, and Christian piety, and which offend true religious sense
either by depraved forms or through lack of artistic
merit or because of mediocrity or pretence, be kept
well away from the house of God and from other
sacred places.

And when churches are to be built, let great care be
taken that they are suitable for the celebration of
liturgical services and for the active participation of
the faithful.

125. The practice of placing sacred images in
churches for people to venerate is to be maintained.
Nevertheless they should be restricted in number and
their relative positions should reflect right order, lest
they cause confusion among the christian people, or
foster devotion of doubtful orthodoxy.

126. When passing judgment on works of art, local
ordinaries should ask the opinion of the diocesan
commission on sacred art and — when occasion demands — the opinions of others who are experts, and
the commissions mentioned in articles 44, 45 and 46.

Ordinaries should ensure that sacred furnishings
and works of value are not disposed of or destroyed,

for they are the adornment of God's house.

127. Bishops, either personally or through suitable priests who are gifted with a knowledge and love of art, should have a special concern for artists, so as to imbue them with the spirit of sacred art and of the sacred liturgy.

It is also desirable that schools or academies of sacred art should be established in those parts of the world where they would be useful for the training of artists.

All artists who, prompted by their talents, desire to serve God's glory in the church should always bear in mind that they are engaged in a kind of holy imitation of God the Creator and that the works they produce are destined to be used in Catholic worship, for the edification of the faithful and to foster their piety and religious formation.

128. The canons and ecclesiastical statutes which govern the provision of the externals of sacred worship should be revised as soon as possible, together with the liturgical books, as laid down in article 25. These laws refer especially to the construction of sacred buildings which are dignified and suitable, the design and construction of altars, the dignity, positioning and security of the eucharistic tabernacle, the suitable siting of the baptistery and its adornment, how to arrange sacred images and regulate decoration and ornamentation. Laws which seem less suited to the reformed liturgy should be corrected or abolished. Those which foster it are to be retained, or introduced if lacking.

In this matter, especially as regards the material and design of sacred furnishing and vestments, in accordance with article 22 of this Constitution, powers are given to territorial conferences of bishops to adapt such things to the needs and customs of their different regions.

129. During their philosophical and theological studies, clerics are to be taught about the history and development of sacred art, and about the basic principles which govern the production of its works. Thus they will be able to appreciate and preserve the church's ancient monuments, and be able to aid by good advice artists who are engaged in producing works of art.

130. The use of pontifical insignia ought to be reserved to those ecclesiastics who are bishops or hold some particular jurisdiction.

Appendix

A DECLARATION OF THE SECOND VATICAN ECUMENICAL COUNCIL ON REVISION OF THE CALENDAR

The Second Vatican Ecumenical Council, recognizing the importance of the wishes of many on assigning the feast of Easter to a fixed Sunday and on a fixed calendar, having carefully considered the results that could follow from the introduction of a new calendar, declares as follows:

1. The sacred council is not opposed to assigning the feast of Easter to a fixed Sunday in the Gregorian Calendar, provided those whom it may concern give their assent, especially Christians who are not in communion with the Apostolic See.

2. The sacred council likewise declares that it does not oppose efforts designed to introduce a perpetual calendar into civil society.

But among the various systems which are being

devised with a view to establishing a perpetual calendar and introducing it into civil life, those and only those are unopposed by the church which retain and safeguard a seven-day week, with Sunday, without the introduction of any days outside the week, so that the succession of weeks may be left intact, unless in the judgment of the Apostolic See there are extremely weighty reasons to the contrary.

a. This translation is based on that made in 1963 by the late Clifford Howell, S.J., who had done much in his native England and elsewhere for the liturgical movement. His translation was later revised by the late Joseph Rodgers, bishop of Killaloe, Ireland. For this edition it has been very considerably revised by AF and Sean Collins, OFM, former director of the Irish Institute of Pastoral Liturgy.

1. Roman Missal, prayer over the gifts, 9th Sunday after Pentecost.

2. See St Ignatius of Antioch: *Ad Ephesios*, 7:2: ed. F. X. Funk, *Patres Apostolici*, I, Tübingen 1901, p. 218.

3. *Sacramentarium Veronense* (Leonianium): ed. C Mohlberg, Rome 1956, n. 1265, p. 162.

4. Roman Missal, Easter Preface.

5. See Augustine, *Enarr. in Ps.* CXXXVIII, 2: CChr. 40, Turnhout, 1956, p. 1991 and prayer after Second Lesson of Holy Saturday (Roman Missal, before renewal of Holy Week).

6. Council of Trent, Session 13, 11 Oct. 1551, Decree on the Holy Eucharist, ch 5: CT, *Diariorum, Actorum, Epistolarum, Tractatuum nova collectio*, ed. Goerresian society, t. VII, *Actorum* part IV, Freiburg im Breisgau 1961, p. 202.

7. Council of Trent, Session 22, 17 Sept. 1562, Teaching *On the Holy sacrifice of the Mass*, ch 2. CT, ed. cit., t. VIII, *Actorum* part V, Freiburg im Breisgau 1919, p. 960.

8. See Augustine, *In Johannis Evangelium Tractatus* VI, ch. 1, n. 7: PL 35, 1428.

8a. The Latin is: *cuius efficacitatem eodem titulo eodemque gradu nulla alia actio ecclesiae adaequat*. [Editor].

9. Roman Missal, prayer after communion for Easter vigil and Easter Sunday.

10. Ibid., opening prayer at Mass of Tuesday of Easter Week.

11. Roman Missal, prayer over the gifts for Monday within the octave of Pentecost.

12. St Cyprian, *De cath. eccl. unitate*, 7: ed. G. Hartel, in CSEL, t. III, 1, Vienna 1868, pp. 215-216; see Letter 66, n. 8, 3: ed. G. Hartel, in CSEL, T. III, 2, Vienna, 1871, pp. 732-733.

13. See council of Trent, session 22, 17 Sept. 1562, Teaching *On the Holy sacrifice of the Mass,* ch. 8: CT, *ed. cit.,* t. VIII, p. 961.

14. See St Ignatius of Antioch: *Ad Magn.* 7; *Ad Philad.* 4, *Ad Smyrn.* 8: ed. F. X. Funk, op. cit., 1, pp. 236, 266, 281.

15. See St Augustine, *In Ioannis Evangelium Tractatus XXVI,* ch. 6, no 13; PL 35, 1613.

16. Roman Breviary: feast of Corpus Christi, Second Vespers, Antiphon for Magnificat.

17. See St Cyril of Alexandria: *Commentarium. in Joannis Evangelium,* Book XI, chs. 11-12: PG 74, 557-565, especially 564-565.

18. Session 21: On Communion under both kinds and of children, ch. 1-3, canons 1-3: CT, *ed. cit.,* t. VIII, pp. 698-699.

19. Council of Trent, Session 24: *On Reform,* ch. 1: CT, ed. cit., t. IX. Actorum part VI, Freiburg im Breisgau 1924, p. 969. See Roman Ritual, Title 8, ch. 2, n. 6.

19a. Literally, "that temporal truth may be restored to the hours". Latin: *ut horis veritas temporis. . . reddatur.* [Editor].

19b. Latin: *octava quaque die.* Sunday is both the first and the eighth day: the first *(prima sabbati)* when God's activity began in creation and in the risen Christ, and the eighth, beyond the sabbath, which is the longed-for eternal day of victory. [Courtesy of Seán Collins, OFM. Editor.]

19c. The Latin *(piis sacrisque exercitiis)* refers to the two kinds of devotional exercises mentioned in number 13 (q. v.): *pia exercitia* and *sacra exercitia.* [Editor].

PASTORAL CONSTITUTION ON THE CHURCH IN THE MODERN WORLD[1]

Gaudium et Spes
7 December, 1965

Preface[1a]

**Solidarity of the Church with
the Whole Human Family**

1. The joys and hopes, the grief and anguish of the people of our time, especially of those who are poor or afflicted, are the joys and hopes, the grief and anguish of the followers of Christ as well. Nothing that is genuinely human fails to find an echo in their hearts. For theirs is a community of people united in Christ and guided by the holy Spirit in their pilgrimage towards the Father's kingdom, bearers of a message of salvation for all of humanity. That is why they cherish a feeling of deep solidarity with the human race and its history.

The Council Addresses All of Humanity

2. Now that the Second Vatican council has studied the mystery of the church more deeply, it addresses not only the daughters and sons of the church and all who call upon the name of Christ, but the whole of humanity as well, and it wishes to set down how it understands the presence and function of the church in the world of today.

The world which the council has in mind is the world of women and men, the entire human family seen in its total environment. It is the world as the theatre of human history, bearing the marks of its travail, its triumphs and failures. It is the world which Christians believe has been created and is sustained by the love of its maker, has fallen into the slavery of sin but has been freed by Christ, who was crucified and rose again in order to break the stranglehold of the evil one, so that it might be fashioned anew according to God's design and brought to its fulfillment.

An Offer of Service to Humankind

3. Though proud of its discoveries and its power, humanity is often concerned about current developments in the world, about humanity's place and role in the universe, about the meaning of individual and collective endeavor, and finally about the destiny of nature and of humanity. And so the council, as witness and guide to the faith of all of God's people, gathered together by Christ, can find no more eloquent expression of this people's solidarity, respect and love for the whole human family, of which it forms part, than to enter into dialogue with it about all these various problems, throwing the light of the Gospel on them and supplying humanity with the saving resources which the church has received from its founder under the promptings of the holy Spirit. It is the human person that is to be saved, human society which must be renewed. It is the human person, therefore, which is the key to this discussion, each individual human person in her or his totality, body and soul, heart and conscience, mind and will.

This is the reason why this holy synod, in proclaiming humanity's noble destiny and affirming that there exists in it a divine seed, offers the human race the sincere cooperation of the church in fostering a sense of sisterhood and brotherhood to correspond to their destiny. The church is not motivated by earthly ambition but is interested in one thing only — to carry on the work of Christ under the guidance of the holy Spirit, who came into the world to bear witness to the truth,[2] to save and not to judge, to serve and not to be served.[3]

Introduction
THE CONDITION OF HUMANITY
IN THE WORLD TODAY

Hope and Anguish

4. In every age, the church carries the responsibility of reading the signs of the times and of interpreting them in the light of the Gospel, if it is to carry out its task. In language intelligible to every generation, it should be able to answer the ever recurring questions which people ask about the meaning of this present life and of the life to come, and how one is related to the other. We must be aware of and understand the aspirations, the yearnings, and the often dramatic features of the world in which we live. An outline of some of the more important features of the modern world forms the subject of the following paragraphs.

Ours is a new age of history with profound and rapid changes spreading gradually to all corners of the earth. They are the products of people's intelligence and creative activity, but they recoil upon them, upon their judgments and desires, both individual and collective, upon their ways of thinking and acting in regard to people and things. We are entitled then to speak of a real social and cultural transformation whose repercussions are felt at the religious level also.

A transformation of this kind brings with it the serious problems associated with any crisis of growth. Increase in power is not always accompanied by control of that power for the benefit of humanity. In probing the recesses of their own minds, people often seem more uncertain than ever of themselves: in the gradual and precise unfolding of the laws of social living, they are uncertain about how to plot its course.

In no other age has humanity enjoyed such an abundance of wealth, resources and economic well-being; and yet a huge proportion of the people of the world is plagued by hunger and extreme need while countless numbers are totally illiterate. At no time have people had such a keen sense of freedom, only to be faced by new forms of social and psychological slavery. The world is keenly aware of its unity and of mutual interdependence in essential solidarity, but at the same time it is split into bitterly opposing camps. We have not yet seen the last of bitter political, social, and economic hostility, and racial and ideological antagonism, nor are we free from the spectre of a war of total destruction. If there is a growing exchange of ideas, there is still widespread disagreement in competing ideologies about the meaning of the words which express our key concepts. There is lastly a painstaking search for a better material world, without a parallel spiritual advancement.

Small wonder then, that many of our contemporaries are prevented by this complex situation from recognizing permanent values and duly applying them to recent discoveries. As a result, they hover between hope and anxiety and wonder uneasily about the present course of events. It is a situation that challenges and even obliges people to respond.

Deep-seated Changes

5. The spiritual uneasiness of today and the changing structure of life are part of a broader upheaval, whose symptoms are the increasing part played on the intellectual level by the mathematical, natural and human sciences and on the practical level by their repercussions on technology. The scientific mentality

has brought about a change in the cultural sphere and on habits of thought, and the progress of technology is now reshaping the face of the earth and has its sights set on the conquest of space.

The human mind is, in a certain sense, increasing its mastery over time — over the past through the insights of history, over the future by foresight and planning. Advances in biology, psychology, and the social sciences not only lead humanity to greater self-awareness, but provide it with the technical means of molding the lives of whole societies as well. At the same time, the human race is giving more and more thought to the forecasting and control of its own population growth.

The accelerated pace of history is such that one can scarcely keep abreast of it. The destiny of the human race is viewed as a complete whole, no longer, as it were, in the particular histories of various peoples: now it merges into a complete whole. And so humankind substitutes a dynamic and more evolutionary concept of nature for a static one, and the result is an immense series of new problems calling for a new endeavor of analysis and synthesis.

Changes in the Social Order

6. As a result, the traditional structure of local communities — family, clan, tribe, village, various groupings and social relationships — is subjected to ever more sweeping changes. Industrialization is on the increase and has raised some nations to a position of affluence, while it radically transfigures ideas and social practices hallowed by centuries. Urbanization too is on the increase, both on account of the expanding number of city dwellers and the spread of an urban way of life into rural settings. New and more effective mass media are contributing to the spread of knowledge and the speedy diffusion far and wide of

habits of thought and feeling, setting off chain reactions in their wake. Nor should one underestimate the effect of emigration on those who, for whatever reason, are led to undertake a new way of life. On the whole, the bonds uniting human beings multiply unceasingly, and *socialization* creates yet other bonds, without, however, a corresponding personal development, and truly personal relationships (*personalization*). It is above all in countries with advanced standards of economic and social progress that this evolution is apparent, but it also affects developing nations, who are eager to share in the benefits of industrialization and urbanization. Peoples like these, especially where ancient traditions are still strong, are at the same time conscious of the need to exercise their freedom in a more mature and personal way.

Changes in Attitudes, Morals and Religion

7. A change in attitudes and structures frequently calls accepted values into question. This is true above all of young people who have grown impatient at times and, indeed, rebellious. Conscious of their own importance in the life of society, they aspire to play their part in it all the earlier. Consequently, it frequently happens that parents and teachers find their tasks increasingly difficult.

Traditional institutions, laws and modes of thought and emotion do not always appear to be in harmony with today's world. This has given rise to a serious disruption of patterns and even of norms of behavior.

As regards religion, there is a completely new atmosphere that conditions its practice. On the one hand people are taking a hard look at all magical world-views and prevailing superstitions and are demanding a more personal and active commitment of faith, so that not a few have achieved a lively sense of the divine. On the other hand, greater numbers are falling away from the practice of religion. In the past it was the exception to repudiate God and religion to the point of abandoning them, and then only in individual cases; but nowadays it seems a matter of course to reject them as incompatible with scientific progress and a new kind of humanism. In many places it is not only in philosophical terms that such trends are expressed, there are signs of them in literature, art, the humanities, the interpretation of history and even civil law: all of which is very disturbing to many people.

Imbalances in the World of Today

8. Such rapid and uneven change, coupled with an increasingly keener awareness of existing inequalities make for the creation and aggravation of differences and imbalances.

On the personal level, there often arises an imbalance between a modern practical outlook and a theoretical way of thinking which fails to master and synthesize the sum total of its ideas. Another imbalance occurs between concern for practical effectiveness and the demands of moral conscience; yet another occurs between life in society and the individual's need for reflection and contemplation. A final imbalance takes the form of conflict between the specialization of human activity and a global view of reality.

On the family level there are tensions arising out of demographic, economic and social pressures, out of conflicts between the generations, and out of new social relationships between the sexes.

On the level of race and social class we find tensions between the affluent and the underdeveloped nations; we find them between international bodies set up in the interests of peace and the desire to spread ideologies along with national or bloc expansionism. In the midst of it all stands humanity, at once the author and the victim of mutual distrust, animosity, conflict and woe.

Broader Aspirations of Humankind

9. Meanwhile there is a growing conviction that humanity is able and has the duty to strengthen its mastery over nature and that there is need to establish a political, social, and economic order at the service of humanity, to assert and develop the dignity proper to individuals and to societies.

Great numbers of people are acutely conscious of being deprived of the world's goods through injustice and unfair distribution and are vehemently demanding their share of them. Developing nations, such as the recently independent states, are anxious to share in the political and economic benefits of modern civilization and to play their part freely in the world, but they are hampered by their economic dependence on the rapidly expanding richer nations and the ever widening gap between them. The hungry nations cry out to their affluent neighbors; women claim parity with men in fact as well as of right, where they have not already obtained it; labourers and agricultural workers insist not just on the necessities of life but also on the opportunity to develop by their labor their personal talents and to play their due role in organizing economic, social, political, and cultural life. Now for the first time in history people are not afraid to think that cultural benefits are for all and should be available to everybody.

These claims are but the sign of a deeper and more widespread aspiration. Women and men as individuals and as members of society crave a life that is full, autonomous, and worthy of their nature as human beings; they long to harness for their own welfare the immense resources of the modern world. Among nations there is a growing movement to set up a worldwide community.

In the light of the foregoing factors there appears the dichotomy of a world that is at once powerful and weak, capable of doing what is noble and what is base, disposed to freedom and slavery, progress and decline, amity and hatred. People are becoming conscious that the forces they have unleashed are in their own hands and that it is up to themselves to control them or be enslaved by them. Here lies the modern dilemma.

Humanity's Deeper Questionings

10. The dichotomy affecting the modern world is, in fact, a symptom of the deeper dichotomy that is rooted in humanity itself. It is the meeting point of many conflicting forces. As created beings, people are subject to many limitations, but they feel unlimited in their desires and their sense of being destined for a higher life. They feel the pull of many attractions and are compelled to choose between them and reject some among them. Worse still, feeble and sinful as they are, they often do the very thing they hate and do not do what they want.[4] And so they feel themselves divided, and the result is a host of discords in social life. Many, it is true, fail to see the dramatic nature of this state of affairs in all its clarity for their vision is in fact blurred by materialism, or they are prevented from even thinking about it by the wretchedness of their plight. Others delude themselves that they have found peace in a world-view now fashionable. There are still others whose hopes are set on a genuine and total emancipation of humankind through human effort alone and look forward to some future earthly paradise where all the desires of their hearts will be fulfilled. Nor is it unusual to find people who, having lost faith in life, extol the kind of foolhardiness which would empty life of all significance in itself and invest

it with a meaning of their own devising. Nonetheless, in the face of modern developments there is a growing body of people who are asking the most fundamental of all questions or are glimpsing them with a keener insight: What is humanity? What is the meaning of suffering, evil, death, which have not been eliminated by all this progress? What is the purpose of these achievements, purchased at so high a price? What can people contribute to society? What can they expect from it? What happens after this earthly life is ended?

The church believes that Christ, who died and was raised for the sake of all,[5] can show people the way and strengthen them through the Spirit so that they become worthy of their destiny: nor is there given any other name under heaven by which they can be saved.[6] The church likewise believes that the key, the center and the purpose of the whole of human history is to be found in its Lord and Master. It also maintains that beneath all those changes there is much that is unchanging, much that has its ultimate foundation in Christ, who is the same yesterday, and today, and forever.[7] And that is why the council, relying on the inspiration of Christ, the image of the invisible God, the firstborn of all creation,[8] proposes to speak to all people in order to unfold the mystery that is humankind and cooperate in tackling the main problems facing the world today.

1. Although it consists of two parts, the Pastoral Constitution "The Church in the World Today" constitutes an organic unity.

The Constitution is called "pastoral" because, while resting on doctrinal principles, it sets out the relation of the church to the world and to the people of today. In Part I, therefore, the pastoral emphasis is not overlooked, nor is the doctrinal emphasis overlooked in Part II.

In Part I the church develops its teaching on humanity, the world it inhabits, and its relationship to women and men. Part II treats at length of various aspects of life and human society today and in particular deals with those questions and problems which seem to have a greater urgency in our day. The result is that in Part II the subject matter which is viewed in the light of doctrinal principles consists of elements, some of which are permanent and some of which are contingent.

The Constitution is to be interpreted according to the general norms of theological interpretation, while taking into account, especially in Part II, the changing circumstances which the subject matter, by its very nature, involves.

1a. With the exception of Part I, chap. 1 (translated by the late Ambrose McNicholl, O.P., University of St Thomas, Rome), the Constitution was translated by Paul Lennon, O.Carm. It was revised for this edition by AF.

2. See Jn 18:37.
3. See Jn 3:17; Mt 20:28; Mk 10:45.
4. See Rom 7:14 ff.
5. See 2 Cor 5:15.
6. See Acts 4:12.
7. See Heb 13:8.
8. See Col 1:15.

Part One

THE CHURCH AND THE HUMAN VOCATION

Responding to the Promptings of the Spirit

11. The people of God believes that it is led by the Spirit of the Lord who fills the whole world. Impelled by that faith, they try to discern the true signs of God's presence and purpose in the events, the needs and the desires which it shares with the rest of humanity today. For faith casts a new light on everything and makes known the full ideal which God has set for humanity, thus guiding the mind towards solutions that are fully human.

The council intends first of all to assess by that light those values which are most highly prized today and to relate them to their divine source. For such values are very good, in so far as they stem from the God-given character of the human person. Frequently, however, thanks to the corruption of the human heart, they are disordered and need to be purified.

What does the church think of humanity? What measures are to be recommended for building up society today? What is the ultimate meaning of human activity in the universe? These questions call for answers. From the answers it will be increasingly clear that the people of God, and the human race of which it forms part, are of service to each other; and the mission of the church will show itself to be supremely human by the very fact of being religious.

Chapter I

THE DIGNITY OF THE HUMAN PERSON

Women and Men in the Image of God

12. Believers and unbelievers agree almost unanimously that all things on earth should be ordained to humanity as to their center and summit.

But what is humanity? People have put forward, and continue to put forward, many views about humanity, views that are divergent and even contradictory. Sometimes they either set it up as the absolute measure of all things, or debase it to the point of despair. Hence humanity's doubt and anguish. The church is keenly sensitive to these difficulties. Enlightened by divine revelation it can offer a solution to them by which the true state of humanity may be described, its weakness explained in such a way that at the same time its dignity and vocation may be perceived in their true light.

For sacred scripture teaches that women and men were created "in the image of God," able to know and

love their creator, and set by him over all earthly creatures[1] that they might rule them, and make use of
them, while glorifying God.[2] "What are women and
men that you are mindful of them, their sons and
daughters that you care for them? You have made
them little less than angels, and crown them with
glory and honor. You have given them dominion over
the works of your hands; you have put all things
under their feet" (Ps 8:5-8).

But God did not create men and women as solitary
beings. From the beginning "male and female God
created them" (Gen 1:27). This partnership of man
and woman constitutes the first form of communion
between people. For by their innermost nature men
and women are social beings; and if they do not enter
into relationships with others they can neither live
nor develop their gifts.

So God, as we read again in the Bible, saw" all the
things that he had made, and they were very good"
(Gen 1:31).

Sin

13. Although set by God in a state of righteousness,
men and women, enticed by the evil one, abused their
freedom at the very start of history. They raised themselves up against God, and tried to attain their goal
apart from him. Although they had known God, they
did not glorify him as God, but their senseless hearts
were darkened, and they served the creature rather
than the creator.[3] What revelation makes known to us
is confirmed by our own experience. For when people
look into their own hearts they find that they are
drawn towards what is wrong and are sunk in many
evils which cannot have come from their good creator. Often refusing to acknowledge God as their
source, men and women have also upset the relationship which should link them to their final destiny;

and at the same time they have broken the right order that should exist within themselves as well as between them and other people and all creatures.

They are therefore divided interiorly. As a result, the entire life of women and men, both individual and social, shows itself to be a struggle, and a dramatic one, between good and evil, between light and darkness. People find that they are unable of themselves to overcome the assaults of evil successfully, so that everyone feels as if in chains. But the Lord himself came to free and strengthen humanity, renewing it inwardly and casting out the "prince of this world" (Jn 12:31), who held it in the bondage of sin.[4] For sin diminished humanity, preventing it from attaining its fulfillment.

Both the high calling and the deep misery which people experience find their final explanation in the light of this revelation.

Humanity's Essential Nature

14. The human person, though made of body and soul, is a unity. In itself, in its very bodily condition, it synthesizes the elements of the material world, which through it are thus brought to their highest perfection and are enabled to raise their voice in spontaneous praise of the creator.[5] For this reason human beings may not despise their bodily life. They are, rather, to regard their bodies as good and to hold them in honor since God has created them and will raise them up on the last day. Nevertheless humanity has been wounded by sin. People find by experience that their bodies are in revolt. Their very dignity therefore requires that they should glorify God in their bodies,[6] and not allow them to serve the evil inclinations of their hearts.

Women and men are not mistaken when they regard themselves as superior to merely bodily creatures and as more than mere particles of nature or nameless units in human society. For by their power to know themselves in the depths of their being they rise above the entire universe of mere objects.[6a] When they are drawn to think about their real selves they turn to those deep recesses of their being where God who probes the heart[7] awaits them, and where they themselves decide their own destiny in the sight of God. So when they recognize in themselves a spiritual and immortal soul, this is not an illusion, a product of their imagination, to be explained solely in terms of physical or social causes. On the contrary, they have grasped the profound truth of the matter.

Dignity of the Intellect, of Truth, and of Wisdom

15. Men and women, sharing in the light of the divine mind, rightly affirm that by their intellect they surpass the world of mere things. By diligent use of their talents through the ages they have indeed made progress in the empirical sciences, in technology, and in the liberal arts. In our time, their attempts to search out the secrets of the material universe and to bring it under their control have been extremely successful. Yet they have always looked for, and found truths of a higher order. For their intellect is not confined to the range of what can be observed by the senses. They can, with genuine certainty, reach to realities known only to the mind, even though, as a result of sin, their vision has been clouded and their powers weakened.

Humanity's intellectual nature finds at last its perfection, as it needs to, in wisdom, which gently draws the human mind to look for and to love what is true and good. Endowed with wisdom, women and men are led through visible realities to those which are invisible.

Our age, more than any of the past, needs such wisdom if all humanity's discoveries are to be ennobled through human effort. Indeed the future of the world is in danger unless wiser people are forthcoming. It should also be pointed out that many nations which are poorer as far as material goods are concerned, yet richer in wisdom, can be of the greatest advantage to others.

It is by the gift of the holy Spirit that humanity, through faith, comes to contemplate and savor the mystery of God's design.[8]

Dignity of Moral Conscience

16. Deep within their consciences men and women discover a law which they have not laid upon themselves and which they must obey. Its voice, ever calling them to love and to do what is good and to avoid evil, tells them inwardly at the right moment: do this, shun that. For they have in their hearts a law inscribed by God. Their dignity rests in observing this law, and by it they will be judged.[9] Their conscience is people's most secret core, and their sanctuary. There they are alone with God whose voice echoes in their depths.[10] By conscience, in a wonderful way, that law is made known which is fulfilled in the love of God and of one's neighbor.[11] Through loyalty to conscience, Christians are joined to others in the search for truth and for the right solution to so many moral problems which arise both in the life of individuals and from social relationships. Hence, the more a correct conscience prevails, the more do persons and groups turn aside from blind choice and endeavor to conform to the objective standards of moral conduct. Yet it often happens that conscience goes astray through ignorance which it is unable to avoid, without thereby losing its dignity. This cannot be said of the person who takes little trouble to find out what is true and good, or when conscience is gradually almost blinded through the habit of committing sin.

The Excellence of Freedom

17. It is, however, only in freedom that people can turn themselves towards what is good. The people of our time prize freedom very highly and strive eagerly for it. In this they are right. Yet they often cherish it improperly, as if it gave them leave to do anything they like, even when it is evil. But genuine freedom is an exceptional sign of the image of God in humanity. For God willed that men and women should "be left free to make their own decisions"[12] so that they might of their own accord seek their creator and freely attain their full and blessed perfection by cleaving to God. Their dignity therefore requires them to act out of conscious and free choice, as moved and drawn in a personal way from within, and not by their own blind impulses or by external constraint. People gain such dignity when, freeing themselves of all slavery to the passions, they press forward towards their goal by freely choosing what is good, and, by their diligence and skill, effectively secure for themselves the means suited to this end. Since human freedom has been weakened by sin it is only by the help of God's grace that people can properly orientate their actions towards God. Before the judgment seat of God everybody will have to give an account of their life, according as they have done either good or evil.[13]

The Mystery of Death

18. It is when faced with death that the enigma of the human condition is most evident. People are tormented not only by pain and by the gradual diminution of their bodily powers but also, and even more, by the dread of forever ceasing to be. But a deep instinct leads them rightly to shrink from and to reject the utter ruin and total loss of their personality. Because they bear in themselves the seed of eternity, which cannot be reduced to mere matter, they rebel

against death. All the helps made available by technology, however useful they may be, cannot set their anguished minds at rest. They may prolong their lifespan; but this does not satisfy their heartfelt longing, one that can never be stifled, for an after-life.

While the imagination is at a loss before the mystery of death, the church, taught by divine revelation, declares that God has created people in view of a blessed destiny that lies beyond the boundaries of earthly misery. Moreover, the christian faith teaches that bodily death, from which people would have been immune had humanity not sinned,[14] will be overcome when that wholeness which they lost through their own fault will be given once again to them by the almighty and merciful Savior. For God has called men and women, and still calls them, to attach themselves with all their being to him in sharing for ever a life that is divine and free from all decay. Christ won this victory when he rose to life, for by his death he freed women and men from death.[15] Faith, therefore, with its solidly based teaching, provides thoughtful people with an answer to their anxious queries about their future lot. At the same time it makes them capable of being united in Christ with their loved ones who have already died, and gives hope that they have found true life with God.

Kinds of Atheism and Its Causes

19. Human dignity rests above all on the fact that humanity is called to communion with God. The invitation to converse with God is addressed to men and women as soon as they are born. For if people exist it is because God has created them through love, and through love continues to keep them in existence. They cannot live fully in the truth unless they freely acknowledge that love and entrust themselves to their creator. Many, however, of our contemporaries

either do not at all perceive, or else explicitly reject, this intimate and vital relationship with God. Atheism must therefore be regarded as one of the most serious problems of our time, and one that deserves more thorough treatment.

The word atheism is used to signify things that differ considerably from one another. Some people expressly deny the existence of God. Others maintain that people cannot make any assertion whatsoever about God. Still others admit only such methods of investigation as would make it seem quite meaningless to ask questions about God. Many, trespassing beyond the boundaries of the positive sciences, either contend that everything can be explained by the reasoning process used in such sciences, or, on the contrary, hold that there is no such thing as absolute truth. With others it is their exaggerated idea of humanity that causes their faith to languish; they are more prone, it would seem, to affirm humanity than to deny God. Yet others have such a faulty notion of God that when they disown this product of their imagination their denial has no reference to the God of the Gospels. There are also those who never enquire about God; religion never seems to trouble or interest them at all, nor do they see why they should bother about it. Not infrequently atheism is born from a violent protest against the evil in the world, or from the fact that certain human ideals are wrongfully invested with such an absolute character as to be taken for God. Modern civilization itself, though not of its very nature but because it is too engrossed in the concerns of this world, can often make it harder to approach God.

Without doubt those who wilfully try to drive God from their heart and to avoid all questions about religion, not following the dictates of their conscience, are not free from blame. But believers themselves often share some responsibility for this situation. For, in general, atheism is not present in people's minds from the beginning. It springs from various causes, among which must be included a critical reaction against religions and, in some places, against the christian religion in particular. Believers can thus have more than a little to do with the rise of atheism. To the extent that they are careless about their instruction in the faith, or present its teaching falsely, or even fail in their religious, moral, or social life, they must be said to conceal rather than to reveal the true nature of God and of religion.

Systematic Atheism

20. Modern atheism often takes a systematic form. There are a number of reasons for this, among them an insistence on human autonomy so great as to put obstacles in the way of any degree of dependence on God. For those who profess atheism of this kind freedom means that humanity constitutes its own end and is the sole maker, in total control, of its own history. They claim that this outlook cannot be reconciled with the assertion of a Lord who is author and end of all things, or that at least it makes such an affirmation altogether unnecessary. The sense of power which modern technical progress produces in people may encourage this outlook.

One form of modern atheism which should not be ignored is that which looks to people's economic and social emancipation for their liberation. It holds that religion, of its very nature, frustrates such emancipation by investing people's hopes in a future life, thus both deceiving them and discouraging them from working for a better form of life on earth. That is why those who hold such views, wherever they gain control of the state, violently attack religion, and in order to spread atheism, especially in the education of young people, make use of all the means by which the civil authority can bring pressure to bear on its subjects.

The Attitude of the Church Towards Atheism

21. The church, faithful to its obligations both to God and humanity, cannot cease, as in the past,[16] to deplore, sadly yet with the utmost firmness, those harmful teachings and ways of acting which are in conflict with reason and with common human experience, and which cast humanity down from the noble state to which it is born. It tries nevertheless to seek out the secret motives which lead the atheistic mind to deny God. Well knowing how important are the problems raised by atheism, and urged by its love for everyone, it considers that these motives deserve an earnest and more thorough scrutiny.

The church holds that to acknowledge God is in no way to diminish human dignity, since such dignity is grounded and brought to perfection in God. Women and men have in fact been placed in the world by God, who created them as intelligent and free beings; but over and above this they are called as daughters and sons to intimacy with God and to share in his happiness. It further teaches that hope in a life to come does not take away from the importance of the duties of this life on earth but rather adds to it by giving new motives for fulfilling those duties. When, on the other hand, people are deprived of this divine support and without hope of eternal life their dignity is deeply impaired, as may so often be seen today. The problems of life and death, of guilt and of suffering, remain unsolved, so that people are frequently thrown into despair.

Meanwhile, everybody remains a question to themselves, one that is dimly perceived and left unanswered. For there are times, especially in the major events of life, when nobody can altogether escape from such self-questioning. God alone, who calls people to deeper thought and to more humble probing, can fully and with complete certainty supply an answer to this questioning.

Atheism must be countered both by properly presenting true teaching and by the full and complete life of the church and of its members. For it is the function of the church to render God the Father and his incarnate Son present and as it were visible, while ceaselessly renewing and purifying itself[16a] under the guidance of the holy Spirit.[17] This is brought about chiefly by the witness of a living and mature faith, one namely that is so well formed that it can see difficulties clearly and overcome them. Many martyrs have borne, and continue to bear, a splendid witness to this faith. This faith should show its fruitfulness by penetrating the entire life, even the worldly activities, of those who believe, and by urging them to be loving and just, especially towards those in need. Lastly, what does most to show God's presence clearly is the familial love of the faithful who, being all of one mind and spirit, work together for the faith of the Gospel[18] and present themselves as a sign of unity.

Although the church altogether rejects atheism, it nevertheless sincerely proclaims that all men and women, those who believe as well as those who do not, should help to establish right order in this world where all live together. This certainly cannot be done without a dialogue that is sincere and prudent. The church therefore deplores the discrimination between believers and unbelievers which some civil authorities unjustly practice, in defiance of the fundamental rights of the human person. It demands effective freedom for the faithful to be allowed to build up God's temple in this world also. It courteously invites atheists to weigh the merits of the Gospel of Christ with an open mind.

For the church knows full well that its message is in harmony with the most secret desires of the human heart, since it champions the dignity of humanity's calling, giving hope once more to those who already despair of their higher destiny. Its message, far from diminishing humanity helps people to develop themselves by bestowing light, life, and freedom. Apart from this message nothing is able to satisfy the human heart:"You have made us for yourself, O Lord, and our heart is restless until it rest in you."[19]

Christ the New Man

22. In reality it is only in the mystery of the Word made flesh that the mystery of humanity truly becomes clear. For Adam, the first man, was a type of him who was to come,[20] Christ the Lord. Christ the new Adam, in the very revelation of the mystery of the Father and of his love, fully reveals humanity to itself and brings to light its very high calling. It is no wonder, then, that all the truths mentioned so far should find in him their source and their most perfect embodiment.

He who is the "image of the invisible God" (Col 1:15),[21] is himself the perfect man who has restored in the children of Adam that likeness to God which had been disfigured ever since the first sin. Human nature, by the very fact that it was assumed, not absorbed, in him, has been raised in us also to a dignity beyond compare.[22] For, by his incarnation, he, the Son of God, has in a certain way united himself with each individual. He worked with human hands, he thought with a human mind. He acted with a human will,[23] and with a human heart he loved. Born of the Virgin Mary, he has truly been made one of us, like to us in all things except sin.[24]

As an innocent lamb he merited life for us by his

blood which he freely shed. In him God reconciled us to himself and to one another,[25] freeing us from the bondage of the devil and of sin, so that each one of us could say with the apostle: the Son of God "loved me and gave himself for me" (Gal 2:20). By suffering for us he not only gave us an example so that we might follow in his footsteps,[26] but he also opened up a way. If we follow this path, life and death are made holy and acquire a new meaning.

Conformed to the image of the Son who is the firstborn of many brothers and sisters,[27] Christians receive the "first fruits of the Spirit" (Rom 8:23) by which they are able to fulfil the new law of love.[28] By this Spirit, who is the "pledge of our inheritance" (Eph 1:14), the entire person is inwardly renewed, even to the "redemption of the body" (Rom 8:23). "If the Spirit of him who raised Jesus from the dead dwells in you, God who raised Christ Jesus from the dead will give life to your mortal bodies also through his Spirit who dwells in you" (Rom 8:11).[29] The Christian is certainly bound both by need and by duty to struggle with evil through many afflictions and to suffer death; but, as one who has been made a partner in the paschal mystery, and as one who has been configured to the death of Christ, will go forward, strengthened by hope, to the resurrection.[30]

All this holds true not only for Christians but also for all people of good will in whose hearts grace is active invisibly.[31] For since Christ died for everyone,[32] and since all are in fact called to one and the same destiny, which is divine, we must hold that the holy Spirit offers to all the possibility of being made partners, in a way known to God, in the paschal mystery.

Such is the nature and the greatness of the mystery of humankind as enlightened for the faithful by the christian revelation. It is therefore through Christ, and in Christ, that light is thrown on the mystery of suf-

fering and death which, apart from his Gospel, over-
whelms us. Christ has risen again, destroying death
by his death, and has given life abundantly to us[33] so
that, becoming sons in the Son, we may cry out in the
Spirit: Abba, Father![34]

1. See Gen 1:26; Wis 2:23.
2. See Ecclus 17:3-10.
3. See Rom 1:21-25.
4. See Jn 8:34.
5. See Dan 3:57-90.
6. See 1 Cor 6:13-20.

6a. The Latin text (*Interioritate enim sua universitatem rerum
excedit: ad haec profunda redit, quando convertitur ad cor . . .*) here
shows most closely its dependence on the French draft prepared
under the direction of Abbé P. Haubtmann. I have had to render the
French *interiorité* and the semi-biblical *revertitur ad cor* by para-
phrasing. Similarly, in (15), with regard to the words *ut humaniora
fiant* as applied to what humanity has discovered. [Translator].

7. See 1 Kg 16:7; Jer 17:10.
8. See Eccl 17:7-8.
9. See Rom 2:14-16.
10. See Pius XII, radio message on rightly forming the christian
conscience in youth, 23 March 1952: AAS 44 (1952), p. 271.
11. See Mt 22:37-40; Gal 5:14.
12. See Eccl 15:14.
13. See 2 Cor 5:10.
14. See Wis 1:13; 2:23-24; Rom 5:21; 6:23; Jas 1:15.
15. See 1 Cor 15:56-57.
16. See Pius XI, Encyclical *Divini Redemptoris,* 19 March 1937:
AAS 29 (1937), pp. 65-106; Pius XII, Encyclical *Ad Apostolorum
Principes,* 29 June 1958: AAS 50 (1958), pp. 601-14; John XXIII,
Encyclical *Mater et Magistra,* 15 May 1961: AAS 53 (1961), pp. 451-
3; Paul VI, Encyclical *Ecclesiam Suam,* 6 August 1964: AAS 56 (1964),
pp. 651-3.

16a. Grammatically the text could read: by ceaselessly renewing
and purifying herself. But this would imply that the church makes
God present only when she renews herself. The text, in trying to be
short, mixes two ideas, that of the presence of God in the world
through the church, and that of a presence made more visible and
striking through a renewal of christian life. [Translator].

17. See Vatican Council II, Dogmatic Constitution on the
Church, *Lumen gentium,* ch. 1, n. 8.
18. See Phil 1:27.
19. St Augustine, *Confessions* 1, 1: PL 32, 661.
20. See Rom 5:14. See Tertullian, *De carnis resurrectione,* 6: "For in

all the form which was moulded in the clay, Christ was in his thoughts as the man who was to be.": PL 2, 802 (848); CSEL, 47, p. 33, lines 12-13.

21. See 2 Cor 4:4.

22. See council of Constantinople II, can. 7: "Neither was God the Word changed into the nature of flesh, nor his flesh changed into the nature of the word.": Denz. 219 (428); see also council Constantinople III: "For as his all-holy and immaculate ensouled flesh was not destroyed (*theothesia ouk anerethé*) by being deified, but persisted in its own state and sphere.": Denz. 291 (556), see council Chalcedon: "Recognized in two natures, without confusion, without change, without division, without separation.": Denz. 291 (302).

23. See council of Constantinople III: "So also his human will was not destroyed by being deified, but was rather preserved.": Denz. 291 (556).

24. See Heb 4:15.

25. See 2 Cor 5:18-19; Col 1:20-22.

26. See I Pet 2:21; Mt 16:24; Lk 14:27.

27. See Rom 8:29; Col 1:18.

28. See Rom 8:1-11.

29. See 2 Cor 4:14.

30. See Phil 3:10, Rom 8:17.

31. See Vatican Council II Constitution on the Church, *Lumen gentium*, n. 16.

32. See Rom 8:32.

33. See *Byzantine Easter Liturgy*.

34. See Rom 8:15 and Gal 4:6; see also 1 Jn 3:1.

Chapter II

THE HUMAN COMMUNITY

The Council's Intention

23. One of the most striking features of today's world, and one due in no small measure to modern technical progress, is the very great increase in mutual interdependence between people. Genuine sororal and fraternal dialogue is not advanced by progress of this sort, however, but takes place at a deeper level in a community of persons which calls for mutual respect for each one's full spiritual dignity. Christian

revelation greatly fosters the establishment of such communion and at the same time promotes deeper understanding of the laws of social living which the creator has inscribed in people's spiritual and moral nature.

Some recent pronouncements of the church's teaching authority have dealt at length with christian teaching on human society.[1] The council, therefore, proposes to repeat only a few of the more important truths and to outline the basis of these truths in the light of revelation. Later, it will deal with some of their implications which have special importance for our day.

Communitarian Nature of the Human Vocation: God's Design

24. God, who has a parent's care for all of us, desired that all men and women should form one family and deal with each other as brothers and sisters. All, in fact, are destined to the very same end, namely God himself, since they have been created in the likeness of God, who "made from one every nation of humankind who live on all the face of the earth" (Acts 17:26). Love of God and of one's neighbor, then, is the first and greatest commandment. Scripture teaches us that love of God cannot be separated from love of one's neighbor: "Any other commandment [is] summed up in this sentence: 'You shall love your neighbor as yourself . . .' therefore love is the fulfilling of the law" (Rom 13:9-10; see 1 Jn 4:20). It goes without saying that this is a matter of the utmost importance to people who are coming to rely more and more on each other and to a world which is becoming more unified every day.

Furthermore, the Lord Jesus, when praying to the Father "that they may all be one . . . even as we are one" (Jn 17:21-22), has opened up new horizons closed to human reason by indicating that there is a certain similarity between the union existing among the divine persons and the union of God's children in truth and love. It follows, then, that if human beings are the only creatures on earth that God has wanted for their own sake, they can fully discover their true selves only in sincere self-giving.[2]

Person and Society: Interdependence

25. The fact that human beings are social by nature indicates that the betterment of the person and the improvement of society depend on each other. Insofar as humanity by its very nature stands completely in need of life in society,[3] it is and it ought to be the beginning, the subject and the object of every social organization. Life in society is not something accessory to humanity: through their dealings with others, through mutual service, and through fraternal and sororal dialogue, men and women develop all their talents and become able to rise to their destiny.

Among the social ties necessary for humanity's development, some correspond more immediately to our innermost nature — the family, for instance, and the political community; others are freely chosen. Nowadays, for various reasons, mutual relationships and interdependence increase from day to day and give rise to a variety of associations and organizations, both public and private. Socialization, as it is called, is not without its dangers, but it brings with it many advantages for the strengthening and betterment of human qualities and for the protection of human rights.[4]

On the one hand, in fulfilling their calling, including their religious calling, men and women are greatly helped by life in society, on the other hand, however, it cannot be denied that they are often turned away from the good and towards evil by the social environment in which they live and in which they have been immersed since their birth. Without doubt frequent upheavals in the social order are in part the result of economic, political, and social tensions. But at a deeper level they come from selfishness and pride, two things which contaminate the atmosphere of society as well. As it is, human beings are prone to evil, but whenever they are confronted with an environment where the effects of sin are to be found, they are exposed to further inducements to sin, which can be overcome only by unremitting effort with the help of grace.

The Common Good

26. Because of the increasingly close interdependence which is gradually extending to the entire world, we are today witnessing an extension of the role of the common good, which is the sum total of social conditions which allow people, either as groups or as individuals, to reach their fulfillment more fully and more easily. The resulting rights and obligations are consequently the concern of the entire human race. Every group must take into account the needs and legitimate aspirations of every other group, and even those of the human family as a whole.[5]

At the same time, however, there is a growing awareness of the sublime dignity of human persons, who stand above all things and whose rights and duties are universal and inviolable. They ought, therefore, to have ready access to all that is necessary for living a genuinely human life: for example, food, clothing, housing, the right freely to choose their state of life and set up a family, the right to education, work, to their good name, to respect, to proper knowledge, the right to act according to the dictates of conscience and to safeguard their privacy, and rightful freedom, including freedom of religion.

The social order and its development must constantly yield to the good of the person, since the order of things must be subordinate to the order of persons and not the other way around, as the Lord suggested when he said that the Sabbath was made for men and women and not men and women for the Sabbath.[6] The social order requires constant improvement: it must be founded in truth, built on justice, and enlivened by love: it should grow in freedom towards a more humane equilibrium.[7] If these objectives are to be attained there will first have to be a renewal of attitudes and far-reaching social changes.

The Spirit of God, who, with wonderful providence, directs the course of time and renews the face of the earth, assists at this development. The ferment of the Gospel has aroused and continues to arouse in human hearts an unquenchable thirst for human dignity.

Respect for the Human Person

27. Coming to topics which are practical and of some urgency, the council lays stress on respect for the human person: everybody should look upon his or her neighbor (without any exception) as another self, bearing in mind especially their neighbor's life and the means needed for a dignified way of life,[8] lest they follow the example of the rich man who ignored Lazarus, who was poor.[9]

Today, there is an inescapable duty to make ourselves the neighbor of every individual, without exception, and to take positive steps to help a neighbor whom we encounter, whether that neighbor be an elderly person abandoned by everyone, a foreign worker who suffers the injustice of being despised, a refugee, an illegitimate child wrongly suffering for a sin of which the child is innocent, or a starving human being who awakens our conscience by calling to mind the words of Christ: "As you did it to one of the least of these my brothers or sisters, you did it to me" (Mt 25:40).

The varieties of crime are numerous: all offenses against life itself, such as murder, genocide, abortion, euthanasia and willful suicide; all violations of the integrity of the human person, such as mutilation, physical and mental torture, undue psychological pressures; all offenses against human dignity, such as subhuman living conditions, arbitrary imprisonment, deportation, slavery, prostitution, the selling of women and children, degrading working conditions where people are treated as mere tools for profit rather than free and responsible persons: all these and the like are criminal: they poison civilization; and they debase the perpetrators more than the victims and militate against the honor of the creator.

Respect and Love for Enemies

28. Those also have a claim on our respect and charity who think and act differently from us in social, political, and religious matters. In fact, the more deeply, through courtesy and love, we come to understand their ways of thinking, the more easily will we be able to enter into dialogue with them.

Love and courtesy of this kind should not, of course, make us indifferent to truth and goodness. Love, in fact, impels the followers of Christ to proclaim to everyone the truth which saves. But we must distinguish between the error (which must always be rejected) and the people in error, who never lose their dignity as persons even though they flounder amid false or inadequate religious ideas.[10] God, who alone is the judge and the searcher of hearts, forbids us to pass judgment on the inner guilt of others.[11]

The teaching of Christ even demands that we forgive injury,[12] and the precept of love, which is the commandment of the New Law, includes all our enemies: "You have heard that it was said, 'You shall love your neighbor and hate your enemy.' But I say to you, love your enemies, do good to them that hate you; and pray for those who persecute and calumniate you" (Mt 5:43-44).

Essential Equality of All: Social Justice

29. All women and men are endowed with a rational soul and are created in God's image; they have the same nature and origin and, being redeemed by Christ, they enjoy the same divine calling and destiny; there is here a basic equality between all and it must be accorded ever greater recognition.

Undoubtedly not all people are alike as regards physical capacity and intellectual and moral powers. But any kind of social or cultural discrimination in basic personal rights on the grounds of sex, race, color, social conditions, language or religion, must be curbed and eradicated as incompatible with God's design. It is deeply to be deplored that these basic personal rights are not yet being respected everywhere, as is the case with women who are denied the chance freely to choose a husband, or a state of life, or to have access to the same educational and cultural benefits as are available to men.

Furthermore, while there are just differences between people, their equal dignity as persons demands that we strive for fairer and more humane conditions. Excessive economic and social disparity between individuals and peoples of the one human race is a source of scandal and militates against social justice, equity, human dignity, as well as social and international peace.

It is for public and private organizations to be at the service of the dignity and destiny of humanity; let them spare no effort to banish every vestige of social and political slavery and to safeguard basic human rights under every political system. And even if it takes a considerable time to arrive at the desired goal, these organizations should gradually align them-selves with spiritual realities, which are the most sub-lime of all.

Need to Transcend an Individualistic Morality

30. The pace of change is so far-reaching and rapid nowadays that it is imperative that no one, out of in-difference to the course of events or because of iner-tia, would indulge in a merely individualistic morality. The best way to fulfil one's obligations of justice and love is to contribute to the common good according to one's means and the needs of others, and also to promote and help public and private organizations devoted to bettering the conditions of life. There are people who profess noble sentiments and who in practice, however, are carelessly indifferent to the needs of society. There are many in various countries who make light of social laws and directives and are not ashamed to resort to fraud and cheating to avoid paying just taxes and fulfilling other social obliga-tions. There are others who neglect the norms of social conduct, such as those regulating public hygiene and speed limits, forgetting that they are endangering their own lives and the lives of others by their carelessness.

All must consider it their sacred duty to count social obligations among their chief duties today and observe them as such. For the more closely the world comes together, the more widely do people's obli-gations transcend particular groups and extend to the whole world. This will be realized only if individuals and groups practise moral and social virtues and fos-ter them in social living. Then, under the necessary help of divine grace, there will arise a generation of new women and men, the molders of a new humanity.

Responsibility and Participation

31. To help individuals to carry out more carefully their obligations in conscience towards themselves and towards the various groups to which they belong, they must be carefully educated to a higher degree of culture through the employment of the immense resources available today to the human race. Above all, we must undertake the training of youth from all social backgrounds if we are to produce the kind of men and women so urgently needed today, men and women who not only are highly cultured but are generous in spirit as well.

But this sense of responsibility will not be achieved unless people are so circumstanced that they are aware of their dignity and are capable of responding to their calling in the service of God and of humanity. For freedom is often crippled by extreme destitution, just as it can wither in an ivory-tower isolation brought on by overindulgence in the good things of life. It can, however, be strengthened by accepting the inevitable constraints of social life, by undertaking the manifold demands of human relationships, and by service to the community at large.

All should therefore be encouraged to play their part in communal enterprises. One must pay tribute to those nations whose systems permit the largest possible number of the citizens to take part in public life in a climate of genuine freedom. At the same time one must bear in mind the concrete circumstances of each nation and the need for strong public authority. However, if all citizens are to be persuaded to take part in the activities of the various groups which make up the social body, such groups must offer sufficient motivation to attract them and dispose them to serve their fellow men and women. One is right in thinking that the future of humanity rests with people who are capable of providing the generations to come with reasons for living and for hope.

The Word Made Flesh and Human Solidarity

32. Just as God did not create people to live as individuals but to come together in the formation of social unity, so he "willed to make women and men holy and to save them, not as individuals without any bond between them, but rather to make them into a people who might acknowledge him and serve him in holiness."[13] From the beginning of the history of salvation, God chose certain people as members of a given community, not as individuals, and revealed his plan to them, calling them "his people" (Ex 3:7-12) and making a covenant on Mount Sinai with them.[14]

This communitarian character is perfected and fulfilled in the work of Jesus Christ, for the Word made flesh willed to take his place in human society. He was present at the wedding feast at Cana, he visited the house of Zacchaeus, he sat down with publicans and sinners. In revealing the Father's love and humanity's sublime calling, he made use of the most ordinary things of social life and illustrated his words with expressions and imagery from everyday life. He sanctified those human ties, above all family ties, which are the basis of social structures. He willingly observed the laws of his country and chose to lead the life of an ordinary craftsman of his time and place.

In his preaching he clearly described an obligation on the part of the daughters and sons of God to treat each other as sisters and brothers. In his prayer he asked that all his followers should be one. As the redeemer of all of humanity he delivered himself up to death for the sake of all: "No one has greater love than this, to lay down one's life for one's friends" (Jn 15:13). His command to the apostles was to preach the Gospel to all nations in order that the human race would become the family of God, in which love would be the fullness of the law.

As the firstborn of many, and by the gift of his Spirit, he established, after his death and resurrection, a new communion of sisters and brothers among all who received him in faith and love; this is the communion of his own body, the church, in which all as members one of the other would render mutual service in the measure of the different gifts bestowed on each.

This solidarity must be constantly increased until that day when it will be brought to fulfillment; on that day humanity, saved by grace, will offer perfect glory to God as the family beloved of God and of Christ their brother.

1. See John XXIII, Encyclical *Mater et Magistra*, 15 May 1961: AAS 53 (1961), pp. 401-64, and Encyclical *Pacem in Terris*, 11 April 1963: AAS 55 (1963), pp. 257-304; Paul VI, *Encyclical Ecclesiam Suam*, 6 August 1964: AAS 56 (1964), pp. 609-59.

2. See Lk 17:33.

3. See St Thomas Aquinas, *I Ethic.*, Lect. 1.

4. See John XXIII, Encyclical. *Mater et Magistra* 15 May 1961: AAS 53 (1961), p. 418. See also Pius XI, Encyclical *Quadragesimo Anno*, 15 May 1931: AAS 23 (1931), p. 222 ff.

5. See John XXIII, Encyclical *Mater et Magistra*: AAS 53 (1961), p. 417.

6. Mk 2:27.

7. See John XXIII, Encyclical *Pacem in Terris*: AAS 55 (1963), p. 266.

8. See Jas 2:15-16.

9. See Lk 16:19-31.

10. See John XXIII, Encyclical *Pacem in Terris*: AAS 55 (1963), pp. 299 and 300.

11. See Lk 6:37-38; Mt 7:1-2; Rom 2:1-11, 14:10-12

12. See Mt 5:43-47.

13. Vatican Council II, Dogmatic Constitution on the Church, *Lumen gentium* , ch 2, n. 9.

14. See Ex 24:1-8.

Chapter III

HUMANITY'S ACTIVITY IN THE UNIVERSE

The Problem

33. Humanity has always tried to develop its life by its own effort and ingenuity. Nowadays, it has extended and continues to extend its mastery over nearly all spheres of nature with the help of science and technology. Thanks, above all, to an increase in all kinds of interchange between nations the human family is gradually coming to recognize itself and constitute itself as one single community world-wide. As a result, it now produces by its own enterprise many things which in former times it expected would come largely from heavenly powers.

In the face of this immense enterprise now involving the whole human race people face many worrying questions. What is the meaning and value of this feverish activity? How ought all of these things be used? To what goal is all this individual and collective enterprise heading? The church is guardian of the deposit of God's word and draws religious and moral principles from it, but it does not always have a ready answer to every question. Still, it is eager to associate the light of revelation with the experience of humanity in trying to clarify the course upon which it has recently entered.

Value of Human Activity

34. Individual and collective activity, that monumental effort of humanity through the centuries to improve living conditions, in itself presents no problem to believers, it corresponds to the plan of God. Men and women were created in God's image and

were commanded to conquer the earth with all it contains and to rule the world in justice and holiness:[1] they were to acknowledge God as maker of all things and refer themselves and the totality of creation to him, so that with all things subject to God, the divine name would be glorified through all the earth.[2]

This holds good also for our daily work. When men and women provide for themselves and their families in such a way as to be of service to the community as well, they can rightly look upon their work as a prolongation of the work of the creator, a service to other men and women, and their personal contribution to the fulfilment in history of the divine plan.[3]

Far from thinking that what human enterprise and ability have achieved is opposed to God's power as if the rational creature is a rival to the creator, Christians are convinced that the achievements of the human race are a sign of God's greatness and the fulfilment of his mysterious design. The more the power of men and women increases the greater is their responsibility as individuals and as members of the community. There is no question, then, of the christian message inhibiting them from building up the world or making them disinterested in the good of others: on the contrary it makes it a matter of stricter obligation.[4]

Regulation of Human Activity

35. Human activity is for the benefit of human beings, proceeding from them as it does. When they work, not only do they transform matter and society, they also perfect themselves. They learn, develop their faculties, emerging from and transcending themselves. Rightly understood, this kind of growth is more precious than any kind of wealth that can be amassed. People are of greater value for what they are than for what they have.[5] Technical progress is of less value than advances towards greater justice, wider

kinship and a more humane social environment. Technical progress may supply the material for human advance but it is powerless to achieve it.

Here then is the norm for human activity — to harmonize with the authentic interests of the human race, in accordance with God's will and design, and to enable people as individuals and as members of society to pursue and fulfil their total vocation.

Rightful Autonomy of Earthly Affairs

36. Many of our contemporaries seem to fear that a close association between human activity and religion will endanger the autonomy of humanity, of organizations and of science. If by the autonomy of earthly affairs is meant the gradual discovery, utilization and ordering of the laws and values of matter and society, then the demand for autonomy is perfectly in order: it is at once the claim of humankind today and the desire of the creator. By the very nature of creation, material being is endowed with its own stability, truth and excellence, its own order and laws. These, as the methods proper to every science and technique must be respected. Consequently, methodical research in all branches of knowledge, provided it is carried out in a truly scientific manner and does not override moral laws, can never conflict with the faith, because the things of the world and the things of faith derive from the same God.[6] The humble and persevering investigators of the secrets of nature are being led, as it were, by the hand of God, even unawares, for it is God, the conserver of all things, who made them what they are. We cannot but deplore certain attitudes, not unknown among Christians, deriving from a shortsighted view of the rightful autonomy of science; they have occasioned conflict and controversy and have misled many into opposing faith and science.[7]

However, if by the term "the autonomy of earthy

affairs" is meant that material being does not depend on God and that humanity can use it as if it had no relation to its creator, then the falsity of such a claim will be obvious to anyone who believes in God. Without a creator there can be no creature. In any case, believers, no matter what their religion, have always recognized the voice and the revelation of God in the language of creatures. Besides, once God is forgotten, the creature itself is left in darkness.

Human Activity Infected by Sin

37. Sacred scripture teaches humankind what has also been confirmed by centuries of experience, namely, that the great advantages of human progress bring with them grave temptations: the hierarchy of values has been disordered, good and evil intermingle, and every person and group are interested only in their own affairs, not in those of others. So it is that the earth has not yet become the scene of true amity; rather, humanity's growing power now threatens to put an end to the human race itself.

The whole of human history has been the story of dour combat with the powers of evil, stretching, as our Lord tells us,[8] from the very dawn of history until the last day. Finding themselves in the battlefield, men and women have to struggle to do what is right, and it is at great cost to themselves, and aided by God's grace, that they succeed in achieving their own inner integrity. Hence the church of Christ, trusting in the design of the creator and accepting that progress can contribute to humanity's true happiness, still feels called upon to echo the words of the apostle: "Do not be conformed to this world" (Rom 12:2). "World" here means a spirit of vanity and malice whereby human activity from being ordered to the service of God and humanity is reduced to being an instrument of sin.

To the question of how this unhappy situation can

be overcome, Christians reply that all these human activities, which are daily endangered by pride and inordinate self love, must be purified and perfected by the cross and resurrection of Christ. Redeemed by Christ and made a new creature by the holy Spirit, a person can, and indeed must, love the things which God has created: it is from God that they have been received, and it is as coming from God's hand that they are seen and revered. Thanks are owed to the divine benefactor for all these things, they are used and enjoyed in a spirit of poverty and freedom: thus a person is brought to a true possession of the world, as having nothing yet possessing everything:[9] "All are yours; and you are Christ's; and Christ is God's" (1 Cor 2:22-23).

Human Activity: Its Fulfillment in the Paschal Mystery

38. The Word of God, through whom all things were made, became man and dwelt among us,[10] a perfect man, he entered world history, taking that history into himself and recapitulating it.[11] He reveals to us that "God is love" (1 Jn 4:8) and at the same time teaches that the fundamental law of human perfection, and consequently of the transformation of the world, is the new commandment of love. He assures those who trust in the charity of God that the way of love is open to all and that the effort to establish a universal communion will not be in vain.

This love is not something reserved for important matters, but must be exercised above all in the ordinary circumstances of daily life. Christ's example in dying for us sinners[12] teaches us that we must carry the cross, which the flesh and the world inflict on the shoulders of any who seek after peace and justice. Constituted Lord by his resurrection and given all authority in heaven and on earth,[13] Christ is now at work in human hearts by the power of his Spirit; not only does he arouse in them a desire for the world to come but he quickens, purifies, and strengthens the generous aspirations of humanity to make life more humane and conquer the earth for this purpose. The gifts of the Spirit are manifold: some are called to testify openly to humanity's yearning for its heavenly home and to keep the awareness of it vividly before people's minds; others are called to dedicate themselves to the service of people on earth and in this way to prepare the way for the kingdom of heaven. But the Spirit makes all of them free, ready to put aside love of self and assume earthly resources into human life, stretching out towards that future day when humanity itself will become an offering accepted by God.[14]

Christ left to his followers a pledge of this hope and food for the journey in the sacrament of faith, in which natural elements, the fruits of human cultivation, are changed into his glorified Body and Blood, as a supper of brotherly and sisterly communion and a foretaste of the heavenly banquet.

39. We do not know the moment of the consummation of the earth and of humanity[15] nor the way the universe will be transformed. The form of this world, distorted by sin, is passing away[16] and we are taught that God is preparing a new dwelling and a new earth in which righteousness dwells,[17] whose happiness will fill and surpass all the desires of peace arising in human hearts.[18] Then death will have been conquered, the daughters and sons of God will be raised in Christ and what was sown in weakness and dishonor will become incorruptible;[19] charity and its works will remain[20] and all of creation, which God made for humanity, will be set free from its bondage to decay.[21]

We have been warned, of course, that it profits us

nothing if we gain the whole world and lose or forfeit ourselves.[22] Far from diminishing our concern to develop this earth, the expectation of a new earth should spur us on, for it is here that the body of a new human family grows, foreshadowing in some way the age which is to come. That is why, although we must be careful to distinguish earthly progress clearly from the increase of the kingdom of Christ, such progress is of vital concern to the kingdom of God, insofar as it can contribute to the better ordering of human society.[23]

When we have spread on earth the fruits of our nature and our enterprise — human dignity, sisterly and brotherly communion, and freedom — according to the command of the Lord and in his Spirit, we will find them once again, cleansed this time from the stain of sin, illuminated and transfigured, when Christ presents to his Father an eternal and universal kingdom "of truth and life, a kingdom of holiness and grace, a kingdom of justice, love and peace."[24] Here on earth the kingdom is mysteriously present; when the Lord comes it will enter into its perfection.

1. See Gen 1:26-27; 9:2-3; Wis 9:2-3.

2. See Ps 8:7 and 10.

3. See John XXIII, Encyclical *Pacem in Terris:* AAS 55 (1963), p. 297.

4. See *Message to all men and women,* issued by the Fathers at the beginning of Vatican Council II, October 1962: AAS 54 (1962), p. 823.

5. See Paul VI, Allocution to the Diplomatic Corps, 7 January 1965: AAS 57 (1965), p. 232.

6. See Vatican Council I, Dogmatic Constitution on the Catholic Faith, *Dei Filius,* ch. 3: Denz. 1785-1786 (3004-3005).

7. See Pius Paschini, *Vita e opere di Galileo Galilei,* 2 vol., Vatican City, 1964.

8. See Mt 24:13; 13:24-30 and 36-43.

9. See 2 Cor 6:10.

10. See Jn 1:3 and 14.

11. See Eph 1:10.

12. See Jn 3:16; Rom 5:8-10.

13. See Acts 2:36; Mt 28:18.

14. See Rom 15:16.

15. See. Acts 1:7.

16. See I Cor 7:31; St Irenaeus *Adversus Haereses,* V, 36, 1: PG 7, 1222.

17. See 2 Cor 5:2; 2 Pet 3:13.

18. See 1 Cor 2:9; Apoc 21:4-5.

19. See I Cor 15:42 and 53.

20. See I Cor 13:8; 3:14.

21. See Rom 8:19-21.

22. See Lk 9:25.

23. See Pius XI, Encyclical *Quadragesimo* Anno: AAS 23 (1931), p. 207.

24. Preface for the Feast of Christ the King.

Chapter IV

ROLE OF THE CHURCH IN THE MODERN WORLD

Mutual Relationship of Church and World

40. All we have said up to now about the dignity of the human person, the community of men and women, and the deep significance of human activity, provides a basis for discussing the relationship between the church and the world and the dialogue between them.[1] The council now intends to consider the presence of the church in the world, and its life and activity there, in the light of what it has already declared about the mystery of the church.

Proceeding from the love of the eternal Father,[2] the church was founded by Christ in time and gathered into one by the holy Spirit.[3] It has a saving and eschatological purpose which can be fully attained only in the next life. But it is now present here on earth and is composed of women and men; they, the members of the earthly city, are called to form the family of the children of God even in this present history of humankind and to increase it continually until the Lord comes. Made one in view of heavenly benefits and enriched by them, this family has been "constituted and organized as a society in the present world"[4] by Christ and "provided with means adapted to its visible and social union."[5] Thus the church, at once "a visible organization and a spiritual community,"[6] travels the same journey as all of humanity and shares the same earthly lot with the world: it is to be a leaven and, as it were, the soul of human society in its renewal by Christ[7] and transformation into the family of God.

That the earthly and the heavenly city penetrate one another is a fact open only to the eyes of faith; moreover, it will remain the mystery of human history, which will be harassed by sin until the perfect revelation of the splendor of the children of God. In pursuing its own salvific purpose not only does the church communicate divine life to humanity but in a certain sense it casts the reflected light of that divine life over all the earth, notably in the way it heals and elevates the dignity of the human person, in the way it consolidates society, and endows people's daily activity with a deeper sense and meaning. The church, then, believes that through each of its members and its community as a whole it can help to make the human family and its history still more human.

Furthermore, the Catholic Church deeply appreciates what other christian churches and ecclesial communities have contributed and are contributing cooperatively to the realization of this aim. Similarly, it is convinced that there is a great variety of help that it can receive from the world in preparing the ground for the Gospel, both from individuals and from society as a whole, by their talents and activity. The council will now outline some general principles for the proper fostering of mutual exchange and help in matters which are in some way common to the church and the world.

What the Chuch Offers to Individuals

41. Contemporary women and men are in process of developing their personality and of increasingly discovering and affirming their rights. The church is entrusted with the task of manifesting to them the mystery of God, who is their final destiny; in doing so it discloses to them the meaning of their own existence, the innermost truth about themselves. The church knows well that God alone, whom it serves, can satisfy the deepest cravings of the human heart, for it can never be fully content with the world and what it has to offer. The church also realizes that men and women are continually being aroused by the Spirit of God and that they will never be utterly indifferent to religion — a fact confirmed by the experience of past ages and by a variety of evidence today. For people will always be keen to know, if only in a general way, what is the meaning of their life, their activity, their death. The very presence of the church recalls these problems to their minds. The most perfect answer to these questions is to be found in God alone, who created women and men in his own image and redeemed them from sin; and this answer is given in the revelation in Christ his Son who became man. To follow Christ the perfect human is to become more human oneself.

By this faith the church can keep the dignity of human nature out of the reach of changing opinions which, for example, either devalue the human body or glorify it. There is no human law so well fitted to safeguard the personal dignity and human freedom as is the Gospel which Christ entrusted to the church; for the Gospel announces and proclaims the freedom of the daughters and sons of God, it rejects all bondage resulting from sin,[8] it scrupulously respects the dignity of conscience and its freedom of choice, it never ceases to encourage the employment of human talents in the service of God and humanity, and, finally, it commends everyone to the charity of all.[9] This is nothing other than the basic law of the christian dispensation. The fact that it is the same God who is at once saviour and creator, Lord of human history and of the history of salvation, does not mean that this divine order deprives creation, and humanity in particular, of their rightful autonomy; on the contrary, it restores and strengthens its dignity.

In virtue of the Gospel entrusted to it, the church proclaims human rights; it acknowledges and holds in high esteem the dynamic approach of today which is fostering these rights all over the world. But this approach needs to be animated by the spirit of the Gospel and preserved from all traces of false autonomy. For there is a temptation to feel that our personal rights are fully maintained only when we are free from every restriction of divine law. But this is the way leading to the extinction of human dignity, not its preservation.

What the Church Offers to Society

42. The union of the human family is greatly consolidated and perfected by the unity which Christ established among the sons and daughters of God.[10]

Christ did not bequeath to the church a mission in the political, economic, or social order: the purpose he assigned to it was religious.[11] But this religious mission can be the source of commitment, direction, and vigor to establish and consolidate the human community according to the law of God. In fact, the church is able, indeed it is obliged, if times and circumstances require it, to initiate action for the benefit of everyone, especially of those in need, such as works of mercy and the like.

The church, moreover, acknowledges the good to be found in the social dynamism of today, especially in progress towards unity, healthy socialization, and civil and economic cooperation. The encouragement of unity is in harmony with the deepest nature of the church's mission, for it is "a sacrament — a sign and instrument, that is, of communion with God and of the unity of the entire human race."[12] It shows to the world that social and exterior union comes from a union of hearts and minds, from the faith and love by which its own indissoluble unity has been founded in the holy Spirit. The impact which the church can have on modern society is due to an effective living of faith and love, not to any external power exercised by purely human means.

By its nature and mission the church is universal in that it is not committed to any one culture or to any political, economic or social system. Hence, it can be a very close bond between the various communities of people and nations, provided they trust the church and guarantee it true freedom to carry out its mission. With this in view the church calls upon its members and upon all people to put aside, in the family spirit of the children of God, all conflict between nations and races and to build up the internal strength of just human associations.

Whatever truth, goodness, and justice is to be found in past or present human institutions is held in high esteem by the council. In addition, the council declares that the church wants to help and foster these institutions insofar as this depends on it and is compatible with its mission. The church desires nothing more ardently than that it should develop in freedom in the service of all, under any regime which recognizes the basic rights of the person and the family, and the requirements of the common good.

What the Church Offers to Human Activity Through its Members

43. The council exhorts Christians, as citizens of both cities, to perform their duties faithfully in the spirit of the Gospel. It is a mistake to think that, because we have here no lasting city, but seek the city which is to come,[13] we are entitled to evade our earthly responsibilities; this is to forget that because of our faith we are all the more bound to fulfil these responsibilities according to each one's vocation.[14] But it is no less mistaken to think that we may immerse ourselves in earthly activities as if these latter were utterly foreign to religion, and religion were nothing more than the fulfilment of acts of worship and the observance of a few moral obligations. One of the gravest errors of our time is the dichotomy between the faith which many profess and their day-to-day conduct. As far back as the Old Testament the prophets vehemently denounced this scandal,[15] and in the New Testament Christ himself even more forcibly threatened it with severe punishment.[16] Let there, then, be no such pernicious opposition between professional and social activity on the one hand and religious life on the other. Christians who shirk their temporal duties shirk their duties towards his neighbor, neglect God himself, and endanger their eternal salvation. Let Christians follow the example of Christ who worked as a craftsman; let them be proud of the opportunity to carry out their earthly activity in such a way as to integrate human, domestic, professional, scientific and technical enterprises with religious values, under whose supreme direction all things are ordered to the glory of God.

It is to the laity, though not exclusively to them,

that secular duties and activity properly belong. When
therefore, as citizens of the world, they are engaged in
any activity either individually or collectively, they will
not be satisfied with meeting the minimum legal
requirements but will strive to become truly proficient
in that sphere. They will gladly cooperate with others
working towards the same objectives. Let them be
aware of what their faith demands of them in these
matters and derive strength from it; let them not hesitate to take the initiative at the opportune moment
and put their findings into effect. It is their task to cultivate a properly informed conscience and to impress
the divine law on the affairs of the earthly city. For
guidance and spiritual strength let them turn to the
clergy; but let them realize that their pastors will not
always be so expert as to have a ready answer to every
problem, even every grave problem, that arises; this is
not the role of the clergy: it is rather the task of lay
people to shoulder their responsibilities under the
guidance of christian wisdom and with careful attention to the teaching authority of the church.[17]

Very often their christian vision will suggest a certain solution in some given situation. Yet it happens
rather frequently, and legitimately so, that some of
the faithful, with no less sincerity, will see the problem quite differently. Now if one or other of the proposed solutions is readily perceived by many to be
closely connected with the message of the Gospel,
they ought to remember that in those cases no one is
permitted to identify the authority of the church
exclusively with his or her own opinion. Let them,
then, try to guide each other by sincere dialogue in a
spirit of mutual charity and with with a genuine concern for the common good above all.

The laity are called to participate actively in the
entire life of the church; not only are they to animate
the world with the spirit of Christianity, they are to be

witnesses to Christ in all circumstances and at the very heart of the human community.

The task of directing the church of God has been entrusted to bishops and they, with their priests, are to preach the message of Christ in such a way that the light of the Gospel will shine on all activities of the faithful. Let all pastors of souls bear in mind that by their daily behavior and concerns[18] they are presenting the face of the church to the world and that people judge from that the power and truth of the christian message. By their words and example and in union with religious and with the faithful, let them show that the church with all its gifts is, by its presence alone, an inexhaustible source of all those virtues of which the modern world stands most in need. Let them prepare themselves by careful study to meet to enter into dialogue with the world and with people of all shades of opinion: let them have in their hearts above all these words of the council: "Since the human race today is tending more and more towards civil, economic and social unity, it is all the more necessary that priests should unite their efforts and combine their resources under the leadership of the bishops and the Supreme Pontiff and thus eliminate division and dissension in every shape or form, so that all humanity may be led into the unity of the family of God."[19]

By the power of the holy Spirit the church is the faithful spouse of the Lord and will never fail to be a sign of salvation in the world; but it is by no means unaware that down through the centuries there have been among its members,[20] both clerical and lay, some who were disloyal to the Spirit of God. Today as well, the church is not blind to the discrepancy between the message it proclaims and the human weakness of those to whom the Gospel has been entrusted. Whatever is history's judgment on these shortcomings, we cannot ignore them and we must combat them assiduously, lest they hinder the spread of the Gospel. The church also realizes how much it needs the maturing influence of centuries of past experience in order to work out its relationship to the world. Guided by the holy Spirit the church ceaselessly exhorts her children "to purification and renewal so that the sign of Christ may shine more brightly over the face of the church."[21]

What the Church Receives from the Modern World

44. Just as it is in the world's interest to acknowledge the church as a social reality and a driving force in history, so too the church is not unaware how much it has profited from the history and development of humankind. It profits from the experience of past ages, from the progress of the sciences, and from the riches hidden in various cultures, through which greater light is thrown on human nature and new avenues to truth are opened up. The church learned early in its history to express the christian message in the concepts and languages of different peoples and tried to clarify it in the light of the wisdom of their philosophers: it was an attempt to adapt the Gospel to the understanding of all and the requirements of the learned, insofar as this could be done. Indeed, this kind of adaptation and preaching of the revealed word must ever be the law of all evangelization. In this way it is possible to create in every country the possibility of expressing the message of Christ in suitable terms and to foster vital contact and exchange between the church and different cultures.[22] Nowadays when things change so rapidly and thought patterns differ so widely, the church needs to step up this exchange by calling upon the help of people who are living in the world, who are expert in its organizations and its forms of training, and who understand

its mentality, in the case of believers and non believers alike. With the help of the holy Spirit, it is the task of the whole people of God, particularly of its pastors and theologians, to listen to and distinguish the many voices of our times and to interpret them in the light of God's word, in order that the revealed truth may be more deeply penetrated, better understood, and more suitably presented.

The church has a visible social structure, which is a sign of its unity in Christ: as such it can be enriched, and it is being enriched, by the evolution of social life, not as if something were missing in the constitution which Christ gave the church, but in order to understand this constitution more deeply, express it better, and adapt it more successfully to our times. The church acknowledges gratefully that, both as a whole and in its individual sons and daughters, it has been helped in various ways by people of all classes and conditions. Whoever contributes to the development of the human community on the level of family, culture, economic and social life, and national and international politics, according to the plan of God, is also contributing in no small way to the community of the church insofar as it depends on things outside itself. The church itself also recognizes that it has benefited and is still benefiting from the opposition of its enemies and persecutors.[23]

Christ: Alpha and Omega

45. Whether it aids the world or whether it benefits from it, the church has but one sole purpose — that the kingdom of God may come and the salvation of the human race may be accomplished. Every benefit the people of God can confer on humanity during its earthly pilgrimage is rooted in the church's being "the universal sacrament of salvation,"[24] at once manifesting and actualizing the mystery of God's love for

humanity.

The Word of God, through whom all things were made, was made flesh, so that as a perfect man he could save all women and men and sum up all things in himself. The Lord is the goal of human history, the focal point of the desires of history and civilization, the center of humanity, the joy of all hearts, and the fulfillment of all aspirations.[25] It is he whom the Father raised from the dead, exalted and placed at his right hand, constituting him judge of the living and the dead. Animated and drawn together in his Spirit we press onwards on our journey towards the consummation of history which fully corresponds to the plan of his love: "to unite all things in him, things in heaven and things on earth" (Eph 1:10).

The Lord himself said: "See, I am coming soon, my reward is with me, to repay according to everyone's work. I am the alpha and the omega, the first and the last, the beginning and the end" (Apoc 22:12-13).

1. Paul VI, Encyclical *Ecclesiam Suam*, III: AAS 56 (1964), pp. 637-659.

2. See Tit 3:4: 'philantropia.'

3. See Eph 1:3, 5-6, 13-14, 23.

4. Vatican Council II, Dogmatic Constitution on the Church, *Lumen gentium*, ch. 1, n. 8.

5. Ibid., ch. 2, n. 9.

6. Ibid., ch. 1, n. 8.

7. Ibid., ch. 4, 38.

8. See Rom 8:14-17.

9. See Mt 22:39.

10. See Vatican Council II, Dogmatic Constitution on the Church, *Lumen gentium*, ch. 2, n. 9.

11. See Pius XII, Allocution to Historians and Artists, 9 March 1956: AAS 48 (1956), p. 212.

12. Vatican Council II, Dogmatic Constitution on the Church, *Lumen gentium*, ch. 1, n. 1.

13. See Heb 13:14.

14. See 2 Th 3:6-13; Eph 4:28.

15. See Is 58:1-12.

16. See Mt 23:3-33; Mk 7:10-13.

17. See John XXIII, Encyclical *Mater et Magistra*, IV: AAS 53

(1961), pp. 456-7: see 1: AAS Loc. cit., pp. 407, 410-411.

18. Vatican Council II, Dogmatic Constitution on the Church, *Lumen gentium*, ch. 3, n. 28.

19. Ibid., n. 28.

20. See St Ambrose, *De virginitate*, ch. Vlll, n. 48: PL 16, 278.

21. Vatican Council II, Dogmatic Constitution on the Church, *Lumen gentium*, ch. 2, n. 15.

22. Vatican Council II, Dogmatic Constitution on the Church, *Lumen gentium*, ch. 2, n. 13.

23. Justin, *Dialogus cum Tryphone* ch. 110: PG 6, 729: ed. Otto, 1897, pp. 391-393: ". . . for the more such persecutions are inflicted upon us, the greater the number of others who will become devout believers in the name of Jesus." See Tertullian, *Apologeticus*, ch. 50, 13: Corpus Christ. ser. Iat. 1, p. 171: "We become even more numerous when you mow us down, for the blood of Christians is a seed!" See Vatican council II, Dogmatic Constitution on the Church, *Lumen gentium*, ch. 2, n. 9.

24. Vatican Council II, Dogmatic Constitution on the Church, *Lumen gentium*, ch. 7, n. 48.

25. See Paul VI, Allocution, Feb. 1965.

Part Two

SOME MORE URGENT PROBLEMS

Preface

46. Having described the dignity of the human person and his and her individual and social role in the universe, the council now draws people's attention, in the light of the Gospel and of human experience, to some more urgent problems deeply affecting the human race at the present day.

Of the many problems which are matters of universal concern nowadays, it may be helpful to concentrate on the following: marriage and the family, culture, economic and social life, politics, the solidarity of peoples, and peace. We must seek light for each of these problems from the principles which Christ has given us; in this way the faithful will receive guidance and all people will be enlightened in their search for solutions to so many complex problems.

Chapter I
THE DIGNITY OF MARRIAGE AND THE FAMILY

Marriage and the Family in the Modern World

47. The well-being of the individual person and of both human and christian society is closely bound up with the healthy state of the community of marriage and the family. Hence, Christians and all who value this community are very pleased to see the various kinds of support which have increased people's esteem for this community of love and their respect for life, and which have also helped married people and parents in their lofty calling. They expect even greater benefits and are endeavouring to achieve them.

However, the dignity of this institution is not so evident everywhere, being obscured by polygamy, the plague of divorce, free love, and similar blemishes; furthermore, married love is too often dishonoured by selfishness, hedonism, and unlawful contraceptive practices. Besides, the economic, social, psychological, and civil climate of today has a severely disruptive effect on family life. There are also the serious and alarming problems arising in many parts of the world as a result of population expansion. On all of these counts an anguish of conscience is being generated. And yet the strength and vigor of the institution of marriage and family shines forth time and again: for the profoundly changing conditions of society today, in spite of the difficulties which they cause, very often reveal in one way or another the true nature of marriage and of the family.

It is for these reasons that the council intends to present certain key points of the church's teaching in a clearer light; and it hopes to guide and encourage Christians and all others who are trying to preserve and to foster the dignity and supremely sacred value of the married state.

Holiness of the Marriage and the Family

48. The intimate partnership of life and the love which constitutes the married state has been established by the creator and endowed by him with its own proper laws; it is rooted in the contract of its partners, that is, in their irrevocable personal consent. It is an institution confirmed by divine law and receiving its stability, in the eyes of society also, from the human act by which the partners mutually surrender themselves to each other; for the good of the partners, of the children, and of society this sacred bond no longer depends on human decision alone. For God himself is the author of marriage and has endowed it with various values and purposes:[1] all of these have a very important bearing on the continuation of the human race, on the personal development and eternal destiny of every member of the family, on the dignity, stability, peace, and prosperity of the family and of the whole human race. By its very nature the institution of marriage and married love are ordered to the procreation and education of the offspring and it is in them that it finds its crowning glory. Thus the man and woman, who "are no longer two but one" (Mt 19:6), help and serve each other by their marriage partnership; they become conscious of their unity and experience it more deeply from day to day. The intimate union of marriage, as a mutual giving of two persons, and the good of the children demand total

fidelity from the spouses and require an unbreakable unity between them.[2]

Christ our Lord has abundantly blessed this love, which is rich in its various features, coming as it does from the spring of divine love and modeled on Christ's own union with the church. Just as of old God encountered his people in a covenant of love and fidelity,[3] so our Savior, the spouse of the church,[4] now encounters christian spouses through the sacrament of marriage. He abides with them in order that by their mutual self-giving spouses will love each other with enduring fidelity, as he loved the church and delivered himself for it.[5] Authentic married love is caught up into divine love and is directed and enriched by the redemptive power of Christ and the salvific action of the church, with the result that the spouses are effectively led to God and are helped and strengthened in their lofty role as fathers and mothers.[6] Spouses, therefore, are fortified and, as it were, consecrated for the duties and dignity of their state by a special sacrament;[7] fulfilling their conjugal and family role by virtue of this sacrament, spouses are penetrated with the spirit of Christ and their whole life is suffused by faith, hope and charity; thus they increasingly further their own perfection and their mutual sanctification, and together they render glory to God.

Inspired by the example and family prayer of their parents, children, and in fact everyone living under the family roof, will more easily set out upon the path of a truly human training, of salvation, and of holiness. As for the spouses, when they are given the dignity and role of fatherhood and motherhood, they will eagerly carry out their duties of education, especially religious education, which primarily devolves on them.

Children as living members of the family contribute in their own way to the sanctification of their parents. With sentiments of gratitude, affection and trust, they will repay their parents for the benefits given to them and will come to their assistance as devoted children in times of hardship and in the loneliness of old age. Widowhood, accepted courageously as a continuation of the calling to marriage, will be honored by all.[8] Families will generously share their spiritual treasures with other families. The christian family springs from marriage,[9] which is an image and a sharing in the partnership of love between Christ and the church; it will show to all people Christ's living presence in the world and the authentic nature of the church by the love and generous fruitfulness of the spouses, by their unity and fidelity, and by the loving way in which all members of the family cooperate with each other.

Married Love

49. The word of God regularly invites engaged and married couples to nourish and cherish their betrothal with chaste love and their marriage with undivided love.[10] Many of our contemporaries, too, have a high regard for true love between husband and wife as manifested in the worthy customs of various times and peoples. Married love is an eminently human love because it is an affection between two persons rooted in the will and it embraces the good of the whole person; it can enrich the sentiments of the spirit and their physical expression with a unique dignity and ennoble them as the special features and manifestations of the friendship proper to marriage. The Lord, wishing to bestow special gifts of grace and divine love on married love, has restored, perfected, and elevated it. A love like that, bringing together the human and the divine, leads the partners to a free and mutual self-giving, experienced in tenderness and action, and permeating their entire lives;[11] this love is

actually developed and increased by its generous exercise. This is a far cry from mere erotic attraction, which is pursued in selfishness and soon fades away in wretchedness.

Married love is uniquely expressed and perfected by the exercise of the acts proper to marriage. Hence the acts in marriage by which the intimate and chaste union of the spouses takes place are noble and honorable; the truly human performance of these acts fosters the self-giving they signify and enriches the spouses in joy and gratitude. Endorsed by mutual fidelity and, above all, consecrated by Christ's sacrament, this love abides faithfully in mind and body in prosperity and adversity and hence excludes both adultery and divorce. The unity of marriage, confirmed by our Lord, is clearly apparent in the equal personal dignity which is accorded to man and wife in mutual and unreserved affection. Outstanding virtue is required for the constant fulfillment of the duties of this christian calling. Married couples, therefore, strengthened by grace for leading a holy life, will perseveringly practice and will pray for a love that is firm, generous, and ready for sacrifice.

Authentic married love will be held in high esteem, and healthy public opinion will be quick to recognize it, if christian spouses are noted for faithfulness and harmony in their love, for their concern for the education of their children and if they play their part in a much needed cultural, psychological and social renewal in matters concerning marriage and the family. It is imperative to give suitable instruction to young people and in good time, especially in their own families, concerning the dignity of married love, its function and its exercise; thus trained in chastity they will be able in due course to marry, after an honourable engagement.

The Fruitfulness of Marriage

50. Marriage and married love are by nature ordered to the procreation and education of children. Indeed children are the supreme gift of marriage and greatly contribute to the well-being of the parents themselves. God said:"It is not good that man should be alone"(Gen 2:18), and "from the beginning (God) made them male and female" (Mt 19:4); wishing to associate them in a special way with his own creative work, God blessed man and woman with the words: "Be fruitful and multiply"(Gen 1:28). Without intending to underestimate the other ends of marriage, it must be said that true married love and the family life which flows from it have this end in view: that the spouses would cooperate generously with the love of the Creator and Savior, who through them will in due time increase and enrich his family.

Married couples should see it as their mission to transmit human life and to educate their children; they should realize that they are thereby cooperating with the love of God the Creator and are, in a certain sense, its interpreters. This involves fulfilling their role responsibly as human beings and Christians, judging matters correctly in a spirit of obedient respect for God, reflecting and working together; it also involves taking into consideration their own well-being and the well-being of their children already born or yet to come, being able to read the signs of the times and assess their own situation on the material and spiritual level, and, finally, an estimation of the good of the family, of society, and of the church. It is the married couple themselves who must in the last analysis arrive at these judgments before God. Married people should realize that in their behavior they may not simply follow their own fancy but must be ruled by conscience — and conscience ought to be in accord with the law of God in the teaching authority of the church, which is the authentic interpreter of divine law. For the divine law throws light on the meaning of married love, protects it and leads it to truly human fulfillment. Whenever christian spouses in a spirit of sacrifice and trust in divine providence[12] carry out their duties of procreation with generous human and christian responsibility, they glorify the Creator and perfect themselves in Christ. Among the married couples who thus fulfil their God-given mission, special mention should be made of those who after prudent reflection and joint decision courageously undertake the rearing of a large family.[13]

But marriage was not instituted solely for the procreation of children: its nature as an indissoluble covenant between two people and the good of the children demand that the mutual love of the partners be properly expressed, that it should grow and mature. Even in cases where despite the intense desire of the spouses there are no children, marriage still retains its character of being a whole manner and communion of life and preserves its value and indissolubility.

Married Love and Respect for Human Life

51. The council realizes that certain situations in modern life often prevent married people from living their married life harmoniously and that they can sometimes find themselves in a position where the number of children cannot be increased, at least for the time being: in cases like these it is quite difficult to preserve the practice of faithful love and the complete intimacy of their lives. But where the intimacy of married life is broken, it often happens that faithfulness is imperilled and the good of the children suffers: then the education of the children as well as the courage to accept more children are both endangered. Some of the proposed solutions to these problems are shame-

ful and some people have not hesitated to suggest the taking of life: the church wishes to emphasize that there can be no conflict between the divine laws governing the transmission of life and the fostering of authentic married love.

God, the Lord of life, has entrusted to women and men the noble mission of safeguarding life and they must carry it out in a manner worthy of themselves. Life must be protected with the utmost care from the moment of conception: abortion and infanticide are abominable crimes. People's sexuality and the faculty of reproduction wonderfully surpass the endowments of lower forms of life; therefore the acts proper to married life are to be ordered according to authentic human dignity and must be held in the greatest reverence. When it is a question of harmonizing married love with the responsible transmission of life it is not enough to take only the good intention and the evaluation of motives into account: objective criteria must be used, criteria drawn from the nature of the human person and human action, criteria which respect the total meaning of mutual self-giving and human procreation in the context of true love; all this is possible only if the virtue of married chastity is seriously practised. In questions of birth regulation the daughters and sons of the church, faithful to these principles, are forbidden to use methods disapproved of by the teaching authority of the church in its interpretation of the divine law.[14]

Let all be convinced that human life and its transmission are realities whose meaning is not limited by the horizons of this life only: their true evaluation and full meaning can only be understood in reference to our eternal destiny.

Fostering Marriage and the Family: A Duty for All

52. The family is, in a sense, a school for human

enrichment. But if it is to achieve the full flowering of its life and mission, it requires an affectionate sharing of souls between the married couple and their commitment to cooperation in the children's upbringing. The father's active presence is very important for the children's education; the mother, too, has a central role in the home, for the children, especially the younger children, depend very much on her; this role must be safeguarded without, however, underrating woman's legitimate social advancement. The education of children should be such that when they grow up they will be able to follow their vocation, including a religious vocation, and choose their state of life fully aware of their responsibility; and if they marry they should be capable of setting up a family in favorable moral, social, and economic circumstances. It is the duty of parents and teachers to guide young people with prudent advice in the establishment of a family; their advice should be willingly listened to, but they should beware of exercising any undue influence, directly or indirectly, to force them into marriage or dictate their choice of partner.

The family is the place where different generations come together and to help one another to grow in wisdom and harmonize the rights of individuals with other demands of social life; as such it constitutes the basis of society. All, therefore, who have influence in the community and in social groups should devote themselves effectively to the welfare of marriage and the family. Civil authority should consider it a sacred duty to acknowledge the true nature of marriage and the family, to protect and support them, to safeguard public morality and promote domestic prosperity. The rights of parents to procreate and educate children in the family must be safeguarded. There should also be welfare legislation and provision of various kinds made for the protection and assistance of those who unfortunately have been deprived of the benefits of family life.

Christians, making the most of the times in which we live[15] and carefully distinguishing the everlasting from the changeable, should actively strive to promote the values of marriage and the family; it can be done by the witness of their own lives and by concerted action along with all people of good will; in this way they will overcome obstacles and make provision for the requirements and the advantages of family life arising at the present day. To this end the christian instincts of the faithful, a correct moral conscience and the wisdom and skill of persons versed in the sacred sciences will have much to contribute.

Experts in other sciences, particularly biology, medicine, social science and psychology, can help secure the welfare of marriage, the family and people's peace of mind if by pooling their findings they try to clarify thoroughly the different conditions favoring the proper regulation of births.

Priests should be properly trained to deal with family matters and to nurture the vocation of married people in their married and family life by different pastoral means, by the preaching of the word of God, by the liturgy, and other spiritual helps. They should strengthen them sympathetically and patiently in their difficulties and comfort them in charity with a view to the formation of families which are shining examples.

Various organizations, especially family associations, should set out by their programs of instruction and activity to strengthen young people and especially young married people, and to prepare them for family, social, and apostolic life.

Let married people themselves, who are created in the image of the living God and constituted in an authentic personal dignity, be united together in equal affection, agreement of mind and mutual holiness.[16] Thus, in the footsteps of Christ, the principle of life,[17] they will bear witness by their faithful love in the joys and sacrifices of their calling, to that mystery of love which the Lord revealed to the world by his death and resurrection.[18]

1. St Augustine, *De bono coniugii:* PL 40, 375-376 and 394; St Thomas Aquinas, *Summa Theologiae,* Suppl. Quaest. 49, art. 3 ad I; *Decretum pro Armenis:* Denz. 702 (1327); Pius XI, Encyclical *Casti Connubii:* AAS 22 (1930), pp. 543-545; Denz. 2227-2238 (3703-3714).

2. See Pius XI, Encyclical *Casti Connubii:* AAS 22 (1930), pp. 546-7: Denz, 2231 (3706).

3. See Hos 2; Jer 3:6-13; Ezek 16 and 23; Is 54.

4. See Mt 9:15; Mk 2:19-20; Lk 5:34-35; Jn 3:29; 2 Cor 11:2; Eph 5:27; Apoc 19:7-8; 21:2 and 9.

5. See Eph 5 25.

6. See Vatican Council II, Dogmatic Constitution on the Church, *Lumen gentium,* 11-12, 34-36, 41.

7. See Pius XI, Encyclical *Casti Connubii:* AAS 22 (1930), p. 583.

8. See 1 Tim 5:3.

9. See Eph 5:32.

10. See Gen 2:22-24; Prov 5:18-20; 31:10-31; Tob 8:4-8; Cant 1:1-3; 2:16; 7:8-11; 1 Cor 7:3-6; Eph 5:25-33.

11. See Pius XI, Encyclical *Casti Connubii:* AAS 22 (1930), pp. 547 and 548; Denz. 2232 (3707).

12. See 1 Cor 7:5.

13. See Pius XII, Allocution, *Tra le visite,* 20 Jan. 1958: AAS 50 (1958), p. 91.

14. See Pius XI, Encyclical *Casti Connubii:* AAS 22 (1930), pp. 559-561; Denz. 2239-2241 (3716-3718); Pius XII, Allocution to the Congress of Italian Midwives, 29 Oct. 1951: AAS 43 (1951), pp. 835-54, Paul VI, Allocution to the Cardinals, 23 June 1964: AAS 56 (1964), pp. 581-9. [By order of Pope Paul VI, a special commission was appointed to study the question of the regulation of births. When it had completed its report, Pope Paul VI issued the encyclical letter 'On the Regulation of Births', *Humanae Vitae,* 25 July, 1968, text in *Vatican Collection* vol 2, pp. 397-416. See also 'Declaration on Procured Abortion', *Questio de abortu,* op. cit., pp 441-53, 'The Christian Family in the Modern World', *Familiaris consortio,* 22 November, 1981, op. cit. pp. 815-898. Ed.]

15. See Eph 5:16; Col 4:5.

16. See *Sacramentarium Gregorianum:* PL 78, 262.

17. See Rom 5:15 and 18; 6:5-11 Gal 2:20.

18. See Eph 5:25-27.

Chapter II

PROPER DEVELOPMENT OF CULTURE

Introduction

53. It is a feature of the human person that it can achieve true and full humanity only by means of culture, that is through the cultivation of the goods and values of nature. Whenever, therefore, there is a question of human life, nature and culture are intimately linked together.

The word "culture" in the general sense refers to all those things which go to the refining and developing of humanity's diverse mental and physical endowments. We strive to subdue the earth by our knowledge and labor; we humanize social life both in the family and in the whole civic community through the improvement of customs and institutions; we express through our works the great spiritual experiences and aspirations of humanity through the ages; we communicate and preserve them to be an inspiration for the progress of many people, even of all humanity.

Hence it follows that culture necessarily has historical and social overtones, and the word "culture" often carries with it sociological and ethnological connotations; in this sense one can speak about a plurality of cultures. For different styles of living and different scales of values originate in different ways of using things, of working and self-expression, of practicing religion and of behavior, of establishing laws and juridical institutions, of developing science and the arts and of cultivating beauty. Thus the heritage of its institutions forms the patrimony proper to each human community; thus, too, is created a well defined, historical milieu which envelops the people of every nation and age, and from which they draw the values needed to foster humanity and civilization.

Section 1: Cultural Situation Today

New Forms of Living

54. The circumstances of life today have undergone such profound changes on the social and cultural level that one is entitled to speak of a new age of human history;[1] hence new ways are opened up for the development and diffusion of culture. The factors which have occasioned it have been the tremendous expansion of the natural and human sciences (including social sciences), the increase of technology, and the advances in developing and organizing the media of communication. As a result, modern culture is characterized as follows: the "exact" sciences foster to the highest degree a critical way of judging; recent psychological advances furnish deeper insights into human behavior; historical studies tend to make us view things under the aspects of change and evolution; customs and patterns of life tend to become more uniform from day to day; industrialization, urbanization, and other factors which promote community living create new mass-cultures which give birth to new patterns of thinking, of acting, and of the use of leisure; heightened media of exchange between nations and different branches of society open up the riches of different cultures to each and every individual, with the result that a more universal form of culture is gradually taking shape, and through it the unity of humankind is being fostered and expressed in the measure that the particular characteristics of each culture are preserved.

Humanity, Author of Culture

55. In each nation and social group there is a growing number of men and women who are conscious that they themselves are the architects and molders of their community's culture. All over the world the

sense of autonomy and responsibility increases with effects of the greatest importance for the spiritual and moral maturity of humankind. This will become clearer to us if we advert to the unification of the world and the duty imposed on us to build up a better world in truth and justice. We are witnessing the birth of a new humanism, where people are defined before all else by their responsibility to their sisters and brothers and at the court of history.

Difficulties and Duties

56. In circumstances such as these it is no wonder that people feel responsible for the progress of culture and nourish high hopes for it, but anxiously foresee numerous conflicting elements which it is up to them to resolve.

Increased exchanges between cultures ought to lead to genuine and fruitful dialogue between groups and nations. What, however, is to be done to prevent such exchanges from disturbing the life of communities, destroying traditional wisdom and endangering each people's native characteristics?

How is the dynamism and expansion of the new culture to be fostered without forfeiting loyalty to inherited traditions? This question is of particular relevance in a culture where the enormous progress of science and technology must be harmonized with a culture nourished by classical studies from various traditions.

As specialization in different branches of knowledge continues to increase so rapidly, how can the requisite synthesis be worked out between them, not to mention the need to safeguard humanity's powers of contemplation and the wonder which lead to wisdom?

What can be done to enable everyone to share in the benefits of culture, when the culture of specialists is becoming every day more complex and esoteric?

Finally, how are we to accept that culture's claim to autonomy is justified, without falling into a humanism which is purely earthbound and even hostile to religion?

In spite of these conflicting issues human culture must evolve today in such a way that it will develop the whole human person harmoniously and integrally, and will help everyone to fulfil the tasks to which they are called, especially Christians who are united in communion at the heart of the human family.

Section 2: Some Principles of Proper Cultural Development

Faith and Culture

57. In their pilgrimage to the heavenly city Christians are to seek and value the things that are above;[2] this involves not less, but greater commitment to working with everyone for the establishment of a more human world. Indeed, the mystery of their faith provides Christians with greater incentive and encouragement to fulfil their role more willingly and to assess the significance of activities capable of assigning to human culture its honored role in the complete vocation of humanity.

By the work of our hands or with the help of technology, we till the earth to produce fruit and to make it a dwelling place fit for all of humanity; we also play our part in the life of social groups. In so doing we are realizing God's plan, revealed at the beginning of time, to subdue the earth[3] and perfect the work of creation; at the same time we are perfecting ourselves and observing the command of Christ to devote ourselves to the service of our sisters and brothers.

Furthermore, when we work in the disciplines of philosophy, history, mathematics and science and when we cultivates the arts, we can greatly help humanity to reach a higher understanding of truth, goodness, and beauty, to make judgments of universal value. Humanity will thus be more fully enlightened by the marvellous wisdom, which was with God from eternity, fashioning all things with God, rejoicing in God's inhabited world, and delighting in humanity's sons and daughters.[4] As a consequence the human spirit, freed from the bondage of material things, can be more easily drawn to the worship and contemplation of the creator. Moreover, humanity is disposed to acknowledge, under the impulse of grace, the word of God, who was in the world as "the true light that enlightens everyone" (Jn 1:9), before becoming flesh to save and gather up all things in himself.[5]

There is no doubt that modern scientific and technical progress can lead to a certain phenomenism or agnosticism; this happens when scientific methods of investigation, which of themselves are incapable of penetrating to the deepest nature of things, are unjustifiably taken as the supreme norm for arriving at truth. There is a further danger that in their excessive confidence in modern inventions people may think that they are sufficient unto themselves and abandon the search for higher values.

But these drawbacks are not necessarily due to modern culture and they should not tempt us to overlook its positive values. Among these values we would like to draw attention to the following: study of the sciences and exact fidelity to truth in scientific investigation, the necessity of teamwork in technology, the sense of international solidarity, a growing awareness of the expert's responsibility to help and defend the rest of humanity, and an eagerness to improve the standard of living of everyone, especially of those who are deprived of responsibility or suffer from cultural destitution. All these can afford a certain kind of preparation for the acceptance of the message of the Gospel and can be infused with divine charity by him who came to save the world.

Relations Between Culture and the Good News of Christ

58. There are many links between the message of salvation and culture. In his self-revelation to his people, fully manifesting himself in his incarnate Son, God spoke in the context of the culture proper to each age. Similarly the church has existed through the centuries in varying circumstances and has utilized the resources of different cultures to spread and explain the message of Christ in its preaching, to examine and understand it more deeply, and to express it more perfectly in the liturgy and in the life of the multiform community of the faithful.

Nevertheless, the church has been sent to all ages and nations and, therefore, is not tied exclusively and indissolubly to any race or nation, to any one particular way of life, or to any set of customs, ancient or modern. The church is faithful to its traditions and is at the same time conscious of its universal mission; it can, then, enter into communion with different forms of culture, thereby enriching both itself and the cultures themselves.

The good news of Christ continually renews the life and culture of fallen humanity; it combats and removes the error and evil which flow from the ever-present attraction of sin. It never ceases to purify and elevate the morality of peoples. It takes the spiritual qualities and endowments of every age and nation and enriches them with heavenly resources, causes them to bear fruit, as it were, from within; it fortifies, completes and restores them in Christ.[6] In this way the church carries out its mission[7] and in that very act it stimulates and advances human and civil culture, as well as contributing by its activity, including liturgical activity, to humanity's interior freedom.

Proper Harmony Between Forms of Culture

59. For the reasons given above, the church recalls to mind that culture must be subordinated to the integral development of the human person, to the good of the community and of the whole of humanity. Therefore one must aim at encouraging the human spirit to develop its faculties of wonder, of understanding, of contemplation, of forming personal judgments and cultivating a religious, moral and social sense.

Culture, since it flows from humanity's rational and social nature, has continual need of proper freedom of development and a legitimate possibility of autonomy according to its own principles. Quite rightly it demands respect and enjoys a certain inviolability, provided, of course, that the rights of the individual and the community, both particular and universal, are safeguarded within the limits of the common good.

Calling to mind the teaching of the first Vatican council, this sacred synod declares that "there are two orders of knowledge" distinct from one another, faith and reason, and that the church does not forbid "that human arts and sciences have recourse to their own principles and methods in their respective fields;" therefore, "it acknowledges this lawful freedom" and affirms the legitimate autonomy of culture and especially of the sciences.[8]

All this demands that, provided they respect the moral order and the common interest, people should be entitled to seek after truth, to express and make known their opinions, to engage in whatever art they please; and, finally, that they should be accurately informed about matters of public interest.[9]

It is not for the public authority to determine how

human culture should develop, but to build up the environment and to provide assistance favorable to such development, without overlooking minorities.[10] This is the reason why one must avoid at all costs the distortion of culture and its exploitation by political or economical forces.

Section 3: Some More Urgent Duties of Christians in Regard to Culture

Recognition of Everyone's Right to Culture and its Implementation

60. It is now possible to remove from most of the human race the curse of ignorance. A duty most appropriate in our times, especially for Christians, is to work untiringly to the end that fundamental economic and political decisions are taken, nationally and internationally, which will ensure the recognition and implementation everywhere of everyone's right to human and civil culture in harmony with personal dignity, without distinction of race, sex, nation, religion, or social circumstances. Hence it is necessary to ensure that there is a sufficiency of cultural benefits available to everybody, especially the benefit of what is called "basic" culture, lest any be prevented by illiteracy and lack of initiative from contributing in an authentically human way to the common good.

Every effort should be made to provide for those who are capable of it the opportunity to pursue higher studies so that as far as possible they may engage in the functions and services, and play the role in society most in keeping with their talents and the skills they acquire.[11] In this way all the individuals and social groups of a particular people will be able to attain a full development of their cultural life in harmony with their capabilities and their traditions.

We must do everything possible to make everyone aware of their right to culture and their duty to develop themselves culturally and to help their sisters and brothers. Sometimes conditions of life and work are such as to stifle people's cultural activities and take away their appetite for culture. This holds true especially for those living in rural areas and for manual workers who ought to be provided with working conditions conducive to their cultural development. At present women are involved in nearly all spheres of life: they ought to be permitted to play their part fully in ways suited to their nature. It is up to everyone to see to it that women's specific and necessary participation in cultural life be acknowledged and developed.

Cultural Education

61. Nowadays much more than in the past it is difficult to form a synthesis of the arts and of the different branches of knowledge. While, in fact, the volume and diversity of the constituent elements of culture are on the increase, there is a decrease in the individual's capability to perceive and harmonize them, so that the notion of "universal humanity" has almost vanished. Still, it remains each one's duty to safeguard the notion of the human person as a totality in which intellect, will, conscience, sisterhood and brotherhood predominate, since these values were established by the creator and wonderfully restored and elevated by Christ.

Education of this kind has its source and its cradle, as it were, in the family; children in an atmosphere of love learn there more quickly the true scale of values and there, too, approved forms of culture are almost naturally assimilated by the developing minds of adolescents.

There are nowadays many opportunities favorable to the development of a universal culture, thanks especially to the increase in book publication and new techniques of cultural and social communication. Shorter working hours are becoming the general rule everywhere and provide greater opportunities for large numbers of people. This leisure time must be properly employed to refresh the spirit and improve the health of mind and body — by means of voluntary activity and study; by means of travel to broaden and enrich people's minds by learning from others; by means of physical exercise and sport, which help to create harmony of feeling even on the level of the community as well as fostering friendly relations between people of all classes, countries, and races. Christians, therefore, should cooperate in the cultural framework and collective activity characteristic of our times, to humanize them and imbue them with a christian spirit. All these advantages, however, are insufficient to confer full cultural development, unless they are accompanied by a deeply thought out evaluation of the meaning of culture and knowledge of the human person.

Proper Harmony Between Culture and Christian Formation

62. Although the church has contributed largely to the progress of culture, it is a fact of experience that there have been difficulties in the way of harmonizing culture with christian thought, arising out of contingent factors. These difficulties do not necessarily harm the life of faith, but can rather stimulate a more precise and deeper understanding of that faith. In fact, recent research and discoveries in the sciences, in history and philosophy bring up new problems which have an important bearing on life itself and demand new scrutiny by theologians. Furthermore, theologians are now being asked, within the methods and limits of theological science, to develop more efficient ways of communicating doctrine to the people of

today, for the deposit and the truths of faith are one thing, the manner of expressing them — provided their sense and meaning are retained — is quite another.[12] In pastoral care sufficient use should be made, not only of theological principles, but also of the findings of secular sciences, especially psychology and sociology: in this way the faithful will be brought to a purer and more mature living of the faith.

In their own way literature and art are very important in the life of the church. They seek to penetrates our nature, our problems and experience as we endeavour to discover and perfect ourselves and the world in which we live; they try to discover our place in history and in the universe, to throw light on our suffering and joy, our needs and potentialities, and to outline a happier destiny in store for us. Hence they can elevate human life, which they express under many forms according to various times and places.

Every effort should be made, therefore, to make artists feel that they are understood by the church in their artistic work and to encourage them, while enjoying a reasonable standard of freedom, to enter into happier relations with the christian community. New art forms adapted to our times and in keeping with the characteristics of different nations and regions should be acknowledged by the church. They may also be brought into the sanctuary whenever they raise the mind to God with suitable forms of expression and in conformity with liturgical requirements.[13] Thus the knowledge of God will be made more widely available; the preaching of the Gospel will be rendered more intelligible and will appear more relevant to people's situations.

Therefore, the faithful ought to work closely with their contemporaries and ought to try to understand their ways of thinking and feeling, as these find expression in current culture. Let the faithful incorporate the findings of new sciences and teachings and the understanding of the most recent discoveries into christian morality and thought, so that their practice of religion and their moral behavior may keep abreast of their acquaintance with science and of the relentless progress of technology: in this way they will succeed in evaluating and interpreting everything with an authentically christian sense of values.

Those involved in theological studies in seminaries and universities should be eager to cooperate with people versed in other disciplines by pooling their resources and their points of view. Theological research, while it deepens knowledge of revealed truth, should not lose contact with its own times, so that experts in various fields may be led to a deeper knowledge of the faith. Collaboration of this kind will be beneficial in the formation of sacred ministers; they will be able to present teaching on God, on humanity, and on the world, in a way more suited to our contemporaries, who will then be more ready to accept their word.[14] Furthermore, it is to be hoped that more of the laity will receive adequate theological formation and that some among them will dedicate themselves professionally to these studies and contribute to their advancement. But for the proper exercise of this role, the faithful, both clerical and lay, should be accorded a lawful freedom of inquiry, of thought, and of expression, tempered by humility and courage in whatever branch of study they have specialized.[15]

1. See the Introduction to this Constitution, nn. 4-10.
2. See Col 3:1-2.
3. See Gen 1:28.
4. See Prov 8:30-31.
5. See St Irenaeus, *Adv. Haer.*, III, 11, 8: ed. Sagnard, p. 200; see ibid., 16, 6, pp. 290-292; 21, 10-22, pp. 370-372; 22, 3, p. 378; etc.
6. See Eph 1:10.
7. See words of Pius XI to Mgr. M. D. Roland-Gosselin "One must never lose sight of the fact that the church's objective is to

evangelize, not to civilize. If it does civilize, it is done through evangelizing" (*Semaines sociales de France,* Versailles, 1936, pp. 461-462).

8. Vatican Council I, Dogmatic Constitution on the Catholic Faith, *Dei filius,* ch. IV: Denz., 1795, 1799 (3015, 3019). See Pius XI, Encyclical *Quadragesimo Anno:* AAS 23 :1931), p. 190.

9. See John XXIII, Encyclical *Pacem in Terris:* AAS 55 (1963), p. 260.

10. See John XXIII, Encyclical *Pacem in Terris:* AAS 55 (1963), p. 283; Pius XII, radio message, 24 Dec. 1941: ASS 34 (1942), pp. 16-17.

11. See John XXIII, Encyclical *Pacem in Terris:* AAS 55 (1963), p. 260.

12. See John XXIII, Speech delivered at the opening of the council: AAS 54 (1962), p. 792.

13. See Constitution on the Sacred Liturgy, *Sacrosanctum Concilium* n. 123; Paul VI, Address to Roman Artists, 7 May 1964: AAS 56 (1964), pp. 439-442.

14. See Vatican Council II, Decree on Priestly Formation, *Optatam Totius,* and on Christian Education, *Gravissimum Educationis.*

15. See Vatican Council II, Dogmatic Constitution on the Church, *Lumen gentium* , ch. 4, n. 37.

Chapter III

ECONOMIC AND SOCIAL LIFE

Some Characteristics of Economic Life Today

63. In the sphere of economics and social life, too, the dignity and vocation of the human person as well as the welfare of society as a whole have to be respected and fostered; for people are the source, the focus and the aim of all economic and social life.

Like all other areas of social life, the economy of today is marked by humanity's growing dominion over nature, by closer and more developed relationships between individuals, groups and peoples, and by the frequency of state intervention. At the same time increased efficiency in production and improved methods of distribution, of productivity and services have rendered the economy an instrument capable of meeting the increasing needs of the human family.

But the picture is not without its disturbing elements. Many people, especially in economically advanced areas, seem to be dominated by economics; almost all of their personal and social lives are permeated with a kind of economic mentality, and this is true of nations that favor a collective economy as well as of other nations. At the very time when economic progress, provided it is directed and organized in a reasonable and human way, could do so much to reduce social inequalities, it serves all too often only to aggravate them; in some places it even leads to a decline in the situation of the underprivileged and to contempt for the poor. In the midst of huge numbers deprived of the bare necessities of life there are some who live in riches and squander their wealth; and this happens in less developed areas as well. Luxury and misery exist side by side. While a few individuals enjoy almost unlimited freedom of choice, the vast majority have no chance whatever of exercising personal initiative and responsibility, and quite often have to live and work in conditions unworthy of human beings.

Similar economic and social imbalances exist between those engaged in agriculture, industry, and the service industries, and even between different areas of the same country. The growing contrast between the economically more advanced countries and others could well endanger world peace.

Our contemporaries are daily becoming more keenly aware of these discrepancies because they are thoroughly convinced that this unhappy state of affairs can and should be rectified by the greater technical and economic resources available in the world today. To achieve this, considerable reform in economic and social life is required along with a universal change of mentality and of attitude. It was for this reason that the church in the course of centuries has worked out in the light of the Gospel principles of justice and equity demanded by right reason for individual and social life and also for international relations. The council now intends to reiterate these principles in accordance with the situation of the world today and will outline certain guidelines, particularly with reference to the requirements of economic development.[1]

Section 1: Economic Development

Ecomonic Development in the Service of Humanity

64. Today, more than ever before, there is an increase in the production of agricultural and industrial goods and in the number of services available, and this is as it should be in view of the population expansion and growing human needs. Therefore we must encourage technical progress and the spirit of enterprise, the wish to create and improve new enterprises, and we must promote adaptation of the means of production and all serious efforts by people engaged in production — in other words everything which contributes to economic progress. The ultimate and basic purpose of economic production does not consist merely in producing more goods, nor in profit or prestige; economic production is meant to be at the service of humanity in its totality, taking into account people's material needs and the requirements of their intellectual, moral, spiritual, and religious life; it is intended to benefit all individuals and groups of people of whatever race or from whatever part of the world. Therefore, economic activity is to be carried out in accordance with techniques and methods belonging to the moral order,[2] so that God's design for humanity may be carried out.[3]

Economic Development Under Man's Direction

65. Economic development must remain under the people's control; it is not to be left to the judgment of a few individuals or groups possessing too much economic power, nor to the political community alone, nor to a few powerful nations. It is only right that, in matters of general interest, as many people as possible, and, in international relations, all nations, should participate in decision making. It is likewise necessary that the voluntary initiatives of individuals and of free associations should be integrated with state enterprises and organized suitably and harmoniously. Nor should development be left to the almost mechanical evolution of economic activity nor to the decision of public authority. Hence we must denounce as false those doctrines which stand in the way of all reform on the pretext of a false notion of freedom, as well as those which subordinate the basic rights of individuals and of groups to the collective organization of production.[4]

All citizens should remember that they have the right and the duty to contribute according to their ability to the progress of their own community and that this must be recognized by the civil authority. Above all in economically underdeveloped areas, where there is urgent need to exploit all available resources, the common good is seriously endangered by those who hoard their resources unproductively and by those who, apart from the personal right to emigrate, deprive their community of much needed material and spiritual assistance.

An End to Excessive Economic and Social Differences

66. To meet the requirements of justice and equity, every effort must be made, while respecting the rights of individuals and national characteristics, to put an

end as soon as possible to the immense economic inequalities which exist in the world, which increase daily and which go hand and hand with individual and social discrimination. Likewise in many areas, in view of the special difficulties of production and marketing in agriculture, rural people must be helped to improve methods of production and marketing, to introduce necessary developments and innovations, and to receive a fair return for their products, lest, as often happens, they remain second-class citizens. Farmers themselves, especially young farmers, ought to set about improving their professional skills, without which the advancement of farming is impossible.[5]

Justice and equity also demand that the sort of mobility which is a necessary feature of developing economies should not be allowed to jeopardize the livelihood of individuals and their families. Every kind of discrimination in wages and working conditions should be avoided in regard to workers who come from other countries or areas and contribute by their work to the economic development of a people or a region. Furthermore, no one, especially public authorities, should treat such workers simply as mere instruments of production, but as persons; they should help them to bring their families with them and to obtain decent housing conditions, and they should try to integrate them into the social life of the country or area to which they have come. However, employment should be found for them so far as possible in their own countries.

Nowadays, when an economy is undergoing change, with the introduction of new forms of industrialization, such as automation, for example, care must be taken to ensure that there is sufficient suitable employment available; opportunities for appropriate technical and professional training should be provided, and safeguards should be put in place to protect the livelihood and human dignity of those who through age or ill health are seriously disadvantaged.

Section 2: Some Principles Governing Economic and Social Life as a Whole

Work, Working Conditions, Leisure

67. Human work which is carried out in the production and exchange of goods or in the provision of economic services, surpasses all other elements of economic life, which are only its instruments.

Human work, whether it is done independently or as an employee, proceeds from the human person, who as it were puts a personal seal on the things of nature and reduces them to her or his will. By their work people ordinarily provide for themselves and their family, associate with others as their brothers and sisters, and serve them; they can exercise genuine charity and be partners in the work of bringing God's creation to perfection. Moreover, we believe by faith that through the homage of work offered to God humanity is associated with the redemptive work of Jesus Christ, whose labor with his hands at Nazareth greatly added to the dignity of work. This is the source of every person's duty to work loyally as well as of their right to work; moreover, it is the duty of society to see to it that, in the prevailing circumstances, all citizens have the opportunity of finding employment. Finally, remuneration for work should guarantee to individuals the capacity to provide a dignified livelihood for themselves and their family on the material, social, cultural and spiritual level corresponding to their roles and productivity, having regard to the relevant economic factors in their employment, and the common good.[6]

Since economic activity is, for the most part, the

fruit of the collaboration of many, it is unjust and inhuman to organize and direct it in such a way that some of the workers are exploited. But it frequently happens, even today, that workers are almost enslaved by the work they do. So-called laws of economics are no excuse for this. The entire process of productive work, then, must be accommodated to the needs of the human person and the nature of his or her life, with special attention to domestic life, that of mothers of families in particular, always taking sex and age into account. Workers should have the opportunity to develop their talents and their personalities in the very exercise of their work. While devoting their time and energy to the performance of their work with a due sense of responsibility, they should nevertheless be allowed sufficient rest and leisure to cultivate their family, cultural, social and religious life. And they should be given the opportunity to develop those energies and talents, which perhaps are little utilised in their professional work.

Co-Responsibility in Enterprise and in the Economic System as a Whole; Labor Disputes

68. It is persons who associate together in business enterprises, people who are free and autonomous, who have been created in the image of God. Therefore, while taking into account the role of every person concerned — owners, employers, management, and employees — and without diminishing the requisite executive unity, the active participation of everybody in administration is to be encouraged.[7] More often, however, decisions concerning economic and social conditions are made not so much within the business itself as by institutions at a higher level, and since it is on these that the future of the employees and their children depends, the employees ought to have a say in decision-making, either in per-

son or through their representatives.

Among the fundamental rights of the individual must be numbered the right of workers to form truly representative union which contribute to the proper structuring of economic life, and also the right to play their part in the activities of such associations without risk of reprisal. Thanks to such organized participation, along with progressive economic and social education, there will be a growing awareness among all people of their role and their responsibility, and, according to the capacity and aptitudes of each one, they will feel that they have an active part to play in the whole task of economic and social development and in the achievement of the common good as a whole.

In the event of economic-social disputes all should strive to arrive at peaceful settlements. The first step is to engage in sincere discussion between all sides; but the strike remains even in today's conditions, a necessary, although an ultimate, instrument for the defence of workers' rights and the satisfaction of their lawful aspirations. As soon as possible, however, avenues should be explored to resume negotiations and effect reconciliation.

Earthly Goods Destined for All

69. God destined the earth and all it contains for all people and nations so that all created things would be shared fairly by all humankind under the guidance of justice tempered by charity.[8] No matter how property is structured in different countries, adapted to their lawful institutions according to various and changing circumstances, we must never lose sight of this universal destination of earthly goods. In their use of things people should regard the external goods they lawfully possess as not just their own but common to others as well, in the sense that they can benefit oth-

ers as well as themselves.[9] Therefore everyone has the right to possess a sufficient amount of the earth's goods for themselves and their family. This has been the opinion of the Fathers and Doctors of the church, who taught that people are bound to come to the aid of the poor and to do so not merely out of their superfluous goods.[10] Persons in extreme necessity are entitled to take what they need from the riches of others.[11] Faced with a world today where so many people are suffering from want, the council asks individuals and governments to remember the saying of the Fathers: "Feed the people dying of hunger, because if you do not feed them you are killing them,"[12] and it urges them according to their ability to share and dispose of their goods to help others, above all by giving them aid which will enable them to help and develop themselves.

In economically less developed societies, it often happens that the common destination of goods is partly achieved by a system of community customs and traditions which guarantee a minimum of necessities to each one. Certain customs must not be considered sacrosanct if they no longer correspond to modern needs; on the other hand one should not rashly do away with respectable customs which, if they are brought up to date, can still be very useful. In the same way, in economically advanced countries the common destination of goods is achieved through a system of social institutions dealing with insurance and security. Family and social services, especially those providing for culture and education, should be further developed. In setting up these different organizations care must be taken to prevent the citizens from slipping into a kind of passivity vis-à-vis society, or of irresponsibility in their duty, or of a refusal to do their fair share.

Investment and Money

70. Investment in its turn should be directed to providing employment and ensuring sufficient income for the people of today and of the future. Those responsible for investment and the planning of the economy — individuals, associations, public authorities — must keep these objectives in mind; they must show themselves to be aware of their serious obligation, on the one hand, to ensure that the necessities for living a decent life are available to individuals and to the community as a whole, and, on the other hand, to provide for the future and strike a rightful balance between the needs of present-day consumption, individual and collective, and the requirements of investment for future generations. Always they must keep before their eyes the pressing needs of underdeveloped countries and areas. In fiscal matters they must be careful not to do harm to their own country, or to any other. Care must also be taken that economically weak countries do not unjustly suffer loss from a change in the value of money.

Ownership, Private Property, Large Estates

71. Property and other forms of private ownership of external goods contribute to self-expression and provide people with the opportunity of exercising a role in society and in the economy; it is very important, then, to facilitate access to some ownership of external goods on the part of individuals and communities.

Private property or some form of ownership of external goods affords each person an indispensable zone for personal and family autonomy and ought to be considered an extension of human freedom. Further, in encouraging the exercise of responsibility it provides one of the conditions for civil liberty.[13] Nowadays the forms of such ownership or property are varied and are becoming more diversified with time. In spite of the social security, the rights, and the services guaranteed by society, all these forms of ownership remain a source of security which must not be underestimated. And this applies not only to ownership of material goods but also to the possession of professional skills.

The right to private ownership is not opposed to the various forms of public ownership. But the transfer of goods from private to public ownership may be undertaken only by competent authority, in accordance with the demands and within the limits of the common good, and it must be accompanied by adequate compensation. Furthermore, the state has the duty to prevent people from abusing their private property to the detriment of the common good.[14] By its nature private property has a social dimension which is based on the law of the common destination of earthly goods.[15] Whenever the social aspect is forgotten, ownership can often become the object of greed and a source of serious disorder, and its opponents easily find a pretext for calling the right itself into question.

In several economically under-developed areas there exist large, and sometimes very large, rural estates which are either very little cultivated or are left uncultivated as speculative ventures, while the majority of the population are landless or have very small holdings and at the same time it is obvious that there is a pressing need to increase agricultural production. Not infrequently those who are hired as labourers or who farm a portion of the land as tenants receive a wage or income unworthy of a human being; they are deprived of decent living conditions and are exploited by entrepeneurs. They lack all sense of security and live in such a state of personal dependence that almost all chance of exercising initiative and responsibility is closed to them and they are denied any cultural advancement or participation in social and political life. Reforms are called for in these different situations: incomes must be raised, working conditions improved, security in employment assured, and personal incentives to work encouraged; insufficiently cultivated estates should be divided up and given to those who will be able to make them productive. When this happens the necessary resources and equipment must be supplied, especially educational facilities and proper cooperative organizations. However, when the common good calls for expropriation, compensation must be made and is to be calculated according to equity, with all circumstances taken into account.

Economic and Social Activity and the Kingdom of Christ

72. Christians engaged actively in modern economic and social progress and in the struggle for justice and charity must be convinced that they have much to contribute to the prosperity of humanity and to world peace. Let them, as individuals and as a group, give a shining example to others. Endowed with the skill and experience so absolutely necessary for them, let them preserve a proper sense of values in their earthly activity in loyalty to Christ and his Gospel, in order that their lives, individual as well as social, may be inspired by the spirit of the Beatitudes, and in particular by the spirit of poverty.

All who in obedience to Christ seek first the kingdom of God will derive from it a stronger and purer motivation for helping all their brothers and sisters and for accomplishing the task of justice under the inspiration of charity.[16]

1. Pius XII, Message, 23 March 1952: AAS 44 (1952), p. 273; John

XXIII, Allocution to the Italian Catholic Workers Association, 1 May 1959: AAS 51 (1959), p. 358.

2. Pius XI, Encyclical *Quadragesimo Anno:* AAS 23 (1931), p. 190 ff.; Pius XII, Message, 23 March 1952: AAS 44 (1952), p. 276 ff.; John XXIII, Encyclical *Mater et Magistra:* AAS 53 (1961), p. 450; Vatican Council II, Decree on the Mass Media, *Inter Mirifica*, ch. 1, n. 6.

3. See Mt 16:26; Lk 16:1-31; Col 3:17.

4. See Leo XIII, Encyclical *Libertas Praestantissimum*, 20 June 1888: AAS 20 (1887-1888), p. 597 ff.; Pius XI, Encyclical *Quadragesimo Anno:* AAS 23 (1931), p. 191 ff.; Pius XI, Encyclical *Divini Redemptoris:* AAS 29 (1937), p. 65 ff.; Pius XII, Christmas Message, 1941: AAS 34 (1942), p. 10 ff.; John XXIII, Encyclical *Mater et Magistra:* AAS 53 (1961). pp. 401-464..

5. For the problem of agriculture see especially John XXIII, Encyclical *Mater et Magistra:* AAS 53 (1961), p. 341 ff.

6. See Leo XIII, Encyclical *Rerum Novarum:* AAS 23 (1890-1891), pp. 649-662; Pius XI, Encyclical *Quadragesimo Anno:* AAS 23 (1931), p. 200; Pius XI, Encyclical *Divini Redemptoris:* AAS 29 (1937), p. 92; Pius XII, Christmas Message, 1942: AAS 35 (1943) p. 20; Pius XII, Radio Message to Spanish workers, 11 March 1951: AAS 43 (1951), p. 215; John XXIII, Encyclical *Mater et Magistra:* AAS 53 (1961), p. 419.

7. See John XXIII, Encyclical *Mater et Magistra:* AAS 53 (1961), pp. 408, 424, 427; the word "curatione" used in the original text is taken from the Latin version of the Encyclical *Quadragesimo Anno:* AAS 23 (1931), p. 199. For the evolution of the question see also: Pius XII, Allocution, 3 June 1950: AAS 42 (1950), pp. 484-8; Paul VI, Allocution, 8 June 1964: AAS 56 (1964), pp. 574-9.

8. See Pius XII, Encyclical *Sertum Laetitiae:* AAS 31 (1939), p. 642; John XXIII, Consistorial Allocution: AAS 52 (1960), pp. 5-ll; John XXIII, Encyclical *Mater et Magistra:* AAS 53 (1961), p. 411.

9. See St Thomas Aquinas, *Summa Theologiae*, II-II, q. 32, a. 5 ad 2; ibid., q.66, a.2; see the explanation in Leo XIII, Encyclical *Rerum Novarum:* AAS 23 (1890-1891), p. 651; see also Pius XII, Allocution, 1 June 1941: AAS 33 (1941), p. 199; Pius XII, Christmas Message, 1954: AAS 47 (1955), p. 27.

10. See St Basil, *Hom. in illud Lucae "Destruam horrea mea,"* n. 2: PG 31, 263; Lactantius, *Divinarum Institutionum*, bk. V on justice: PL 6, 565 B; St Augustine, *In Ioann. Ev.*, tr. 50, n. 6: PL 35, 1760; St Augustine, *Enarratio in Ps. CXLVII*, 12: PL 37, 1922; St Gregory the Great, *Homiliae in Ev.*, hom. 20: PL 76, 1165; St Gregory the Great, *Regulae Pastoralis liber*, part III, c. 21: PL 77, 87; St Bonaventure, *In 111 Sent.*, d. 33, dub. 1 (ed. Quaracchi III, 728); St Bonaventure, In IV Sent., d. 15, p. 11, a. 2, q. 1 (ed. cit IV, 371 b) q. de superfluo (ms. Assisi, Bibl, commun. 186, ff. 112a-113a); St Albert the Great, In 111 Sent., d. 33, a. 3, sol. 1 (ed. Borgnet XXVIII, 611); St Albert the Great, In IV Sent., d. 15, a. 16 (ed. cit. XXIX, 494-497). As regards the deter-

mination of what is superfluous today see John XXIII, Radio-Television Message, 11 Sept. 1962: AAS 54 (1962), p. 682: "It is the duty of everyone, the compelling duty of Christians, to calculate what is superfluous by the measure of the needs of others and to see to it that the administration and distribution of created goods be utilized for the advantage of all."

11. In this case the old principle holds good: "In extreme necessity all goods are common, that is, they are to be shared." On the other hand for the scope, the extension, and the way this principle is to be applied in the text, besides accepted modern authors, see St Thomas Aquinas, *Summa Theologiae*, II-II, q. 66, a. 7. Clearly, for the correct application of the principle all the moral conditions required must be fulfilled.

12. See Gratian, *Decretum*, c. 21, dist. LXXXVI: ed. Friedberg I, 302. This axiom is found already in PL 54, 591a and PL 56, 1132b; see *Antonianum*, 27 (1952), 349-366.

13. See Leo XII, Encyclical *Rerum Novarum:* AAS 23 (1890-1891), pp. 643-6; Pius XI, Encyclical *Quadragesimo Anno* :AAS 23 (1931), p. 191; Pius XII, Radio Message, 1 June 1941: AAS 33 (1941), p. 199; Pius XII, Christmas Message, 1942: AAS 35 (1943), p. 17; Pius XII, Radio Message, I Sept. 1944: AAS 36 (1944), p. 253; John XXIII, Encyclical *Mater et Magistra:* AAS 53 (1961), pp. 428ff.

14. See Pius XI, Encyclical *Quadragesimo Anno:* AAS 23 (1931), p. 214; John XXIII, Encyclical *Mater et Magistra:* AAS 53 (1961), p. 429.

15. See Pius XII, Radio message for Pentecost 1941: AAS 44 (1941), p. 199 John XXIII, Encyclical *Mater et Magistra:* AAS 53 (1961), p 430.

16. For the right use of goods according to the teaching of the New Testament see Lk 3:11; 10:30 ff.; 11:41; Mk 8:36, 12:29-31; 1 Pet 5:3; Jas 5:1-6; 1 Tim 6:8; Eph 4:28; 2 Cor 8:13 f.; 1 Jn 3:17-18.

Chapter IV

THE POLITICAL COMMUNITY

Modern Public Life

73. In our times profound transformations are to be noticed in the structure and institutions of nations; they are the accompaniment of cultural, economic, and social development. These transformations exer-

cise a deep influence on political life, particularly as regards the rights and duties of the individual, in the exercise of civil liberty and in the achievement of the common good; and they affect the organization of the relations of citizens with each other and with the state.

A clearer awareness of human dignity has given rise in various parts of the world to a movement to establish a politico-juridical order which will provide better protection for the rights of women and men in public life — the right of free assembly and association, for example, the right to express one's opinions and to profess one's religion privately and publicly. The guarantee of the rights of the person is, indeed, a necessary condition for citizens, individually and collectively, to play an active part in public life and administration.

Linked with cultural, economic, and social progress there is a growing desire among many to assume greater responsibilities in the organization of political life. Many people are becoming more willing to ensure that the rights of minority groups in their country are safeguarded, without overlooking the duties of these minorities towards the political community; there is also an increase in tolerance for others who differ in opinion and religion; at the same time wider cooperation is taking place to enable all citizens, and not just a few privileged individuals, to exercise their rights effectively as persons.

People condemn those political systems which flourish in some parts of the world and which diminish civil and religious liberty, make many people the victims of political passions and crimes, cease to exercise authority in the interests of the common good, but rather in the interests of a particular faction or of the government.

There is no better way to establish political life on

a truly human basis than by encouraging an interior sense of justice, of good will and of service to the common good, and by consolidating people's basic convictions as to the true nature of the political community and the aim, proper exercise, and the limits of public authority.

Nature and Purpose of the Political Community

74. Individuals, families, and the various groups which make up the civil community, are aware of their inability to achieve a truly human life by their own unaided efforts; they see the need for a wider community where each one will make a specific contribution to an even broader implementation of the common good.[1] For this reason they set up various forms of political communities. The political community, then, exists for the common good: this is its full justification and meaning and the source of its specific and basic right to exist. The common good embraces the sum total of all those conditions of social life which enable individuals, families, and organizations to achieve complete and effective fulfillment.[2]

The people who go to make up the political community are many and varied; quite rightly, then, they may have widely differing points of view. Therefore, lest the political community be jeopardized because all individuals follow their own opinion, an authority is needed to guide the energies of all towards the common good — not mechanically or despotically, but by acting above all as a moral force based on freedom and a sense of responsibility. It is clear that the political community and public authority are based on human nature, and therefore that they need to belong to an order established by God; nevertheless, the choice of the political regime and the appointment of rulers are left to the free decision of the citizens.[3]

It follows that political authority, either within the

political community as such or through organizations representing the state, must be exercised within the limits of the moral order and directed towards the common good, understood in the dynamic sense of the term, according to the juridical order legitimately established or due to be established. Citizens, then, are bound in conscience to obey.[4] Accordingly, the responsibility, the status, and the importance of the rulers of a state are clear.

When citizens are being oppressed by a public authority which oversteps its competence, they should not refuse whatever is objectively demanded of them by the common good; but it is legitimate for them to defend their own rights and those of their fellow citizens against abuses of this authority within the limits of the natural law and the law of the Gospel.

The concrete forms of structure and organization of public authority adopted in political communities will vary according to people's differing characters and historical developments; but their aim should always be the formation of human persons who are cultured, peace-loving, and well disposed towards all, to the benefit of the whole human race.

Participation by All in Public Life

75. It is fully in accord with human nature that politico-juridical structures be devised which will increasingly and without discrimination provide all citizens with effective opportunities to play a free, active part in the establishment of the juridical foundations of the political community, in the administration of public affairs, in determining the aims and the terms of reference of public bodies, and in the election of political leaders.[5] All citizens ought to be aware of their right and duty to promote the common good by casting their votes. The church praises and esteems

those who devote themselves to the public good and who take upon themselves the burdens of public office in order to be of service.

If the citizens' cooperation and their sense of responsibility are to produce the favorable results expected of them in the normal course of public life, a system of positive law is required which provides for a suitable division of the functions and organs of public authority and an effective and independent protection of citizens' rights. The rights of all individuals, families, and organizations and their practical implementation must be acknowledged, protected, and fostered,[6] together with the public duties binding on all citizens. Among these duties, it is worth mentioning the obligation to render to the state whatever material and personal services are required for the common good. Governments should take care not to put obstacles in the way of family, cultural or social groups, or of organizations and intermediate institutions, nor to hinder their lawful and constructive activity; rather, they should eagerly seek to promote such orderly activity. Citizens, on the other hand, either individually or in association, should take care not to vest too much power in public authority nor to make untimely and exaggerated demands for favors and subsidies, lessening in this way the responsible role of individuals, families, and social groups.

The growing complexity of modern situations makes it necessary for public authority to intervene more frequently in social, cultural and economic matters in order to achieve conditions more favorable to the free and effective pursuit by citizens and groups of the advancement of people's total well-being. The understanding of the relationship between socialization[7] and personal autonomy and progress will vary according to different areas and the development of peoples. However, if restrictions are imposed temporarily for the common good on the exercise of human rights, these restrictions are to be lifted as soon as possible after the situation has changed. In any case it is inhuman for public authority to fall back on totalitarian methods or dictatorship which violate the rights of persons or social groups.

Citizens should cultivate a generous and loyal spirit of patriotism, but without narrow-mindedness, so that they will always keep in mind the welfare of the entire human family which is formed into one by various kinds of links between races, peoples, and nations.

Christians must be conscious of their specific and proper role in the political community; they should be a shining example by their sense of responsibility and their dedication to the common good; they should show in practice how authority can be reconciled with freedom, personal initiative with solidarity and the needs of the social framework as a whole, and the advantages of unity with the benefits of diversity. They should recognize the legitimacy of differing points of view on the organization of worldly affairs and should show respect for the individual citizens and groups who defend their opinions by legitimate means. Political parties, for their part, must support whatever in their opinion is conducive to the common good, but must never put their own interests before the common good.

So that all citizens will be able to play their part in political affairs, civil and political education is vitally necessary for the population as a whole and for young people in particular, and must be diligently attended to. Those with a talent for the difficult yet noble art of politics,[8] or whose talents in this matter can be developed, should prepare themselves for it, and, setting aside their own convenience and material interests, they should engage in political activity. They must

combat injustice and oppression, arbitrary domination and intolerance by individuals or political parties,
and they must do so with integrity and wisdom. They
must dedicate themselves to the welfare of all in a
spirit of sincerity and fairness, of love and of the
courage demanded by political life.

The Political Community and the Church

76. It is very important, especially in a pluralist
society, to have a proper understanding of the relationship between the political community and the
church, and to distinguish clearly between the activities of Christians, acting individually or collectively in
their own name as citizens guided by the dictates of a
christian conscience, and what they do together with
their pastors in the name of the church.

The church, by reason of her role and competence,
is not identified with any political community nor is it
tied to any political system. It is at once the sign and
the safeguard of the transcendental dimension of the
human person.

The political community and the church are
autonomous and independent of each other in their
own fields. They are both at the service of the personal and social vocation of the same individuals, though
under different titles. Their service will be more efficient and beneficial to all if both institutions develop
better cooperation according to the circumstances of
place and time. For humanity's horizons are not confined to the temporal order; living in human history
they retain the fullness of their eternal calling. The
church, for its part, being founded on the love of the
Redeemer, contributes towards the spread of justice
and charity among nations and in the nations themselves. By preaching the truths of the Gospel and clar-
ifying all sectors of human activity through its teaching and the witness of its members, the church re-

spects and encourages the political freedom and responsibility of the citizens.

Since the apostles, their successors with their helpers have been given the task of proclaiming Christ, Savior of the world, to women and men, they rely in their apostolate on the power of God, who often shows forth the force of the Gospel in the weakness of its witnesses. Those who devote themselves to the ministry of God's word should employ the ways and means which are suited to the Gospel, which differ in many respects from those obtaining in the earthly city.

Nevertheless, there are close links between the things of earth and those things in the human condition which transcend the world, and the church utilizes temporal realities as often as its mission requires it. But it does not pin its hopes on privileges accorded to it by civil authority; indeed, it will give up the exercise of certain legitimate rights whenever it becomes clear that their use will compromise the sincerity of its witness, or whenever new circumstances call for a different approach. But at all times and in all places, the church should be genuinely free to preach the faith, to proclaim its teaching about society, to carry out its task among people without hindrance, and to pass moral judgments even in matters relating to politics, whenever the fundamental human rights or the salvation of souls requires it. The means, the only means, it may use are those which are in accord with the Gospel and the welfare of humanity according to the diversity of times and circumstances.

With loyalty to the Gospel in the fulfillment of its mission in the world, the church, whose duty it is to foster and elevate all that is true, all that is good, and all that is beautiful in the human community,[9] consolidates peace between peoples for the glory of God.[10]

1. See John XXIII, Encyclical *Mater et Magistra*: AAS 53 (1961), p.417.

2. See John XXIII, ibid.

3. See Rom 13:1-5.

4. See Rom 13:5.

5. See Pius XII, Christmas Message 1942: AAS 35 (1043), pp. 9-24; Christmas Message 1944: AAS 37 (1945), pp. 11-17, John XXIII, Encyclical *Pacem in Terris:* AAS 55 (1963), pp. 263, 271, 277, 278

6. See Pius XII, Radio Message, 1 June 1941: AAS 33 (1941), p. 200; John XXIII, Encyclical *Pacem in Terris:* AAS 55 (1963), pp. 273-274.

7. See John XXIII, Encyclical *Mater et Magistra:* AAS 53 (1961), p. 415-418.

8. See Pius XI, Allocution to the Directors of the Catholic University Federation: *Discorsi di Pio XI* ed. Bertetto, Torino, vol. 1 (1960), p. 743.

9. See Vatican Council II, Dogmatic Constitution on the Church, *Lumen gentium,* n. 13.

10. See Lk 2:14.

Chapter V

FOSTERING OF PEACE AND ESTABLISHMENT OF A COMMUNITY OF NATIONS

Introduction

77. In our generation, which has been marked by the persistent and severe hardships and anxiety resulting from the ravages of war and the threat of war, the whole human race faces a moment of supreme crisis in its advance towards maturity. Humanity has gradually come closer together and is everywhere more conscious of its own unity; but it will not succeed in accomplishing the task awaiting it, that is, the establishment of a truly human world for all over the entire earth, unless all devote themselves

to the cause of true peace with renewed vigor. Thus the message of the Gospel, which epitomizes the highest ideals and aspirations of humanity, throws a new light in our times when it proclaims that the advocates of peace are blessed "for they shall be called children of God" (Mt 5:9).

Accordingly, the council proposes to set down the true and noble nature of peace, to condemn the savagery of war, and to encourage Christians to cooperate with all in securing a peace based on justice and charity and in promoting the means necessary to attain it, under the help of Christ, author of peace.

Nature of Peace

78. Peace is more than the absence of war: it cannot be reduced to the maintenance of a balance of power between opposing forces nor does it arise out of despotic dominion, but it is appropriately called "the effect of righteousness" (Is 32:17). It is the fruit of that right ordering of things with which the divine founder has invested human society and which must be brought about by humanity in its thirst for an ever more perfect reign of justice. But while the common good of humanity ultimately derives from the eternal law, it depends in the concrete upon circumstances which change with time; consequently, peace will never be achieved once and for all, but must be built up continually. Since, moreover, human nature is weak and wounded by sin, the achievement of peace requires a constant effort to control the passions and unceasing vigilance by lawful authority.

But this is not enough. Peace cannot be achieved on earth unless people's welfare is safeguarded and people freely and in a spirit of mutual trust share with one another the riches of their minds and their talents. A firm determination to respect the dignity of other individuals and peoples along with the deliberate practice of friendliness are absolutely necessary for the achievement of peace. Accordingly, peace is also the fruit of love, for love goes beyond what justice can achieve.

Peace on earth, which flows from love of one's neighbor, symbolizes and has its origin in the peace of Christ who proceeds from God the Father. Christ, the Word made flesh, the prince of peace, reconciled all men and women to God by the cross, and, restoring the unity of all in one people and one body, he abolished hatred in his own flesh.[1] Having been lifted up through his resurrection he poured forth the Spirit of love into people's hearts. Therefore, all Christians are urged to speak the truth in love (see Eph 4:15) and join with all peace-loving people in pleading for peace and trying to achieve it. In the same spirit, we cannot but express our admiration for all who forgo the use of violence to vindicate their rights and have recourse to those other means of defence which are available to weaker parties, provided it can be done without detriment to the rights and duties of others and of the community.

To the extent that people are sinners, the threat of war hangs over them and will so continue until the coming of Christ; but insofar as they can vanquish sin by coming together in charity, violence itself will be vanquished and they will make these words come true:"They shall beat their swords into ploughshares, and their spears into pruning hooks; nation shall not lift up sword against nation, neither shall they learn war any more" (Is 2:4).

Section 1: Avoidance of War

Curbing the Savagery of War

79. Even though recent wars have wrought immense material and moral havoc on the world, the

devastation of battle still rages in some parts of the world. Indeed, now that every kind of weapon produced by modern science is used in war, the savagery of war threatens to lead the combatants to barbarities far surpassing those of former ages. Moreover, the complexity of the modern world and the network of relations between countries means that covert wars can be prolonged by new, insidious and subversive methods. In many cases terrorist methods are regarded as new ways of waging war.

Faced by this deplorable state of humanity the council wishes to remind people that the natural law of peoples and its universal principles still retain their binding force. The conscience of humanity firmly and ever more emphatically proclaims these principles. Any action which deliberately violates these principles and any order which commands such actions is criminal, and blind obedience cannot excuse those who carry them out. The most infamous among such activities is the rationalised and methodical extermination of an entire race, nation, or ethnic minority. These must be condemned as frightful crimes; and we cannot commend too highly the courage of those who openly and fearlessly resist those who issue orders of this kind.

On the question of warfare, there are various international conventions, signed by many countries, aimed at rendering military action and its consequences less inhuman; they deal with the treatment of wounded and interned prisoners of war and with various related questions. These agreements must be honored; indeed public authorities and specialists in these matters must do all in their power to improve these conventions and thus bring about a better and more effective curbing of the savagery of war. Moreover, it seems just that laws should make humane provision for the case of conscientious objectors who refuse to carry arms, provided they accept some other form of community service.

War, granted, has not ceased to be part of the human scene. As long as the danger of war persists and there is no international authority with the necessary competence and power, governments cannot be denied the right of lawful self-defense, once all peaceful efforts have failed. State leaders and all who share the burdens of public administration have the duty to defend the interests of their people and to conduct such grave matters with a deep sense of responsibility. However, it is one thing to wage a war of self-defense; it is quite a different matter to seek to conquer another nation. The possession of war potential does not justify the use of force for political or military objectives. Nor does the mere fact that war has unfortunately broken out mean that all is fair between the warring parties.

All those who enter the military service in loyalty to their country should look upon themselves as the custodians of the security and freedom of their people; and when they carry out their duty properly, they are contributing to the maintenance of peace.

Total Warfare

80. The proliferation of scientific weapons has immeasurably magnified the horror and wickedness of war. Warfare conducted with such weapons can inflict immense and indiscriminate havoc which goes far beyond the bounds of legitimate defense. Indeed, if the kind of weapons now stocked in the arsenals of the great powers were to be employed to the fullest, the result would be the almost complete reciprocal slaughter of one side by the other, not to speak of the widespread devastation that would follow in the world and the deadly after-effects resulting from the use of such weapons.

All these factors force us to undertake a completely fresh appraisal of war.[2] People of the present generation should realize that they will have to render an account of their warlike behavior; the destiny of generations to come depends largely on the decisions they make today.

With these considerations in mind, the council, endorsing the condemnations of total warfare issued by recent popes,[3] declares: Every act of war directed to the indiscriminate destruction of whole cities or vast areas with their inhabitants is a crime against God and humanity, which merits firm and unequivocal condemnation.

The hazards peculiar to modern warfare consist in the fact that they expose those possessing recently developed weapons to the risk of perpetrating crimes like these and, by an inexorable chain of events, of urging people to even worse acts of atrocity. To obviate the possibility of this happening at any time in the future, the bishops of the world gathered together to implore everyone, especially government leaders and military advisers, to give unceasing consideration to their immense responsibilities before God and before the whole human race.

The Arms Race

81. Undoubtedly, weapons are not built up merely for use in wartime. Since the defensive strength of any nation is thought to depend on its capacity for immediate retaliation, the stockpiling of arms which grows from year to year serves, in a way hitherto unthought of, as a deterrent to potential attackers. Many people look upon this as the most effective way known at the present time for maintaining some sort of peace among nations.

Whatever one may think of this form of deterrent, people are convinced that the arms race, which quite a few countries have entered, is no infallible way of maintaining real peace and that the resulting so-called balance of power is no sure and genuine path to achieving it. Rather than eliminating the causes of war, the arms race serves only to aggravate the position. As long as extravagant sums of money are poured into the development of new weapons, it is impossible to devote adequate aid in tackling the misery which prevails at the present day in the world. Instead of eradicating international conflict once and for all, the contagion is spreading to other parts of the world. New approaches, based on reformed attitudes, will have to be made in order to remove this stumbling block, to free the earth from its pressing anxieties, and give back to the world a genuine peace.

Therefore, we declare once again: the arms race is one of the greatest curses on the human race and the harm it inflicts on the poor is more than can be endured. And there is every reason to fear that if it continues it will bring forth those lethal disasters which are already in preparation. Warned by the possibility of the catastrophes which humanity has created, let us profit by the respite we now enjoy, thanks to the divine favor, to take stock of our responsibilities and find ways of resolving controversies in a manner worthy of human beings. Providence urgently demands of us that we free ourselves from the age-old bondage of war. If we refuse to make this effort, there is no knowing where we will be led on the fatal path we have taken.

Total Outlawing of War:
International Action to Prevent War

82. It is our clear duty to spare no effort to achieve the complete outlawing of war by international agreement. This goal, of course, requires the establishment of a universally acknowledged public autho-

rity vested with the effective power to ensure security for all, regard for justice, and respect for law. But before this desirable authority can be constituted, it is necessary for existing international bodies to devote themselves resolutely to the discovery of better means of achieving common security. But since peace must be born of mutual trust between peoples instead of being forced on nations through dread of arms, all must work to put an end to the arms race and make a real beginning of disarmament, not unilaterally indeed but at an equal rate on all sides, on the basis of agreements and backed up by genuine and effective guarantees.[4]

In the meantime, one must not underestimate the efforts already made or now under way to eliminate the danger of war. On the contrary, support should be given to the good will of numerous individuals who are making every effort to eliminate the havoc of war; those people, although burdened by the weighty responsibilities of their high office, are motivated by a consciousness of their very grave obligations, even though they cannot ignore the complexity of the present situation. We must beseech the Lord to give them the strength to tackle with perseverance and carry out with courage this task of supreme love for humanity which is the resolute building up of a lasting peace. In our day, this work demands that they enlarge their thoughts and their spirit beyond the confines of their own country, that they put aside nationalistic selfishness and ambitions to dominate other nations, and that they cultivate deep reverence for the whole of humanity which is painstakingly advancing towards greater maturity.

The problems of peace and disarmament have been examined carefully and ceaselessly and there have been international conferences on the subject; these are to be considered the first steps towards the solution of such important questions and must be further pursued with even greater insistence, with a view to obtaining concrete results in the future. But people should beware of leaving these problems to a few people while being unconcerned about their own attitudes. Governments, who are at once the guardians of their own people and the promoters of the welfare of the whole world, rely to a large extent on public opinion and public attitudes. Their peace-making efforts will be in vain, as long as people are divided and at odds with each other because of hostility, contempt and distrust, or because of racial hatred and ideological obduracy. Hence there is a very urgent need for re-education and a new orientation of public opinion. Those engaged in the work of education, especially education of youth, and the people who mold public opinion, should regard it as their most important task to instill peaceful sentiments in people's minds. Every one of us needs a change of heart; we must set our gaze on the whole world and look to those tasks we can all perform together in order to bring about the betterment of our race.

But let us not be buoyed up with false hope. For unless animosity and hatred are put aside, and firm, honest agreements about world peace are concluded, humanity may, in spite of the wonders of modern science, go from the grave crisis of the present day to that dismal hour, when the only peace it will experience will be the dread peace of death. The church, however, living with these anxieties, even as it makes these statements, has not lost hope. It intends to propose to our age over and over again, in season and out of season, the apostle's message: "Behold, now is the acceptable time" for a change of heart; "behold, now is the day of salvation."[5]

Section 2: Establishment of an
International Community

Causes of Discord: Remedies

83. If peace is to be established, the first condition is to root out those causes of discord between people which lead to wars, especially injustice. Much discord is caused by excessive economic inequalities and by delays in correcting them. Other causes are a desire for power and contempt for people, and at a deeper level, envy, distrust, pride, and other selfish passions. People cannot put up with such an amount of disorder; the result is that, even in the absence of war, the world is constantly beset by strife and violence. Similar evils bedevil relations between nations. If these are to be remedied or prevented and if unlimited recourse to violence is to be restrained, it is of the greatest importance that international bodies work more effectively and more resolutely to coordinate their efforts. And finally, people should work unsparingly to set up bodies to promote peace.

The Community of Nations and
International Organizations

84. Close ties of dependence between individuals and peoples are on the increase world-wide nowadays; consequently, to facilitate effective and successful work for the universal common good the community of nations needs to establish an order suited to its present responsibilities, especially its obligations towards the many areas of the world where intolerable want still prevails. To reach this goal, organizations of the international community, for their part, should set about providing for people's various needs both in the areas of social life covering food, hygiene, education and employment and, in certain particular situations here and there, seeing to the welfare of devel-

oping countries, to alleviate the miseries of refugees dispersed throughout the world, and to assist migrants and their families.

Existing international and regional organizations certainly deserve well of the human race. They represent the first attempts to lay the foundations on an international level for a community of all of humanity to try to solve the very serious problems of our times, and specifically to encourage progress everywhere and to prevent all wars. The church is glad to view the spirit of true community existing in all spheres between Christians and non-Christians as it seeks to intensify its untiring efforts to alleviate human misery.

International Cooperation in Economic Matters

85. The present solidarity of humanity calls for greater international cooperation in economic matters. Indeed, although nearly all peoples have achieved political independence, they are far from being free from excessive inequalities and from undue dependency and far from being immune to serious internal difficulties.

The development of a nation depends on human and financial resources. The citizens of every nation must be prepared by education and professional training to undertake the various tasks of economic and social life. This involves the help of experts from abroad, who, while they are the bearers of assistance, should not behave as overlords but as helpers and fellow workers. Material aid for developing nations will not be forthcoming unless there is a profound change in the prevailing conventions of commerce today. Other forms of aid from affluent nations should take the form of grants, loans, or investments; they should be given in a spirit of generosity and without greed on one side, and accepted with complete honesty on the other.

The establishment of an authentic economic order on a worldwide scale can come about only by abolishing profiteering, nationalistic ambitions, desire for political domination, schemes of military strategy, and intrigues for spreading and imposing ideologies. Different economic and social systems have been suggested; it is to be hoped that experts will find in them a common basis for a just world commerce; it will come about if all people forgo their own prejudices and show themselves ready to enter into sincere dialogue.

Some Useful Norms

86. The following norms seem useful for such cooperation:

(a) Developing nations should be firmly convinced that their express and unequivocal aim is the total human development of their citizens. They should not forget that progress has its roots and its strength before all else in the work and talent of their citizens. They should not forget that progress is based, not only on foreign aid, but on the full exploitation of native resources and on the development of their own talents and traditions. Those who are in positions of influence should give outstanding example in this matter.

(b) The most important task of the affluent nations is to help developing nations to meet their obligations. Accordingly, they should undertake within their own confines the spiritual and material adjustments which are needed for the establishment of worldwide cooperation. They should look to the welfare of the weaker and poorer nations in business dealings with them, for the revenues the latter make from the sale of home-produced goods are needed for their own support.

(c) It is for the international community to coordinate and stimulate development, but in such a way as to distribute with the maximum fairness and efficiency the resources set aside for this purpose It is also its task to organize economic affairs on a world scale, without transgressing the principle of subsidiarity, so that business will be conducted according to the norms of justice. Organizations should be set up to promote and regulate international commerce, especially with less developed nations, in order to compensate for losses resulting from excessive inequality of power between nations. This kind of organization accompanied by technical, cultural, and financial aid, should provide developing nations with all that is necessary for them to achieve adequate economic success.

(d) In many instances there is a pressing need to reassess economic and social structures, but caution is called for with regard to proposed solutions which may be untimely, especially those which offer material advantage while militating against people's spiritual nature and advancement. For "one does not live on bread alone but on every word that comes from the mouth of God" (Mt 4:4). Every branch of the human race possesses in itself and in its nobler traditions some part of the spiritual treasure which God has entrusted to humanity, even though many do not know its source.

87. International cooperation is vitally necessary in the case of those peoples who very often in the midst of many difficulties are faced with the special problems arising out of rapid increases in population. There is a pressing need to harness the full and willing cooperation of all, particularly of the richer countries, in order to explore how the necessary food and education can be furnished and shared with the entire human community. Some peoples could im-

prove their standard of living considerably if they were properly trained to substitute new techniques of agricultural production for antiquated methods and adapt them prudently to their own situation. The social order would also be improved and a fairer distribution of land ownership would be assured.

A government has, assuredly, in the matter of the population of its country, its own rights and duties, within the limits of its proper competence, for instance as regards social and family legislation, the migration of country-dwellers to the city, and information concerning the state and needs of the nation. Nowadays some people are gravely disturbed by this problem; it is to be hoped that there will be catholic experts in these matters, particularly in universities, who will diligently study the problems and pursue their researches further.

Since there is a widespread opinion that the population expansion of the world, or at least of some particular countries, should be kept in check by all possible means and by every kind of intervention by public authority, the council exhorts all people to beware of solutions, whether advocated publicly or privately or imposed at any time, which transgress the natural law. Because in virtue of the inalienable right to marriage and the procreation of children, the decision regarding the number of children depends on the judgment of the parents and is in no way to be left to the public authority. Since the parents' judgment presupposes a properly formed conscience, it is of great importance that all should have an opportunity to cultivate a genuinely human sense of responsibility which will take account of the circumstances of time and place and will respect the divine law; to attain this goal a change for the better must take place in educational and social conditions. Above all, religious formation, or at least full moral training, must be available. People should be discreetly informed of scientific advances in research into methods of birth regulation, whenever the value of these methods has been thoroughly proved and their conformity with the moral order established.

Role of Christians in International Aid

88. Christians should willingly and wholeheartedly support the establishment of an international order that includes a genuine respect for legitimate freedom and amity towards all. It is all the more urgent, now that the greater part of the world is in such poverty: it is as if Christ himself were appealing to the charity of his followers through the mouths of these poor people. Let us not be guilty of the scandal whereby some nations, most of whose citizens bear the name of Christians, enjoy an abundance of riches, while others lack the necessities of life and suffer from hunger, disease, and all kinds of misery. For the spirit of poverty and charity is the glory and witness of the church of Christ.

We must praise and assist those Christians, especially those young Christians, who volunteer their services to help other individuals and nations. Indeed it is the duty of the entire people of God, following the teaching and example of the bishops, to alleviate the hardships of our times within the limits of its means, giving generously, as was the ancient custom of the church, not merely out of what is superfluous but also out of necessities.

Without being rigid and altogether uniform in the matter, methods of collection and distribution of aid should be systematically conducted in dioceses, nations, and throughout the world and in collaboration with suitable institutes.

Effective Presence of the Church in the International Community

89. The church, in preaching the Gospel to everyone and dispensing the treasures of grace in accordance with its divine mission, makes a contribution to the consolidation of peace over the whole world and helps to strengthen the foundations of communion among people and nations. This it does by imparting knowledge of the divine and the natural law. Accordingly, the church ought to be present in the community of peoples, to foster and stimulate cooperation among them; motivated by the sole desire of being of service to all, it contributes both through official channels and through the full and sincere collaboration of all Christians. This goal will be more effectively achieved if all the faithful are conscious of their responsibility as people and as Christians and work in their own environments to stimulate generous cooperation with the international community. In their religious and civil education special attention should be given to the training of youth in this matter.

Role of Christians in International Organizations

90. An outstanding example of international activity on the part of Christians is their contribution, either individually or collectively, to organizations set up or on the way to being set up to foster cooperation between nations. Different catholic international bodies can assist the community of nations on the way to peace, sisterhood and brotherhood; these bodies should be strengthened by increasing the number of their trained members, by increasing the subsidies they need so badly, and by suitable coordination of their forces. Nowadays, efficiency of action and the need for dialogue call for concerted effort. Organizations of this kind, moreover, contribute more than a little to the instilling of a feeling of universali-

ty, which is certainly appropriate for Catholics, and to the formation of truly worldwide solidarity and responsibility.

Finally, it is to be hoped that, in order to fulfil their role in the international community properly, Catholics will seek to cooperate actively and positively with our separated sisters and brothers, who profess the charity of the Gospel along with us, and also with all who long for true peace.

Taking into account the immensity of the hardships which still afflict a large part of humanity, and with a view to fostering everywhere the justice and love of Christ for the poor, the council suggests that it would be most opportune to create some organization of the universal church whose task it would be to encourage the catholic community to promote the progress in areas which are in want and foster social justice between nations.

1. See Eph 2:16; Col 1:20-22.

2. See John XXIII, Encyclical *Pacem in Terris:* AAS 55 (1963), p. 291: "Therefore in this age of ours, which prides itself on its atomic power, it is irrational to think that war is a proper way to obtain justice for violated rights."

3. See Pius XII, Allocution, 30 Sept. 1954: AAS 46 (1954), p. 589; Christmas Message 1954: AAS 47 (1955), pp 15 ff.; John XXIII, Encyclical *Pacem in Terris:* AAS 55 (1963), pp. 286- 291; Paul VI, Address to the United Nations, 4 Oct. 1965: AAS 57 (1965), pp. 877-885.

4. See John XXIII, Encyclical *Pacem in Terris*, where the reduction of arms is treated: AAS 55 (1963), p. 287.

5. See 2 Cor 6:2.

CONCLUSION

ROLE OF INDIVIDUAL CHRISTIANS
AND OF LOCAL CHURCHES

91. Drawn from the treasury of the church's teachings, the proposals of this council are intended for all people, whether they believe in God or whether they do not explicitly acknowledge God; they are intended to help them to a keener awareness of their own destiny, to fashion a world better suited to the surpassing dignity of humanity, to strive for a more deeply rooted sense of universal sisterhood and brotherhood, and to meet the pressing appeals of our times with a generous and common effort of love.

Faced with the wide variety of situations and forms of human culture in the world, this conciliar program is deliberately general on many points; indeed, while the teaching presented is that already accepted in the church, it will have to be pursued further and amplified because it often deals with matters which are subject to continual development. Still, we have based our proposals on the word of God and the spirit of the Gospel. Hence we entertain the hope that many of our suggestions will succeed in effectively assisting all people, especially after they have been adapted to different nations and mentalities and put into practice by the faithful under the direction of their pastors.

Dialogue
92. In virtue of its mission to enlighten the whole world with the message of the Gospel and to gather together in one spirit all women and men of every nation, race and culture, the church shows itself as a sign of that amity which renders possible sincere dialogue and strengthens it.

Such a mission requires us first of all to create in the church itself mutual esteem, reverence and harmony, and to acknowledge all legitimate diversity; in this way all who constitute the one people of God will be able to engage in ever more fruitful dialogue, whether they are pastors or other members of the faithful. For the ties which unite the faithful together are stronger than those which separate them: let there be unity in what is necessary, freedom in what is doubtful, and charity in everything.[1]

At the same time our thoughts go out to those brothers and sisters and those communities who are not yet living in full communion with us; yet we are united by our worship of the Father, the Son, and the holy Spirit and the bonds of love. We are also mindful that the unity of Christians is today awaited and desired by many non-believers. For the more this unity is realized in truth and charity under the powerful impulse of the holy Spirit, the more will it be a harbinger of unity and peace throughout the whole world. Let us, then, join our forces, in ways more suitable and effective today for achieving this lofty goal, and let us pattern ourselves daily more and more after the spirit of the Gospel and work together in a spirit of brotherhood and sisterhood to serve the human family which has been called to become in Christ Jesus the family of the children of God.

Our thoughts also go out to all who acknowledge God and who preserve precious religious and human elements in their traditions; it is our hope that frank dialogue will spur us all on to receive the impulses of the Spirit with fidelity and act upon them with alacrity.

For our part, our eagerness for such dialogue, conducted with appropriate discretion and leading to truth by way of love alone, excludes nobody; we would like to include those who respect outstanding human values without realizing who the author of those values is, as well as those who oppose the church and persecute it in various ways. Since God the Father is the beginning and the end of all things, we are all called to be brothers and sisters; we ought to work together without violence and without deceit to build up the world in a spirit of genuine peace.

A World to be Built Up and Brought to Fulfillment

93. Mindful of the words of the Lord: "By this all will know that you are my disciples, if you have love for one another" (Jn. 13:35), Christians can yearn for nothing more ardently than to serve the people of this age successfully with increasing generosity. Holding loyally to the Gospel, enriched by its resources, and joining forces with all who love and practice justice, they have shouldered a weighty task here on earth and they must render an account of it to him who will judge all people on the last day. Not everyone who says "Lord, Lord," will enter the kingdom of heaven, but those who do the will of the Father[2] and who courageously set to work. It is the Father's will that we should recognize Christ our brother in the persons of all men and women and should love them with an active love, in word and in deed, thus bearing witness to the truth; and it is his will that we should share with others the mystery of his heavenly love. In this way people all over the world will awaken to a lively hope, the gift of the holy Spirit, that they will one day be admitted to the haven of surpassing peace and happiness in their homeland radiant with the glory of the Lord.

"Now to him who by the power at work within us is able to do far more abundantly than all that we ask or think, to him be glory in the church and in Christ Jesus to all generations, for ever and ever. Amen" (Eph 3:20-21).

1. See John XXIII, Encyclical *Ad Petri Cathedram,* 29 June 1959: AAS 55 (1959), p. 513.
2. See Mt 7:21.

DECREE ON THE PASTORAL OFFICE OF BISHOPS IN THE CHURCH[a]

Christus Dominus
28 October, 1965

Introduction

1. Christ the Lord, the Son of the living God, came to redeem his people from their sins[1] that all humanity might be sanctified. Having been sent by the Father, he in turn sent his apostles[2] whom he sanctified by conferring on them the holy Spirit so that they also might glorify the Father on earth and procure humanity's salvation "for the building up of the body of Christ" (Eph 4:12) which is the church.

2. In this church of Christ the Roman pontiff, as the successor of Peter, to whom Christ entrusted the care of his sheep and his lambs, has been granted by God supreme, full, immediate and universal power in the care of souls. As pastor of all the faithful his mission is to promote the common good of the universal church and the particular good of all the churches. He is therefore endowed with the primacy of ordinary power over all the churches.

The bishops also have been designated by the holy Spirit to take the place of the apostles as pastors of souls[3] and, together with the supreme pontiff and subject to his authority, they are commissioned to perpetuate the work of Christ, the eternal Pastor.[4] For

Christ commanded the apostles and their successors and gave them the power to teach all nations, to sanctify people in truth and to give them spiritual nourishment. By virtue, therefore, of the holy Spirit who has been given to them, bishops have been constituted true and authentic teachers of the faith, pontiffs and pastors.[5]

3. United in one college or body for the instruction and pastoral government of the universal church, the bishops, in shared solicitude for all the churches, exercise their episcopal function, which was given them at their episcopal consecration[6] in communion with the supreme pontiff and subject to his authority. Each of them exercises this function individually in that portion of the Lord's flock which has been entrusted to him, each bishop having responsibility for the particular church assigned to him. On occasion a number of bishops will cooperate to provide for the needs common to different churches.

Accordingly the sacred synod, having regard to the conditions of human society which have brought about a new order of things, has promulgated the following decrees in order to determine more exactly the pastoral functions of bishops.[7]

a. Translated by Matthew Dillon, O.S.B., Edward O'Leary, O.P, revised by AF. Paul VI's Apostolic Letter, *Ecclesiae Sanctae,* which contains detailed directives for implementing this decree, is to be found in *Vatican Collection,* vol 1, pp. 591 ff.

1. See Mt 1:21.

2. See Jn 20:21.

3. See Vatican I, fourth session, part 1 of Dogmatic Constitution on the Church of Christ, *Pastor aeternus,* ch. 3: Denz. 1828 (3061).

4. See Vatican I, fourth session, Introduction to Dogmatic Constitution on the Church of Christ, *Pastor aeternus:* Denz. 1821 (3050).

5. See Vatican II, Dogmatic Constitution on the Church, *Lumen gentium,* ch. 3, nn. 21, 24, 25.

6. See Vatican II, Dogmatic Constitution on the Church, *Lumen gentium,* ch. 3, n. 21.

7. See John XXIII, Apostolic constitution *Humanae Salutis,* Dec. 25, 1961: AAS 54 (1962) p. 6.

Chapter I

THE BISHOPS IN RELATION TO THE UNIVERSAL CHURCH

I. The Role of the Bishops in the Universal Church

4. The bishops, by virtue of their sacramental consecration and their hierarchical communion with the head of the college and its other members, are constituted members of the episcopal body.[1] "The order of bishops is the successor to the college of the apostles in their role as teachers and pastors, and in it the apostolic college is perpetuated. Together with its head, the Supreme Pontiff, and never apart from him, it is the subject of supreme and full authority over the universal church; but this power cannot be exercised without the consent of the Roman Pontiff."[2] This authority "is exercised in a solemn way in an ecumenical council."[3] Accordingly, the sacred synod decrees that all bishops who are members of the episcopal college have the right to take part in an ecumenical council. "This same collegiate power can be exercised in union with the pope by the bishops residing in different parts of the world, provided the head of the college summon them to collegiate action, or at least approve or freely admit the corporate action of the unassembled bishops, so that a truly collegiate action may result."[4]

5. Selected from different regions of the world in accordance with criteria determined or to be determined by the Roman pontiff, bishops will render to the supreme Pastor a more effective auxiliary service in a council which will be known by the special name of synod of bishops.[5] Since this council will be representative of the entire catholic episcopate, it will reflect the participation of all the bishops in hierarchical

communion in the care of the universal church.[6]

6. Bishops, as legitimate successors of the apostles and members of the episcopal college, should appreciate that they are closely united to each other and should be solicitous for all the churches. By divine institution and by virtue of their apostolic office, they all share joint responsibility for the church.[7]

They should be especially solicitous for those parts of the world in which the word of God has not yet been proclaimed or in which, mainly on account of the scarcity of priests, the faithful are in danger of abandoning the practice of the christian life or even of losing the faith itself. Bishops should, therefore, do their utmost to ensure that the work of evangelization and the apostolate are fully supported and promoted by the faithful. It should, moreover, be their special care that suitable priests, as well as lay and religious auxiliaries, be trained for those missions and regions where there are insufficient priests. They should arrange also, as far as it is possible, that some of their priests should go to these missions or dioceses to exercise the sacred ministry there, either permanently or for a fixed period.

Furthermore, bishops should bear it in mind that in the expenditure of ecclesiastical resources they must take into account the needs not only of their own dioceses but of other individual churches, since they too form part of the one church of Christ. Let it be their care also to give help according to their resources when other dioceses or regions are afflicted by disaster.

7. Above all, they should extend their brotherly care to those bishops who suffer calumny and hardship for the name of Christ, who are in prison or prevented from exercising their ministry. They should display an active fraternal interest in them so that their sufferings may be lessened and alleviated by the prayers

and help of their brethren.

II. Bishops and the Apostolic See

8. (a) Bishops, as successors of the apostles, enjoy as of right in the dioceses assigned to them all ordinary, special and immediate power which is necessary for the exercise of their pastoral office, but always without prejudice to the Roman pontiff's right, by virtue of his office, to reserve certain matters to himself or to some other authority.

(b) Individual diocesan bishops have the power to dispense from the general law of the church in particular cases those faithful over whom they normally exercise authority. It must, however, be to their spiritual benefit and may not cover a matter which has been specially reserved to the supreme authority of the church.

9. In exercising his supreme, full and immediate authority over the universal church the Roman pontiff employs the various departments of the Roman Curia, which act in his name and by his authority for the good of the churches and in the service of the sacred pastors. It is very much the desire of the Fathers of the sacred council that these departments, which have indeed rendered excellent service to the Roman pontiff and to the pastors of the church, should be reorganized in a manner more appropriate to the needs of our time and of different regions and rites, especially in regard to their number, their titles, their competence, their procedures and how they coordinate their activities. It is also very much their wish that the functions of papal legates be more precisely determined, keeping in mind the pastoral role proper to bishops.

10. Furthermore, since these departments have been instituted for the good of the universal church it is desirable that their members, officials and consul-

tors, as well as papal legates, may be chosen, as far as it is possible, on a more representative basis, so that the offices or central agencies of the church may have a truly universal ethos. It is also recommended that more bishops, especially diocesan bishops, be co-opted to membership of these departments. They will be better able to inform the supreme pontiff on the thinking, the hopes and the needs of all the churches. Finally, the Fathers of the council judge that it would be most advantageous if these departments were to have more frequent recourse to the advice of lay people distinguished for virtue, knowledge and experience so that they also may have an appropriate role in the affairs of the church.

1. See Vatican II, Dogmatic Constitution on the Church, *Lumen gentium,* ch 3, n. 22.
2. Ibid.
3. Ibid.
4. Ibid.
5. See Paul VI, Motu proprio *Apostolica Sollicitudo,* 15 Sept. 1965: AAS 57 57 (1965) pp. 775-780.
6. See Vatican II, op. cit., n. 27-28..
7. See Pius XII, Encyclical *Fidei Donum,* 21 Apr. 1957: AAS 49 (1957) p. 237. See also Benedict XV, Apostolic letter *Maximum Illud,* 30 Nov. 1919: AAS 11 (1919) p. 440; Pius XI, Encyclical *Rerum Ecclesiae,* 28 Feb. 1926: AAS 18 (1926) pp. 68 ff.

Chapter II

BISHOPS IN RELATION TO THEIR OWN CHURCHES OR DIOCESES

I. Diocesan Bishops

11. A diocese is a section of God's people entrusted to a bishop to be guided by him with the assistance of

his clergy so that, loyal to its pastor and formed by him into one community in the holy Spirit through the Gospel and the Eucharist, it constitutes one particular church in which the one, holy, catholic and apostolic church of Christ is truly present and active.

Individual bishops to whose charge particular dioceses are committed, under the authority of the supreme pontiff, care for their flocks in the name of God, as their proper, ordinary and immediate pastors, teaching, sanctifying and governing them. They should, however, recognize the rights which are conferred by law on patriarchs or other hierarchical authorities.[1]

Bishops should devote themselves to their apostolic office as witnesses of Christ to all. They should not confine their concern to those who already acknowledge the prince of pastors but should also devote their energies wholeheartedly to those who have strayed in any way from the path of truth or who have no knowledge of the gospel of Christ and of his saving mercy. Their aim should be that ultimately all may walk "in all goodness, justice and truth." (Eph 5:9)

12. Bishops, in the exercise of their teaching office, are to proclaim to humanity the gospel of Christ. This is one of their principal duties.[2] Fortified by the Spirit they should call people to belief or should strengthen them when they already have a living faith. They should expound to them the mystery of Christ in its entirety: that is, all those truths ignorance of which means ignorance of Christ. They should also teach them the divinely revealed manner of giving glory to God and thus attaining eternal happiness.[3]

They should show that worldly things and human institutions are ordered, according to the plan of God the Creator, towards the salvation of humanity, and that they can therefore make no small contribution to the building up of the body of Christ.

Let them explain also how high a value, according to the Church's teaching, should be placed on the human person, on personal liberty and bodily life itself; how highly we should value the family, its unity and stability, the procreation and education of children; human society with its laws and professions, its labor and leisure, its arts and technology, its poverty and affluence. They should also explain how to set about solving the very serious problems concerning the ownership, increase and just distribution of material goods, concerning peace and war, and the sisterly and brotherly coexistence of all peoples.[4]

13. Bishops should present Christ's teaching in a manner relevant to the needs of the times, providing a response to those difficulties and problems which people find especially distressing and burdensome. They should also safeguard this doctrine, teaching the faithful themselves to defend and spread it. In presenting this doctrine they should proclaim the maternal solicitude of the church for all, whether they be Catholics or not, and should be especially solicitous for the poor and weaker folk whom the Lord has commissioned them to evangelize.

Since it is the Church's job to communicate with the human society in which it lives[5] the bishops should make it their special care to approach people and to initiate and promote dialogue with them. These discussions on religious matters should be marked by clarity of expression as well as by humility and courtesy, so that truth may be combined with charity, and understanding with love. The discussions should likewise be characterized by due prudence allied, however, to confidence. This, by encouraging friendship, is conducive to a union of minds.[6]

Bishops should also employ the various methods available nowadays for proclaiming christian doctrine. These are, first of all, preaching and catechetical instruction, which always hold pride of place. There is also doctrinal instruction in schools and universities, conferences and meetings of every kind. Finally, there are public statements made by way of comment on events, as well as the press and other media of communication, all of which should be used for the promulgation of the gospel of Christ.[7]

14. Bishops should be especially concerned about catechetical instruction. Its function is to develop in women and men a living, explicit and active faith, enlightened by doctrine. It should be very carefully imparted, not only to children and adolescents but also to young people and even to adults. In imparting this instruction, the teachers must observe an order and method suited not only to the matter in hand but also to the character, the ability, the age and the lifestyle of their audience. This instruction should be based on holy scripture, tradition, liturgy, and on the teaching authority and life of the church.

They should, furthermore, ensure that catechists are adequately prepared for their task, being well instructed in the doctrine of the church and possessing both a practical and theoretical knowledge of the laws of psychology and of educational method.

They should take steps to reestablish or to improve the adult catechumenate.

15. In exercising their sanctifying mission bishops should be mindful that they have been chosen from among the people of God and appointed for their sake in what pertains to God, to offer gifts and sacrifices for sins. It is the bishops who enjoy the fullness of the sacrament of orders, and both priests and deacons are dependent on them in the exercise of their power. The former, in order that they may be prudent cooperators with the episcopal order, have been consecrated true priests of the New Testament; deacons, having been ordained for the ministry, serve the peo-

ple of God in union with the bishop and his clergy. It is therefore bishops who are the principal dispensers of the mysteries of God, and it is their function to control, promote and protect the entire liturgical life of the church entrusted to them.[8]

They should therefore see to it that the faithful know and live the paschal mystery more deeply through the Eucharist, forming one closely-knit body, united by the charity of Christ;[9] "devoting themselves to prayer and the ministry of the word" (Acts 6:4).[10] They should aim to make of one mind in prayer all who are entrusted to their care, and to ensure their advancement in grace through the reception of the sacraments, and that they become faithful witnesses to the Lord.

Since their task is to make people perfect, bishops should be zealous in promoting the holiness of their clergy, religious and laity according to the vocation of each individual,[11] remembering that they themselves are obliged to give an example of sanctity in charity, humility and simplicity of life. Let them so sanctify the churches entrusted to them that the ethos of the universal church of Christ may be fully reflected in them. They should, therefore, make every effort to foster vocations to the priesthood and to the religious life, and should encourage missionary vocations especially.

16. In exercising their office of fathers and pastors, bishops should be with their people as those who serve,[12] as good shepherds who know their sheep and whose sheep know them, as true fathers who excel in their love and solicitude for all, to whose divinely conferred authority all readily submit. They should so unite and mold their flock into one family that all, conscious of their duties, may live and act as one in charity.

In order to accomplish these things effectively,

bishops, "being ready for every good work" (2 Tim 2:21) and "enduring all things for the sake of the elect" (2 Tim 2:10) should arrange their own lives to meet the needs of the times. Their priests, who assume a part of their duties and concerns, and who give themselves to them daily so zealously, should be the objects of their particular affection. They should regard them as sons and friends.[13] They should always be ready to listen to them, in an atmosphere of mutual trust, thus facilitating the pastoral work of the entire diocese.

Bishops should be solicitous for the welfare — spiritual, intellectual, and material — of their priests, so that they may live holy and pious lives, and exercise a faithful and fruitful ministry. With this end in view they should encourage courses and arrange for special conferences for their priests from time to time. These could take the form of extended retreats for the renewal of their spiritual lives or courses intended to deepen their knowledge of ecclesiastical studies, especially of sacred scripture and theology, of the more important social questions, or of new kinds of pastoral ministry. Bishops should be compassionate and helpful to those priests who are in any kind of danger or who have failed in some respect.

In order to be able to provide for the welfare of the faithful as their individual circumstances demand, they should try to keep themselves informed of their needs in the social circumstances in which they live. To this end they should employ suitable methods, especially social research. They should be solicitous for all, whatever their age, condition or nationality, whether they are natives, visitors or foreign immigrants. In exercising this ministry they should ensure that the faithful are duly involved in church affairs; they should recognize their right and duty to play their part in building up the mystical body of Christ.

Bishops should be friendly in their dealings with the separated sisters and brothers and should urge the faithful also to exercise all kindness and charity in their regard, encouraging ecumenism as it is understood by the church.[14] The non-baptized also should be the object of their solicitude so that on them too may shine the charity of Christ of whom bishops are the witnesses before all humanity.

17. The various forms of the apostolate should be encouraged. Close collaboration and the coordination of all the apostolic works under the direction of the bishop should be promoted in the diocese as a whole or in its different parts. Thus, all the undertakings and organizations, whether their object be catechetical, missionary, charitable, social, familial, educational, or any other pastoral purpose, will act together in harmony, and the unity of the diocese will be more clearly evident.

Care should be taken to remind the faithful of their obligation to promote the apostolate according to their state of life and ability, and they should be urged to participate in or assist the various works of the lay apostolate, especially Catholic Action. Those associations also should be inaugurated or encouraged which have, either directly or indirectly, a supernatural object such as the attainment of a more perfect life, the preaching of the gospel of Christ to all, the promotion of christian doctrine or of public worship, the pursuit of social aims, or the practice of works of piety or charity.

The forms of the apostolate should be duly adapted to the needs of the times, taking into account the human conditions, not merely spiritual and moral but also social, demographic and economic. This can be done effectively with the help of social and religious research conducted by institutes of pastoral sociology, the establishment of which is strongly recommended.

18. Special concern should be shown for those members of the faithful who, on account of their way of life are not adequately catered for by the ordinary pastoral ministry of the parochial clergy or are entirely deprived of it. These include the many migrants, exiles and refugees, sailors and airmen, itinerants and others of this kind. Suitable pastoral methods should be developed to provide for the spiritual life of people on holidays.

Conferences of bishops, and especially national conferences, should give careful consideration to the more important questions relating to such groups. By common agreement and combined efforts they should issue appropriate directives and devise suitable ways of catering for their spiritual needs. In doing this they should give due consideration especially to the norms determined,[15] or to be determined, by the holy See, adapting them to their own times, places and people.

19. In the exercise of their apostolic function, which is directed towards the salvation of souls, bishops enjoy as of right full and perfect freedom and independence from all civil authority. It is, therefore, unlawful to obstruct them directly or indirectly in the exercise of their ecclesiastical office or to prevent them from communicating freely with the apostolic see and other ecclesiastical authorities or with their subjects.

In fact, the sacred pastors in devoting themselves to the spiritual care of their flock are in fact promoting social and civil progress and prosperity. With this end in view they cooperate actively with the public authorities in a manner consonant with their office and fitting for bishops, enjoining obedience to just laws and prescribing reverence for legitimately constituted authority.

20. Since the apostolic office of bishops was instituted by Christ the Lord and is directed to a spiritual and supernatural end, the holy ecumenical council asserts that the competent ecclesiastical authority has the proper, special, and, as of right, exclusive power to appoint and install bishops. Therefore in order to safeguard the liberty of the church and the better and more effectively to promote the good of the faithful, it is the desire of the holy council that for the future no rights or privileges be conceded to the civil authorities in regard to the election, nomination or presentation to bishoprics. The civil authorities in question, whose good will towards the church the sacred synod gratefully acknowledges and fully appreciates, are respectfully asked to initiate discussions with the holy See with the object of freely waiving the aforesaid rights and privileges which they at present enjoy by agreement or custom.

21. As the pastoral office of bishops is so important and onerous, diocesan bishops and others whose juridical position corresponds to theirs are earnestly requested to resign from their office if on account of advanced age or from any other grave cause they become less able to carry out their duties. This they should do on their own initiative or when invited to do so by the competent authority. If the competent authority accepts the resignation it will make provision for the adequate support of those who have retired and for the special rights to be accorded to them.

II. Diocesan Boundaries

22. For a diocese to fulfill its purpose it is necessary that the nature of the church be clearly manifested in the people of God belonging to the diocese. Bishops must be able to carry out their pastoral function effectively among their people, and finally the spiritual

welfare of the people of God must be catered for as perfectly as possible. This requires not only a proper determination of the territorial limits of the diocese but also a reasonable distribution of clergy and resources in accordance with the needs of the apostolate. All these things contribute to the good, not only of the clergy and the faithful who are directly involved, but also of the entire church.

Therefore as regards diocesan boundaries the sacred synod decrees that, insofar as the good of souls requires it, a prudent revision of diocesan boundaries be undertaken as soon as possible. This can be done by dividing, distributing or uniting dioceses, changing their boundaries, or appointing a more suitable place for the episcopal see, or finally, and especially in those dioceses which comprise larger cities, by establishing a new internal organization.

23. In revising diocesan boundaries a first care should be the preservation of the organic unity of each diocese, as in a healthy living body. This applies to persons, offices and institutions. Due weight being given in individual cases to the particular circumstances, the following general criteria should be borne in mind:

(1) In determining diocesan boundaries the variety of the composition of the People of God should be taken into consideration as far as possible, since this may materially contribute to more effective pastoral care.

At the same time an effort should be made to ensure as far as possible that the demographic groupings remain united with the civil offices and institutions which constitute their organic structure. For this reason the territory of each diocese should form a continuous whole.

The limits of civil boundaries should also be taken into account where they occur, as well as the special

characteristics — psychological, economic, geographical or historical — of people and regions.

(2) The size of the diocesan territory and the number of its inhabitants should as a general rule be such
that on the one hand the bishop himself, assisted perhaps by others, is able to duly exercise his pontifical
functions and carry out his pastoral visitations in it.
He should also be in a position to control and coordinate effectively all the apostolic activities in his diocese, and especially to know his priests and all the
religious and lay people who are involved in diocesan
activities. On the other hand, a diocese should provide sufficient and suitable scope for the bishop and
his priests to employ usefully all their energies in the
ministry, taking into account the needs of the universal church.

(3) Finally, for the more effective exercise of the
ministry of salvation the norm should be that each
diocese would have enough priests capable of properly caring for the people of God. Offices, institutions
and activities should be in place which are suited to a
particular diocese and which experience shows to be
necessary for its efficient administration and for its
apostolate. Lastly, resources for the care of personnel
and the maintenance of institutions should be already
in hand or at least it should be foreseen that they will
be provided from elsewhere.

Accordingly, where there are believers of different
rites, the bishop of that diocese should make provision for their spiritual needs either by providing
priests of those rites, or special parishes, or by appointing episcopal vicars, with the necessary faculties.
If necessary, such a vicar may be ordained bishop.
Alternatively, the bishop himself may perform the
functions of an Ordinary for each of the different rites.
And if the apostolic See judges that, on account of
some special circumstances, none of these alterna-

tives are practicable, a special hierarchy should be established for each different rite.[16]

Likewise in similar circumstances provision should be made for the faithful of a different language group either by appointing priests who speak that language, or by creating special parishes, or by appointing an episcopal vicar well versed in it. If it is deemed appropriate he may be ordained bishop, or the matter may be dealt with in some other more practicable way.

24. The competent episcopal conferences should examine all matters relating to the changes and alterations to be made in dioceses in their territories, in accordance with nn. 22, 23. This is without prejudice to the discipline of the Oriental church. A special episcopal commission may be established for the purpose, but the views of the bishops of the provinces or regions involved should always be given special consideration. Finally, they should present their recommendations and wishes to the Apostolic See.

III. Those Who Cooperate with the Diocesan Bishop in His Pastoral Task

A. Coadjutor and Auxiliary Bishop

25. In governing their dioceses, bishops must take the good of the Lord's flock as their main objective. This will often demand the appointment of auxiliary bishops, when the bishop of the diocese is unable to perform his duty well enough for the good of souls on his own, either because the diocese is too big, the people too numerous, there is a special pastoral problem, or for some other reason. Sometimes indeed special circumstances may require that a coadjutor bishop be appointed to assist the diocesan bishop. Suitable faculties should be given to these coadjutors and auxiliary bishops so that, without prejudice to the unity of the diocesan administration or to the author-

ity of the diocesan bishop, their labors may be more effective and the dignity of the episcopal office duly safeguarded.

Since coadjutors and auxiliary bishops are chosen to share the burdens of the diocesan bishop, they should so perform their ministry that in all matters they act in singleminded accord with him. They should show all respect and reverence for the bishop of the diocese, who for his part should have a fraternal affection for his coadjutors or auxiliaries and should hold them in esteem.

26. When the good of souls requires it the diocesan bishop should not hesitate to ask for one or more auxiliaries, who will be appointed for the diocese, without however any right of succession.

If it is not expressly provided in the letters of nomination, the diocesan bishop should appoint one or more of his auxiliary bishops as vicars general or at least episcopal vicars. They will, however, be dependent on his authority. He may think it well to consult them in deciding matters of greater importance, especially questions of pastoral significance.

Unless it has been otherwise provided by the competent authority, the powers and faculties conferred by law on auxiliary bishops are not terminated by the departure from office of the diocesan bishop. It is indeed desirable, unless there are grave reasons to the contrary, that the responsibility of governing the diocese during the vacancy of the see should be entrusted to the auxiliary bishop, or if there are several, to one of them.

A coadjutor bishop — one nominated with the right of succession, that is — should always be appointed vicar general by the diocesan bishop. More extensive faculties may, in particular cases, be granted to him by the competent authority.

For the greater present and future good of the diocese the diocesan bishop and his coadjutor should consult each other on matters of major importance.

B. The Diocesan Curia and Councils

27. In the diocesan curia the office of vicar general is preeminent. When, however, the good government of the diocese requires it, the bishop may appoint one or more episcopal vicars who by the very fact of their appointment will enjoy, in specified parts of the diocese, or in specific matters, or in regard to the faithful of particular rites, that authority which is conferred by the general law on the vicar general.

Among the cooperators of the bishop in the government of the diocese are included the priests who constitute his senate or council, such as the cathedral chapter, the council of consultors, or other committees according to the circumstances and character of different localities. These councils, and especially the cathedral chapters, should be reorganized, as far as is necessary, to suit contemporary needs.

Priests and lay people who are attached to the diocesan curia should be mindful that they are collaborating in the pastoral work of the bishop.

The diocesan curia should be so organized that it serves the bishop, not only for diocesan administration, but also for pastoral activity.

It is highly desirable that in every diocese a special pastoral council be established, presided over by the diocesan bishop himself, in which clergy, religious, and laity specially chosen for the purpose will participate. It will be the function of this council to investigate and consider matters relating to pastoral activity and to formulate practical conclusions concerning them.

C. The Diocesan Clergy

28. All priests, whether diocesan or religious, share

and exercise with the bishop the one priesthood of Christ. They are thus constituted providential cooperators of the episcopal order. The diocesan clergy have, however, a primary role in the care of souls because, being incardinated in or appointed to a particular church, they are wholly dedicated in its service to the care of a particular section of the Lord's flock, and accordingly form one priestly body and one family of which the bishop is the father. In order to allot the sacred ministries more suitably and more equitably among his priests, the bishop must have the requisite liberty in making appointments to ministries and benefices. All rights and privileges which in any way restrict that liberty should accordingly be abrogated.

The relations between the bishop and the diocesan clergy should be based before all else on supernatural charity, so that their unity of purpose will make their pastoral activity more effective. Therefore, to ensure an increasingly effective apostolate, the bishop should be willing to engage in dialogue with his priests, individually and collectively, not merely occasionally, but if possible, regularly. Furthermore, the diocesan priests should be united among themselves and should be genuinely zealous for the spiritual welfare of the whole diocese. They should bear in mind that the worldly goods which they acquire through their ecclesiastical functions are closely connected with their sacred office, and they should therefore contribute liberally to the material needs of the diocese, according to the bishop's directives.

29. Priests to whom the bishop entrusts a pastoral duty or apostolic work of a trans-parochial nature collaborate even more closely with him, whether they are assigned to a certain portion of the diocese, a special group of the faithful, or a particular kind of work.

Outstanding assistance is rendered also by those priests to whom the bishop entrusts various apostolic activities in schools or in other institutions or associations.

Moreover, those priests who are involved in trans-diocesan activities should be shown particular solicitude especially by the bishop in whose diocese they reside, since they are engaged in apostolic work of great importance.

30. Parish priests are in a special sense collaborators with the bishop. To them, as to pastors in their own right, is given the care of souls in a specific section of the diocese, under the authority of the bishop.

(1) In exercising the care of souls parish priests and their assistants should carry out their work of teaching, sanctifying and governing in such a way that the faithful and the parish communities may feel that they are truly members both of the diocese and of the universal church They should therefore collaborate both with other parish priests and with those priests who are exercising a pastoral function in the district (such as vicars forane and deans) or who are engaged in works of an extra-parochial nature, so that the pastoral work of the diocese may be made more effective by a spirit of unity. Furthermore, the care of souls should always be inspired by a missionary spirit, so that it extends with due prudence to all those who live in the parish. And if the parish priest cannot make contact with certain groups of people he should call to his aid others, including lay people, to assist him in matters relating to the apostolate.

For the better ordering of the care of souls, priests are strongly recommended to live in common, especially those attached to the same parish. This on one hand is helpful to their apostolate work, and on the other gives to the faithful an example of charity and unity.

(2) In their role as teachers it is the duty of parish priests to preach the word of God to all the faithful so

that they, being firmly rooted in faith, hope and charity, may grow in Christ, and the christian community may give that witness to charity which the Lord commended.[17] They should likewise by means of catechetical instruction lead all the faithful, according to their capacity, to a full knowledge of the mystery of salvation. In providing this instruction, they should invoke the help not only of religious, but of the laity by establishing the Confraternity of Christian Doctrine.

In carrying out their work of sanctification, parish priests should ensure that the celebration of the eucharistic sacrifice is the center and culmination of the entire life of the christian community. It should also be their aim to ensure that the faithful receive spiritual nourishment from frequent and devout reception of the sacraments and from an attentive and fervent participation in the liturgy. Parish priests must bear constantly in mind how much the sacrament of penance contributes to the development of the christian life and should therefore be readily available for the hearing of the confessions of the faithful. If necessary, they should call on other priests who are fluent in different languages to help in this work.

In the exercise of their pastoral ministry parish priests should make it their business to get to know their parishioners. Since they are the shepherds of all the individual sheep they should endeavor to stimulate the growth of the christian life in each one of the faithful, in families, in associations, especially those dedicated to the apostolate, and, finally, in the parish as a whole. They should, therefore, visit homes and schools as their pastoral function requires of them. They should have a special interest in adolescents and young people; they should extend a paternal charity towards the poor and the sick. Finally, they should have a special care for workers, and should urge the faithful to support apostolic activities.

(3) Curates, as co-workers with the parish priest, should be willing and zealous in the daily exercise of their pastoral ministry under the authority of the parish priest. Parish priests and curates should be as brothers towards each other; mutual charity and respect should prevail, and they should assist each other by advice, practical help and example, in harmony and with shared zeal providing for the needs of the parish.

31. In forming a judgment as to the suitability of a priest for governing a parish, the bishop should take into consideration not only his learning but also his piety, his zeal for the apostolate, and those other gifts and qualities which are necessary for the proper care of souls.

Basically, however, parochial responsibility has to do with the good of souls. It follows that, if a bishop is more easily and efficiently to make provision for parishes, all rights whatsoever of presentation, nomination and reservation should be abrogated, without prejudice, however, to the rights of religious. Regulations for a competition, whether general or particular, should also be abolished where they exist.

Each parish priest should enjoy that security of tenure in his parish which the good of souls requires. Therefore the distinction between removable and irremovable parish priests should be dropped and the procedure for the transfer or removal of a parish priest should be reexamined and simplified so that the bishop, while observing the principles of natural and canonical justice, may more suitably provide for the good of souls.

Parish priests who on account of advanced years or for some other grave reason are unable to perform their duties adequately and fruitfully are urged to tender their resignation spontaneously, or when the bishop invites them to do so. The bishop will make suitable provision for the support of those who retire.

32. Finally, the same concern for the salvation of souls should be the motive for determining or reconsidering the erection or suppression of parishes and other changes of this kind. The bishop may act in these matters on his own authority.

D. Religious

33. All religious, including for the purposes of this section, members of other institutes professing the evangelical counsels, are under an obligation, in accordance with the particular vocation of each, to work zealously and diligently for the building up and growth of the whole mystical body of Christ and for the good of particular churches. It is their duty to promote these objectives primarily by means of prayer, works of penance, and by the example of their own lives. The sacred synod strongly urges them to develop an ever-increasing esteem and zeal for these practices. But, at the same time, with due consideration for the special character of each religious institute, they should also with ever-increasing zeal apply themselves to the external works of the apostolate.

34. Religious priests, who have been ordained to the priesthood to be prudent cooperators with the episcopal order, can nowadays be of even greater help to bishops in view of the more pressing needs of souls. Thus, they may be said in a certain sense to belong to the diocesan clergy inasmuch as they share in the care of souls and in the practice of apostolic works under the authority of the bishops. The other members, too, of religious institutes, both men and women, also belong in a special sense to the diocesan family and render valuable help to the sacred hierarchy, and in view of the growing needs of the apostolate they can and should constantly increase the aid they give.

35. In order, however, that the works of the apostolate may always be carried out harmoniously in individual dioceses and that the unity of diocesan discipline be preserved intact, the following fundamental principles are decreed:

(1) Religious should at all times treat the bishops, as the successors of the apostles, with loyal respect and reverence. Moreover, whenever legitimately called upon to do apostolic work, they must carry out these duties in such a way as to be the auxiliaries of the bishop and subject to him. Furthermore, religious should comply promptly and faithfully with the requests or desires of the bishops when they are asked to undertake a greater share in the ministry of salvation. Due consideration should be given to the character of a particular institute and to its constitutions, which may, if necessary, be adapted for this purpose in accord with the principles of this decree of the council.

Especially in view of the urgent needs of souls and of the lack of diocesan clergy, those religious institutes which are not dedicated to a purely contemplative life may be called upon by the bishop to help in various pastoral ministries. The special character of each religious institute should be taken into consideration. Superiors should make every effort to cooperate, even taking responsibility for parishes on a temporary basis.

(2) Religious who are engaged in the external apostolate should be inspired by the spirit of their own institute, should remain faithful to the observance of their rule, and should be obedient to their superiors. Bishops should not fail for their part to insist on this obligation.

(3) The privilege of exemption whereby religious are assigned to the control of the supreme pontiff, or of some other ecclesiastical authority, and are

exempted from the jurisdiction of bishops, relates primarily to the internal organization of their institutes. Its purpose is to ensure that everything is suitably and harmoniously arranged within them, and the perfection of the religious life promoted.[18] The privilege ensures also that the supreme pontiff may employ these religious for the good of the universal church,[19] or that some other competent authority may do so for the good of the churches under its jurisdiction. This exemption, however, does not prevent religious being subject to the jurisdiction of the bishops in the individual dioceses in accordance with the general law, insofar as is required for the performance of their pastoral duties and the proper care of souls.[20]

(4) All religious, whether exempt or non-exempt, are subject to the authority of the local ordinary in the following matters: public worship, without prejudice, however, to the diversity of rites; the care of souls; preaching to the people; religious and moral education, catechetical instruction and liturgical formation of the faithful, especially of children. They are also subject to diocesan rules regarding the comportment proper to the clerical state and also the various activities relating to the exercise of their sacred apostolate. Catholic schools conducted by religious are also subject to the local ordinaries as regards their general policy and supervision without prejudice, however, to the right of the religious to manage them. Likewise, religious are obliged to observe all those prescriptions which episcopal councils or conferences legitimately decree as binding on all.

(5) Organized cooperation should be encouraged between the various religious institutes and between them and the diocesan clergy. There should be the closest possible coordination of all apostolic works and activities. This will depend mainly on a supernatural attitude of heart and mind grounded on charity.

It is the responsibility of the apostolic see to foster this coordination in regard to the universal church; it is for each bishop to do so in his own diocese, and for the patriarchs and episcopal synods and conferences in their territories.

There should be consultations beforehand between bishops or episcopal conferences and religious superiors or conferences of major superiors, with regard to apostolic activities to be undertaken by religious.

(6) In order to promote harmonious and fruitful relations between bishops and religious, bishops and superiors should meet at regular intervals and as often as seems opportune to discuss matters relating to the apostolate in their territory.

1. See Vatican II, Decree on the Catholic Eastern Churches, *Orientalium Ecclesiarum,* nn. 7-11.

2. See Council of Trent, fifth session, Decree on reform ch. 2: Mansi 33, 30; twenty-fourth session, Decree on reform ch. 4, Mansi 33, 159; Vatican II, Dogmatic Constitution on the Church ch. 3, art. 25.

3. See Vatican II, Dogmatic Constitution on the Church, *Lumen gentium,* ch 3, n 25.

4. See John XXIII, Encyclical *Pacem in terris,* 11 Apr. 1963 passim: AAS 55 (1963) pp. 257-304.

5. See Paul VI, Encyclical *Ecclesiam suam,* 6 Aug. 1964. AAS 56 (1964) p. 639.

6. See Paul VI, op. cit. AAS 56 (1964) pp. 644-645.

7. See Vatican II, Decree on the Mass Media, *Inter mirifica.*

8. See Vatican II, Constitution on the Sacred Liturgy, *Sacrosanctum Concilium,* 4 Dec. 1963; Paul VI, Motu proprio *Sacram Liturgiam,* 25 Jan. 1964. AAS 56 (1964) pp. 139 ff.

9. See Pius XII, Encyclical *Mediator Dei,* 20 Nov. 1947: AAS 39 (1947) pp. 521 ff; Paul VI, Encyclical *Mysterium Fidei,* 3 Sept. 1965: AAS 57 (1965) pp. 753-774.

10. See Acts 1:14 and 2:46.

11. See Vatican II, Dogmatic Constitution on the Church, *Lumen gentium,* ch. 6, nn. 44-45.

12. Lk 22:26-27.

13. Jn 15:15

14 See Vatican II, Decree on Ecumenism, *Unitatis* redintegratio.

15 See St Pius X, Motu proprio *Iampridem,* 19 Mar 1914: AAS 6

(1914) pp 173 ff; Pius XII, Apostolic Constitution *Exsul Familia,* 1 Aug 1952: AAS 44 (1952) pp 649 ff; Pius XII, *Regulations for the Apostolate of the Sea,* 21 Nov 1957: AAS 50 (1958) pp 375-383

16 See Vatican II, Decree on the Catholic Eastern Churches, Orientalium *Ecclesiarum,* n 4.

17 See Jn 13:35

18. See Leo XIII, Apotolic Constitution *Romanos Pontifices,* 8 May 1881: *Acta Leonis* XIII, vol. 2, 1882, p. 234.

19. See Paul VI, Allocution, 23 May 1964: AAS 56 (1965) pp. 570-571.

20. See Pius XII, Allocution, 8 Dec. 1950: AAS 43 (1951) p. 28.

Chapter III

CONCERNING THE COOPERATION OF BISHOPS FOR THE COMMON GOOD OF A NUMBER OF CHURCHES

I. Synods, Councils and Especially Episcopal Conferences

36. From the earliest ages of the church, bishops in charge of particular churches, inspired by a spirit of fraternal charity and by zeal for the universal mission entrusted to the apostles, have pooled their resources and their aspirations in order to promote both the common good and the good of individual churches. With this end in view, synods, provincial councils and, finally, plenary councils were established in which the bishops determined on a common program to be followed in various churches both for teaching the truths of the faith and for regulating ecclesiastical discipline.

This sacred ecumenical synod expresses its earnest hope that these admirable institutions — synods and councils — may flourish with renewed vigor so that the growth of religion and the maintenance of discipline in the various churches may increasingly be more effectively provided for in accordance with the needs of the times.

37. It is often impossible, nowadays especially, for bishops to exercise their office suitably and fruitfully unless they establish closer understanding and cooperation with other bishops. Since episcopal conferences — many such have already been established in different countries — have produced outstanding examples of a more fruitful apostolate, this sacred synod judges that it would be in the highest degree helpful if in all parts of the world the bishops of each country or region would meet regularly, so that by sharing their wisdom and experience and exchanging views they may jointly formulate a program for the common good of the church.

Therefore, the sacred synod issues the following decrees concerning episcopal conferences:

38. (1) An episcopal conference is a form of assembly in which the bishops of a certain country or region exercise their pastoral office jointly, in order to enhance the Church's beneficial influence on all women and men, especially by devising forms of the apostolate and apostolic methods suitably adapted to the circumstances of the times.

(2) Members of the episcopal conferences include all local ordinaries of whatever rite (but not vicars general), coadjutor and auxiliary bishops and other titular bishops to whom the apostolic See or the episcopal conferences have entrusted some special work. Other titular bishops and papal legates, in view of their special position in the region, are not *de jure* members of the conference.

The local ordinaries and coadjutors have a deliberative vote. The statutes of the conference will determine whether auxiliary bishops and other bishops entitled to attend the conference be given a deliberative or consultative voice.

(3) Each episcopal conference will draw up its own statutes, which will be subject to the approval of the apostolic See. These statutes will provide, among other things, for the setting up of those offices which are required for the effectiveness of the conference, for example, a permanent council of bishops, episcopal commissions and a general secretariat.

(4) Decisions of the episcopal conference, provided they have been legitimately approved by at least two thirds of the votes of the prelates who have a deliberative vote in the conference, and provided they have been confirmed by the apostolic See, shall have the force of law, but only in those cases in which it is so prescribed by the common law, or when it has been so declared by a special mandate of the apostolic See promulgated on its own initiative or at the request of the conference itself.

(5) When the special circumstances require it, bishops of different countries may, subject to the approval of the apostolic See, establish one joint conference. Moreover, contacts between episcopal conferences of different countries are to be encouraged for the promotion of the common good.

(6) It is strongly recommended to prelates of the Oriental churches that when engaged in the improvement of morals in their own church and in the promotion of activities beneficial to religion, they should take into consideration the common good of the whole of a region in which there happen to be churches of different rites. They should meet representatives of other rites and discuss matters with them, in accordance with rules to be determined by the competent authority.

II. The Boundaries of Ecclesiastical Provinces and the Establishment of Ecclesiastical Regions

39. The good of souls requires well-adjusted boun-

daries, not only of dioceses, but also of ecclesiastical provinces; it may indeed call for the establishment of ecclesiastical regions in order that better provision may be made for the needs of the apostolate in accordance with social and local circumstances. In this way easier and more fruitful relations may be established between bishops themselves and between them and their metropolitans and other bishops of the same country, and also between bishops and the civil authorities.

40. Therefore, in order to achieve these objectives, the sacred synod decrees the following:

(1) The boundaries of ecclesiastical provinces should be reviewed as soon as is practicable, and the rights and privileges of metropolitans should be determined according to new and carefully-devised regulations.

(2) As a general rule all dioceses, and other territorial divisions which in law are equivalent to dioceses, should be incorporated in an ecclesiastical province. Thus, those dioceses which are now immediately subject to the apostolic See and which are not united with any other diocese should either be consolidated into new ecclesiastical provinces, if that is practicable, or should be joined to the nearest and most suitable provinces. They should be made subject to the authority of the metropolitan archbishops in accordance with the common law.

(3) Whenever it seems expedient, ecclesiastical provinces should be consolidated into ecclesiastical regions, the organization of which is to be determined by law.

41. The competent episcopal conferences should examine the question of the boundaries of provinces of this kind and the establishment of regions in accordance with the provisions concerning the boundaries

of dioceses in nn. 23, 24, and should submit their decisions to the apostolic See.

III. Bishops Discharging an Inter-Diocesan Function

42. As the needs of the apostolate make joint control and promotion of certain pastoral activities increasingly necessary, it is desirable that some offices be established for the service of all or several dioceses in a particular region or nation, and these may be entrusted to a bishop.

The sacred synod recommends also that fraternal relations and unity of purpose in their pastoral zeal for souls should prevail between the prelates or bishops exercising these functions and the diocesan bishops and the episcopal conferences. These relations should be determined by the common law.

43. The spiritual welfare of military personnel, on account of the special nature of their life, should be the object of particular solicitude. A special military vicariate should therefore, if possible, be established in every country. The vicar and his chaplains should go about this difficult work with the utmost zeal and in harmonious cooperation with diocesan bishops.[1]

Diocesan bishops should for this purpose release to the military vicar a sufficient number of priests well equipped for this difficult work. They should also give every encouragement to undertakings intended to promote the spiritual welfare of military personnel.[2]

General Directive

44. The sacred synod prescribes that in the revision of the Code of Canon Law, suitable laws should be drawn up in conformity with the principles enunciated in this decree, due consideration being given to the comments made by individual commissions or the Fathers of the council.

The sacred synod further decrees that general directories concerning the care of souls be compiled for the use both of bishops and parish priests so that they may have definite directives to guide them in the discharge of their particular pastoral function.

A special directory should also be compiled concerning the pastoral care of special groups of the faithful according to the various circumstances of different countries or regions, and also a directory for the catechetical instruction of the christian people in which the fundamental principles of this instruction and its organization will be dealt with and the preparation of books relating to it. In the preparation of these directories, due consideration should be given to the views expressed both by the commissions and by the conciliar fathers.

1. See Consistorial Congregation, Instruction to Military Ordinaries, 23 April 1951: AAS 43 (1951), pp. 562-565; also Formula Regarding the Conferring of the Status of Military Ordinariates, 20 Oct. 1956; AAS 49 (1957), pp. 150-163; also Decree on *Ad Limina* Visits of Military Ordinariates, 28 Feb. 1959 AAS 51 (1959), pp. 272-274; also Decree on the Granting of Faculties for Confessions to Military Chaplains, 27 Nov. 1960: AAS 53 (1961), pp. 49-50; also Instruction of Sacred Congregation of Religious on Religious Military Chaplains, 2 Feb. 1955: AAS 47 (1955), pp. 93-97.

2. See Consistorial Congregation, Letter to the cardinals, archbishops, bishops, and other ordinaries of Spanish-speaking nations, 21 June 1951: AAS 43 (1951) p. 566.

DECREE ON THE MINISTRY AND LIFE OF PRIESTS[a]

Presbyterorum Ordinis
7 December, 1965

Introduction

1. This sacred council has already on several occasions drawn the attention of the world to the excellence of the order of priests in the church.[1] Since however, a most important and increasingly difficult role is being assigned to priests in the renewal of Christ's church, it seems useful to treat the priesthood at greater length and depth. What is said here applies to all priests and especially to those who are engaged in the care of souls. It is to be applied to religious priests insofar as its provisions suit their circumstances.

Through the sacred ordination and mission which they receive from the bishops, priests are promoted to the service of Christ the teacher, priest and king; they are given a share in his ministry, through which the church here on earth is being unceasingly built up into the people of God, Christ's body and the temple of the Spirit. Consequently, the council declares and decrees what follows, with the aim of giving more effective support to the ministry of priests and making better provision for their life in the often vastly changed circumstances of the pastoral and human scene.

himself builds up, sanctifies and rules his body. Hence the priesthood of presbyters, while presupposing the sacraments of initiation, is conferred by a special sacrament which, by the anointing of the holy Spirit, puts a special stamp on them and so conforms them to Christ the priest in such a way that they are able to act in the person of Christ the head.[8]

Since they share in their measure in the apostles' role, priests are given by God the grace to be the ministers of Jesus Christ among the nations, fulfilling the sacred task of the Gospel, that the offering of the gentiles may be made acceptable and sanctified in the holy Spirit (see Rom 15:16, Greek text). For it is by the apostolic proclamation of the Gospel that the people of God is called and gathered so that all who belong to this people, sanctified as they are by the holy Spirit, may offer themselves "a living sacrifice, holy and acceptable to God" (Rom 12:1). Through the ministry of priests, the spiritual sacrifice of the faithful is completed in union with the sacrifice of Christ the only mediator, which in the Eucharist is offered through the priests' hands in the name of the whole church in an unbloody and sacramental manner until the Lord himself shall come (see 1 Cor 11:26). The ministry of priests is directed to this and finds its consummation in it. For their ministration, which begins with the announcement of the Gospel, draws its force and power from the sacrifice of Christ and tends to this, that "the whole redeemed city, that is, the whole assembly and community of the saints should be offered as a universal sacrifice to God through the High Priest who offered himself in his passion for us that we might be the body of so great a head."[9]

Therefore what priests try to achieve by their ministry and life is to procure the glory of God the Father in Christ. That glory consists in people's conscious, free, and grateful acceptance of God's plan as completed in Christ and their manifestation of it in their

Chapter I

THE PRIESTHOOD IN THE
CHURCH'S MISSION

Nature of the Priesthood

2. The Lord Jesus "whom the Father consecrated and sent into the world" (Jn 10:36) gave his whole mystical body a share in the anointing of the Spirit with which he was anointed (see Mt 3:16; Lk 4:18; Acts 4:27; 10:38). In that body all the faithful are made a holy and kingly priesthood, they offer spiritual sacrifices to God through Jesus Christ, and they proclaim the mighty acts of him who has called them out of darkness into his admirable light (see 1 Pet 2:5, 9). Therefore there is no such thing as a member who does not have a share in the mission of the whole body. Rather, all of the members ought to reverence Jesus in their hearts (see 1 Pet 3:15) and by the spirit of prophecy give testimony to Jesus.[2]

However, the Lord also appointed certain men as ministers, in order that they might be united in one body in which "all the members have not the same function" (Rom 12:4). These men held in the community of the faithful the sacred power of order, that of offering sacrifice and forgiving sins,[3] and exercised the priestly office publicly on behalf of men and women in the name of Christ. Thus Christ sent the apostles as he himself had been sent by the Father,[4] and then through the apostles made their successors, the bishops, sharers in his consecration and mission.[5] The function of the bishops' ministry was handed over in a subordinate degree to priests[6] so that they might be appointed in the order of the priesthood and be co-workers with the episcopal order[7] for the proper fulfillment of the apostolic mission that had been entrusted to it by Christ.

Because it is joined with the episcopal order the priesthood shares in the authority by which Christ whole life. Thus priests, whether they devote themselves to prayer and adoration, or preach the word, or offer the eucharistic sacrifice and administer the other sacraments, or perform other services for people, are contributing at once to the increase of God's glory and people's growth in the divine life. And all these activities, since they flow from the paschal mystery of Christ, will find their consummation in the glorious coming of the same Lord, when he shall have delivered up the kingdom to God his Father (see 1 Cor 15:24).

Place of Priests in the World

3. Priests, while being chosen from the midst of humanity and appointed to act on its behalf in what pertains God, to offer gifts and sacrifices for sins (see Heb 5:1), live with the rest of humanity as with brothers and sisters. So also the Lord Jesus the Son of God, a man sent by the Father to humankind, lived among us and wished to be like his brothers and sisters in all things except sin (see Heb 2:17; 4:15). The apostles in their turn imitated him, and St. Paul the teacher of the gentiles, the man "set apart for the Gospel of God" (Rom 1:1), declares that he became all things to all people that he might save all (see 1 Cor 9:19-23, Vulgate).

The priests of the New Testament are, it is true, by their vocation and ordination, set apart in some way within the people of God, but this is not in order that they should be separated from that people or from any person, but that they should be completely consecrated to the task for which God chooses them (see Acts 13:2). They could not be the servants of Christ unless they were witnesses and dispensers of a life other than that of this earth. On the other hand they would be powerless to serve people if they remained aloof from their life and circumstances.[10] Their very ministry makes a special claim on them not to conform themselves to this world (see Rom 12:2); however, it requires at the same time that they should live among people in this world and that, as good shepherds, they should know their flock and should also seek to lead back those who do not belong to this fold, so that they too may hear the voice of Christ and there may be one fold and one shepherd (see Jn 10:14-16).

Priests will be helped to achieve this by cultivating those qualities which are rightly held in high esteem in human relations, qualities such as goodness of heart, sincerity, strength and constancy of mind, careful attention to justice, courtesy and others which the apostle Paul recommends when he says:"Whatever is true, whatever is honorable, whatever is just, whatever is pure, whatever is lovely, whatever is gracious, if there is any excellence, if there is anything worthy of praise, think about these things" (Phil 4: 8).[11]

a. Translated by Archbishop Joseph Cunnane, of Tuam, and revised by the late Michael Mooney and Enda Lyons of St Jarlath's College, Tuam, Co. Galway. Revised for this edition by AF. Regulations for the implementation of this decree are given in *Ecclesiae Sanctae*, 1, which is in Vatican Collection, vol. 2, pp. 591-610.

1. Vatican Council II, Constitution on the Sacred Liturgy, *Sacrosanctum Concilium;* Dogmatic Constitution on the Church, *Lumen gentium;* Decree on the Pastoral Office of Bishops in the Church, *Christus Dominus;* Decree on the Training of Priests, *Optatam totius.*

2. See Apoc 19:10; Vatican Council II, Dogmatic Constitution on the Church, *Lumen gentium*, n. 35.

3. See Council of Trent, Session 23, ch I and can. 1: Denz. 957 and 961 (1764 and 1771).

4. See Jn 20:21; Vatican Council II, Dogmatic Constitution on the Church, *Lumen gentium*, n. 18.

5. See Vatican Council II, Dogmatic Constitution on the Church, *Lumen gentium*, n. 28.

6. See ibid.

7. See Roman Pontifical, Ordination of a Priest, Preface. These words are already found in the *Sacramentary of Verona* (ed. L. C. Möhlberg, Rome 1956, p 122); Missale Francorum (ed. L. C. Möhl-

berg, Rome 1957, p. 9); in the *Liber Sacramentorum Romanae Ecclesiae* (ed. L. C. Mπhlberg, Rome 1960, p. 25); in the *Pontificale Romano-Germanicum* (ed. Vogel-Elze, Vatican City 1963, vol. 1, p. 34).

8. See Vatican Council II, Dogmatic Constitution on the Church, *Lumen gentium,* n. 10.

9. St Augustine, *De civitate Dei,* 10, 6: PL 41, 284.

10. "Such anxiety for religious and moral perfection is more and more demanded even by the external conditions in which the church lives out its life. For it cannot remain immovable and indifferent to the changes in the human scene around it which in many ways influence its policy and impose limits and conditions upon it. It is quite clear that the church is not isolated from the human community, but is situated in it, and hence that its members are influenced and guided by it, and that they absorb its culture, obey its laws, adopt its customs. The church's involvement in human society is constantly giving rise to difficult problems. These are particularly serious at present . . . The Apostle of the Gentiles addressed this exhortation to the Christians of his time: 'Bear not the yoke with unbelievers. For what has justice to do with injustice? Or what has light to with darkness? . . . Or what part have the faithful with the unbeliever?' (2 Cor 6:14-15). For this reason those who at present hold the position of educators and teachers in the church must impress upon catholic youth their outstanding dignity and the duty arising from this of living in this world but not according to the values of this world. This will be in conformity with the prayer made by Christ for his disciples: 'I pray not that you would take them out of the world, but that you would keep them from evil. They are not of the world, as I am not of the world' (Jn. 17-16). The church makes this prayer its own.

"At the same time however such a difference as this does not imply separation. It does not profess neglect, nor fear, not contempt. For when the church makes a distinction between itself and the human race, so far is it from setting itself in opposition to it that it rather is joined with it" (Paul VI, Encyclical *Ecclesiam suam,* 6 August 1964: AAS, 56 (1964), pp. 627 and 638).

11. See St. Polycarp, *Epist. ad Philippenses,* VI, I: "Let priests also be disposed to pity, merciful to all, leading back the erring, visiting all the sick, not neglecting the widow, the orphan or the poor. Rather let them be always solicitous for good in God's sight and that of the people, refraining from all anger, acceptance of persons, unjust judgment, completely avoiding all avarice, slow to believe evil against anyone. Let them not be over-severe in judgment, knowing that we are all sinners" (ed. F. X. Funk, *Patres Apostolici,* I p. 303).

Chapter II

THE MINISTRY OF PRIESTS

I. Functions of Priests

Priests as Ministers of God's Word

4. The people of God is formed into one in the first place by the word of the living God,[1] which is quite rightly expected from the mouth of priests.[2] For since nobody can be saved who has not first believed,[3] it is the first task of priests as co-workers of the bishops to preach the Gospel of God to all.[4] In this way they carry out the Lord's command "Go into all the world and preach the Gospel to every creature" (Mk 16:15)[5] and thus establish and increase the people of God. For by the saving word of God faith is aroused in the heart of unbelievers and is nourished in the heart of believers. By this faith then the congregation of the faithful begins and grows, according to the saying of the apostle: "Faith comes from what is heard, and what is heard comes by the preaching of Christ" (Rom 10:17).

Priests owe it to everybody to share with them the truth of the Gospel[6] in which they rejoice in the Lord. Therefore, whether by their exemplary behavior they lead people to glorify God;[7] or by their preaching proclaim the mystery of Christ to unbelievers; or teach the christian message or explain the church's doctrine; or endeavor to treat of contemporary problems in the light of Christ's teaching — in every case their role is to teach not their own wisdom but the word of God and to issue a pressing invitation to all men and women to conversion and to holiness.[8] Moreover, the priest's preaching, often very difficult in present-day conditions, if it is to become more effective in moving the minds of his hearers, must expound the word of

God not merely in a general and abstract way but by an application of the eternal truth of the Gospel to the concrete circumstances of life.

Thus the ministry of the word is exercised in many different ways according to the needs of the hearers and the spiritual gifts of preachers. In non-christian territories or societies people are led by the proclamation of the Gospel to faith and the saving sacraments.[9] In the christian community on the other hand, especially for those who seem to have little understanding or belief underlying their practice, the preaching of the word is required for the sacramental ministry itself, since the sacraments are sacraments of faith, which is born of the word and is nourished by it.[10] This is especially true of the liturgy of the word within the celebration of Mass where there is an indivisible unity between the proclamation of the Lord's death and resurrection, the response of the hearers and the offering itself by which Christ confirmed the new covenant in his blood. In this offering the faithful share both by their prayer and by the reception of the sacrament.[11]

Priests as Ministers of the Sacrament and the Eucharist

5. God, who alone is the holy one and sanctifier, has willed to take people as collaborators and helpers, humble servants in his work of sanctification. The purpose then for which priests are consecrated by God through the ministry of the bishop is that they should be made sharers in a special way in Christ's priesthood and, by carrying out sacred functions, act as ministers of him who through his Spirit continually exercises his priestly role for our benefit in the liturgy.[12] By Baptism priests make men and women part of the people of God; by the sacrament of Penance they reconcile sinners with God and the church; by the

anointing of the sick they console those who are ill; and especially by the celebration of Mass they offer Christ's sacrifice sacramentally. But in the celebration of all the sacraments — as St Ignatius Martyr already asserted in the early church[13] — priests are hierarchically united with the bishop in various ways and so make him present in a certain sense in every assembly of the faithful.[14] But the other sacraments, and indeed all ecclesiastical ministries and works of the apostolate are bound up with the Eucharist and are directed towards it.[15] For in the most blessed Eucharist is contained the entire spiritual wealth of the church,[16] namely Christ himself our Pasch and our living bread, who gives life to people through his flesh — that flesh which is given life and gives life by the holy Spirit. Thus people are invited and led to offer themselves, their works and all creation in union with Christ. For this reason the Eucharist appears as the source and the summit of all preaching of the Gospel: catechumens are gradually led forward to participation in the Eucharist, while the faithful who have already been consecrated in Baptism and Confirmation are fully incorporated in the body of Christ by the reception of the Eucharist.

Therefore the eucharistic celebration is the center of the assembly of the faithful over which the priest presides. Hence priests teach the faithful to offer the divine victim to God the Father in the sacrifice of the Mass and with the victim to make an offering of their lives. In the spirit of Christ the pastor, they instruct them to submit their sins to the church with a contrite heart in the sacrament of Penance, so that they may be daily more and more converted to the Lord, remembering his words:"Repent, for the kingdom of heaven is at hand" (Mt 4:17). They teach them to take part in the celebrations of the sacred liturgy in such a way as to achieve sincere prayer in them also. They guide them to the exercise of an ever more perfect spirit of prayer throughout their lives in proportion to each one's graces and needs. They lead all the faithful on to the observance of the duties of their particular state in life, and those who are more advanced to practise the evangelical counsels in the ways suited to their individual cases. Finally they train the faithful so that they will be able to sing in their hearts to the Lord with psalms and hymns and spiritual canticles, giving thanks always for all things in the name of our Lord Jesus Christ to God the Father.[17]

By praying, the Divine Office priests themselves should extend to the different hours of the day the praise and thanksgiving they offer in the celebration of the Eucharist. By the Office they pray to God in the name of the church for the whole people entrusted to them and in fact for the whole world.

The house of prayer in which the most holy Eucharist is celebrated and reserved, where the faithful assemble, and where is worshipped the presence of the Son of God our Saviour, offered for us on the sacrificial altar for the help and solace of the faithful — this house ought to be in good taste and a worthy place for prayer and sacred ceremonial.[18] In it pastors and faithful are called upon to respond with grateful hearts to the gift of himself who through his humanity is unceasingly pouring the divine life into the members of his body.[19] Priests ought to go to the trouble of properly cultivating liturgical knowledge and art so that by means of their liturgical ministry God the Father, Son, and holy Spirit may be daily more perfectly praised by the christian communities entrusted to their care.

Priests as Rulers of God's People

6. Priests exercise the role of Christ as Pastor and Head in proportion to their share of authority. In the

name of the bishop they gather the family of God as sisters and brothers endowed with the spirit of unity and lead it in Christ through the Spirit to God the Father.[20] For the exercise of this ministry, as for the rest of the priests' functions, a spiritual power is given them, a power whose purpose is to build up the church.[21] And in building up the church priests ought to treat everybody with the greatest kindness after the example of our Lord. Their behaviour towards people should not be motivated by a desire to please them,[22] but by the demands of christian teaching and life. They should teach them and warn them as their dearest children,[23] according to the words of the apostle: "Be urgent in season and out of season, convince, rebuke, and exhort, be unfailing in patience and in teaching" (2 Tim 4:2).[24]

For this reason it is the priests' part as instructors of the people in the faith to see to it, either personally or through others, that all the believers are led in the holy Spirit to the full development of their vocation in accordance with the Gospel teaching, and to sincere and active charity and the liberty with which Christ has set us free.[25] Very little good will be achieved by ceremonies, however beautiful, or societies, however flourishing, if they are not directed towards training people to reach christian maturity.[26] To encourage this maturity priests will make themselves available to help people solve their problems and determine the will of God in the great or small crises of life. Christians must also be trained not to live only for themselves. Rather, in accordance with the demands of the new law of charity, all, since they have received grace, ought to minister it to others.[27] All should thus carry out their duties in a christian manner in the community of their sisters and brothers.

Although priests should serve everybody, the poor and the weaker ones have been committed to their care in a special way. It was with these that the Lord himself associated,[28] and the preaching of the Gospel to them is given as a sign of his messianic mission.[29] Priests will be especially diligent in their care for young people and also for married couples and parents. It is desirable that these should meet in friendly groups to help each other live more easily and more fully as Christians in a way of life that is often difficult. Priests should keep in mind that all religious, men and women, being a particularly privileged group in the Lord's house, are deserving of special care for their spiritual progress for the good of the whole church. Finally, priests ought to be especially devoted to the sick and the dying, visiting them and comforting them in the Lord.[30]

The pastor's task is not limited to individual care of the faithful. It extends by right also to the formation of a genuine christian community. But a properly cultivated community spirit must embrace not only the local church but the universal church. A local community ought not merely to promote the care of its own faithful, but should be imbued with the missionary spirit and should smooth the path to Christ for all people. But it must regard as its special charge those under instruction and the newly converted who are being gradually formed to know and live the christian life.

However, no christian community is built up which does not grow from and hinge on the celebration of the most holy Eucharist. From this all education for community spirit must begin.[31] This eucharistic celebration, to be full and sincere, ought to lead on the one hand to the various works of charity and mutual help, and on the other hand to missionary activity and the various forms of christian witness.

In addition, the ecclesial community exercises a truly motherly function in leading souls to Christ by its charity, its prayer, its example and its penitential works. For it constitutes an effective instrument for showing or smoothing the path towards Christ and his church for those who have not yet found faith, while also encouraging, supporting and strengthening believers for their spiritual struggles.

In building up a community of Christians, priests can never be the servants of any human ideology or party. Rather, their task as heralds of the Gospel and pastors of the church is the attainment of the spiritual growth of the body of Christ.

II.   Priests' Relations With Others

Relations Between Bishops and the Priestly Body

7. All priests share with the bishops the one identical priesthood and ministry of Christ. Consequently the very unity of their consecration and mission requires their hierarchical union with the order of bishops.[32] This unity is best shown on some occasions by liturgical concelebration, and priests also affirm their union with the bishops in the eucharistic celebration.[33] Bishops, therefore, because of the gift of the holy Spirit that has been given to priests at their ordination, will regard them as their indispensable helpers and advisers in the ministry and in the task of teaching, sanctifying and shepherding the people of God.[34] This has been forcefully emphasized from the earliest ages of the church by the liturgical texts. These solemnly pray to God for the pouring out upon the priest to be ordained of "the spirit of grace and counsel, that he may help and govern the people in a pure heart,"[35] just as in the desert the spirit of Moses was made grow into the minds of the seventy wise men[36] "whom he employed as helpers and easily governed countless multitudes among the people."[37]

On account of this common sharing in the same

priesthood and ministry, bishops are to regard their priests as brothers and friends[38] and are to take the greatest possible interest in their welfare both temporal and spiritual. For on their shoulders especially falls the burden of sanctifying their priests;[39] therefore they are to exercise the greatest care in the on-going formation of their diocesan body of priests.[40] They should be glad to listen to their priests' views and to consult them and hold conference with them about matters that concern the needs of pastoral work and the good of the diocese. But for this to be put into practice a group or senate of priests[41] should be set up in a way suited to present-day needs[42] and in a form and with rules to be determined by law. This group would represent the body of priests and by their advice could effectively help the bishop in the management of the diocese.

Priests for their part should keep in mind the fullness of the sacrament of order which bishops enjoy and should reverence in their persons the authority of Christ the supreme Pastor. They should therefore be attached to their bishop with sincere charity and obedience.[43] Priestly obedience, inspired through and through by the spirit of co-operation, is based on that sharing of the episcopal ministry which is conferred on priests by the sacrament of order and the canonical mission.[44]

There is all the more need in our day for close union between priests and bishops because nowadays apostolic enterprises must necessarily for various reasons take on many different forms. And not only that, but they must often overstep the boundaries of one parish or diocese. Hence no priest is sufficiently equipped to carry out his mission alone and as it were single-handed. He can only do so by joining forces with other priests, under the leadership of those who are rulers of the church.

Brotherly Bond and Cooperation Among Priests

8. All priests, who are constituted in the order of priesthood by the sacrament of order, are bound together by an intimate sacramental brotherhood; but in a special way they form one priestly body in the diocese to which they are attached under their own bishop. For even though they may be assigned different duties, yet for their people they fulfill the one priestly service. Indeed all priests are sent to cooperate in the same work. This is true whether the ministry they exercise be parochial or supra-parochial; whether their task be research or teaching, or even if they engage in manual labor and share the lot of the workers, where that appears to be of advantage and has the approval of the competent authority; or finally if they carry out other apostolic works or those directed towards the apostolate. They all contribute to the same purpose, namely the building up of the body of Christ, and this, especially in our times, demands many kinds of duties and fresh adaptations.

For this reason it is of great importance that all priests, whether diocesan or regular, should help each other, so that they may be fellow-workers in the service of truth.[45] Each is joined to the rest of the members of this priestly body by special ties of apostolic charity, of ministry and of fellowship. This is signified liturgically from ancient times by the fact that the priests present at an ordination are invited to impose hands, along with the ordaining bishop, on the chosen candidate, and when priests concelebrate the sacred Eucharist in a spirit of harmony. So priests are all united with their brother priests by the bond of charity, prayer, and total cooperation. In this way is made manifest the consummation of that unity which Christ wished for his own, that the world might know that the Son had been sent by the Father.[46]

From this it follows that older priests should sincerely accept younger priests as brothers and help them in facing the first tasks and responsibilities of their ministry. They should make an effort also to understand their outlook even though it may be different from their own, and should give kindly encouragement to their projects. Young priests for their part are to respect the age and experience of their elders; they ought to consult with them on matters concerning the care of souls and willingly co-operate with them.

Under the influence of the spirit of brotherhood priests should not forget hospitality,[47] and should cultivate kindness and the sharing of goods.[48] They should be particularly concerned about those who are sick, about the afflicted, the overworked, the lonely, the exiled, the persecuted.[49] They should also be happy to gather together for relaxation, remembering the words by which the Lord himself invited his weary apostles: "Come apart into a desert place and rest a little" (Mk 6:31).

Moreover, in order to enable priests to find mutual help in cultivating the intellectual and spiritual life, to promote better cooperation among them in the ministry, to safeguard them from possible dangers arising from loneliness, it is necessary to develop some kind of common or shared life for them. This can take different forms according to varying personal and pastoral needs: by priests' living together where this is possible, or by their sharing a common table, or at least meeting at frequent intervals. Associations of priests are also to be highly esteemed and diligently promoted, when by means of rules recognized by the competent authority they foster priestly holiness in the exercise of the ministry through a suitable and properly approved rule of life and through brotherly help, and so aim at serving the whole order of priests.

Finally, because of the same brotherly bond of

priesthood, priests ought to realize that they have an obligation towards those in difficulties. They should offer timely help to them, even by discreetly warning them where necessary. They ought always to treat with fraternal charity and compassion those who have failed in any way. They should pray earnestly to God for them and never cease to show themselves genuine brothers and friends to them.

Relations of Priests with Lay People

9. Even though the priests of the new law by reason of the sacrament of order fulfill the preeminent and essential function of father and teacher among the people of God and on their behalf, still they are disciples of the Lord along with all the faithful and have been made partakers of his kingdom by God, who has called them by his grace.[50] Priests, in common with all who have been reborn in the font of Baptism, are brothers among brothers and sisters[51] as members of the same body of Christ which all are commanded to build.[52]

Priests should, therefore, lead as men who do not seek the things that are their own but the things that are Jesus Christ's.[53] They should unite their efforts with those of the lay faithful and conduct themselves among them after the example of the Master, who came among humankind "not to be served but to serve, and to give his life as a ransom for many" (Mt. 20:28). Priests are to be sincere in their appreciation and promotion of lay people's dignity and of the special role the laity have to play in the church's mission. They should also have an unfailing respect for the just liberty which belongs to everybody in civil society. They should be willing to listen to lay people, give brotherly consideration to their wishes, and recognize their experience and competence in the different fields of human activity. In this way they will be able to recognize along with them the signs of the times.

While testing the spirits to discover if they be of God,[54] they must discover with faith, recognize with joy, and foster diligently the many and varied charismatic gifts of the laity, whether these be of a humble or more exalted kind. Among the other gifts of God which are found abundantly among the faithful, special attention ought to be devoted to those graces by which a considerable number of people are attracted to greater heights in the spiritual life. Priests should confidently entrust to the laity duties in the service of the church, giving them freedom and opportunity for activity and even inviting them, when opportunity offers, to undertake projects on their own initiative.[55]

Finally, priests have been placed in the midst of the laity so that they may lead them all to the unity of charity, "loving one another with mutual affection; outdoing one another in sharing honor" (Rom 12:10). Theirs is the task, then, of bringing about agreement among divergent outlooks in such a way that nobody may feel a stranger in the christian community. They are to be at once the defenders of the common good, for which they are responsible in the bishop's name, and at the same time the unwavering champions of truth lest the faithful be carried about with every wind of doctrine.[56] Those who have abandoned the practice of the sacraments, or even perhaps the faith, are entrusted to priests as special objects of their care. They will not neglect to approach these as good shepherds.

Priests should bear in mind the guidelines on ecumenism[57] and should not forget those Christians who do not enjoy complete ecclesiastical union with us.

They will regard as committed to their charge all those who fail to recognize Christ as their Saviour.

The faithful for their part ought to realize that they have obligations to their priests. They should treat them with filial love as their fathers and pastors. They should also share their priests' anxieties and help them as far as possible by prayer and active work so that they may be better able to overcome difficulties and carry out their duties more successfully.[58]

III. The Distribution of Priests, Priestly Vocations

Proper Distribution of Priests

10. The spiritual gift which priests have received at ordination does not prepare them merely for a limited and circumscribed mission, but for the fullest, in fact the universal mission of salvation "to the end of the earth" (Acts 1:8). The reason is that every priestly ministry shares in the fullness of the mission entrusted by Christ to the apostles. For the priesthood of Christ, of which priests have been truly made sharers, is necessarily directed to all peoples and all times, and is not confined by any bounds of blood, race, or age, as was already typified in a mysterious way by the figure of Melchizedek.[59]

Priests, therefore, should bear in mind that they ought to care for all the churches. For this reason priests of dioceses which are blessed with greater abundance of vocations should be prepared to offer themselves willingly — with the permission or encouragement of their own ordinary — for ministry in countries or missions or tasks that are hampered by shortage of clergy.

In addition, the rules about incardination and excardination should be revised in such a way that, while this ancient institution remains intact, it will answer better to the pastoral needs of today. Where the nature of the apostolate demands this, not only should the proper distribution of priests be made easier but also the carrying out of special pastoral projects for the benefit of different social groups in any region or among any race in any part of the world. For this purpose international seminaries can with advantage be set up, special dioceses, or personal prelacies and other institutions to which, by methods to be decided for the individual undertaking and always without prejudice to the rights of local ordinaries, priests can be attached or incardinated for the common good of the whole church.

As far as possible, however, priests are not to be sent alone into a new territory, especially if they are not yet well versed in its language and customs. Rather, after the example of Christ's disciples,[60] they should at least be sent in groups of two or three so that they may be of mutual help to one another. It is advisable also to pay careful attention to their spiritual life and their mental and bodily health. Where possible, places and conditions of work are to be prepared for them to suit each one's personal circumstances.

It is also of the greatest advantage that those who go to a new territory should take the trouble to learn not only the language of the place but also the special psychological and social characteristics of the people they wish to serve in humility, and should establish the most perfect possible communication with them. In this way they will be following the example of St. Paul, who could say of himself: "For though I am free with respect to all, I have made myself a slave to all, that I might win more of them. To the Jews I became as a Jew, in order to win Jews" (1 Cor 9:19-20).

Priests' Care for Priestly Vocation

11. The pastor and bishop of our souls[61] set up his church in such a way that the people whom he chose and acquired by his blood[62] should always and until the end of the world have its own priests, to ensure that Christians would never be like sheep without a shepherd.[63] The apostles recognised this intention of

Christ and under the guidance of the holy Spirit considered it their duty to choose ministers who should "be able to teach others also" (Tim 2:2). In fact this duty is of to the very nature of the priestly mission which makes the priest share in the anxiety of the whole church lest laborers should ever be wanting to the people of God here on earth.

However, since "a common interest exists . . . between the pilot of the ship and the passengers,"[64] the whole christian people ought to be made aware that it is their duty to cooperate in their various ways, both by earnest prayer and by other means available to them,[65] to ensure that the church will always have those priests who are needed for the fulfilment of its divine mission. First, then, priests are to make it their most cherished object to make clear to people the excellence and necessity of the priesthood. They do this by their preaching and by the personal witness of a life that shows clearly a spirit of service and a genuine paschal joy. They should spare no trouble or inconvenience in helping younger or older men whom they seriously judge suitable for so great a ministry to prepare themselves so that they can be called at some time by the bishops, in full liberty of spirit and without external pressure. In the pursuit of this objective diligent and prudent spiritual direction is of the greatest advantage.

Parents, teachers, and all who are in any way concerned in the education of boys and young men ought to train them in such a way that they will know of the Lord's concern for his flock and be alive to the needs of the church. In this way, when the Lord calls, they will be prepared to answer generously with the prophet: "Here am I! Send me" (Is 6:8). However, it is emphatically not to be expected that the voice of the Lord calling should come to the future priest's ears in some extraordinary way. Rather, it must be perceived and judged through the signs by which God's will becomes known to prudent Christians in everyday life. And these signs are to be studied attentively by priests.[66]

Therefore organizations for the promotion of vocations, whether diocesan or national, are strongly recommended to priests.[67] In sermons, in catechetical instruction and in periodicals the needs of the church both local and universal are to be made known clearly. The meaning and excellence of the priestly ministry is to be highlighted — a ministry in which the many trials are balanced by such great joys, and especially one in which, as the Fathers teach, the greatest witness of love can be given to Christ.[68]

1. See 1 Pet 1:23; Acts 6:7; 12:24. "(The apostles) preached the word of truth and produced churches" (St Augustine, *Comment. on Ps.*, 44, 23: PL 36, 508).

2. See Mal 2:7; 1 Tim 4: 11-13; 2 Tim 4:5; Tit 1:9.

3. See Mk 16:16.

4. See 2 Cor 11:7. What is said of bishops holds also for priests, since they are the co-workers of the bishops. See *Statuta Ecclesiae Antiqua*, ch. 3 (ed. Munier, Paris 1960, p. 79); *Decretum Gratiani*, C. 6, D. 88 (ed. Friedberg, I 307); Council of Trent, Decree *De reform.*, Session 5, c. 2, n. 9 (*Conc. Oec. Decreta*, ed. Herder, Rome 1963, p. 645); Session 24, c. 4 (p. 739); Vatican Council II, Dogmatic Constitution on the Church *Lumen gentium*, n. 25.

5. See *Constitutiones Apostolorum*, II, 26, 7: "Let (priests) be the teachers of divine knowledge, since the Lord himself also commanded us, saying: Going teach ye, etc." (ed. F. X. Funk, *Diadascalia et Constitutiones Apostolorum*, I, Paderborn 1905, p. 105). *Leonine Sacramentary* and other sacramentaries down to the *Roman Pontifical* Preface for the Ordination of a Priest: "By this providence, O Lord, you have added teachers of the faith to the apostles of your Son, and through them they filled the whole earth with preachers [or: preaching] of the second rank." *Book of Orders of the Mozarabic Liturgy*, Preface for the Ordination of a Priest: "The teacher of peoples and the ruler of subjects, let him keep the catholic faith in well-ordered fashion, and announce true salvation to all" (ed. M. Ferotin, Paris 1904, col. 55).

6. See Gal 2:5.

7. See 1 Pet 2:12.

8. See the Rite of Ordination of a Priest in the Alexandrian

church of the Jacobites:"... Gather your people to the word of doctrine like a nurse who cherishes her children" (H. Denzinger, *Ritus Orientalium,* vol. II, Wurzburg 1863, p. 14).

9. See Mt 28:19; Mk 16:16; Tertullian, *On Baptism,* 14, 2 (CCh, Latin series, 1, p. 289, 11-13); St. Athanasius, *Adv. Arianos,* 2, 42 (PG 26, 237); St Jerome, *Comment. on Mat.,* 28, 19: PL 26, 218 BC:"First they teach all nations, then they baptize with water those who have been taught. For it cannot be that the body should receive the sacrament of Baptism unless the soul has previously received the truth of the faith"; St Thomas Aquinas, *Expositio primae Decretalis,* §1:"When our Saviour was sending his disciples to preach he gave them three injunctions. First, that they should teach the faith; secondly that they should initiate believers through the sacraments" (ed. Marietti, *Opuscula Theologica,* Turin Rome 1954, 1138).

10. See Vatican Council II, Constitution on the Sacred Liturgy, *Sacrosanctum Concilium,* n. 35, 2.

11. See ibid., nn. 33, 35, 48, 52.

12. See ibid., n. 7 (pp. 100-101); Pius XII, Encyclical *Mystici Corporis,* 29 June 1943: AAS 35 (1943), p. 230.

13. St. Ignatius Martyr, *Smyrn.,* 8, 1-2 (ed. F. X. Funk, p. 282, 6-15); *Constitutiones Apostolorum,* VIII, 12, 3 (ed. F. X. Funk, p. 496); VIII, 29, 2 (p. 532).

14. See Vatican Council II, Dogmatic Constitution on the Church, *Lumen gentium,* n 28:.

15. "The Eucharist is as it were the completion of the spiritual life and the summit of all the sacraments" (St Thomas Aquinas, *Summa Theologiae* III, q 73 a 3 c); see *Summa Theologiae* III, q 65, a 3

16. See St Thomas Aquinas, *Summa Theologiae* III, q. 65, a. 3, ad 1; q. 79, a. 1, c. et ad 1.

17. See Eph 5:19-20.

18. See St Jerome, *Epist.,* 114, 2-"... and consecrated chalices and sacred vestments and the other things that have to do with the worship of the Lord's passion ... because of their association with the body and Blood of the Lord are to be venerated with the same reverence as his body and Blood" (PL 22, 934). See Vatican Council II, Constitution on the Sacred Liturgy, *Sacrosanctum Concilium,* nn. 122-127.

19. "Moreover, let them not omit to make each day a visit to the most blessed sacrament, which is to be reserved in the most noble place and in the most honorable way possible in churches, according to liturgical laws, since this visit will be at once a proof of gratitude, a pledge of love and an act of the adoration due to Christ present in this same sacrament": Paul VI, Encyclical *Mysterium Fidei,* 3 September 1965: AAS 57 [1965], p 771.

20. See Vatican Council II, Dogmatic Constitution on the Church, *Lumen gentium,* n. 286.

21. See 2 Cor 10:8; 13:10.

22. See Gal 1:10.

23. See I Cor 4:14.

24. See *Didascalia,* II, 34, 3; II, 46, 6; II, 47, 1; *Constitutiones Apostolorum,* II, 47, 1: ed. F. X. Funk, *Didascalia et Constitutiones,* I, pp. 116, 142 and 143.

25. See Gal 4:3; 5:1 and 13.

26. See St Jerome, *Epist.,* 58, 7: "What use is it that walls glitter with gems while Christ dies in the person of one who is poor?": PL 22, 584.

27. See 1 Pet 4:10 ff.

28. See Mt 25:34-35.

29. See Lk 4:18.

30. Other classes can be mentioned, e.g., migrants, itinerants, etc. These are dealt with in the Decree on the Pastoral Function of Bishops in the Church, *Christus Dominus.*

31. See *Didascalia,* II, 59, 1-3: "In your teaching tell the people to visit the church and never to stay away, but to assemble always and not impoverish the church, by staying away, and make the body of Christ a member less . . . . Therefore since you are members of Christ do not separate yourselves from the church by failing to be united; for having Christ your head according to his promise present and communicating with you, do not neglect yourselves or alienate the Saviour from his members or divide or disperse his body . . .": ed. F. X. Funk, 1, p. 170; Paul VI, Allocution to the Italian clergy at the 13th "Week of pastoral renewal," at Orvieto, 6 September 1963: AAS 55 (1963), pp. 750 ff.

32. See Vatican Council II, Dogmatic Constitution on the Church *Lumen gentium,* 21 November 1964, n. 28.

33. See the so-called *Ecclesiastical Constitution of the Apostles,* XVIII: Priests are fellow-participants in the mysteries and fellow-soldiers of the bishops (ed. Th. Schermann, *Die allgemeine Kirchenordnung,* I, Paderborn 1914, p. 26; A. Harnack, T. u. U., II, 4, p. 13, n. 18 and 19); Pseudo-Jerome, *On the Seven Orders of the church* : ". . . in the blessing, they are sharers in the mysteries with the bishops" (ed. A. W Kalff, Wurzburg 1937, p. 45); St Isidore of Seville, *On Ecclesiastical Offices,* c. VII-"They are set over the church of God and in the celebration of the Eucharist they are the associates of the bishops, as they are also in teaching the people and in the office of preaching" (PL 83, 787).

34. See *Didascalia,* II, 28, 4: ed. F. X. Funk, p. 108; *Apostolic Constitutions,* II, 28-34; II, 34, 3: ibid., pp. 109 and 117.

35. *Apostolic Constitutions,* VIII, 16, 4: ed. F X. Funk, I, p 522, 13; see *Summary of Apostolic Constitutions,* VI: ibid, 11, p. 80, 3-4, *Testament of the Lord:* ". . . give him the Spirit of grace, counsel, and magnanimity, the spirit of the priesthood . . . to help and govern your people in work, in fear, in a pure heart": trans. I. E. Rahmani, Mainz 1899, p. 69. So also in *Apostolic Tradition:* ed. B. Botte, *La*

Tradition Apostolique, Munster i. W. 1963, p. 20.

36. See Num 11:16-25

37. *Roman Pontifical,* "Ordination of a Priest," Preface; these words are already contained in the *Leonine, Gelasian* and *Gregorian Sacramentaries.* Similar expressions are found in the eastern liturgies; see *Apost. Trad.:*"... look upon your servant and impart to him the spirit of grace and counsel, that he may aid the priests and rule your people in a clean heart, as you looked upon the people of your choice and commanded Moses to choose elders whom you filled with your spirit which you have given to your servant": from the ancient Latin version of Verona, ed. B. Botte, *La Tradition Apostolique de S. Hippolyte. Essai de reconstruction,* Munster i. W. 1963, p. 20; *Apost. Const.* Vlll, 16, 4: ed. F. X. Funk, 1, p 522, 16-17; *Summary of Apost. Const.* 6: ed. F. X. Funk, 11, p. 20, 5-7; *Testament of the Lord*: trans I. E. Rahmani, Mainz 1899, p. 69, *Euchology of Serapion, XXVII:* ed. F. X. Funk, *Didascalia et Constitutiones,* 11, p. 190, lin 1-7; *Rite of Ordination in the Maronite Liturgy:* trans. H. Denzinger, *Ritus Orientalium,* 11, Wurzburg 1863, p 161. Among the Fathers can be cited: Theodore of Mopsuesta, In I Tim. 3, 8: ed Swete, II, pp. 119-121; Theodore, *Questions on Numbers,* XVIII: PG 80, 372 b.

38. See Vatican Council II, Dogmatic Constitution on the Church, *Lumen gentium,* n. 28.

39. See John XXIII, Encyclical *Sacerdotii Nostri primordia,* I August 1959: AAS 51 (1959), p. 576; St. Pius X, Exhortation to the Clergy *Haerent animo,* 4 August 1908: S. Pii X Acta, vol. IV (1908), pp. 237 ff.

40. See Vatican Council II, Decree on the Pastoral Office of Bishops in the Church, *Christus Dominus,* nn. 15 and 16.

41. St Ignatius Martyr, *Magnesians,* 6, 1:"I exhort you to strive to do all things in the peace of God, the bishop presiding in the place of God and the priests in the place of the senate of apostles, and the deacons who are so dear to me having entrusted to them the ministry of Jesus Christ who was with the Father before all ages and finally appeared": ed F. X. Funk, p. 234, 10-13; St Ignatius Martyr, *Trallians,* 3, 1; "Likewise let all reverence the deacons as Jesus Christ, as also the bishop who is the image of the Father, the priests as the senate of God and the council of apostles: without these one cannot speak of a church": ibid., p. 244, 10-12; St. Jerome, *Commentary on Isaiah,* 11, 3: PL 24, 61 A: "We also have in the church our senate, the group of priests."

42. In established law the Cathedral Chapter is regarded as the bishop's "senate and council": CIC, c. 391, or in its absence the group of diocesan consultors: see ClC, canons. 423-428. But it is desirable to reform these institutions in such a way as to make better provision for present-day needs. Clearly this group of priests differs from the pastoral council spoken of in the Decree on the Pastoral Office of Bishops in the Church, *Christus Dominus,* n 27,

which includes lay people and whose function is confined to investigating questions of pastoral activity. On the question of priests as counsellors of bishops see *Didascalia*, 11, 28, 4: ed. F. X. Funk, 1, p 108; also *Apost. Const.*, 11, 28, 4: ed F. X. Funk, I, p. 109; St Ignatius Martyr, *Magnesians*, 6, 1: ed. F. X Funk, p. 244, 10-12; Origen, *Against Celsus*, 3, 30: Priests are counsellors or *bouleutai*: PG 11, 157 d-960 a.

43. See Paul VI, Allocution to the parish priests and Lenten preachers of Rome, in the Sistine Chapel, 1 March 1965: AAS 57 (1965), p. 326

44. See *Apost. Const.*, Vlll, 47, 39: "Priests . . . should do nothing without the decision of the bishop; for it is to him that the people of the Lord has been entrusted and from him an account of their souls will be demanded": ed F. X. Funk, p. 577.

45. See 3 Jn 8.

46. See Jn 17:23.

47. See Heb 13:1-2.

48. See Heb 13:16.

49. See Mt 5:10.

50. See 1 Th 2:12; Col 1:13.

51. See Mt 23: 8. "From the very fact that we wish to be people's pastors, fathers and teachers it follows that we must act as their brothers": Paul VI, Encyclical *Ecclesiam suam* 6 August 1964: AAS 58 [1964], p. 647.

52. See Eph 4:7 and 16; *Apost. Const*, Vlll, 1, 20: "The bishop moreover should not set himself up over the deacons or priests, nor the priests over the people; for the structure of the assembly is made up of members of both": ed F. X. Funk, 1, p. 467.

53. See Phil 2:21.

54. See 1 Jn 4:1.

55. See Vatican Council II, Dogmatic Constitution on the Church, *Lumen gentium*, n. 37.

56. See Eph 4:14.

57. See Vatican Council II, Decree on Ecumenism, *Unitatis redintegratio*.

58. See Vatican Council II, Dogmatic Constitution on the Church, *Lumen gentium*, n. 37.

59. See Heb 7:3.

60. See Lk 10:1.

61. See 1 Pet 2:25.

62. See Acts 20:28.

63. See Mt 9:36

64. *Roman Pontifical*, "Ordination of a Priest."

65. See Vatican Council II, Decree on the Training of Priests, *Optatum totius*, n. 2.

66. "The voice of God which calls expresses itself in two different ways that are marvellous and converging: one interior, that of

grace, that of the holy Spirit, that inexpressible interior attraction which the silent and powerful voice of the Lord exercises in the unfathomable depths of the human soul; and the other one external, human, sensible, social, juridical, concrete, that of the qualified minister of the word of God, that of the Apostle, that of the hierarchy, an indispensable instrument instituted and willed by Christ as a concrete means of translating into the language of experience the message of the word and the divine precept Such is the teaching of catholic doctrine with St Paul: *How shall they hear without a preacher . . . Faith comes from hearing:* Rom 10:14 and 17": Paul VI, Allocution, 5 May 1965: *L'Osservatore Romano,* 6 May 1965, p 1.

67. See Vatican Council II, Decree *Optatam totius,* on Priestly Training, 28 October 1965, n. 2.

68. This is the teaching of the Fathers when they explain Christ's words to Peter:"Do you love me? . . . Feed my sheep"(Jn. 21:17): so St John Chrysostom, *On The Priesthood,* II, 1-2: PG 47-48, 633; St Gregory the Great, *Pastoral Rule,* part 1. ch. 5: PL 77, 19 A.

Chapter III

THE LIFE OF PRIESTS

I. Priests' Call to Perfection

Call of Priests to Holiness

12. By the sacrament of order priests are made in the image of Christ the priest as servants of the Head, so that as co-workers with the episcopal order they may build up the body of Christ, the church. Like all Christians they have already received in the consecration of Baptism the sign and gift of their great calling and grace. So they are enabled and obliged even in the midst of human weakness[1] to seek perfection, according to the Lord's word:"You, therefore, must be perfect, as your heavenly Father is perfect"(Mt 5:48).

But priests are especially bound to attain perfection. They are consecrated to God in a new way by their ordination and are made the living instruments of Christ the eternal priest, and so are enabled to accomplish throughout all time that wonderful work of his which with supernatural efficacy restored the whole human race.[2] Since every priest in his own way assumes the person of Christ he is endowed with a special grace. By this grace the priest, through his service of the people committed to his care and all the people of God, is able the better to pursue the perfection of Christ, whose place he takes. The human weakness of his flesh is remedied by the holiness of him who became for us a high priest "holy, innocent, undefiled, separated from sinners" (Heb 7:26).

Christ, whom the Father sanctified or consecrated and sent into the world,[3] "gave himself for us to redeem us from all iniquity and to purify for himself a people of his own who are zealous for good deeds" (Tit 2:14), and in this way through his passion entered into his glory.[4] In a similar way, priests, who are consecrated by the anointing of the holy Spirit and sent by Christ, mortify the works of the flesh in themselves and dedicate themselves completely to the service of the people, and so are able, in the holiness with which they have been enriched in Christ, to grow towards the perfection of humanity.[5]

In this way they are made strong in the life of the spirit by exercising the ministration of the Spirit and of justice,[6] provided they are prepared to listen to the inspiration of the Spirit of Christ who gives them life and guidance. For it is through the sacred actions they perform every day, as through their whole ministry which they exercise in union with the bishop and their fellow priests, that they are set on the right course to perfection of life. The very holiness of priests is of the greatest benefit for the fruitful fulfillment of their ministry. While it is possible for God's grace to carry out the work of salvation through unworthy ministers, yet God ordinarily prefers to show his wonders through those who are more responsive to the impulse and guidance of the holy Spirit and who, because of their intimate union with Christ and their holiness of life, are able to say with St Paul: "It is no longer I who live, but Christ who lives in me" (Gal 2:20).

For this reason this sacred council, in the hope of attaining its pastoral objectives of interior renewal, of worldwide diffusion of the Gospel, and of dialogue with the modern world, issues the strongest appeal to all priests to strive always by the use of all suitable means commended by the church[7] towards that greater holiness that will make them daily more effective instruments for the service of all God's people.

The Exercise of the Threefold Priestly Function both Demands and Fosters Holiness

13. Priests will acquire holiness in their own distinctive way by exercising their functions sincerely and tirelessly in the Spirit of Christ.

Since they are ministers of the word of God, they read and hear every day the word of God which they must teach to others. If they endeavour at the same time to make it part of their own lives, they will become daily more perfect disciples of the Lord, according to the saying of the apostle Paul to Timothy: "Practice these duties, devote yourself to them; so that all may see your progress. Take heed to yourself and to your teaching; hold to that, for in doing so you will save both yourself and your hearers" (1 Tim 4:15-16). For by seeking more effective ways of conveying to others what they have meditated on,[8] they will savor more profoundly the "unsearchable riches of Christ" (Eph 3:8) and the many-sided wisdom of God.[9] By keeping in mind that it is the Lord who opens hearts[10] and that the excellence comes not from themselves

but from the power of God,[11] they will be more intimately united with Christ the Teacher and will be
guided by his Spirit in the very act of teaching the
word. And by this close union with Christ they share
in the charity of God, the mystery of which was kept
hidden from all ages[12] to be revealed in Christ.

Priests as ministers of the sacred mysteries, especially in the sacrifice of the Mass, act in a special way
in the person of Christ who gave himself as a victim
to sanctify men and women. And this is why they are
invited to imitate what they handle, so that as they
celebrate the mystery of the Lord's death they may
take care to mortify their members from vices and
concupiscences.[13]

In the mystery of the eucharistic sacrifice, in which
priests fulfil their principal function, the work of our
redemption is continually carried out.[14] For this reason
the daily celebration of the Eucharist is earnestly recommended. This celebration is an action of Christ and
the church even if it is impossible for the faithful to be
present.[15] So when priests unite themselves with the
action of Christ the Priest they daily offer themselves
completely to God, and by being nourished with
Christ's body they share in the charity of him who
gives himself as food to the faithful.

In the same way they are united with the intention
and the charity of Christ when they administer the
sacraments. They do this in a special way when they
show themselves to be always available to administer
the sacrament of Penance whenever it is reasonably
requested by the faithful. In reciting the Divine Office
they lend their voice to the church which perseveres
in prayer in the name of the whole human race, in
union with Christ who "always lives to make intercession for them" (Heb 7:25).

While they govern and shepherd the people of
God, they are encouraged by the love of the good
shepherd to give their lives for their sheep.[16] They, too,

are prepared for the supreme sacrifice, following the example of those priests who even in our own times have not held back from laying down their lives. Since they are the instructors in the faith and have themselves "confidence to enter the sanctuary by the blood of Jesus" (Heb 10:19), they approach God "with a true heart in full assurance of faith" (Heb 10:22). They set up a steadfast hope for their faithful people,[17] so that they may be able to comfort all who are in distress by the exhortation wherewith God also exhorts them.[18] As rulers of the community they cultivate the form of asceticism suited to a pastor of souls, renouncing their own convenience, seeking not their own good, but that of the many, that they may be saved,[19] always making further progress towards a more perfect fulfillment of their pastoral work and, where the need arises, prepared to break new ground in pastoral methods under the guidance of the Spirit of love who breathes where he wills.[20]

Unity and Harmony of Priests

14. In today's world, with the many tasks which people have to do and the great variety of problems facing them and very often needing to be solved very quickly, there is often danger for those whose energies are divided among different activities. Priests who are perplexed and distracted by the multiplicity of tasks facing them may be very concerned about how they can unify their interior life and their program of external activity. This cannot be achieved merely by an outward arrangement of ministerial tasks nor by the practice of spiritual exercises alone, though this may help to foster such unity. Priests can bring unity into their lives by following the example of Christ the Lord as they carry out their ministry: his food was to do the will of him who sent him to accomplish his work.[21]

For in truth, to continue to do the will of his Father

unceasingly in the world through the church, Christ works through his ministers. Thus, he remains the constant principle and source of the unity of their lives. Therefore priests will unify their lives by uniting themselves with Christ in recognition of the Father's will and in the gift of themselves to the flock entrusted to them.[22] In this way, by adopting the role of the good shepherd they will find in the practise of pastoral charity itself the bond of priestly perfection which will harmonise their lives and activity. Such pastoral charity[23] is derived chiefly from the eucharistic sacrifice, which is the centre and root of the priest's entire life, in the sense that in a priestly spirit he tries to apply to himself what is enacted on the altar of sacrifice. But this cannot be achieved except through priests themselves penetrating ever more intimately through prayer into the mystery of Christ.

To verify the unity of their lives in practice priests should examine all their projects in order to discover what is God's will:[24] to learn, that is to say, how far their projects are in conformity with the standards of the church's Gospel mission. Faithfulness to Christ cannot be separated from faithfulness to his church. Hence pastoral charity demands that priests, if they are not to run in vain,[25] should always work within the bond of union with the bishops and their fellow priests. If they act in this manner, priests will find unity of life in the unity of the church's own mission. In this way they will be united with their Lord and through him with the Father in the holy Spirit, and can be filled with consolation and abounding joy.[26]

II. Special Spiritual Requirements in the Life of the Priest

Humility and Obedience

15. Among the virtues especially demanded by the

ministry of priests must be counted that disposition of mind by which they are always prepared to seek not their own will but the will of him who has sent them.[27] The divine task for the fulfilment of which they have been set apart by the holy Spirit[28] transcends all human strength and human wisdom; for "God chose what is weak in the world to shame the strong" (l Cor 1:27).

Therefore, the true minister of Christ is conscious of his own weakness and labors in humility. He tries to find out what is well-pleasing to God[29] and, bound as it were in the Spirit,[30] he is guided in all things by the will of him who wishes all women and men to be saved. He is able to discover and carry out that will in the course of his daily routine by humbly placing himself at the service of all those who are entrusted to his care by God, in the office that has been committed to him and the variety of events that make up his life.

The priestly ministry, being the ministry of the church itself, can be exercised only in the hierarchical union of the whole body of the church. Hence pastoral charity urges priests to act within this communion and in obedience to dedicate their own wills to the service of God and their fellow Christians. They will accept and carry out in the spirit of faith the commands and suggestions of the Pope and of their bishop and other superiors. They will most gladly spend themselves and be spent [31] in whatever office is entrusted to them, however lowly and poorly rewarded. By acting in this way, they preserve and strengthen the indispensable unity with their brothers in the ministry and especially with those whom the Lord has appointed the visible rulers of his church. They also work towards the building up of the body of Christ, which grows "by every joint with which it is supplied."[32] This obedience, which leads to the more mature freedom of the sons and daughters of God, by its nature demands that priests in the exercise of their duties should be moved by charity prudently to seek new methods of advancing the good of the church. At the same time it also demands that while putting forward their schemes with confidence and being insistent in making known the needs of the flock entrusted to them, they should always be prepared to submit to the judgment of those who exercise the chief function in ruling God's church.

By this humility and by responsible and willing obedience, priests conform themselves to Christ. They reproduce the sentiment of Jesus Christ who "emptied himself, taking the form of a servant . . . and became obedient unto death"(Phil 2:7-9), and who by this obedience overcame and redeemed the disobedience of Adam, as the apostle declares "For as by one man's disobedience many were made sinners, so by one man's obedience many will be made righteous" (Rom 5:19).

Celibacy to be Embraced and Esteemed as a Gift

16. Perfect and perpetual continence for the sake of the kingdom of heaven was recommended by Christ the Lord.[33] It has been freely accepted and laudably observed by many Christians down through the centuries as well as in our own time, and has always been held in especially high esteem by the church as a feature of priestly life. For it is at once a sign of pastoral charity and an incentive to it as well as being in a special way a source of spiritual fruitfulness in the world.[34] It is true that it is not demanded of the priesthood by its nature. This is clear from the practice of the primitive church[35] and the tradition of the eastern churches where in addition to those — including all bishops — who are given the grace to choose to observe celibacy, there are also many excellent mar-

ried priests. While recommending ecclesiastical celibacy this sacred council does not by any means aim at changing that different discipline which is lawfully practiced in the eastern churches. Rather the council affectionately exhorts all those who have received the priesthood in the married state to persevere in their holy vocation and continue to devote their lives fully and generously to the flock entrusted to them.[36]

There are many ways in which celibacy is in harmony with the priesthood. For the whole mission of the priest is dedicated to the service of the new humanity which Christ, the victor over death, raises up in the world through his Spirit and which is born "not of blood nor of the will of the flesh nor of the will of man, but of God" (Jn 1:13). By preserving virginity or celibacy for the sake of the Kingdom of heaven[37] priests are consecrated in a new and excellent way to Christ. They more readily join themselves to him with undivided heart[38] and dedicate themselves more freely in him and through him to the service of God and of men and women. They are less encumbered in their service of his kingdom and of the task of heavenly regeneration. In this way they become better fitted for a broader acceptance of fatherhood in Christ. By means of celibacy, then, priests profess before humanity their willingness to be dedicated with undivided loyalty to the task entrusted to them, namely that of espousing the faithful to one husband and presenting them as a chaste virgin to Christ.[39] They recall that mystical marriage, established by God and destined to be fully revealed in the future, by which the church holds Christ as her only spouse.[40] Moreover they are made a living sign of that world to come, already present through faith and charity, a world in which the children of the resurrection shall neither marry nor be given in marriage.[41]

For these reasons, based on the mystery of Christ

and his mission, celibacy, which at first was recommended to priests, was afterwards in the Latin church imposed by law on all who were to be promoted to holy Orders. This sacred council approves and confirms this legislation so far as it concerns those destined for the priesthood, and feels confident in the Spirit that the gift of celibacy, so appropriate to the priesthood of the New Testament, is liberally granted by the Father, provided those who share Christ's priesthood through the sacrament of order, and indeed the whole church, ask for that gift humbly and earnestly.

This sacred council also exhorts all priests who, with trust in God's grace, have of their own free choice accepted consecrated celibacy after the example of Christ, to hold fast to it with courage and enthusiasm, and to persevere faithfully in this state, appreciating that glorious gift that has been given them by the Father and is so clearly praised by the Lord,[42] and keeping before their eyes the great mysteries that are signified and fulfilled in it. And the more that perfect continence is considered by many people to be impossible in the world of today, so much the more humbly and perseveringly in union with the church ought priests to demand the grace of fidelity, which is never denied to those who ask.

At the same time they will employ all the helps to fidelity, both supernatural and natural, which are available to everybody. Especially they should never neglect to follow the rules of asceticism which are approved by the experience of the church and are as necessary as ever in the modern world. So this sacred council asks that not only priests but all the faithful would cherish this precious gift of priestly celibacy, and that all of them would ask God always to give this gift abundantly to his church.

Relation with the World and Worldly Goods: Voluntary Poverty

17. Priests can learn, by brotherly and friendly association with each other and with other people, to cultivate human values and appreciate created goods as gifts of God. While living in the world they should yet realize that according to the word of our Lord and Master they are not of the world.[43] By using the world, then, as those who do not use it[44] they will come to that liberty by which they will be freed from all inordinate anxiety and will become docile to the divine voice in their daily life. From this liberty and docility grows that spiritual insight through which is found a right attitude to the world and to earthly goods.

This attitude is of great importance for priests, since the church's mission is carried out in the midst of the world and since created goods are absolutely necessary for people's personal progress. Let priests be thankful for everything that the heavenly Father has given them towards a proper standard of living. However, they ought to judge everything they meet in the light of faith, so that they will be guided towards the right use of things in accordance with God's will and will reject anything that is prejudicial to their mission.

Priests as men whose "portion and inheritance" (Num 18:20) is the Lord ought to use temporal goods for those purposes only for which Christ's teaching and the church's directives allow them to be used. They are to manage ecclesiastical property, properly so called, according to the nature of the case and the norm of ecclesiastical laws and with the help, as far as possible, of skilled lay people. They are to apply this property always to those purposes for the achievement of which the church is allowed to own temporal goods. These are: the organization of divine worship, the provision of decent support for the clergy, and the exercise of works of the apostolate and of charity, especially for the benefit of those in need.[45]

Priests, just like bishops, without prejudice to particular law,[46] are to use money acquired by them on the occasion of their exercise of some ecclesiastical office primarily for their own decent support and the fulfilment of the duties of their state. They should be willing to devote whatever is left over to the good of the church or to works of charity. So they are not to regard an ecclesiastical office as a source of profit, and are not to spend the income accruing from it for increasing their own private fortunes.[47] Hence priests, far from setting their hearts on riches,[48] must always avoid all avarice and carefully refrain from all appearance of trafficking.

In fact, priests are invited to embrace voluntary poverty. By it they become more clearly conformed to Christ and more ready to devote themselves to their sacred ministry. For Christ being rich became poor for our sakes, that through his poverty we might be rich.[49] The apostles by their example gave testimony that the free gift of God was to be given freely.[50] They knew both how to abound and to suffer need.[51] Even some kind of use of property in common, like the community of goods which is praised in the history of the primitive church, [52] provides an excellent opening for pastoral charity. By this way of life priests can laudably put into practice the spirit of poverty commended by Christ.

Guided then by the Spirit of the Lord, who anointed the Saviour and sent him to preach the Gospel to the poor,[53] priests and bishops alike are to avoid everything that might in any way antagonize the poor. More than the rest of Christ's disciples they are to put aside all appearance of vanity in their surroundings. Each is to arrange his house in such a way that it never appears unapproachable to anyone and that nobody, even the humblest, is ever afraid to visit it.

III. Helps for the Priest's Life

Helps Toward Fostering Interior Life

18. To enable them to foster union with Christ in all of life's circumstances, priests, in addition to the conscientious performance of their ministry, have at their disposal the means both general and particular, new and old, which the holy Spirit has never ceased to raise up among the people of God and which the church recommends and in fact sometimes commands[54] for the sanctification of her members. Over and above all other spiritual helps are those activities in which Christians are nourished by the word of God from the double table of holy scripture and the Eucharist.[55] Everybody knows how important their continuous use is for the personal sanctification of priests.

The ministers of sacramental grace are intimately united to Christ the Saviour and Pastor through the fruitful reception of the sacrament of Penance. If it is prepared for by a daily examination of conscience, it is a powerful incentive to the essential conversion of heart to the love of the Father of mercies. Under the light of a faith that has been nourished by spiritual reading, priests can diligently search for the signs of God's will and the inspirations of his grace in the varied events of life. In this way, they will become daily more docile in the demands of the mission they have undertaken in the holy Spirit. They always find a wonderful example of such docility in the Blessed Virgin Mary, who under the guidance of the holy Spirit made a total dedication of herself for the mystery of people's redemption.[56] Priests should always venerate and love her, with a filial devotion and worship, as the mother of the supreme and eternal priest, as queen of apostles, and as protectress of their ministry.

As a help towards faithful performance of their ministry, priests should be deeply attached to daily conversation with Christ the Lord in their visits to the most blessed sacrament and in their personal devotion to it. They should be glad to devote time to a spiritual retreat and should have a high regard for spiritual direction. In various ways, in particular through the approved practice of mental prayer and the different forms of vocal prayer which they freely choose to practice, priests are to seek and perseveringly ask of God the true spirit of adoration. By this spirit they themselves, and with them the people entrusted to their care, will unite themselves with Christ the Mediator of the New Testament, and will be able as adopted sons and daughters to cry, "Abba! Father!" (Rom 8:15).

Study and Pastoral Knowledge

19. Priests are charged by the bishop in the ceremony of ordination that they are to be "mature in learning" and that their teaching should be "a spiritual medicine for the people of God."[57] A sacred minister's learning ought itself be sacred in the sense of being derived from a sacred source and directed to a sacred purpose. Primarily, then, it is drawn from reading and meditating on sacred scripture.[58] It is also fruitfully nourished by the study of the Fathers and Doctors of the church and the other traditional classics. Moreover, if priests are to give adequate answers to the problems discussed by people at the present time, they should be well versed in the statements of the church's magisterium and especially those of the councils and the popes. They should also consult the best approved writers in theology.

Secular culture and even sacred science are advancing at an unprecedented rate in our time. Priests are therefore urged constantly to strive to attain an adequate knowledge of things divine and human. In this way they will be better equipped for dialogue with their contemporaries.

To facilitate the study and the more effective learning of methods of evangelization and the apostolate, every attention is to be given to providing priests with suitable helps. Examples of these are the organization of courses or congresses suited to the conditions of each region, the setting up of centers for pastoral studies, the founding of libraries, and the proper direction of studies by suitable persons.

In addition bishops, either individually or in collaboration with others, should consider more effective ways of arranging that their priests would be able to attend a course of study at certain times, especially for a few years after ordination.[59] The aim of such a course should be to give them an opportunity of increasing their knowledge of pastoral methods and theological science, and at the same time of strengthening their spiritual life and sharing their pastoral experiences with their brother priests.[60] By these and other suitable helps, special attention may be given to helping newly appointed parish priests also, as well as priests assigned to new pastoral work or sent to another diocese or country.

Finally, bishops should see to it that some priests devote themselves to deeper study of the sacred sciences. This will ensure that there will never be any lack of suitable teachers for the education of clerics. It will also ensure that the rest of the priests and the faithful will be helped to acquire the knowledge of religion that they need, and that the sound progress in sacred studies so very necessary for the church will be encouraged.

The Provision of Just Remuneration for Priests

20. Completely devoted as they are to the service of God in the fulfilment of the office entrusted to them, priests are entitled to receive a just remuneration. For "the laborers deserve their wages" (Lk 10:7)[61] and "the Lord commanded that they who proclaim the Gospel should get their living by the Gospel" (1 Cor 9:14). For this reason, insofar as provision is not made from some other source for the just remuneration of priests, the faithful are duty bound to provide a decent and fitting livelihood for their priests. The obligation arises from the fact that the priests are working for the lay people's benefit. Bishops are bound to warn the faithful of their obligation in this regard. They should also, either individually for their own dioceses or better still by acting together in a common territory, see to it that rules are drawn up by which due provision is made for the decent support of those who hold or have held any office in God's service.

Taking into consideration the conditions of different places and times as well as the nature of the office they hold, the remuneration to be received by each priest should be fundamentally the same for all living in the same circumstances. It should be in keeping with their status and in addition should be sufficient to ensure that they are able to pay those who work in their service and also are able to give to those in need. The church has always from its very beginnings esteemed highly the ministry to the poor. Moreover, priests' remuneration should be such as to allow the priest a proper holiday each year. The bishop should see to it that priests are able to have a holiday.

The actual office which sacred ministers fulfill should be regarded as of primary importance. For this reason the so-called system of benefices is to be abandoned or else reformed in such a way that the beneficiary dimension — that is, the right to the revenues attached to an endowed office — shall be regarded as secondary and the principal emphasis in law given to the ecclesiastical office itself. This should in future be understood as any office conferred in a permanent fashion and to be exercised for a spiritual purpose.

Common Funds to be Set up: Social Security for Priests to be Organized

21. The example of the faithful in the primitive church of Jerusalem should be always kept in mind. There "they had everything in common" (Acts 4:32) and "distribution was made to each as any had need" (Acts 4:35). It is an excellent arrangement, at least in places where the support of the clergy depends completely or to a great extent on the offerings of the faithful, that the money offered in this way should be collected by some kind of diocesan agency. The bishop would administer this agency with the help of priests appointed for this purpose and also of lay experts in financial matters, where the advantage of such appointment may make it advisable.

It is also desirable that as far as possible there should be set up in each diocese or region a common fund to enable bishops to satisfy obligations to people employed in the service of the church and to meet the various needs of the diocese. From this fund too, richer dioceses would be able to help poorer ones, so that the abundance of the one may supply the want of the other.[62] This common fund also should be made up mainly of moneys from the offerings of the faithful as well as from those coming from other sources to be determined by law.

Moreover, in countries where social security has not yet been adequately organized for the benefit of clergy, episcopal conferences are to make provision, in keeping with ecclesiastical and civil law, for the setting up of diocesan organizations (even federated with one another), or organizations for different dioceses grouped together, or an association catering for the whole territory: the purpose of these being that under the supervision of the hierarchy satisfactory provision should be made both for preventive and remedial treatment, and for the proper support of priests who suffer from ill health, disability or old age.

Priests should assist this organization when it has been set up, moved by a spirit of solidarity with their brother priests, sharing their hardships,[63] and at the same time realizing that in this way they can, without anxiety for their future, practice poverty with a readier appreciation of the Gospel and devote themselves completely to the salvation of souls. Those responsible should do their utmost to have such organizations combined on an international scale, so as to give them more stability and strength and promote their wider diffusion.

1. See 2 Cor 12:9.
2. See Pius XI, Encyclical *Ad catholici sacerdotii,* 20 December 1935: AAS 28 (1936), p 10.
3. See Jn 10:36.
4. See Lk 24:26.
5. See Eph 4:13.
6. See 2 Cor 3:8-9.
7. See among others: St Pius X, Exhortation to the Clergy, *Haerent animo,* 4 August 1908: S. Pii X Acta, vol. IV (1908), p. 237 ff.; Pius XI, Encyclical *Ad catholici sacerdotii,* 20 December 1935: AAS 28 (1936), p. 5 ff.; Pius XII, Apostolic Exhortation, *Menti Nostrae,* 23 September 1950: AAS 42 (1950), p. 657 ff.; John XXIII, Encyclical *Sacerdotii Nostri primordia,* 1 August 1959: AAS 51 (1959), p. 545 ff.
8. See St Thomas Aquinas *Summa Theologiae,* II-II, q. 188, a 7.
9. See Heb 3: 9-10.
10. See Acts 16:14.
11. See 2 Cor 4:7.
12. See Eph 3:9.
13. *Roman Pontifical,* "Ordination of a Priest."
14. See *Roman Missal,* Prayer over the offerings, of Ninth Sunday after Pentecost.
15. "The Mass, even though it is celebrated privately is still not

private, but is the act of Christ and the church. The church, in the sacrifice which it offers, learns to offer itself as a universal sacrifice and applies the unique and infinite redemptive power of the sacrifice of the cross to the whole world for its salvation. For every Mass that is celebrated is offered not merely for the salvation of some souls but for that of the whole world . . . Therefore we recommend with paternal insistence to priests, who are our especial joy and our crown in the Lord, that . . . they celebrate Mass worthily and devoutly every day": Paul VI, Encyclical *Mysterium Fidei*, 3 September 1965: AAS 57 [1965], pp. 761-762). See Vatican Council II, Constitution on the Sacred Liturgy, *Sacrosanctum Concilium*, nn. 26 and 27.

16. See Jn 10:11.

17. See 2 Cor 1:7.

18. See 2 Cor 1:4.

19. See 1 Cor 10:33.

20. See Jn 3:8.

21. See Jn 4:34.

22. See 1 Jn 3:16.

23. "Let it be the duty of love to shepherd the Lord's flock": St Augustine, *Treatise on John*, 123, 5: PL 35, 1967).

24. See Rom 12:2.

25. See Gal 2:2.

26. See 2 Cor 7:4.

27. See Jn 4:34; 5:30; and 6:38.

28. See Acts 13:2.

29. See Eph 5:10.

30. See Acts 20:22.

31. See 2 Cor 12:15.

32. See Eph 4:11-16.

33. See Mt 19:12.

34. See Vatican Council II, Dogmatic Constitution on the Church, *Lumen gentium*, n. 42.

35. See 1 Tim 3:2-5; Tit 1:6.

36. See Pius XI, Encyclical *Ad catholici sacerdotii*: AAS 28 (1936), p. 28.

37. See Mt 19:12.

38. See 1 Cor 7:32-34.

39. See 2 Cor 11:2.

40. See Vatican Council II, Dogmatic Constitution on the Church *Lumen gentium*, 21 November 1964, nn. 42 and 44; Decree on the Up-to-date Renewal of Religious Life, *Perfectae caritatis*, n. 12.

41. See Lk 20:35-36; Pius XI, Encyclical *Ad catholici sacerdotii*, 20 December 1935: AAS 28 (1936), pp. 24-28; Pius XII Encyclical *Sacra Virginitas*, 25 March 1954: AAS 46 (1954), pp. 169-172

42. See Mt 19:11.

43. See Jn 17:14-16.

44. See 1 Cor 7:31.

45. Council of Antioch, can. 25: Mansi 2, 1328; *Decree of Gratian,* c. 23, C. 12, q. 1 (ed. Friedberg, I, pp. 684-685).

46. This is to be understood especially of the laws and customs in force in the Eastern churches.

47. Council of Paris, a. 829, can. 15: M.G.H., sect. III, *Concilia,* t. 2, par. 6, 622; Council of Trent, Session 25, On reform, cap. 1.

48. See Ps 62:11 Vg. 61.

49. See 2 Cor 8:9.

50. See Acts 8:9.

50. See Acts 8:18-25.

51. See Phil 4:12.

52. See Acts 2:42-47.

53. See Lk 4:18.

54. See ClC, can. 125 ff.

55. See Vatican Council II, Decree on the Up-to-date Renewal of Religious Life, *Perfectae caritatis,* n. 6; Dogmatic Constitution on Divine Revelation *Dei verbum,* n. 21.

56. See Vatican Council II, Dogmatic Constitution on the Church *Lumen gentium,* n. 65.

57. *Roman Pontifical,* "Ordination of a Priest."

58. See Vatican Council II, Dogmatic Constitution on Divine Revelation, *Dei verbum,* on Divine Revelation, 18 November 1965, n. 25.

59. This course is not the same as the pastoral course to be completed immediately after ordination and dealt with in the Decree on the Training of Priests, *Optatam totius,* n. 22.

60. See Vatican Council II, Decree on the Pastoral Office of Bishops in the church, *Christus Dominus* n. 16.

61. See Mt 10:10; 1 Cor 9:7; 1 Tim 5:18.

62. See 2 Cor 8:14.

63. See Phil 4:14.

Conclusion and Exhortation

22. This sacred council, while keeping in mind the joys of the priestly life, cannot pass over the difficulties too which priests encounter in the circumstances of their life today. It knows also how much economic and social conditions, and even people's morals, are being transformed, and how much their sense of

values is undergoing change. Hence, it is that the church's ministers, and even sometimes the faithful, in the midst of this world feel themselves estranged from it and are anxiously seeking suitable methods and words by which they may be able to communicate with it. The new obstacles opposing the faith, the apparent fruitlessness of the work done, the bitter loneliness they experience — these can bring for priests the danger of a feeling of frustration.

But this world as it is entrusted today to the church as the object of its love and service, this is the world God has so loved as to give his only-begotten Son for it.[1] The truth is that this world, caught as it is in the grip of much sin yet enriched too with many possibilities, provides the church with the living stones[2] which are built together into a habitation of God in the Spirit.[3] The same holy Spirit, while urging the church to open new avenues of approach to the modern world, also suggests and fosters suitable adaptations of the priestly ministry.

Let priests remember that in carrying out their task they are never alone but are supported by the almighty power of God. Believing in Christ who has called them to share in his priesthood, let them devote themselves to their office with all trust, knowing that God is powerful to increase charity in them.[4] Let them remember too that they have their brothers in the priesthood and indeed the entire world's believers, as allies.

For all priests are cooperating in carrying out God's saving plan, the mystery of Christ or the sacrament hidden from eternity in God.[5] Only gradually is this mystery carried into effect by the united efforts of the different ministries for the building up of the body of Christ until the measure of its age be fulfilled. Since all these truths are hidden with Christ in God[6] it is by faith especially that they can be perceived. For the leaders of the people of God must needs walk by faith, following the example of the faithful Abraham who by faith "obeyed when he was called to go out to a place which he was to receive as an inheritance; and he went out, not knowing where he was to go" (Heb 11:8).

Indeed the dispenser of the mysteries of God can be compared to the person who cast the seed into the earth, of whom the Lord said that he "should sleep and rise night and day, and the seed should sprout and grow, he knows not how" (Mk 4:27). The Lord Jesus who said "Be of good cheer, I have overcome the world" (Jn 16:23), did not by these words promise complete victory to his church in this world. This sacred council rejoices that the earth which has been sown with the seed of the Gospel is now bringing forth fruit in many places under the guidance of the Spirit of the Lord. This Spirit is filling the world and has stirred up a truly missionary spirit in the hearts of many priests and faithful. For all this the sacred council affectionately offers its thanks to all the priests of the world: "Now to him who by the power at work within us is able to do far more abundantly than all that we ask or think, to him be glory in the church and in Christ Jesus . . ." (Eph 3:20-21).

1. See Jn 3:16.
2. See 1 Pet 2:5.
3. See Eph 2:22.
4. See *Roman Pontifical,* "Ordination of a Priest."
5. See Eph 3:9.
6. See Col 3:3.

DECREE ON THE TRAINING OF PRIESTS[a]

Optatam Totius
28 October, 1965

This holy council is fully aware that the desired renewal of the whole church depends to a great extent on a priestly ministry animated by the spirit of Christ.[1] It proclaims the supreme importance of priestly formation and affirms some of its primary principles, whereby laws tested by the experience of centuries are confirmed and new elements are introduced to correspond with the constitutions and decrees of this council and with the changed conditions of our time. Priestly formation, by reason of the very unity of the catholic priesthood, is necessary for all priests, diocesan and religious, of whatever rite. Thus, the following directives, which primarily concern diocesan clergy, need to be adapted for all priests, with due allowance for the different categories.

I. Program of Priestly Formation in Different Countries

1. Given the great diversity of peoples and countries, only laws of a general nature can be laid down. In each country and rite, therefore, a specific "Program of priestly formation" shall be established by the episcopal conference,[2] to be reviewed at suitable intervals and approved by the holy See, so that the

general rules may be adapted to the special circumstances of time and place, and the formation of priests will always be in keeping with the pastoral needs of the areas in which they minister.

II. More Active Encouragement of Priestly Vocations

2. To foster priestly vocations[3] is the duty of the entire christian community, and this is done first of all through living a full christian life. Most helpful in this are families whose faith, charity and piety make them the first seed-bed of vocations, and parishes in whose fruitful life the young people themselves are involved. Let teachers and all who in any way have responsibility for the formation of boys and young men, especially catholic associations, train the young people in their care to recognize and readily follow the divine call. Let all priests be apostolically zealous to foster vocations as much as possible, and let their own humble, hard-working and cheerful lives, together with their mutual friendship and brotherly cooperation, attract young people to the priesthood.

It is for the bishops, however, to stimulate their people to foster vocations and to coordinate resources and efforts. Sparing no sacrifice, they should help in a fatherly way those whom they consider called to the Lord's service.

This active cooperation of the entire people of God in fostering vocations is a response to the action of divine providence, which bestows suitable gifts on those chosen by God to share in the hierarchical priesthood of Christ and helps them with divine grace. At the same time it entrusts to the rightful ministers of the church the task of calling those candidates considered suitable and who seek so great an office with proper intention and full freedom, and of consecrating them by the seal of the holy Spirit to the worship of God and the service of the church.[4]

The council first of all recommends the traditional forms of collaboration, such as fervent prayer and christian penance. It urges more thorough instruction of the faithful through preaching and catechesis or the media, to explain to them the need for the priesthood, its nature and its immense value. Moreover, it lays down that, following the papal documents on the subject, organizations for vocations, whether already established or yet to be set up in dioceses, regions or countries, should methodically and consistently coordinate all pastoral action for fostering vocations, and promote it with both discretion and zeal, not neglecting whatever suitable help may be found in the insights of modern psychology and sociology.[5]

But the work of fostering vocations must generously transcend the limits of individual dioceses, countries, religious families and rites. It must look to the needs of the church as a whole and bring help to those regions which more urgently need workers for the Lord's vineyard.

3. Where junior seminaries are set up to cultivate the seeds of vocation, the students are to be trained by means of special religious formation and above all by spiritual direction to follow Christ their Redeemer with a generous mind and a pure heart. Under the fatherly supervision of superiors, with the cooperation of parents as occasion offers, they are to lead a life suitable to the age, maturity and development of young people, in keeping with the principles of sound psychology. Nor should they be deprived of social contact and contact with their families.[6] Moreover, what is laid down for major seminaries in the following paragraphs applies also to minor seminaries whenever it is in keeping with their purpose and program. Study courses in the minor seminary are to

be such that the students can continue them elsewhere without disadvantage should they choose
another state of life.

The same care should be taken to nourish the
seeds of vocation in those institutes which in various
places serve the same purpose as minor seminaries
and also among students educated in other schools or
systems. Special encouragement should also be given
to institutes and enterprises which cater for those
who discover a vocation at a later age.

III. Major Seminaries

4. Major seminaries are needed for priestly formation. Their entire formation program should aim at
enabling students to be formed as true pastors of
souls,[7] following the example of our Lord Jesus Christ,
teacher, priest and shepherd. Let students therefore
be trained for the ministry of the word, so that they
acquire an ever better understanding of the revealed
word of God, take it to heart by meditating on it and
give it expression in their speech and conduct. Let
them be trained for the ministry of worship and sanctification so that by prayer and sharing in liturgical
celebrations they may carry on the work of salvation
through the eucharistic sacrifice and the sacraments.
They are to be prepared for the pastoral ministry in
order to learn how to represent Christ to people,
Christ who "came not to be served, but to serve, and
to give his life as a ransom for many" (Mk 10:45; see
Jn 13:12-17), and to become the servants of all in
order to win over many (see 1 Cor 9:19).

All aspects of their training, therefore — spiritual,
intellectual and disciplinary — are to be coordinated
by joint action with this pastoral purpose in view all
directors and teachers must diligently cooperate to
achieve it, in loyal fidelity to the authority of the

bishop.

5. Since the formation of students depends both on sensible rules and still more on suitable educators, seminary rectors and teachers should be chosen from among persons of the highest calibre,[8] and they should be prepared by sound teaching, appropriate pastoral experience and spiritual and pedagogical training. To this end special colleges are to be set up, or at least suitable courses organized, as well as regular meetings of seminary directors.

Directors and teachers should realize how greatly the outcome of the students' formation is affected by their own way of thinking and acting. Led by the rector, they should cultivate among themselves a close harmony of mind and action; they should form with one another and with the students a family such as the Lord had in mind when he prayed: "that they may be one" (Jn 17:11), and nourish in the students a delight in their vocation. The bishop, by his keen and affectionate care, should encourage the seminary staff and show himself a true father in Christ to the students. Finally, all priests should look on the seminary as the very heart of the diocese and should gladly help and support it.[9]

6. Taking into account his age and development, each candidate's motivation should be tested, as should his freedom to choose. His spiritual, moral and intellectual stability should be examined, as should his physical and psychological health and any possible hereditary traits. The same goes for his ability to carry the burden of priesthood and perform his pastoral duties.[10] Even though there is a regrettable shortage of priests[11] the entire process of selection and assessment must be marked by decisiveness. God will not permit his church to be deprived of ministers if those worthy are promoted, while those not suitable are early on directed in a fatherly way to follow

another calling and are helped to engage in the lay apostolate, conscious of their vocation as Christians.

7. Where individual dioceses are unable to provide adequate seminaries of their own, shared seminaries should be established and maintained jointly for several dioceses or for the whole region or country, so that the solid training of the students, which is the primary consideration here, will be more effectively ensured. Such seminaries, whether regional or national, are to be governed by statutes laid down by the bishops involved,[12] and approved by the holy See.

In large seminaries, the students should be appropriately divided into smaller groups to allow for better personal development of individuals, while retaining unity of programme and studies.

IV. Greater Attention to Spiritual Training

8. Spiritual formation should be closely allied to doctrinal and pastoral training, and with the help of the spiritual director in particular[13] it should be conducted in such a way that the students learn to live in holy, familiar and attentive union with the Father, through his Son Jesus Christ in the holy Spirit. Those who, through ordination, are to take on the likeness of Christ the priest, should learn to cling to him as friends by intimately sharing their entire lives with him.[14] They should so live his paschal mystery themselves that they will know how to initiate into it the people entrusted to their care. Let them be taught to seek Christ in faithful meditation on God's word and in active sharing in the sacred mysteries of the church, especially the holy Eucharist and the Divine Office.[15] Let them seek him too in the person of the bishop who sends them and in the people to whom they are sent, especially the poor, the little ones, the sick, sinners and unbelievers. Let them love and be

devoted with filial trust to the most blessed Virgin Mary, given as a mother to the disciple by Christ Jesus dying on the cross.

Let the exercises of piety traditionally commended by the venerable practice of the church be zealously encouraged, but care must be taken that spiritual formation not be reduced to pious exercises alone nor merely develop religious sentiment. Rather let the students learn to live according to the gospel pattern, grounded in faith, hope and charity, so that by practising these virtues they may acquire a spirit of prayer,[16] strengthen and protect their vocation, add vigor to the other virtues and grow in zeal to win all people to Christ.

9. Let the students be so imbued with the mystery of the church as explained by this holy council especially that, bound to the vicar of Christ in humble and filial love, and, after ordination, loyal to their own bishop as faithful helpers, working in close harmony with their fellow-priests, they will bear witness to that unity which attracts people to Christ.[17] Let them learn to share generously in the life of the whole church, mindful of the words of St Augustine:"People possess the holy Spirit in the measure in which they love the church of Christ."[18] Let the students realize that they are not destined for a life of power and honors, but are destined to be totally dedicated to the service of God and pastoral ministry. They must be trained with special care in priestly obedience, a humble life-style and the spirit of self-denial,[19] so that they will readily give up what may be lawful but not expedient, and learn to conform themselves to the crucified Christ.

Students should be well informed about the burdens they are to carry, and no difficulty of the priestly life should be passed over. However, they should not be almost totally preoccupied with the element of danger in their future work. Rather, they should be trained to strengthen their spiritual life as much as possible in the actual exercise of their pastoral activity.

10. Students who follow the venerable tradition of priestly celibacy as laid down by the holy and firm rules of their own rite should be carefully trained for this state. As celibate, they give up marriage for the sake of the kingdom of heaven (see Mt 19:12), hold fast to the Lord with that undivided love[20] so much in harmony with the new covenant, bear witness to the resurrection in the world to come (see Lk 20:36)[21] and receive the best possible help to the lasting achievement of that perfect charity by which they can become all things to all people in the priestly ministry.[22] They must become deeply convinced of how eagerly that state ought to be undertaken, not just as a precept of ecclesiastical law, but as a precious gift to be humbly sought from God — a gift to which, inspired by the holy Spirit and helped by divine grace, they must freely and generously respond. Students should have a proper understanding of the duties and dignity of christian marriage, representing the love between Christ and his church (see Eph 5:22-33). They should realize, however, the greater excellence of virginity consecrated to Christ,[23] so that they may commit themselves to the Lord with a maturely considered and magnanimous free choice and a total dedication of mind and body.

They are to be warned of the dangers their chastity will encounter, especially in present-day society,[24] but they should learn how, with suitable natural and supernatural safeguards, to integrate their giving up of marriage in such a way that not only will their life and work suffer no harm from celibacy, but they themselves will acquire greater mastery of mind and body, grow in maturity and receive more fully the blessedness promised by the gospel.

11. The principles of christian education are to be

religiously observed and appropriately supplemented by the latest findings of sound psychology and pedagogy. A well-planned formation program should therefore develop in the students a proper degree of human maturity, showing itself in a certain stability of character, in the ability to make carefully considered decisions, and in a sound judgment of events and people. Let them form habits of self-control,[24a] develop strength of character and in general learn to value those qualities which are most appreciated among people and are a credit to a minister of Christ,[25] such as sincerity of spirit, constant concern for justice, fidelity to one's promises, courtesy in behaviour, and modesty and charity in speech.

The discipline of seminary life should be regarded not merely as a safeguard for common life and charity, but as a necessary part of a formation program geared towards the achievement of self-control, the development of solid personal maturity and those other qualities most helpful for orderly and fruitful activity in the church. But the discipline is to be applied in such a way that the students make it their own, so that they accept the authority of superiors from inner conviction and for reasons of conscience (see Rom 13:5) as well as from supernatural motives. Standards of discipline should be in keeping with the age of the students, so that as they gradually acquire self-mastery, they will learn to use their freedom wisely, act energetically on their own initiative[26] and work harmoniously with colleagues and laity.

The entire training program is to be so organized that, with its atmosphere of piety, recollection and mutual support, it becomes a kind of initiation to the students' future lives as priests.

12. To provide a more solid foundation for the spiritual formation of students and to enable them to embrace their vocation with greater conviction, the

bishops must set aside a suitable period of time for more intensive spiritual training. It is for them also to consider the advisability of an interruption of studies or the organization of a sound training period in pastoral work, to ensure a more adequate testing of the candidates for the priesthood. Given the variety of circumstances in different regions, it will be for the bishops to decide whether the age at present required by common law for holy orders should be raised, and whether students at the end of their theological course should minister as deacons for an appropriate period of time before being ordained to the priesthood.

V. The Revision of Ecclesiastical Studies

13. Before seminarians begin their strictly ecclesiastical studies, they should have already completed those courses in science and the humanities which are required in their country for entry to higher studies, and should also have acquired a sufficient knowledge of Latin to enable them to understand and use the many scientific sources and church documents.[27] They should be required to study the liturgical language of their own rite and warmly encouraged to acquire an adequate knowledge of the languages of holy scripture and tradition.

In the revision of ecclesiastical studies, the primary aim is to coordinate philosophy and theology in such a way that together they open the minds of the students more and more to the mystery of Christ, which touches the whole of human history, continually influences the church, and is at work particularly in priestly ministry.[28]

So that this vision be communicated to the students from the very beginning of their training, their ecclesiastical studies should begin with an introductory course of appropriate length. In this initiation course the mystery of salvation is to be presented in such a way that students will see the meaning, arrangement and pastoral aim of their studies, and at the same time be helped to make faith the foundation and inner principle of their whole lives and be strengthened to accept their vocation with personal dedication and joyful heart.

15. Philosophical subjects should be taught in such a way that students are first of all gradually led to a solid and coherent knowledge of human nature, the world and God, guided by the philosophical tradition of lasting value.[29] At the same time they should take account of modern philosophical developments, particularly those of influence in their own country, as well as recent progress in the sciences, so that with a proper understanding of the present age, they will be equipped for dialogue with people of their time.[30] The history of philosophy should be taught in a way that enables students to grasp the basic principles of the various systems, hold fast to elements proved to be true and recognize and refute the roots of error.

The actual teaching should arouse in the students a love of rigorous investigation, observation and demonstration of truth, together with an honest awareness of the limits of human knowledge. Careful attention should be paid to the close connection between philosophy and the real problems of life, as well as to the questions which engage the minds of the students. The students themselves must be helped to see the links between philosophical arguments and the mysteries of salvation studied in theology in the higher light of faith.

16. Theological subjects should be taught in the light of faith under the guidance of the Church's magisterium[31] so that students will accurately draw catholic teaching from divine revelation, enter deeply into

its meaning, use it to nourish their spiritual lives[32] and be able to proclaim, explain and defend it in their priestly ministry.

Students are to be trained most diligently in the study of scripture, which ought to be the very soul of all theology.[33] After a suitable introduction, let them be carefully initiated into exegetical method, study closely the main themes of divine revelation and find inspiration and nourishment in daily reading of the sacred books and meditation on them.[34]

The following order should be observed in dogmatic theology: let biblical themes be treated first, then what the Fathers of the church (both east and west) have contributed to the faithful transmission and explanation of the revealed truths, followed by the later history of dogma, including its relation to the general history of the church.[35] Then, in order to throw the fullest light possible on the mysteries of salvation, let them learn through speculation guided by St. Thomas to enter into them more deeply and see how they are interconnected,[36] to recognize how they are present and active in liturgical celebration[37] and in the whole life of the church. Let them also learn to use the light of divine revelation in seeking the solution to human problems, to apply its eternal truths to the changing condition of human life, and to communicate these truths in a way the modern world can understand.[38]

In like manner the other theological subjects should be renewed through a more lively contact with the mystery of Christ and the history of salvation. Special care is to be taken for the improvement of moral theology. Its scientific presentation, drawing more fully on the teaching of holy scripture, should highlight the lofty vocation of the christian faithful and their obligation to bring forth fruit in charity for the life of the world. In the same way the teaching of canon law and church history should take account of the mystery of the church as presented in the dogmatic constitution "On the church" of this holy council. Liturgy, which is to be regarded as the first and ever necessary source of true christian spirit, should be taught in the spirit of articles 15 and 16 of the Constitution on the Sacred Liturgy.[39]

With due regard for the conditions in different countries, students should be introduced to a fuller knowledge of the churches and ecclesial communities separated from the apostolic Roman See, to enable them to play their part in the work of christian reunion according to the decisions of this council.[40]

They should also be introduced to a knowledge of whatever other religions are most commonly found in this or that region, in order to recognize what, by God's providence, is good and true in them, and learn to reject what is false and share the full light of truth with those who lack it.

17. Since doctrinal training should aim not at mere communication of ideas, but at a genuine and profound formation of students, teaching methods need to be revised, both as regards lectures, discussions and seminars and in encouraging the personal study by students in private or in small groups. Great care must be taken with the unity and solidity of the whole training programme, avoiding the multiplication of courses and lectures and omitting topics that have little or no importance today or should be left to higher academic studies.

18. It is the responsibility of bishops to see that young men of suitable character, virtue and talent be sent to special institutes, faculties or universities for more scientific training in sacred sciences and other appropriate subjects, to enable them to meet the various needs of the apostolate, but their spiritual and pastoral formation must by no means be neglected,

especially if they are not yet ordained.

VI. Strictly Pastoral Training

19. The pastoral concern which should characterize the whole formation program[41] also requires that students be especially trained in what is relevant to the sacred ministry, that is, in catechesis and preaching, liturgy and administration of the sacraments, works of charity, meeting the needs of those in error and of unbelievers, and in all other pastoral duties. Let them be carefully trained in the art of directing souls, through which all members of the church can be guided towards a fully committed and apostolic christian life and helped to fulfil the duties of their state. With equal care let them learn to help religious women and men to persevere in the grace of their vocation and to make progress according to the spirit of their institute.[42]

In general, those gifts are to be cultivated in students which are most conducive to dialogue with people, such as the ability to listen to others and to open their hearts in a spirit of charity to the various kinds of human need.[43]

20. They should be taught how to use correctly the various aids provided by pedagogy, psychology and sociology,[44] according to the norms of ecclesiastical authority. They should also be taught how to inspire and encourage apostolic activity among the laity,[45] how to promote various and more effective forms of apostolate, and be filled with that truly catholic spirit which looks beyond the boundaries of diocese, country or rite to respond to the needs of the whole church, always ready in spirit to preach the gospel everywhere.[46]

21. Since students must learn how to exercise the ministry not only in theory but also in practice, and

should be able to act on their own initiative as well as cooperate with others, during the course of their studies and in holiday time they should be initiated into pastoral practice by appropriate experiences. These should be carried out according to the age of the students and the circumstances of the place, decided by the bishops, under the guidance of men with pastoral experience, always keeping in mind the outstanding power of supernatural helps.[47]

VII. Ongoing Formation

22 Since priestly formation, especially in view of the conditions of modern life, needs to be continued and perfected even after the normal course of studies,[48] it is for the bishops' conference in each country to provide the best means to achieve this, such as pastoral institutes cooperating with selected parishes, regular conferences, and appropriate projects in which younger priests can be gradually introduced to priestly life and apostolic activity from the spiritual, intellectual and pastoral point of view, and thus renew and develop this life and activity.

Conclusion

The Fathers of this holy council, continuing the work begun by the Council of Trent, confidently entrust to seminary directors and teachers the duty of training Christ's future priests in the spirit of that renewal promoted by the council itself. At the same time, they most strongly exhort those preparing for the sacred ministry to develop a keen awareness that the hopes of the church and the salvation of souls are being committed to them, and urge them by their joyful acceptance of the regulations in this decree to bring forth most abundant and lasting fruit.

a. Freshly translated for this edition by Sean Fagan, SM, Rome, who had been part of the original team of translators.

1. It is according to Christ's own will that the progress of the whole people of God should depend in the highest degree on the ministry of priests, as is clear from the words he used to appoint the apostles and their successors and helpers as heralds of the gospel, leaders of the new chosen people and stewards of the mysteries of God. This is supported by statements of church Fathers and saints and a whole series of papal documents. See especially:

St Pius X, Exhortation to the Clergy *Haerent animo*, 4 August 1908: St Pii X Acta IV, pp. 237-264.

Pius XI, Encyclical Ad *catholici Sacerdotii*, 20 December 1935: AAS 28 (1936), especially pp. 37-52.

Pius XII, Apostolic Exhortation *Menti Nostri*, 23 September 1950: AAS 42 (1950), pp. 657-702.

John XXIII, Encyclical *Sacerdotii Nostri primordia*, 1 August 1959: AAS 51 (1959), pp. 545-579.

Paul VI, Apostolic Letter *Summi Dei Verbum*, 4 November 1963: AAS 55 (1963), pp. 979-995.

2. The whole course of priestly training, i.e. the organization of the seminary, spiritual formation, course of studies, the common life and rule of the students, and pastoral practice, should be adapted to local conditions. The general principles of this adaptation should be decided by episcopal conferences for the diocesan clergy and in a similar manner by the competent superiors for religious (see. the General Statutes attached to the Apostolic Constitution *Sedes Sapientiae*, art. 19).

3. Almost everywhere one of the chief anxieties of the church today is the dearth of vocations.

See Pius XII, Apostolic Exhortation *Menti Nostrae:* " . . both in catholic countries and in mission territories, the number of priests is insufficient to cope with the increasing demands": AAS 42 (1950), p. 682.

John XXIII"The problem of ecclesiastical and religious vocations is a daily preoccupation with the Pope....Vocations are the object of his prayer, the ardent longing of his soul": from the Allocution to the First International Congress on Religious Vocations, 16 December 1961: *L'Osservatore Romano*, 17 December 1961).

4. Pius XII, Apostolic Constitution *Sedes Sapientiae*, 31 May 1956: AAS 48 (1956), p. 357. Paul VI, Apostolic Letter *Summi Dei Verbum*, 4 November 1963: AAS 55 (1963), pp. 984 ff.

5. See especially: Pius XII, Motu proprio *Cum nobis*, on the establishment of the Pontifical Work for priestly vocations, 4 November 1941: AAS 33 (1941), p. 479; with the attached statutes and rules promulgated by the Sacred Congregation for Seminaries and Universities, 8 September 1943. The Motu proprio *Cum supremae*, on the Pontifical Work for religious vocations, 11 February 1955: AAS 47 (1955), p. 266; with the attached statutes and rules

promulgated by the Sacred Congregation for Religious: ibid., pp. 298-301; Vatican Council II, Decree on the Up-to-date Renewal of Religious Life, *Perfectae caritatis*, n. 24; Decree on the Pastoral Office of Bishops in the Church, *Christus Dominus*, n. 15.

6. See Pius XII, Apostolic Exhortation *Menti Nostrae*, 23 September 1950: AAS 42 (1950), p. 685.

7. See Vatican Council II, Dogmatic Constitution on the Church, *Lumen gentium*, n. 28

8. See Pius XI, Encyclical *Ad Catholici Sacerdotii*, 20 December 1935: AAS 28 (1936), p. 37: "In the first place let careful choice be made of superiors and professors.... Give these sacred colleges priests of the greatest virtue, and do not hesitate to withdraw them from tasks which seem indeed to be of greater importance, but which cannot be compared with this supremely important matter, the place of which nothing else can supply." This principle of choosing the best men for the seminaries is again insisted on by Pius XII in his Apostolic Letter to the hierarchy of Brazil, 23 April 1947, *Discorsi e Radiomessaggi* IX, pp. 579-580.

9. With regard to this general duty of priests to give their support to seminaries see Paul VI, Apostolic Letter *Summi Dei Verbum*, 4 November 1963: AAS 53 (1963), p. 984.

10. See Pius XII, Apostolic Exhortation *Menti Nostrae*, 23 September 1950. AAS 42 (1950), p. 684; see. also the Sacred Congregation for the Sacraments, circular letter *Magna equidem* to Bishops, 27 December 1935, n. 10. For religious see. the General Statutes attached to the Apostolic Constitution *Sedes Sapientiae*, 31 May 1956, art. 33; Paul VI Apostolic Letter *Summi Dei Verbum*, 4 November 1963: AAS 55 (1963), pp. 987 f.

11. See Pius XI, Encyclical *Ad Catholici Sacerdotii*, 20 December 1935: AAS 28 (1936), p. 41.

12. It is decreed that in drawing up the statutes of regional or national seminaries, all bishops concerned will take part, setting aside canon 1357, par. 4, of the Code of Canon Law.

13. See Pius XII, Apostolic Exhortation *Menti Nostrae*, 23 September 1950: AAS 42 (1950), p. 674; Sacred Congregation of Seminaries and Universities, *La Formazione spirituale del candidato al sacerdozio*, Vatican City, 1965.

14. See St Pius X, Exhortation to the catholic clergy, *Haerent animo*, 4 August 1908: St Pii X Acta, IV, pp 242-244; Pius XII, Apostolic Exhortation *Menti Nostrae*, 23 September 1950: AAS 42 (1950), pp. 659-661; John XXIII, Encyclical Sacerdotii *Nostri Primordia*, 1 August 1959: AAS 51 (1959), pp. 550 ff.

15. See Pius XII, Encyclical *Mediator Dei*, 20 November 1947: AAS 39 (1947), pp. 547 ff. and 572 f.; John XXIII, Apostolic Exhortation *Sacrae Laudis*, 6 January 1962: AAS 54 (1962), p. 69; Vatican Council II, Constitution on the Sacred Liturgy, *Sacrosanctum Concilium*, art. 16 and 17; Sacred Congregation of Rites, Instruction on the Proper Implementation of the Constitution on the Sacred

Liturgy, 26 September 1964, nn 14-17: *Vatican Collection*, vol. 1, pp. 48-49.

16. See John XXIII, Encyclical *Sacerdotii Nostri Primordia:* AAS 51 (1959), pp. 559 f.

17. See Vatican Council II, Dogmatic Constitution on the Church, *Lumen gentium*, n. 28.

18. St Augustine, *In Ioannem tract.* 32, 8: PL 35, 1646.

19. See Pius XII, Apostolic Exhortation *Menti Nostrae:* AAS 42 (1950), pp. 626 f., 685, 690; John XXIII, Encyclical *Sacerdotii Nostri Primordia:* AAS 51 (1959), pp. 551-553, 556 f.: Paul VI, Encyclical *Ecclesiam suam*, 6 August 1964: AAS 56 (1964), pp. 634 f.; Vatican council II Dogmatic Constitution on the Church, *Lumen gentium*, especially n. 8.

20. See Pius XII, Encyclical *Sacra Virginitas*, 25 March 1954: AAS 46 (1954), pp. 165 ff.

21. See St Cyprian, *De habitu virginum*, 22: PL 4, 475; St Ambrose, *De virginibus*, I, 8, 52: PL 16, 202 f.

22. See Pius XII, Apostolic Exhortation *Menti Nostrae:* AAS 42 (1950), p. 663.

23. See Pius XII, Encyclical *Sacra Virginitas*, loc. cit., pp. 170-174.

24. See Pius XII, Apostolic Exhortation *Menti Nostrae*, loc. cit., pp. 664 and 690 f.

24a. The Latin of the phrase is *'Alumni propriam indolem recte componere assuescant'*. Translators seem divided as to what exactly it means. Some take it, as we and Tanner have done, to refer to self-control — thus, the translation published in French by Editions du Cerf: 'Que *les seminaristes prennent l'habitude de dominer leur temperament'*. Others, however, take it to refer to the development of their abilities by the students. Thus Abbott: 'They should be practised in an intelligent organization of their proper talents' and that published by the English Catholic Truth Society: 'The students should know how to make the most of their own abilities', and the Italian translation published by the *L'Osservatore Romano: 'Gli alunni si abituino a perfezionare come si deve la propria indole'*. [Translator].

25. See Paul VI, Apostolic Letter *Summi Dei Verbum*, 4 November 1963: AAS 55 (1963), p. 991.

26. See Pius XII, Apostolic Exhortation *Menti Nostrae*, loc. cit., p. 686.

27. See Paul VI, Apostolic Letter *Summi Dei Verbum*, loc. cit., p. 993.

28. See Vatican Council II, Dogmatic Constitution on the Church, *Lumen gentium*, nn. 7 and 28.

29. See Pius XII, Encyclical *Humani Generis*, 12 August 1980: AAS 42 (1950), pp. 571-575.

30. See Paul VI, Encyclical *Ecclesiam suam*, 6 August 1964: AAS 56 (1964), pp. 637 ff.

31. See Pius XII, Encyclical *Humani Generis:* AAS 42 (1950), pp. 567-569; Allocution *Si diligis*, 31 May 1954: AAS 46 (1954), pp 314

f.; Paul VI, Allocution in the Pontifical Gregorian University, 12 March 1964 AAS 56 (1964), pp. 364 f.; Vatican Council II, Dogmatic Constitution on the Church, *Lumen gentium*, n. 25: AAS 5 (1965), pp. 29-31.

32. See St Bonaventure, *Itinerarium mentis in Deum*, Prol., n. 4: "Let no one think he will find sufficiency in a reading which lacks unction, an enquiry which lacks devotion, a search which arouses no wonder, a survey without enthusiasm, industry without piety, knowledge without love, intelligence without humility, application without grace, contemplation without wisdom inspired by God": St. Bonaventure, *Opera Omnia, V,* Quaracchi 1891, p. 296.

33. See Leo XIII, Encyclical *Providentissimus Deus*, 18 November 1893: AAS 26 (1893-94), p. 283.

34. See Pontifical Biblical Commission, *Instructio de Sacra Scriptura recte docenda*, 13 May 1950: AAS 42 (1950), p. 502.

35. See Pius XII, Encyclical *Humani Generis*, 12 August 1950: AAS 42 (1950), p. 568 f.: 'The sacred sciences are being constantly rejuvenated by the study of their sacred sources, while on the other hand that speculation which neglects the deeper examination of the sacred deposit becomes sterile, as we know from experience."

36. See Pius XII, Address to Seminarians, 24 June 1939: AAS 31 (1939), p. 247: "Emulation in seeking and propagating the truth is not suppressed, but is rather stimulated and given its true direction by commending the teaching of St Thomas." Paul VI, Address in Gregorian University, 12 March 1964: AAS 56 (1964), p. 365: "Let (teachers) listen with respect to the Doctors of the church, among whom St. Thomas Aquinas holds the principal place. For so great is the power of the angelic Doctor's genius so sincere his love of truth, and so great his wisdom in investigating the deepest truths, in illustrating them, and linking them together with a most fitting bond of unity, that his teaching is a most efficacious instrument not only for safeguarding the foundations of the faith, but also in gaining the fruits of healthy progress with profit and security." See also his Allocution to the Sixth International Thomistic Congress, 10 September 1965.

37. See Vatican Council II, Constitution on the Sacred Liturgy, *Sacrosanctum Concilium*, nn. 7 and 16: AAS 56 (1964), pp. 100 f. and 104 f.

38. See Paul VI, Encyclical *Ecclesiam Suam*, 6 August 1964: AAS 56 (1964), p. 640 f.

39. Vatican Council II, Constitution on the Sacred Liturgy, *Sacrosanctum Concilium,* nn. 10, 14, 15, 16; Sacred Congregation of Rites, Instruction on the Proper Implementation of the Constitution on the Sacred Liturgy, 26 September 1964, nn. 11 and 12: Vatican Collection, vol. 1, pp 47-48..

40. See Vatican Council II, Decree on Ecumenism, *Unitatis redintegratio*, nn 1, 9, 10.

41. The perfect idea of the pastor can be seen in the recent documents of the popes dealing specifically with the life, qualities and

training of priests, especially:

St. Pius X, Exhortation to the Clergy *Haerent animo,* St Pii X Acta, IV, pp. 237 ff.;

Pius XI, Encyclical Ad *Catholici Sacerdotii:* AAS 28 (1936), pp. 5 ff.;

Pius XII, Apostolic Exhortation *Menti Nostri:* AAS 42 (1950), pp. 657 ff.;

John XXIII, Encyclical *Sacerdotii Nostri primordia:* AAS 51 (1959), pp. 545 ff.;

Paul VI, Apostolic Letter *Summi Dei Verbum:* AAS 55 (1963), pp. 979 ff.

Much information about pastoral training is also given in the encyclicals *Mystici Corporis* (1943); *Mediator Dei* (1947); *Evangelii Praecones* (1951); *Sacra Virginitas* (1954); *Musicae sacrae Disciplina* (1955); *Princeps Pastorum* (1959), and in the Apostolic Constitution *Sedes Sapientiae* (1956) for religious.

Pius XII, John XXIII and Paul VI have often thrown light on the ideal of the good shepherd in their allocutions to seminarians and priests.

42. As regards the importance of that state which is set up by the profession of the evangelical counsels, see Vatican Council II, Dogmatic Constitution on the Church, *Lumen gentium,* chapter VI: AAS 57 (1965), pp. 49-55; Decree on the Up-to-date Renewal of Religious Life, *Perfectae caritatis.*

43. See Paul VI, Encyclical *Ecclesiam suam:* AAS 56 (1964), *passim,* especially pp. 635 f. and 640 ff.

44. See especially John XXIII, Encyclical *Mater et Magistra,* 15 May 1961: AAS 53 (1961), pp. 401 ff.

45. See especially Vatican Council II, Dogmatic Constitution on the Church, *Lumen gentium,* n. 33.

46. See Vatican Council II, Dogmatic Constitution on the Church, *Lumen gentium,* n. 17.

47. Very many papal documents sound a warning against the danger of neglecting the supernatural goal in pastoral activity, and of minimizing the value of supernatural means, at least in practice; see especially the documents recommended in note 41.

48. More recent documents of the holy See urge that special attention be paid to newly ordained priests. The following are specially recommended:

Pius XII, Motu proprio *Quandoquidem,* 2 April 1949- AAS 41 (1949), pp. 165-167; Apostolic Exhortation *Menti Nostrae,* 23 September 1950: AAS 42 (1950); Apostolic Constitution (for religious) *Sedes Sapientiae,* 31 May 1956, and the General Statutes attached to it; Address to the priests of the 'Convictus Barcinonensis,' 14 June 1957, *Discorsi e Radiomessaggi,* XIX, pp. 271-273.

Paul VI, address to the priests of the Gian Matteo Giberti Institute, of the diocese of Verona, 11 March 1964.

DECREE ON THE UP-TO-DATE RENEWAL OF RELIGIOUS LIFE[a]

Perfectae Caritatis

28 October, 1965

1. In the constitution, *Lumen Gentium*, the holy synod has already shown that the quest for perfect charity by means of the evangelical counsels traces its origins to the teaching and example of the divine Master, and that it is a very clear symbol of the heavenly kingdom. Now, however, it proposes to deal with the life and discipline of those institutes whose members take vows of chastity, poverty and obedience, and to make provision for their needs in today's world.

From the church's earliest times there were women and men who set out to follow Christ more freely and to imitate him more closely by practicing the evangelical counsels. In their different ways they led lives dedicated to God. Many of them, under the inspiration of the holy Spirit, became hermits or founded religious families, which the church, by virtue of its authority, gladly accepted and approved. Thus, in keeping with the divine purpose, a wonderful variety of religious communities came into existence. This has helped considerably to equip the church for every good work (see 2 Tim 3:17) and for ministry aimed at building up the body of Christ (see Eph 4:12). It has also enabled it to display the assorted gifts of its sons and daughters, like a bride adorned for her husband (see Apoc 21:2), and to manifest in itself the manifold wisdom of God (see Eph 3:10).

Amid such a great variety of gifts, all those who are called by God to the practice of the evangelical counsels, and who make faithful profession of them, bind themselves to the Lord in a special way. They follow Christ virginal and poor (see Mt 8:20; Lk 9:58) who, by obedience unto death on the cross (see Phil 2:8), redeemed humanity and made it holy. Under the impulse of love, which the holy Spirit pours into their hearts (see Rom 5:5), they live more and more for Christ and for his body, the church (see Col 1:24). The more fervently, therefore, they join themselves to Christ by this gift of their entire life, the fuller does the church's life become and the more vigorous and fruitful its apostolate.

In order that the church of today may derive greater benefit from the outstanding worth of a life consecrated by the profession of the counsels and from the vital function which it performs, the holy synod makes the following provisions. These deal only with the general principles of the up-to-date renewal of the life and discipline of religious orders and, while leaving their special characters intact, of societies of common life without vows, and of secular institutes. Particular norms for their interpretation and application will be determined after the council by the competent authority.

2. The up-to-date renewal of the religious life comprises both a constant return to the sources of christian life in general and to the primitive inspiration of the institutes, and their adaptation to the changed conditions of our time. This renewal, under the impulse of the holy Spirit and with the guidance of the church, must be promoted in accordance with the fol-

lowing principles:

(a) Since the ultimate norm of the religious life is the following of Christ as it is put before us in the Gospel, this must be taken by all institutes as the supreme rule.

(b) It is to the church's advantage that each institute has its own proper character and function. Therefore the spirit and aims of each founder should be faithfully acknowledged and maintained, as indeed should each institute's sound traditions, for all of these constitute an institute's heritage.

(c) All institutes should share in the life of the church. They should make their own and should promote to the best of their ability, each in a manner suited to its own character, the church's initiatives and undertakings in biblical, liturgical, dogmatic, pastoral, ecumenical, missionary and social matters.

(d) Institutes should see to it that their members have a proper understanding of people, of the contemporary situation and of the needs of the church, this to the end that, evaluating the contemporary world wisely in the light of faith, and fired with apostolic zeal, they may be more helpful to people.

(e) Before all else, religious life is ordered to the following of Christ by its members and to their becoming united with God by the profession of the evangelical counsels. For this reason it has to be accepted that even the best-contrived adaptations to the needs of our time will be of no avail unless they are animated by a spiritual renewal, which must always be assigned primary importance even in the development of the active ministry.

3. The manner of life, of prayer and of work should be suited to the physical and psychological conditions of today's religious. It should also, in so far as this is permitted by an institute's character, be in harmony with the demands of the apostolate, with the require-

ments of culture and with the social and economic climate, especially in mission territories.

The mode of government of the institutes should also be examined using the same criteria

For this reason, constitutions, directories, books of customs, of prayers, of ceremonies and such like should be suitably revised, obsolete prescriptions being suppressed, and should be brought into line with this synod's documents.

4. Effective renewal and authentic adaptation cannot be achieved save with the cooperation of all the members of an institute.

However, it is for the competent authorities, alone, and especially for general chapters, to establish the norms for up-to-date renewal and to legislate for it, as also to provide for sufficient prudent experimentation. The approval of the Holy See and of the local ordinaries must be sought when the law requires it. In matters which concern the destiny of an institute as a whole, however, superiors should find appropriate means of consulting their members and should take their views into consideration. For the appropriate renewal of convents of nuns suggestions and advice may be obtained also from assemblies of federated houses or from other lawfully convened groupings.

All should remember, however, that hope for renewal lies more in stricter observance of the rule and constitutions than in the multiplication of laws.

5. The members of each institute should recall, first of all, that when they made profession of the evangelical counsels they were responding to a divine call, to the end that, not merely being dead to sin (see Rom 6:11) but renouncing worldly things as well, they might live for God alone. They have dedicated their entire lives to God's service. This constitutes a special consecration, which is deeply rooted in their baptismal consecration and is a fuller expression of it.

Since this gift of themselves has been accepted by the church, they should be aware that they are dedicated to the church's service too. This service of God should stimulate and foster their practice of the virtues, especially the virtues of humility and obedience, fortitude and chastity, by which they share in Christ's self-emptying (see Phil 2:7-8) and at the same time in his life in the Spirit (see Rom 8: 1-13).

Religious, therefore, faithful to their profession and leaving all things for Christ (see Mk 10:28), follow him (see Mt 19:21), regarding this as the one thing necessary (see Lk 10:42), listen to his words (see Lk 10:39) and are solicitous for all that is his (see 1 Cor 7:32).

The members of every institute, therefore, ought to seek God, and God alone, before all else; they should join contemplation, by which they cleave to God by mind and heart, to apostolic love, by which they endeavour to be identified with the work of redemption and the spread of the kingdom of God.

6. Those who make profession of the evangelical counsels should seek and love above all else God who has first loved us (see 1 Jn 4:10). In all circumstances they should take care to foster a life hidden with Christ in God (see Col 3:3), which is the source and stimulus of love of the neighbor, for the salvation of the world and the building-up of the church. The very practice of the evangelical counsels is animated and governed by this charity.

For this reason, members of institutes should assiduously cultivate the spirit and practice of prayer, drawing on the authentic sources of christian spirituality. In the first place, let them have the sacred scripture at hand daily, so that they might learn "the surpassing worth of knowing Christ Jesus" (Phil 3:8) by reading and meditating on the divine scriptures. They should celebrate the sacred liturgy, especially the holy mystery of the Eucharist, with their hearts and their lips, according to the mind of the church, and they should nourish their spiritual lives from this richest of sources.

Thus, refreshed at the table of the divine law and of the sacred altar, let them love the members of Christ as sisters and brothers, let them reverence and love their pastors in a filial spirit; let them more and more live and think with the church, and let them dedicate themselves wholeheartedly to its mission.

7. There are institutes which are entirely ordered towards contemplation, in such wise that their members give themselves over to God alone in solitude and silence, in constant prayer and penance cheerfully accepted. No matter how pressing the needs of the active ministry, these are always assured an honored place in the mystical body of Christ, in which "all the members do not have the same function" (Rom 12:4). They offer to God an exceptional sacrifice of praise; their holiness and its abundant fruits lend luster to God's people, their example inspires them and they enrich the church with their hidden apostolic fruitfulness. They are thus an ornament to the church and a fount of heavenly graces. However, their way of life should be revised in accordance with the aforesaid principles and criteria of up-to-date renewal, the greatest care being taken to preserve both their withdrawal from the world and the exercises which belong to the contemplative life.

8. In the church there are very many institutes, clerical and lay, engaged in different kinds of apostolic work and endowed with gifts which vary according to the grace that is given to them. The administrator is given the gift of administration, the teacher the gift of doctrine, the preacher persuasiveness. Liberality is given to those who give to others, and cheerfulness to those who perform works of mercy (see Rom 12:5-8).

"There are varieties of gifts, but the same Spirit" (1 Cor 12:4).

In these institutes, apostolic and charitable activity is of the very nature of religious life, as their own holy ministry and work of charity, entrusted to them by the church and to be performed in its name. For this reason, the entire religious life of the members should be imbued with an apostolic spirit, and all their apostolic activity with a religious spirit. In order, therefore, that the members may first answer their call to follow Christ and to serve Christ himself in his members, their apostolic activity must needs have its source in intimate union with him. It is thus that their very love for God and their neighbor is fostered.

Consequently, these institutes should adjust their observances and customs to the needs of their particular apostolate. Since however the active religious life takes many forms, this diversity should be taken into account when its up-to-date renewal is being undertaken, and in the various institutes the members' lives in the service of Christ should be sustained by means which are proper and suited to each institute.

9. The venerable institution of monastic life should be faithfully maintained and should flourish increasingly in both East and West in accordance with its true spirit. Through long centuries it has deserved well of both the church and of civil society. The principal duty of monks is to present to the divine majesty a service at once humble and noble within the walls of the monastery, either living a withdrawn life dedicated entirely to divine worship, or legitimately undertaking apostolic activities or works of christian charity. While preserving, therefore, the nature of their own institutions they should renovate their ancient holy traditions and should so adapt them to the present-day needs of souls that monasteries will, as it were, be seedbeds of growth for the christian people.

There are religious orders which, from their rule or institution combine the apostolic life with choral office and monastic observances. These should adapt their way of life to the needs of their proper apostolates, at the same time loyally preserving their form of life, for it has been of considerable service to the church.

10. Religious congregations of laymen and laywomen are thoroughly adequate for the profession of the evangelical counsels. The holy synod holds them in high esteem, for they serve the church well in the exercise of its pastoral duty to educate the young, care for the sick, and perform other ministries. It confirms the members in their vocation and encourages them to adapt their lives to modern requirements.

The holy synod declares that there is nothing to prevent some members of institutes of brothers being admitted to holy orders — the lay character of the institutes remaining intact — by provision of their general chapter and in order to meet the need for priestly ministration in their houses.

11. While it is true that secular institutes are not religious institutes, at the same time they embody a true and full profession of the evangelical counsels in the world, recognized by the church, conferring a consecration on men and women, clerical and lay, living in the world. Therefore the members should make it their chief aim to give themselves to God totally in perfect charity. The institutes themselves ought to preserve their own special character — their secular character, that is to say — to the end that they may be able to carry on effectively and everywhere the apostolate in the world and, as it were, from the world, for which they were founded.

Let them know quite clearly, at the same time, that they will be unable to accomplish so great a task unless the members have so thorough a grounding in matters divine and human that they will indeed be leaven in the world, for the strengthening and increase of the body of Christ. Superiors therefore should devote great care to the formation, especially the spiritual formation, of their subjects, and also to their ongoing formation.

12. Chastity "for the sake of the kingdom of heaven" (Mt 19:22), which religious profess, must be esteemed an exceptional gift of grace. It uniquely frees the hearts of women and men (see 1 Cor 7:32-35), so that they become more fervent in love for God and for all humanity. For this reason it is a special symbol of heavenly benefits, and for religious it is a most effective way of dedicating themselves wholeheartedly to the divine service and the works of the apostolate. Thus, for all Christ's faithful, religious recall that wonderful marriage made by God which will be made fully manifest in the age to come, and in which the church has Christ alone for her spouse.

Religious, therefore, at pains to be faithful to what they have professed, should believe our Lord's words and, relying on God's help, they should not presume on their own strength. They should practise mortification and custody of the senses. Nor should they neglect the natural means which promote health of mind and body. Thus, they should not be influenced by the false teachings which allege that perfect continence is impossible or inimical to human development and, by a spiritual instinct, they should reject whatever endangers chastity. Further, let all, and especially superiors, remember that chastity is preserved more securely when the members live a common life in true sisterly and brotherly love.

The observance of perfect continence touches intimately the deeper inclinations of human nature. For this reason, candidates ought not to go forward, nor should they be admitted, to the profession of chastity except after really adequate testing, and unless they are sufficiently mature, psychologically and affectively. Not only should they be warned against the dangers to chastity which they may encounter, they should be taught to take on the celibacy they have dedicated to God in a manner beneficial to their entire personality.

13. Voluntary poverty, in Christ's footsteps, is a symbol of Christ which is much esteemed, especially nowadays. Religious should cultivate it diligently and, if needs be, express it in new forms. It enables them to share in the poverty of Christ who for our sake became poor, though he was rich, so that we might become rich through his poverty (see 2 Cor 8:9; Mt 8:20).

With regard to religious poverty it is by no means enough to be subject to superiors in the use of property. Religious should be poor in fact and in spirit, having their treasures in heaven (see Mt 6:20).

They should, each in their own assigned tasks, consider themselves bound by the common law of labor, and while by this means they are provided with whatever they need for their sustenance or their work, they should reject all undue solicitude, putting their trust in the providence of the heavenly Father (see Mt 6:25).

Religious congregations may, in their constitutions, permit their members to renounce their inheritances, both those which have already been acquired and those which may be acquired in the future.

The institutes themselves should endeavor, taking local conditions into account, to bear a quasi-collective witness to poverty. They should willingly contribute part of what they possess for the other needs of the church and for the support of the poor, whom all religious should love in the heart of Christ (see Mt 19:21; 25:34-46; Jas 2:15-16;1 Jn 3:17). Provinces and houses of the different institutes should share their resources with one another, those who have more helping those who are in need.

While institutes have the right, provided this is allowed by their rules and constitutions, to possess whatever they need for their temporal life and work, they should avoid any semblance of luxury, excessive wealth and accumulation of property.

14. By their vow of obedience, religious offer the full surrender of their own wills as a sacrifice of themselves to God, and by this means they are united more permanently and securely with God's saving will. After the example of Jesus Christ, who came to do his Father's will (see Jn 4:34; 5:30; Heb 10:7; Ps 39:9) and "taking the form of a servant" (Phil 2:7) learned obedience through what he suffered (see Heb 5:8), religious moved by the holy Spirit subject themselves in faith to those who hold God's place, their superiors. Through them they are led to serve all their sisters and brothers in Christ, just as Christ ministered to his sisters and brothers in submission to the Father and laid down his life for the redemption of many (see Mt 20:28; Jn 10:14-18). They are thus bound more closely to the church's service and they endeavor to attain to the measure of the stature of the fullness of Christ (see Eph 4:13).

Religious, therefore, should be humbly submissive to their superiors, in a spirit of faith and of love of God's will, and in accordance with their rules and constitutions. They should bring their powers of intellect and will and their gifts of nature and grace to bear on the execution of commands and on the fulfillment of the tasks given to them, realizing that they are contributing towards the building up of the body of Christ, according to God's plan. In this way, far from lowering the dignity of the human person, religious obedience leads it to maturity by increasing the freedom of the sons and daughters of God.

Superiors will have to render an account of the souls committed to their care (Heb 13:17). They should be docile to God's will in performing the task laid upon them and should exercise authority in a spirit of service of their sisters or brothers, thus reflecting God's love for them.

They should govern their subjects in the realization that they are children of God and with respect for them as human persons, fostering in them a spirit of voluntary submission. In particular, therefore, they should allow them due liberty with regard to the sacrament of penance and the direction of conscience. They should train their subjects to cooperate with them by applying themselves to their ordinary duties and to new undertakings with an active and responsible obedience. Superiors therefore, ought to listen to their subjects willingly and ought to invite their cooperation as something beneficial to the institute and to the church, retaining however their own authority to decide and to prescribe what is to be done.

Chapters and councils should faithfully discharge the role committed to them in government and, each of them in its own way, should give expression to the involvement and the concern of all the members of the community for the good of the whole.

15. Common life, in prayer and the sharing of the same spirit, should be constant, after the example of the early church, in which the company of believers was of one heart and mind (see Acts 4:32). It should be nourished by the teaching of the Gospel and by the sacred liturgy, especially by the Eucharist (see Acts 2:42). As members of Christ and members of a family, religious should outdo each another in mutual esteem (see Rom 12:10), carrying one another's burdens (see Gal 6:12). A community gathered together

as a true family in the Lord's name enjoys the Lord's presence (see Mt 18:20), through the love of God which is poured into their hearts by the holy Spirit (see Rom 5:5). For love sums up the law (see Rom 13:10) and is the bond which makes us perfect (see Col 3:14); by it we know that we have crossed over from death to life (see 1 Jn 3:14). Indeed, the unity between the sisters and brothers is a sign that Christ has come (see Jn 13:35; 17:21) and is a source of great apostolic power.

In order to strengthen the familial bond between the members of an institute, those who are called lay brothers, cooperators, or some such name should be associated more closely with the life and work of the community. Unless there are strong arguments to the contrary, it should be the aim to arrive at but one category of sisters in women's institutes. The only distinction between persons that should then be retained is that demanded by the different tasks to which sisters are assigned by God's special vocation or by reason of their special aptitudes.

Men's monasteries and institutes which are not entirely lay can, of their nature, admit clerics and laymen, in accordance with the constitutions, on an equal footing and with equal rights and obligations, apart from those arising from sacred orders.

16. Papal enclosure is to be maintained for nuns whose life is wholly contemplative. However, it should be adjusted to suit the conditions of time and place, abolishing obsolete practices after consultation with the monasteries themselves. Other nuns, however, who are engaged in the external apostolate by virtue of their own rule are to be exempted from papal enclosure so that they can the better fulfill their apostolic tasks. The enclosure prescribed by the constitutions must be maintained, however.

17. Religious dress, as a symbol of consecration,

must be simple and modest, at once poor and becoming. In addition, it must be in keeping with the requirements of health and must be suited to the time and place and to the needs of the apostolate. The dress, of men or of women, which is not in conformity with these norms ought to be changed.

18. The up-to-date renewal of institutes depends very much on the training of the members. For this reason, non-clerical religious men and religious women should not be assigned to apostolic tasks immediately after the noviciate. Their religious, apostolic, doctrinal and technical training should, rather, be continued, as is deemed appropriate, in suitable establishments. They should also acquire whatever academic degrees they need.

Lest the adaptation of religious life to the needs of our time be merely external and lest those whose rule assigns them to the active ministry should prove unequal to the task, they should be properly instructed, in keeping with each one's intellectual calibre and personal bent, concerning the behavior patterns, the emotional attitudes, and the thought processes of modern society. The elements of the education should be so harmoniously fused that it will help achieve balance in the lives of the religious.

All through their lives, religious should endeavor assiduously to perfect their spiritual, doctrinal and technical culture. Superiors, as far as they are able, should provide for them the opportunity, assistance and the time for this.

It is also the task of superiors to see to it that counsellors, spiritual directors and professors are carefully selected and are properly trained.

19. When it is proposed to found a new religious institute it must be asked, seriously: is it necessary, or at least very useful, and can it develop? Otherwise, institutes may be imprudently founded which are

useless or lacking in sufficient vitality. In young churches particular attention should be paid to the promotion and cultivation of forms of religious life which take into account the character and way of life of the inhabitants, and the local customs and conditions.

20. Institutes should maintain and faithfully perform their specific apostolates. Further, mindful of what is useful for the universal church and for the dioceses, they should adapt their ministry to what the locality and the times require. They should employ appropriate and even new methods, rejecting those which nowadays are less suited to the spirit and native genius of their institutes.

It is vital that the missionary spirit be maintained in religious institutes and be adapted to modern conditions, in keeping with each institute's character, so that the preaching of the Gospel to all nations may be more effective.

21. Institutes and monasteries, however, which the Holy See, having consulted the local ordinaries concerned, judges not to offer any reasonable hope of further development, are to be forbidden to receive more novices. If possible, they are to be amalgamated with more flourishing institutes or monasteries whose aims and spirit are similar to their own.

22. Institutes and independent monasteries should, as opportunity offers and with the approval of the Holy See, form federations, if they belong in some measure, to the same religious family. Failing this, they should form unions, if they have almost identical constitutions and customs, have the same spirit, and especially if they are few in number. Or they should form associations if they have the same or similar active apostolates.

23. Conferences or councils of major superiors, erected by the Holy See, are to be welcomed. They can

contribute a great deal towards the fuller achievement of the purpose of the individual institutes, towards fostering more effective cooperation for the good of the church, towards a more equitable distribution of ministers of the Gospel in a given territory, and towards dealing with the problems which are common to all religious. They should establish suitable coordination and cooperation with episcopal conferences with regard to the exercise of the apostolate.

Conferences of this type can also be established for secular institutes.

24. Priests and christian educators should seriously set about meeting adequately the church's need for new growth through religious vocations carefully and suitably screened. Even ordinary preaching should deal more frequently with the evangelical counsels and with choosing the religious state. Parents should nurture and protect religious vocations in their children by educating them in christian virtues.

Religious institutes have the right to publicize themselves in order to foster vocations, and they also have the right to seek candidates. However, they must do this with due prudence and they must observe the norms laid down by the Holy See and the local ordinary.

Religious should remember that the example of their own lives is the best commendation of their institutes and is an invitation to others to take on the religious life.

25. Religious institutes, for which these norms of up-to-date renewal have been established, should respond generously to the divine call and should be prompt in performing the task allotted to them in the church today. The holy synod holds in high esteem their way of life in chastity, poverty and obedience, a way of life of which Christ the Lord himself is the exemplar. It reposes great hope in their work, which

is so fruitful, whether it be hidden or public. All religious, therefore, with undiminished faith, with charity towards God and their neighbor, with love for the cross and with the hope of future glory, should spread the good news of Christ throughout the whole world, so that their witness will be seen by all and that our Father in heaven will be glorified (Mt 5:16). Thus, through the prayers of the gentle Virgin Mary, Mother of God, "whose life is a model for all" (St Ambrose, De Virginitate, 2, 2, n. 15) may they increase daily and may they bring more abundant fruits of salvation.

a. Translated and revised by A. F. The document's title, *Decretum de accomodata renovatione vitae religiosae,* has been translated in various ways. Literally it means "The decree on the accomodated renewal of the religious life." In his authoritative *The Theology of Vatican II,* p. 18, Bishop Christopher Butler said: "although, so far as I am aware, the fact has never been publicly stated, I take it that the term *accomodata renovatio* ('accommodated renewal') is here offered as a Latin translation of *aggiornamento.*"He goes on to quote the description of that renewal in no 2 of the decree as comprising: (a) "a constant return to the sources of christian life in general and to the original inspiration of the institutes", and (b) "their adaptation to the changed conditions of our time". He went on: "The former process is covered by the word *renewal* (which therefore does not mean changing but recovering one's origins) and the latter by the word *accommodated.*"

"Up-to-date" is another way of saying "adapted to modern times", hence the rendering of the title as: "The Up-to-date Renewal of the Religious Life." In the document itself I have translated *accommodata* as "up-to-date". Other versions are "appropriate renewal" (Abbott and Vorgrimler), "sensitive renewal" (Tanner), "renewal and adaptation", which is also used in the official French translation. The Italian translation, which one would have expected to use *aggiornamento,* opts for "rinnovamento" ("renewal") on its own. Paul VI's Apostolic Letter, *Ecclesiae Sanctae,* which contains directives on the implementation of the Decree, is in *Vatican Collection,* vol. 1, pp. 624 ff. [Editor].

DECREE ON THE APOSTOLATE OF LAY PEOPLE[a]

Apostolicam actuositatem
18 November, 1965

Introduction

1. Because it wants to intensify the apostolic activity of God's people,[1] the council now turns with solicitude to the christian laity. Mention has already been made in other documents of the laity's special and indispensable role in the church's mission.[2] Indeed, the church can never be without the lay apostolate; it is something that derives from the lay person's very vocation as a Christian. Scripture clearly shows how spontaneous and fruitful was this activity in the church's early days (see Acts 11:19-21; 18:26; Rom 16:1-16; Phil 4:3).

No less fervent a zeal on the part of lay people is called for today; present circumstances, in fact, demand from them a more extensive and more vigorous apostolate. For continuing population increases, progress in science and technology, and growing interdependence between people worldwide have immensely enlarged the field of the lay apostolate, a field that is in great part open to the laity alone. These developments have in addition given rise to new problems which require the laity's careful attention. All the more urgent has this apostolate become, now that autonomy — as is only right — has been reached in numerous sectors of human life, sometimes accompanied by a certain loss of moral and religious values, seriously jeopardizing the christian life. Besides, in many regions where priests are very few in number or, as is sometimes the case, are denied freedom to exercise their ministry, the church can only with difficulty make its presence and action felt without the help of the laity.

A sign of this urgent and many-faceted need is the manifest action of the holy Spirit making lay people nowadays increasingly aware of their responsibility and encouraging them everywhere to serve Christ and the church.[3]

The council intends to explain in this decree the nature of the lay apostolate, its character and the various forms it can take; it will state fundamental principles and give pastoral directives for its more effective exercise. These are all to serve as norms in the revision of canon law on the lay apostolate.

a. Translated by Father Finnian, OCSO, revised for this edition by AF.

1. See John XXIII, Apostolic Constitution *Humanae Salutis*, 25 Dec. 1961: AAS 54 (1962) p. 7-10.

2. See Vatican Council II, Dogmatic Constitution on the Church, *Lumen Gentium*, ch. IV, no. 33 ff.; Constitution on the Sacred Liturgy, *Sacrosanctum Concilium*, nos. 26-40; Decree on the Media, *Inter mirifica*; Decree on Ecumenism, *Unitatis redintegratio*; Decree on the Pastoral Office of Bishops in the Church, *Christus Dominus*: nos. 16, 17, 18; Declaration on Christian Education, *Gravissimum educationis*, nos. 3, 5, 7.

3. See Pius XII, Allocution To the cardinals 18 Feb. 1946: AAS 38 (1946) pp. 101-102; Idem, Sermon to young catholic workers, 25 Aug. 1957: AAS 49 (1957) p. 843.

Chapter I

THE VOCATION OF LAY PEOPLE TO THE APOSTOLATE

Participation of Laity in the Church's Mission

2. The church was founded so that by spreading Christ's kingdom throughout the world to the glory of God the Father, every man and woman may share in the saving work of redemption,[1] and so that through them the entire world may be truly directed towards Christ. Every activity of the mystical body, with this in view, goes by the name of apostolate, which the church exercises through all its members, though in various ways. In fact, the christian vocation is, of its nature, a vocation to the apostolate as well. In the organism of a living body no member is purely passive: sharing in the life of the body each member also shares in its activity. The same is true in the body of Christ which is the church, the whole body, "when each part is working properly, promotes the body's growth" (Eph 4:16). Between the members of this body there exists, further, such a unity and solidarity (see Eph 4:16) that members who fail to do their best to promote the growth of the body must be considered unhelpful both to the church and to themselves.

In the church, there is diversity of ministry but unity of mission. To the apostles and their successors, Christ has entrusted the office of teaching, sanctifying and governing in his name and by his power. Lay people too, sharing in the priestly, prophetical and kingly office of Christ, play their part in the mission of the whole people of God in the church and in the world.[2] In the concrete, their apostolate is exercised when they work to evangelize people and make them holy; it is exercised, too, when they endeavor to have the Gospel spirit permeate and improve the temporal order, going about it in a way that bears clear witness to Christ and helps forward the salvation of humanity. The characteristic of the lay state being a life led in the midst of the world and of secular affairs, lay people are called by God to make of their apostolate, through the vigor of their christian spirit, a leaven in the world.

Foundations of the Lay Apostolate

3. Lay people's right and duty to be apostles derives from their union with Christ their head. Inserted as they are in the mystical body of Christ by baptism and strengthened by the power of the holy Spirit in confirmation, it is by the Lord himself that they are assigned to the apostolate. If they are consecrated a royal priesthood and a holy nation (see 1 Pet 2:4-10), this is so that in all their actions they may offer spiritual sacrifices and bear witness to Christ all the world over. Charity, which is, as it were, the soul of the whole apostolate, is given to them and nourished in them by the sacraments, and especially by the Eucharist.[3]

The apostolate is lived in faith, hope and charity poured out by the holy Spirit into the hearts of all the members of the church. And the precept of charity, which is the Lord's greatest commandment, urges all Christians to work for the glory of God through the coming of his kingdom and for the communication of eternal life to all, that they may know the only true God and Jesus Christ whom he has sent (see Jn 17:3).

On all Christians, accordingly, rests the noble obligation of working to bring all people the whole world over to hear and accept the divine message of salvation.

The holy Spirit sanctifies the people of God through the ministry and the sacraments and, for the exercise of the apostolate, gives the faithful special gifts besides (see 1 Cor 12:7), "allotting them to each just as the Spirit chooses" (1 Cor 12:11), so that, putting at the service of others the grace received, all may be "good stewards of God's varied gifts," (1 Pet 4:10), for the building up of the whole body in charity (see Eph 4:16). From the reception of these charisms, even the most ordinary ones, there follow for all christian believers the right and duty to use them in the church and in the world for the good of humanity and the development of the church, to use them in the freedom of the holy Spirit who "chooses where to blow" (Jn 3:8), and at the same time in communion with the sisters and brothers in Christ, and with the pastors especially. It is for the pastors to pass judgment on the authenticity and good use of these gifts, not certainly with a view to quenching the Spirit but to testing everything and keeping what is good (see 1 Th 5:12, 19, 21).[4]

The Spirituality of Lay People

4. Christ, sent by the Father, is the source of the church's entire apostolate. Clearly then, the fruitfulness of the apostolate of lay people depends on their living union with Christ; as the Lord said himself: "Those who abide in me and I in them bear much fruit, for separated from me you can do nothing" (Jn 15:5). This life of intimate union with Christ in the church is maintained by the spiritual helps shared by all the faithful, especially by active participation in the liturgy.[5] Lay people should so use these aids that, while doing what is expected of them in the world in the ordinary conditions of life, they do not separate their union with Christ from their ordinary life, but actually grow closer to him by doing their work according to God's will. This is the path along which lay people must advance, fervently, joyfully, overcoming difficulties with prudent, patient effort.[6] Family

cares should not be foreign to their spirituality, nor any other temporal interest; in the words of the apostle: "Whatever you are doing, whether speaking or acting, do everything in the name of the Lord Jesus Christ, giving thanks to God the Father through him" (Col 3:17).

A life like this calls for a continuous exercise of faith, hope and charity. Only the light of faith and meditation on the word of God can enable us to find everywhere and always the God "in whom we live and exist" (Acts 17:28); only thus can we seek his will in everything, see Christ in everyone, acquaintance or stranger, make sound judgments on the true meaning and value of temporal realities both in themselves and in relation to our final end.

Those with such faith live in the hope of the revelation of the daughters and sons of God, keeping in mind the cross and resurrection of the Lord.

On life's pilgrimage they are hidden with Christ in God, are free from slavery to riches, are in search of the goods that last for ever. Generously they exert all their energies in extending God's kingdom, in making the christian spirit a vital energizing force in the temporal sphere. In life's trials they draw courage from hope,"convinced that present sufferings are no measure of the future glory to be revealed in us" (Rom 8:18).

Prompted by the love that comes from God, they do good to everyone, especially to their brothers and sisters in the faith (see Gal 6:10), putting aside "all ill will and deceit, all hypocrisy, envy and slander" (1 Pet 2:1), in this way attracting people to Christ. Divine love, "poured into our hearts by the holy Spirit who has been given to us" (Rom 5:5), enables lay people to express concretely in their lives the spirit of the Beatitudes. Following Jesus in his poverty, want does not depress them, nor is plenty a cause for pride.

Imitating the humble Christ, they do not long for empty glory (see Gal 5:26). They try, rather, to please God rather than people, always ready to abandon everything for Christ (see Lk 14:26) and to endure persecution in the cause of right (see Mt 5:10), having in mind the Lord's saying: "If any want to become my followers let them renounce themselves and take up their cross and follow me" (Mt 16:24). Preserving christian friendship with one another, they help each other in their needs.

This lay spirituality will take its particular character from the circumstances of one's state in life — married and family life, celibacy, widowhood — from one's state of health and from one's professional and social activity. Whatever their circumstances, all have received suitable talents and these should be cultivated, as should also the personal gifts they have from the holy Spirit.

Similarly, lay people who have followed their particular vocation and become members of any of the associations or institutions approved by the church aim sincerely at making their own the forms of spirituality proper to these bodies.

They should also hold in high esteem professional competence, family and civic sense, and the virtues related to social behavior such as honesty, sense of justice, sincerity, courtesy, moral courage; without them there is no true christian life.

A perfect model of this apostolic spiritual life is the Blessed Virgin Mary, Queen of Apostles. While on earth her life was like that of any other, filled with labors and the cares of the home; always, however, she remained intimately united to her Son and cooperated in an entirely unique way in the Saviour's work. And now, assumed into heaven, "her motherly love keeps her attentive to her Son's brothers and sisters, still on pilgrimage amid the dangers and difficulties of life, until they arrive at the happiness of the fatherland."[7] All should have a genuine devotion to her and entrust their lives to her motherly care.

1. See Pius XI, Encyclical Rerum *Ecclesiae:* AAS 18 (1926) p. 65.

2. See Vatican Council II, Dogmatic Constitution on the Church, *Lumen Gentium,* no. 33.

3. See Vatican Council II, Dogmatic Constitution on the Church, *Lumen Gentium,* no. 33. See also no. 10.

4. See ibid., no. 12.

5. See Vatican Council II, Constitution on the Sacred Liturgy, *Sacrosanctum Concilium,* no. 11.

6. See Vatican Council II, Dogmatic Constitution on the Church, *Lumen Gentium,* no. 32. See also nos. 40-4.

7. See ibid., no. 62. See also no. 65.

Chapter II

OBJECTIVES

5. The work of Christ's redemption concerns essentially the salvation of men and women; it takes in also, however, the renewal of the whole temporal order. The mission of the church, consequently, is not only to bring people the message and grace of Christ but also to permeate and improve the whole range of temporal things. The laity, carrying out this mission of the church, exercise their apostolate therefore in the world as well as in the church, in the temporal order as well as in the spiritual. These orders are distinct; they are nevertheless so closely linked that God's plan is, in Christ, to take the whole world up again and make of it a new creation, initially here on earth, totally at the end of time. The layperson, at one and the same time a believer and a citizen of the world, has only a single conscience, a christian conscience, by which to be guided continually in both domains.

The Apostolate of Evangelization and Sanctification

6. The church's mission is concerned with people's salvation; and people win salvation through faith in Christ and his grace. The apostolate of the church therefore, and of each of its members, aims primarily at announcing to the world, by word and action, the message of Christ and communicating to it the grace of Christ. The principal means of bringing this about is the ministry of the word and of the sacraments. This is entrusted in a special way to the clergy, but the laity also have a highly important part to play, the part namely of "helping on the cause of truth" (3 Jn 8). It is in this sphere most of all that the lay apostolate and the pastoral ministry complement each other.

Lay people have countless opportunities for exercising the apostolate of evangelization and sanctification. The very witness of a christian life, and good works done in a supernatural spirit, are effective in drawing women and men to the faith and to God; and that is what the Lord has said: "Your light must shine so brightly before people that they can see your good works and glorify your Father who is in heaven" (Mt 5:16).

This witness of life, however, is not the sole element in the apostolate; the true apostle is on the lookout for occasions to proclaim Christ by word, either to unbelievers to draw them towards the faith, or to the faithful to instruct them, strengthen them, call them to a more fervent life; "for Christ's love urges us on" (2 Cor 5:14), and in everyone's heart the apostle's words should find an echo: "Woe to me if I do not preach the Gospel" (1 Cor 9:16).[1]

At a time when new questions are being put and when grave errors aiming at undermining religion, the moral order and human society itself are rampant, the council appeals to the laity to take a more active part, according to their talents and knowledge and in fidelity to the mind of the church, in the explanation and defense of christian principles and in the correct application of them to the problems of our times.

The Renewal of the Temporal Order

7. That women and men, working in harmony, should renew the temporal order and make it increasingly more perfect: such is God's design for the world.

All that goes to make up the temporal order — personal and family values, culture, economic interests, the trades and professions, political institutions, international relations, and so on, as well as their gradual development — all these are not merely helps to humanity's last end, they possess a value of their own, placed in them by God, both in themselves or as parts of the integral temporal structure: "And God saw all that he had made and found it very good" (Gen 1:31). This natural goodness of theirs receives an added dignity from their relation with the human person, for whose use they have been created. And then, too, God has willed to gather together all that was natural, all that was supernatural, into a single whole in Christ, "so that in everything he would have the primacy" (Col 1:18). Far from depriving the temporal order of its autonomy, of its specific ends, of its own laws and resources, or its importance for human well-being, this design, on the contrary, increases its energy and excellence, raising it at the same time to the level of people's integral vocation here below.

In the course of history the use of temporal things has been tarnished by serious defects. Under the influence of original sin people have often fallen into very many errors about the true God, human nature and the principles of morality. As a consequence human conduct and institutions became corrupted, the human person itself being held in contempt. Again in our own days many have placed their trust to an immoderate degree in the conquests of science and technology, lapsing into a kind of idolatry of the temporal; they become its slaves rather than its masters.

It is the task of the church as a whole to make women and men capable of establishing the proper scale of values in the temporal order and to direct it towards God through Christ. Pastors have the duty to set out clearly what is the purpose of creation and the use to be made of the world, and to provide moral and spiritual helps for the renewal of the temporal order in Christ.

Lay people ought themselves to take on as their distinctive task this renewal of the temporal order. Guided by the light of the Gospel and the mind of the church, prompted by christian love, they should act directly in this domain and in their own way. As citizens among citizens they must bring to their cooperation with others their own special competence, and act on their own responsibility; everywhere and always they have to seek the justice of the kingdom of God. The temporal order is to be renewed in such a way that, while its own principles are fully respected, it is harmonized with the principles of the christian life and adapted to the various conditions of time, place and people. Among the tasks of this apostolate christian social action is preeminent. The council desires to see it extended today to every sector of life, including the cultural sphere.[2]

Charitable Works and Social Aid

8. While every apostolic activity should find in charity its origin and driving force, certain works are of their nature a most eloquent witness to charity;

and Christ has willed that these should be signs of his messianic mission (see Mt 11:4-5).

The greatest commandment of the law is to love God with one's whole heart and one's neighbor as oneself (see Mt 22:37-40). Christ has made this love of the neighbor his personal commandment and has enriched it with a new meaning when he willed himself, along with his brothers and sisters, to be the object of this charity saying: "just as you did it to one of the least of these who are members of my family, you did it to me" (Mt 25:40). In assuming human nature he has united to himself all humanity in a supernatural solidarity which makes of it one single family. He has made charity the distinguishing mark of his disciples, in the words: "By this will everyone know you for my disciples, by your love for one another" (Jn 13:35).

In the early days the church linked the "agape" to the eucharistic supper, and by so doing showed itself as one body around Christ united by the bond of charity. So too, in all ages, love is its characteristic mark. While rejoicing at initiatives taken elsewhere, it claims charitable works as its own mission and right. That is why mercy to the poor and the sick, charitable works and works of mutual aid for the alleviation of all kinds of human need, are especially esteemed in the church.[3]

Today these activities and works of charity have become much more urgent worldwide; now that means of communication are more rapid, distances between people have been more or less eliminated, people in every part of the globe have become as members of a single family. Charitable action today can and should reach all women and men and all needs.

Wherever women and men are to be found who are in want of food and drink, of clothing, housing, medicine, work, education, the means necessary for leading a truly human life, wherever there are men and women suffering from misfortune or illness, men and women suffering exile or imprisonment, christian charity should search them out, comfort and care for them and give them the assistance that will relieve their needs. This obligation is especially binding on the more affluent individuals and nations.[4]

If such charitable activity is clearly to be above all criticism, people should see in their neighbors the image of God in which they have been created, and Christ the Lord to whom all that is given to the needy is really offered. The liberty and dignity of the person helped must be respected with the greatest sensitivity. Purity of intention should not be stained by any self-seeking or desire to dominate.[5] The demands of justice must first of all be satisfied; what is already due in justice is not to be offered as a gift in charity. The causes of evils, and not merely their effects, should be eliminated. The aid contributed should be organized in such a way that beneficiaries are gradually freed from their dependence on others and become self-supporting.

The laity should therefore highly esteem, and support as far as they can, private or public works of charity and social assistance movements, including international schemes. By these channels effective help is brought to individuals and nations in need. They should collaborate in this with all men and women of good will.[6]

1. See Pius XI, Encyclical *Ubi arcano,* 23 Dec. 1922: AAS 14 (1922) p. 659; Pius XII, Encyclical *Summi Pontificatus,* 20 Oct. 1939: AAS 31 (1939) pp. 442-443.

2. See Leo XIII, Encyclical *Rerum Novarum:* AAS 23 (1890-1891) p. 647; Pius XI, Encyclical *Quadragesimo Anno:* AAS 23 (1931) p. 190; Pius XII, Radio message, 1 June 1941: AAS 33 (1941) p. 207.

3. See John XXIII, Encyclical *Mater et Magistra:* AAS 53 (1961) p. 402.

4. See ibid., pp. 440-441.

5. See ibid., pp. 442-443.

6. See Pius XII, Allocution *Ad Pax Romana* M.l.l.C., 25 April 1957: AAS 49 (1957) pp. 298-299; and especially John XXIII, *Ad Conventum Consilii 'Food and Agriculture* Organization' (FAO), 10 Nov. 1959: AAS 51 (1959) pp. 856, 866.

Chapter III

THE VARIOUS FIELDS OF THE APOSTOLATE

9. The lay apostolate, in all its many aspects, is exercised both in the church and in the world. In either case different fields of apostolic action are open to the laity. We propose to mention here the chief among them: church communities, the family, the young, the social environment, national and international spheres. Since in our days women are taking an increasingly active share in the entire life of society, it is very important that their participation in the various sectors of the church's apostolate should likewise develop.

Church Communities

10. Sharing in the function of Christ, priest, prophet and king, the laity have an active part of their own in the life and activity of the church. Their activity within the church communities is so necessary that without it the apostolate of the pastors will frequently be unable to obtain its full effect. Following in the footsteps of the men and women who assisted Paul in the proclamation of the Gospel (see Acts 18:18-26; Rom 16:3), lay persons of a genuinely apostolic spirit supply the needs of their brothers and sisters and are a source of consolation to the pastors no

less than to the rest of the faithful (see 1 Cor 16:17-18). Nourished by their active participation in the liturgical life of their community, they engage zealously in its apostolic works; they attract people towards the church who had been perhaps very far away from it; they ardently cooperate in the spread of the word of God, particularly by catechetical instruction; by their expert assistance they increase the efficacy of the care of souls as well as of the administration of the goods of the church.

The parish offers an outstanding example of community apostolate, for it gathers into one all the human diversities that are found there and inserts them into the universality of the church.[1] The laity should develop the habit of working in the parish in close cooperation with their priests,[2] of bringing before the ecclesial community their own problems, world problems, and questions regarding humanity's salvation, to examine them together and solve them by general discussion. According to their abilities the laity ought to cooperate in all the apostolic and missionary enterprises of their ecclesial family.

The laity will continuously cultivate the "feeling for the diocese," of which the parish is a kind of cell; they will be always ready at the invitation of their bishop to make their own contribution to diocesan undertakings. Indeed they will not confine their cooperation within the limits of the parish or diocese, but will endeavor, in response to the needs of the towns and rural districts[3] to extend it to interparochial, interdiocesan, national and international spheres. This widening of horizons is all the more necessary in the present situation, in which the increasing frequency of population shifts, the development of active solidarity and the ease of communications no longer permit any part of society to live in isolation. The laity will therefore be concerned for the needs of the people of

God scattered throughout the world. Especially will they make missionary works their own by providing them with material means and even with personal service. It is for Christians a duty and an honor to give God back a portion of the goods they have received from him.

The Family

11. The Creator made the married state the beginning and foundation of human society; by his grace he has made of it, too, a great mystery in Christ and in the church (see Eph 5:32), and so the apostolate of married persons and of families has a special importance for both church and civil society.

Christian couples are, for each other, for their children and for their relatives, cooperators of grace and witnesses of the faith. They are the first to pass on the faith to their children and to educate them in it. By word and example they form them to a christian and apostolic life; they offer them wise guidance in the choice of vocation, and if they discover in them a sacred vocation they encourage it with every care.

To give clear proof in their own lives of the indissolubility and holiness of the marriage bond; to assert with vigor the right and duty of parents and guardians to give their children a christian upbringing; to defend the dignity and legitimate autonomy of the family: this has always been the duty of married persons; today, however, it has become the most important aspect of their apostolate. They and all the faithful, therefore, should collaborate with men and women of good will in seeing that these rights are perfectly safeguarded in civil legislation; that in social administration consideration is given to the requirements of families in the matter of housing, education of children, working conditions, social security and taxes; and that in emigration regulations family life is perfectly safeguarded.[4]

The mission of being the primary vital cell of society has been given to the family by God. This mission will be accomplished if the family, by the mutual affection of its members and by family prayer, presents itself as a domestic sanctuary of the church; if the whole family takes its part in the church's liturgical worship; if, finally, it offers active hospitality, and practises justice and other good works for the benefit of all its sisters and brothers who suffer from want. Among the various works of the family apostolate the following may be listed: adopting abandoned children, showing a loving welcome to strangers, helping with the running of schools, supporting adolescents with advice and help, assisting engaged couples to make a better preparation for marriage, taking part in catechism-teaching, supporting married people and families in a material or moral crisis, and, in the case of the aged, providing them not only with what is indispensable but also procuring for them a fair share of the fruits of economic progress.

Everywhere and always, but especially in regions where the first seeds of the Gospel are being sown, or where the church is still in its infancy or finds itself in a critical situation, christian families bear a very valuable witness to Christ before the world when all their life they remain attached to the Gospel and give clear examples of christian marriage.[5]

To attain the ends of their apostolate more easily it can be of advantage for families to organise themselves into groups.[6]

Young People

12. Young people exert a very important influence in modern society.[7] Their living conditions, their mental attitudes, their relations with their families, have been completely transformed. Often, they enter too

rapidly a new social and economic environment. While their social and even political importance is on the increase daily, they seem unequal to the weight of these new responsibilities.

The growth of their social importance demands from them a corresponding apostolic activity; and indeed their natural character inclines them in this direction. Buoyed up by their natural ardor and exuberant energy, when awareness of their own personality ripens in them they shoulder their responsibilities and are eager to take their place in social and cultural life. If this enthusiasm is penetrated with the spirit of Christ, animated by a sense of obedience and love of the pastors of the church, a very rich harvest can be expected from it. The young should become the first apostles to the young, in direct contact with them, exercising the apostolate by themselves among themselves, taking account of their social environment.[8]

Adults should be anxious to enter into friendly dialogue with the young. Through this, despite the difference in age, adults and young people could get to know each other and share with each other their own personal riches. It is by example first of all and, on occasion, by sound advice and practical help that adults should persuade the young to undertake the apostolate. The young, on their side, will treat their elders with respect and confidence; and though by nature inclined to favor what is new, they will have due esteem for praiseworthy traditions.

Children too have an apostolate of their own. In their own measure they are true living witnesses of Christ among their companions.

Apostolate of Like Towards Like

13. The apostolate in one's social environment: that

is the attempt to infuse with the christian spirit the mentality and behavior, laws and structures of the community in which one lives. So much is it the special work and responsibility of lay people that it cannot be properly carried out by any others. In this area lay people can conduct the apostolate of like towards like. There the witness of their life is completed by the witness of their word.[9] It is amid the surroundings of their work that they are best qualified to be of help to their brothers and sisters, in the surroundings of their profession, of their study, residence, leisure or local group.

The laity accomplish the church's mission in the world principally by that blending of behaviour and faith which makes them the light of the world. They achieve this by that uprightness in all their dealings which persuades everyone to love the true and the good and which attracts them ultimately to Christ and the church; by that love which bids them share the living conditions and labors, the sufferings and yearnings of their sisters and brothers, and thereby prepare all hearts, gently, imperceptibly, for the action of saving grace. They also bring to their mission that full awareness of their personal responsibility in the development of society which persuades them to perform their family, social and professional duties with christian generosity. In this way their conduct gradually makes itself felt in the surroundings where they live and work.

This apostolate should reach out to every single person in the environment and must not exclude any good, spiritual or temporal, that can be done for them. Genuine apostles are not content, however, with just that. They are also very serious about revealing Christ by word to those around them. It is a fact that many men and women cannot hear the Gospel and come to acknowledge Christ except through the lay people with whom they associate.

The National and International Levels

14. There is a vast apostolate on the national and international planes and it is there that the laity especially are the channels of christian wisdom. In their patriotism and in their fidelity to their civic duties Catholics will feel themselves bound to promote the true common good; they will make the weight of their convictions so influential that, as a result, the exercise of civil authority will be just and laws will accord with the moral precepts and the common good. Catholics versed in politics and, as should be the case, firm in the faith and christian teaching, should not hesitate to enter public life; for by fulfilling their duties they can work for the common good and at the same time prepare the way for the Gospel.

Catholics should be ready to collaborate with all men and women of good will in the promotion of all that is true, just, holy, all that is worthy of love (see Phil 4:8). They are to enter into dialogue with them, approaching them with understanding and courtesy, and are to search for means of improving social and public institutions along the lines of the Gospel.

Particularly worthy of note among the signs of our times is the ever growing and inescapable sense of the solidarity of all peoples. It is the task of the lay apostolate to take pains in developing this sense and transforming it into a really sincere desire for communion. The laity should have an awareness also of the international sector, of the doctrinal and practical problems and solutions that are brought forward there, in particular those concerned with newly-developing nations.[10]

Everyone who works in foreign countries or brings

them aid must remember that relations among peoples should be a real familial interchange in which both parties give and at the same time receive. Those who travel abroad on international activities, on business or on holiday, should keep in mind that no matter where they may be they are the travelling messengers of Christ, and should conduct themselves as such.

1. See Pius X, Apostolic Letter *Creationis duarum novarum paroeciarum*, I June 1905: ASS 3 (1905) pp. 65-67; Pius II, Allocution *Ad fideles Paroeciae S. Saba*, 11 Jan. 1953: *Discorsi e Radiomessaggi di SS. Pio Xll*, 14 (1952-1953) pp. 449-454; John XXIII, Allocution *Clero et christifidelibus e diocesi suburbicaria Albanensi, ad Arcem Gandulfi habita*, 16 Aug. 1962: AAS 54 (1962) pp. 656-660.

2. See Leo XIII, Allocution, 28 Jan. 1894 Acts 14 (1894) pp. 424-425.

3. See Pius XII Allocution *Ad Parochos, etc.*, 6 Feb. 1951: *Discorsi e Radiomessaggi di SS. Pio XII* 12 (1950 1951) pp. 437 443; 8 March 1952: ibid., 14 (1952-1953) pp. 5-10; 27 March 1953: ibid., 15 (1953-1954) pp. 27-35; 28 Feb. 1954: ibid., pp. 585-590.

4. Pius XI, Encyclical Casti *Connubii*: AAS 22 (1930) p. 554; Pius XII, Radio message, 1 June 1941: AAS 33 (1941) p. 203; Idem, *Delegatis ad Conventum Unionis Internationalis sodalitatum ad iura familiae tuenda*, 20 Sept. 1949: AAS 41 (1949) p. 552; Idem, *Ad patres familias e Gallia Romam peregrinantes*, 18 Sept. 1951, p. 731: AAS 45 (1953) p. 41; Idem, Radio Message at Christmas 1952: AAS 45 (1953) p. 41; John XXIII, Encyclical *Mater et Magistra*, 15 May 1961: AAS 53 (1961) pp. 429, 439.

5. See Pius XII, Encyclical *Evangelii Praecones*, 2 June 1951: AAS 43 (1951) p. 514.

6. See Pius XII, *Delegatis ad Conventum Unionis Internationalis sodalitatum ad iura familiae tuenda*, 20 Sept. 1949: AAS 41 (1949) p. 552.

7. See Pius X, Allocution *Ad catholicam Associationem Iuventutis Gallicae de pietate, scientia et actione*, 25 Sept. 1904: AAS 37 (1904-1905) pp. 296-300.

8. See Pius XII, Letter, *Dans quelques semaines*, to the archbishop of Montreal: De conventibus a juvenibus operariis christianis canadiensibus indictis, 24 May 1947: AAS 39 (1974) p. 257; Radio Message *Ad J.O.C. Bruxelles*, 3 Sept. 1950: AAS 42 (1950) pp. 640 641.

9. See Pius X1, Encyclical Quadragesimo *Anno*, 15 May 1931: AAS 23 (1931) pp. 225 — 226.

10. See John XXIII Encyclical *Mater et Magistra*, 15 May 1961: AAS 53 (1961) pp. 448-450.

Chapter IV

THE DIFFERENT FORMS OF
THE APOSTOLATE

15. The laity can exercise their apostolic activity either singly or grouped in various communities or associations.

Individual Apostolate

16. The apostolate to be exercised by the individual — which flows abundantly from a truly christian life (see Jn 4:11) — is the starting point and condition of all types of lay apostolate, including the organized apostolate; nothing can replace it.

The individual apostolate is everywhere and always in place; in certain circumstances it is the only one appropriate, the only one possible. All lay people, whatever their condition, are called to it, are obliged to it, even if they do not have the opportunity or possibility of collaborating in associations.

The apostolate, through which the laity build up the church, sanctify the world and persuade it to live in Christ, can take on many forms.

A special form of the individual apostolate is the witness of an entire lay life motivated by faith, hope and charity; it is a sign very much in keeping with our times, and a manifestation of Christ living in his faithful. Then, by the apostolate of the word, which in certain circumstances is absolutely necessary, the laity proclaim Christ, explain and extend his teachings, according to their condition and competence, and faithfully profess those teachings.

Moreover, cooperating as citizens of this world in all that has to do with the construction and regulation of the temporal order, the laity should, by the light of faith, endeavour to find the higher motives that should govern their behavior in the home and in professional, cultural and social life; they should too, given the opportunity, let these motives be seen by others, conscious that by so doing they become cooperators with God the creator, redeemer and sanctifier, and give him glory.

Finally, the laity should vitalize their lives with charity and, to the extent of each person's capability, give concrete expression to it in works.

All should remember that by public worship and by prayer, by penance and the willing acceptance of the toil and hardships of life by which they resemble the suffering Christ (see 2 Cor 4:10; Col 1:24), they can reach all men and women and contribute to the salvation of the entire world.

Individual Apostolate in Certain Circumstances

7. There is an imperative need for the individual apostolate in those areas where the church's freedom is seriously diminished. In such difficult circumstances the laity take over as far as possible the work of priests, jeopardizing their own freedom and sometimes their lives; they teach christian doctrine to those around them, train them in a religious way of life and in catholic attitudes, encourage them to receive the sacraments frequently and to cultivate piety, especially eucharistic piety.[1] The council renders God most heartfelt thanks that in our own times he is still raising up lay people of heroic courage in the midst of persecution; the council embraces them with gratitude and fatherly affection.

The individual apostolate has a special role in regions where Catholics are few and scattered. In such circumstances the laity who exercise only the personal apostolate — whether from the reasons mentioned above or from particular motives arising, among other things, from their professional activity — can gather for discussion into small groups with no rigid form of rules or organization. This is particularly appropriate in the present instance, for it ensures the continual presence before the eyes of others of a sign of the church's community, a sign that will be seen as a genuine witness of love. Thus, by affording mutual spiritual aid, by friendship and the exchange of personal experiences, they are given the courage to surmount the difficulties of too isolated a life and activity and can increase the yield of their apostolate.

Group Apostolate

18. The faithful are called as individuals to exercise an apostolate in their various situations. They must, however, remember that people are social by nature and that it has been God's pleasure to assemble those who believe in Christ and make of them the people of God (see 1 Pet 2:5-10), a single body (see 1 Cor 12:12). The group apostolate is in happy harmony therefore with a fundamental need in the faithful, a need that is both human and christian. At the same time it offers a sign of the communion and unity of the church in Christ, who said: "Where two or three are gathered together in my name, I am there in the midst of them" (Mt 18:20).

For that reason Christians will exercise their apostolate in concert.[2] They will be apostles both in their families and in the parishes and dioceses, which express the communitarian character of the apostolate; apostles too in the free associations they will have decided to form among themselves.

The group apostolate is very important also for another reason: often, either in ecclesial communities or in various other environments, the apostolate calls for concerted action. Organizations created for group apostolate afford support to their members, train them for the apostolate, carefully assign and direct their apostolic activities; and as a result a much richer harvest can be hoped for from them than if each person were acting on her or his own.

In present circumstances it is supremely necessary that wherever the laity are at work the apostolate under its collective and organized form should be strengthened. In actual fact, only a well-knit combination of efforts can attain all the aims of the modern apostolate and defend its values.[3] From this point of view it is particularly important for the apostolate to establish contact with the group attitudes and social conditions of the persons who are its object; otherwise these will often be incapable of withstanding the pressure of public opinion or of social institutions.

Various Types of Group Apostolate

19. There is a great variety of apostolic associations.[4] Some serve the general apostolic purposes of the church; others aim specifically at evangelization and sanctification; others work for the permeation of the temporal order by the christian spirit; and others engage in works of mercy and of charity as their special way of bearing witness to Christ.

First among these associations to be given consideration should be those which favor and promote a more intimate unity between the faith of the members and their everyday life. Associations are not ends in themselves; they are meant to be of service to the church's mission to the world. Their apostolic value depends on their conformity with the church's aims, as well as on the christian witness and evangelical spirit of each of their members and of the association as a whole.

As a consequence of the progress of institutions and the rapid evolution of modern society, the universal nature of the church's mission requires that the apostolic initiatives of Catholics should increasingly develop international associations of various kinds. Catholic international organizations will the more surely gain their object, the more closely the groups that compose them, as well as their members, are linked to them.

While preserving intact the necessary link with ecclesiastical authority,[5] the laity have the right to establish and direct associations,[6] and to join existing ones. Dissipation of forces must, however, be avoided; this would happen if new associations and works were created without sufficient reason, if old ones now grown useless were retained, if out-of-date methods continued to be employed. It will not always be a wise procedure, either, to transfer indiscriminately into some particular country forms that have originated in another.[7]

Catholic Action

20. Several decades ago lay people, dedicating themselves increasingly to the apostolate, in many countries formed themselves into various kinds of movements and societies which, in closer union with the hierarchy, have pursued and continue to pursue properly apostolic ends. Among these institutions, as indeed among other similar older ones, special mention must be made of those which, though using differing methods, have yielded abundant fruit for the kingdom of Christ. Deservedly praised and promoted by the popes and numerous bishops, they have received from them the name of Catholic Action, and have most often been described by them as a collaboration of the laity in the hierarchical apostolate.[8]

These types of apostolate, whether or not they go by the name of Catholic Action, are today doing a work of great value. They are constituted by the combination of all the following characteristics:

(a) The immediate aim of organizations of this sort is the church's apostolic purpose. In other words, the evangelization and sanctification of men and women and the christian formation of their consciences, so as to enable them to imbue with the Gospel spirit the various social groups and environments.

(b) The laity, cooperating in their own particular way with the hierarchy, contribute their experience and assume responsibility for the direction of these organizations, for the investigation of the conditions in which the church's pastoral work is to be carried on, for the elaboration and execution of their plan of action.

(c) The laity act in unison after the manner of an organic body, to display more strikingly the community aspect of the church and to render the apostolate more productive.

(d) The laity, whether coming of their own accord or in response to an invitation to action and direct cooperation with the hierarchical apostolate, act under the higher direction of the hierarchy, which can authorize this cooperation, besides, with an explicit mandate.

Organizations which, in the judgment of the hierarchy, combine all these elements should be regarded as Catholic Action, even if they have forms and names that vary according to the requirements of localities and peoples.

The council most earnestly commends those institutions which certainly meet the requirements of the church's apostolate in many countries; it invites the priests and laity working in them to develop more and more the characteristics mentioned above, and always to give familial cooperation in the church to all other forms of the apostolate.

Special Commendation

21. Proper esteem is to be shown for all associations of the apostolate; those, however, which the hierarchy has praised, commended, or decided to establish with a view to meeting more urgent needs of time and place, should be held in the greatest esteem by priests, religious and lay people, and developed each in its own way. And among these organizations the international associations or societies of Catholics are especially worthy of mention today.

22. Deserving of special respect and praise in the church are the laity, single or married, who, permanently or for a time, put their person and their professional competence at the service of institutions and their activities. It is a great joy to the church to see the continuing increase in the number of lay people who are offering their personal service to associations and works of the apostolate, whether in their own country or abroad, or, above all, in the catholic communities of the missions and of the young churches.

Pastors are to welcome these lay persons with joy and gratitude. They will see to it that their conditions satisfy as perfectly as possible the requirements of justice, equity and charity, chiefly in the matter of resources necessary for the maintenance of themselves and their families. They should also be provided with the necessary training and with spiritual comfort and encouragement.

1. See Pius XII, Allocution *Ad I Conventum ex Omnibus Gentibus Laicorum Apostolatui provehendo*, 15 Oct. 1951: AAS 43 (1951) p. 788.
2. See Pius XII, Allocution *Ad I Conventum ex Omnibus Gentibus Laicorum Apostolatui provehendo*, 15 Oct. 1951: AAS 43 (1951) pp. 787-788.
3. See Pius XII, Encyclical *Le pélerinage de Lourdes*, 2 July 1957: AAS 49 (1957) p. 615.

4. See Pius XII, Allocution *Ad Consilium Foederationis interna-tionalis virorum catholicorum,* 8 Dec. 1956: AAS 49 (1957) pp. 26-27.

5. See below, ch. V, no. 24.

6. See Decree of the Sacred Congregation of the Council, *Corrienten.*, 13 Nov. 1920: AAS 13 (1921) p. 139.

7. See John XXIII, Encyclical *Princeps Pastorum,* 10 Dec. 1959. AAS 51 (1959) p. 856.

8. See Pius XI, Letter *Quae nobis,* to Cardinal Bertram, 13 Nov. 1928: AAS 20 (1928) p. 385. See also Pius XII, Allocution *Ad A.C. Italicam,* 4 Sept. 1940: AAS 32 (1940) p. 362.

Chapter V

THE ORDER TO BE OBSERVED

23. The lay apostolate, individual or collective, must be set in its true place within the apostolate of the whole church. Union with those whom the holy Spirit has appointed to rule the church of God (see Acts 20:28) is an essential element of the christian apostolate. No less necessary is collaboration among the different undertakings of the apostolate; it is the hierarchy's place to systematise this collaboration.

It is of vital importance that there be mutual esteem among all forms of the church's apostolate as well as proper coordination — while allowing full scope for each one's special character — in order to promote that the spirit of unity which will ensure familial charity will be clearly evident in the church's whole apostolate, as well as ensuring the accomplishment of common aims and the avoidance of ruinous rivalries.[1]

This is especially important when some particular action in the church calls for the agreement and apostolic cooperation of secular and regular clergy, of religious and of the laity.

Relations With the Hierarchy

24. The hierarchy's duty is to favor the lay apostolate, furnish it with principles and spiritual assistance, direct the exercise of the apostolate to the common good of the church, and see to it that doctrine and order are safeguarded.

Yet the lay apostolate allows of different kinds of relations with the hierarchy, depending on the various forms and objects of this apostolate.

Very many apostolic enterprise are to be found in the church which owe their origin to lay enterprise and which are run by lay people. Such enterprises enable the church, in certain circumstances, to fulfil her mission more effectively; these therefore are often praised and commended by the hierarchy.[2] But no enterprise may lay claim to the name "catholic" if it does not have the approval of legitimate ecclesiastical authority.

Certain types of the lay apostolate are explicitly recognized by the hierarchy, though in different ways.

Ecclesiastical authority, looking to the common good of the church, may also, from among apostolic associations and undertakings whose immediate goal is spiritual, choose some which it will especially promote and for which it may assume a special responsibility. Thus, to organize the apostolate as circumstances demand, the hierarchy can unite more closely a given form of the apostolate with its own apostolic functions, without, however, changing the specific nature of either or the distinction between the two, and consequently without depriving the laity of their rightful freedom to act on their own initiative. This action of the hierarchy has received the name of "mandate" in various ecclesiastical documents.

Finally, the hierarchy entrusts the laity with certain tasks more closely connected with the duties of pastors: in the teaching of christian doctrine, for example, in certain liturgical actions, in the care of souls. In virtue of this mission the laity are fully subject to superior ecclesiastical control in the exercise of these charges.

As for works and institutions of the temporal order, the duty of the ecclesiastical hierarchy is the teaching and authentic interpretation of the moral principles to be followed in this domain. It is also in its province to judge, after mature reflection and with the help of qualified persons, the conformity of such works or institutions with moral principles, and to pronounce in their regard concerning what is required for the safeguard and promotion of the values of the supernatural order.

Relations with the Clergy and with Religious

25. Bishops, parish priests and other priests of the secular and regular clergy will remember that the right and duty of exercising the apostolate are common to all the faithful, whether clerics or lay; and that in the building up of the church the laity too have parts of their own to play.[3] For this reason they will work as brothers with the laity in the church and for the church, and will have a special concern for the laity in their apostolic activities.[4] A careful choice will be made of priests with the ability and appropriate training to assist special forms of the lay apostolate.[5] Those who take part in this ministry in virtue of a mission received from the hierarchy represent the hierarchy in this pastoral action of theirs. Ever faithfully attached to the spirit and teaching of the church they will promote good relations between laity and hierarchy, they will devote their energies to fostering the spiritual life and the apostolic sense of the catholic associations confided to them; their wise advice will be there to help these in their apostolic labors; their encouragement will be given to their

enterprises. In constant dialogue with the laity, they will make painstaking search for methods capable of making apostolic action more fruitful; they will develop the spirit of unity within the association, and between it and others. Lastly, religious brothers and sisters will hold lay apostolic works in high regard; and will gladly help in promoting them in accordance with the spirit and rules of their institute;[6] they will strive to support, assist and complete the ministrations of the priest.

Special Councils

26. In dioceses, as far as possible, councils should be set up to assist the church's apostolic work, whether in the field of evangelization and sanctification or in the fields of charity, social relations and the rest, the clergy and religious working with the laity in whatever way proves satisfactory. These councils can see to the coordination of the various lay associations and undertakings, the autonomy and particular nature of each remaining intact.[7] Such councils should be established too, if possible, at parochial, inter-parochial, inter-diocesan level, and also on the national and international planes.[8]

In addition, a special secretariat should be established at the holy See for the service and promotion of the lay apostolate. This secretariat will act as a center which, with the proper equipment, will supply information about the different apostolic initiatives of the laity. It will undertake research into the problems arising today in this domain; and with its advice will assist the hierarchy and laity in the field of apostolic activities. The various apostolic movements and institutes of the lay apostolate all the world over should be represented in this secretariat. Clerics and religious should also be there to collaborate with the laity.

Cooperation With Other Christians and Non-Christians

27. The common patrimony of the Gospel and the resultant common duty of bearing a christian witness make it desirable, and often imperative, that Catholics cooperate with other Christians, either in activities or in societies; this collaboration can be carried on by individuals and by ecclesial communities, and at the national or international level.[9]

It frequently happens that Christians working for apostolic ends are required to collaborate with people who, though not Christians, acknowledge certain human values held by all humankind.

Through this dynamic, yet prudent, cooperation,[10] which is of great importance in temporal activities, the laity bears witness to Christ the Saviour of the world, and to the unity of the human family.

1. See Pius XI, Encyclical *Quamvis Nostra*, 30 April 1936: AAS 28 (1936) pp. 160-161.

2. See Sacred Congregation of the Council, Resolution *Corrienten.*, 13 Nov. 1920: AAS 13 (1921) pp. 137-140.

3. See Pius XII, *Ad II Conventum ex Omnibus Gentibus Laicorum Apostolatui provehendo*, 5 Oct. 1957: AAS 49 (1957) p. 927.

4. See Vatican Council II, Dogmatic Constitution on the Church, *Lumen Gentium*, no. 37.

5. See Pius XII, Apostolic Exhortation *Menti Nostrae*, 23 Sept. 1950: AAS 42 (1950) p. 660.

6. See Vatican Council II, Decree on the Up-to-date Renewal of Religious Life, *Perfectae caritatis*, no. 8.

7. See Benedict XIV, *De Synodo Dioecesana*, book III, ch. IX, no. VII-VIII: *Opera omnia in tomos XVII distributa*, tome XI (Prato 1884), pp. 76-77.

8. See Pius XI, Encyclical *Quamvis Nostra*, 30 April 1936; AAS 28 (1936) pp. 160-161.

9. See John XXIII, Encyclical *Mater et Magistra*, 15 May 1961: AAS 53 (1961) pp. 456-457; Vatican Council II, Decree on Ecumenism, *Unitatis redintegratio*, no. 12.

10. See Vatican Council II, Decree on Ecumenism, *Unitatis redintegratio*, no. 12; see also Dogmatic Constitution on the Church, *Lumen Gentium*, no. 15.

Chapter VI

TRAINING FOR THE APOSTOLATE

The Need for Training

28. A training, at once many-sided and complete, is indispensable if the apostolate is to be fully effective. This is required, not only by the continuous spiritual and doctrinal progress of lay people themselves, but also by the variety of circumstances, persons and duties to which they should adapt their activity. This education to the apostolate must rest on those foundations which the council has in other places set down and expounded.[1] Not a few types of apostolate require, besides the education common to all Christians, a specific and individual training, by reason of the diversity of persons and circumstances.

Principles of Training

29. Since the laity participate in the church's mission in their own way, their apostolic training acquires a special character precisely from the secularity proper to the lay state and from its particular type of spirituality.

Education for the apostolate presupposes an integral human education suited to each one's abilities and conditions. For lay people ought to be, through an intimate knowledge of the contemporary world, well integrated into their own society and its culture.

But in the first place they should learn to accomplish the mission of Christ and the church, living by faith in the divine mystery of creation and redemption, moved by the holy Spirit who gives life to the people of God and urging everyone to love God the Father, and in him to love the world of men and women. Such an education must be considered the foundation and condition of any fruitful apostolate.

Besides spiritual formation, solid grounding in doctrine is required: in theology, ethics and philosophy, at least, proportioned to the age, condition and abilities of each one. The importance too of a general culture linked with a practical and technical training is something which should by no means be overlooked.

If good human relations are to be cultivated, then it is necessary for genuine human values to stand at a premium, especially the art of living and working on friendly terms with others and entering into dialogue with them.

Training for the apostolate cannot consist only in being taught theory; on that account there is need, right from the start of training, to learn gradually and prudently to see all things in the light of faith, to judge and act always in its light, to improve and perfect oneself by working with others, and in this way to enter actively into the service of the church.[2] Inasmuch as the human person is continuously developing and new problems are forever arising, this education should be steadily perfected; it requires an ever more thorough knowledge and a continual adaptation of action. While meeting all its demands, concern for the unity and integrity of the human person must be kept always in the foreground, in order to preserve and intensify its harmony and equilibrium.

In this way lay people actively insert themselves deeply into the very reality of the temporal order and take their part competently in the work of the world. At the same time, as living members and witnesses of the church, they bring its presence and its action into the heart of the temporal sphere.[3]

Those Who Train Others for the Apostolate
30. Training for the apostolate should begin from the very start of a child's education. But it is more par-

ticularly adolescents and youths who should be initiated into the apostolate and imbued with its spirit.
This training should be continued all through life, to
fit them to meet the demands of fresh duties. It is
clear, then, that those with responsibility for christian
education have also the duty of attending to this
apostolic education.

It rests with parents to prepare their children from
an early age, within the family circle, to discern God's
love for everyone; they will teach them little by little
— and above all by their example — to be concerned
about their neighbors' needs, material and spiritual.
The whole family, accordingly, and its community life
should become a kind of apprenticeship to the apostolate.

Children must be trained, besides, to go beyond
the confines of the family and take an interest in both
ecclesial and temporal communities. Their integration
into the local parish community should succeed in
bringing them the awareness of being living, active
members of the people of God. Priests, for their part,
should not lose sight of this question of training for
the apostolate when catechizing, preaching and
directing souls, and in other functions of the pastoral
ministry.

Schools and colleges and other catholic educational institutions should foster in the young a catholic
outlook and apostolic action. If the young do not receive this type of education, either because they do
not attend these schools, or for some other reason, all
the greater is the responsibility for it that devolves
upon parents, pastoral and apostolic bodies. As for
teachers and educators, who by their calling and position practice an outstanding form of lay apostolate,
adequate learning and a thorough grasp of pedagogy
is a prerequisite to any success in this branch of education.

The various lay groups and associations dedicated to the apostolate or to any other supernatural end should look after this education to the apostolate with care and constancy, in ways consistent with their objectives and limits.[4] Frequently they are the ordinary channel of adequate apostolic training; doctrinal, spiritual and practical. The members, gathered in small groups with their companions or friends, evaluate the methods and results of their apostolic action, and measure their everyday behavior by the Gospel.

The training should be pursued in such a way as to take account of the entire range of the lay apostolate, an apostolate that is to be exercised in all circumstances and in every sector of life in the professional and social sectors especially — and not confined within the precincts of the associations. In point of fact, all lay people should undertake their own preparation for the apostolate. Especially for adults does this hold true; for as the years pass, self-awareness expands and so allows each one to acquire a clearer view of the talents with which God has enriched their lives and to bring in better results from the exercise of the charisms given them by the holy Spirit for the good of their sisters and brothers.

Fields Calling for Specialized Training

31. Different types of apostolate require their own appropriate methods of training:

(a) The apostolate of evangelization and sanctification: the laity are to be specially trained for engaging in dialogue with others, believers or non-believers, their aim being to set the message of Christ before the eyes of all.[5] But as materialism under various guises is today spreading far and wide, even among Catholics, the laity should not only make a careful study of catholic doctrine, especially points that are called into question, but should confront materialism of every type with the witness of evangelical life.

(b) The christian renewal of the temporal order: the laity are to be instructed in the true meaning and value of temporal goods, both in themselves and in their relation to all the aims of the human person. The laity should gain experience in the right use of goods and in the organization of institutions, paying heed always to the common good in the light of the principles of the church's moral and social teaching. They should acquire such a knowledge of social teaching especially, its principles and conclusions, as will fit them for contributing to the best of their ability to the progress of that teaching, and for making correct application of these same principles and conclusions in individual cases.[6]

(c) Works of charity and mercy bear a most striking testimony to christian life; therefore, an apostolic training which has as its object the performance of these works should enable the faithful to learn from childhood how to sympathize with their brothers and sisters, and help them generously when in need.[7]

Aids to Training

32. Many aids are now at the disposal of the laity who devote themselves to the apostolate: namely, seminars, congresses, recollections, retreats, frequent meetings, conferences, books and periodicals; all these enable them to deepen their knowledge of holy scripture and catholic doctrine, nourish the spiritual life, and become acquainted also with world conditions and discover and adopt suitable methods.[8]

These educational aids take into account the various types of apostolate exercised in this or that particular area.

With this end in view higher centers or institutes have been created; these have already given excellent results.

The council rejoices at initiatives of this kind now flourishing in certain regions; it desires to see them take root in other places too, wherever the need for them makes itself felt.

Moreover, centers of documentation and research should be established, not only in theology but also in anthropology, psychology, sociology, methodology, for the benefit of all fields of the apostolate. The purpose of such centers is to create a more favorable atmosphere for developing the aptitudes of the laity, men and women, young and old.

Exhortation

33. The council, then, makes to all the laity an earnest appeal in the Lord to give a willing, noble and enthusiastic response to the voice of Christ, who at this hour is summoning them more urgently, and to the urging of the holy Spirit. The younger generation should feel this call to be addressed in a special way to themselves; they should welcome it eagerly and generously. It is the Lord himself, by this council, who is once more inviting all the laity to unite themselves to him ever more intimately, to consider his interests as their own (see Phil 2:5), and to join in his mission as Saviour. It is the Lord who is again sending them into every town and every place where he himself is to come (see Lk 10:1). He sends them on the church's apostolate, an apostolate that is one yet has different forms and methods, an apostolate that must all the time adapt to the needs of the moment; he sends them on an apostolate where they are to show themselves his cooperators, doing their full share continually in the work of the Lord, knowing that in the Lord their labor cannot be lost (see Cor 15:58).

1. See Dogmatic Constitution on the Church, *Lumen Gentium*, chs 2, 4, 5; see also Decree on Ecumenism, *Unitatis redintegratio* nos. 4, 6, 7, 12; see also above, no. 4.

2. See Pius XII, *Ad VI Conferentiam internationalem 'boy-scouts'*, 6 June 1952: AAS 44 (1952) pp. 579-580; John XXIII, Encyclical *Mater et Magistra*, 15 May 1961 AAS 53 (1961) p. 456.

3. See Vatican Council II, Dogmatic Constitution on the Church, *Lumen Gentium*, no. 33.

4. See John XXIII, Encyclical *Mater et Magistra*, 15 May 1961: AAS 53 (1961) p. 455.

5. See Pius XII, Encyclical *Sertum laetitiae*, 1 Nov. 1939: AAS 31 (1939) pp. 635-644; see Idem, *Ad 'Laureati Act. Cath. It.*, 24 May 1953: AAS 45 (1953), pp. 411-415.

6. See Pius XII, Allocution *Ad congressum Universalem Foederationis Juventutis Femineae Catholicae*, 18 April 1952: AAS 44 (1952) pp. 414-419; see Idem, Allocution *Ad Associationem Christianam Operariorum Italiae* (A.C.L.I.), 1 May 1955: AAS 47 (1955) pp. 403-404.

7. See Pius XII, *Ad Delegatos Conventus Sodalitatum Caritas*, 27 April 1952: AAS 44 (1952), pp. 470-471.

8. See John XXIII, Encyclical *Mater et Magistra*, 15 May 1961: AAS 53 (1961) p. 454.

DECREE ON THE CHURCH'S MISSIONARY ACTIVITY[a]

Ad Gentes Divinitus
7 December, 1965

Introduction

1. Having been sent by God to the nations to be "the universal sacrament of salvation,"[1] the church, in obedience to the command of her founder (Mt 16:15) and because it is demanded by her own essential universality, strives to preach the gospel to all. The apostles, on whom the church was founded, following the footsteps of Christ "preached the word of truth and brought churches to birth."[2] It is the duty of their successors to carry on this work so that "the word of God may speed on and triumph" (2 Th 3:1), and the kingdom of God be proclaimed and renewed throughout the whole world.

In the present state of things which gives rise to a new situation for humanity, the church, the salt of the earth and the light of the world (see Mt 5:13-14), is even more urgently called upon to save and renew every creature, so that all things might be restored in Christ, and so that in him men and women might form one family and one people of God.

And so this sacred synod, while it thanks God for the outstanding work done through the generous labor of the whole church, proposes to outline the principles of missionary activity. It wishes to unite the efforts of all the faithful, so that the people of God, following the narrow way of the cross, might everywhere spread the kingdom of Christ, the Lord and beholder of the ages (see Eccl 36:19), and prepare the way for his coming.

a. Translated by Redmond Fitzmaurice, O.P, who also revised it for this edition.
1. See Vatican Council II, Dogmatic Constitution on the Church, *Lumen gentium*, 48.
2. St. Augustine, *Enarr.* in Ps. 44, 23 (PL 36, 508; CChr. 38, 510).

Chapter I

DOCTRINAL PRINCIPLES

2. The church on earth is by its very nature missionary since, according to the plan of the Father, it has its origin in the mission of the Son and the holy Spirit.[1] This plan flows from "fountain-like love," the love of God the Father. As the principle without principle from whom the Son is generated and from whom the holy Spirit proceeds through the Son, God, great and mercifully kind, freely creates us and moreover, graciously calls us to share in his life and glory. He generously pours out, and never ceases to pour out, his divine goodness, so that he who is creator of all things might at last become "all in all" (1 Cor 15:28), thus simultaneously assuring his own glory and our happiness. It pleased God to call men and women to share in his life and not merely singly, without any bond between them; he formed them into a people, in which his children who had been scattered were gathered together (see Jn 11:52).

3. This universal plan of God for the salvation of humanity is not carried out only secretly, as it were, in people's souls, nor by the efforts, including religious efforts, by which they seek God in many ways "and perhaps grope for him and find him — though indeed he is not far from each one of us" (see Acts 17:27); for these efforts need to be enlightened and corrected, although in the loving providence of God they may lead one to the true God and be a preparation for the gospel.[2] However, in order to establish a relationship of peace and communion with himself, and in order to establish communion among people, sinners though they are, God decided to enter into the history of humankind in a new and definitive manner, by sending his own Son in human flesh, so that through him he might snatch men and women from the power of darkness and of Satan (see Col 1:13; Acts 10:38) and in him reconcile the world to himself. He appointed him, through whom he made the world,[3] to be heir of all things, that he might restore all things in him (see Eph 1:10).

Jesus Christ was sent into the world as the true Mediator between God and humanity. Since he is God, "in him the whole fullness of deity dwells bodily" (Col 2:9); as man he is the new Adam, "full of grace and truth" (Jn 1:14), who has been constituted head of a restored humanity. So the Son of God entered the world by means of a true incarnation that he might make men and women sharers in the divine nature; though rich, he was made poor for our sake, that by his poverty we might become rich (2 Cor 8:9). The Son of man did not come to be served, but to serve and to give his life as a ransom for many, that is for all (see Mk 10:45). The fathers of the church constantly proclaim that what was not assumed by Christ was not healed.[4] Now Christ took a complete human nature just as it is found in us, wretched and poor as we are, but one that was without sin (see Heb 4:15; 9:28). Christ, "whom the Father sanctified and sent into the world" (Jn 10:36), said of himself: "The Spirit of the Lord is upon me, because he anointed me; to bring good news to the poor he sent me, to heal the broken-hearted, to proclaim to the captive release, and sight to the blind" (Lk 4:8); and on another occasion: "The Son of man has come to seek and to save what was lost" (Lk 9:10).

Now, what was once preached by the Lord, or fulfilled in him for the salvation of humankind, must be proclaimed and extended to the ends of the earth (Acts 1:8), starting from Jerusalem (see Lk 24:27), so that what was accomplished for the salvation of all may, in the course of time, achieve its universal effect.

4. To do this, Christ sent the holy Spirit from the Father to exercise inwardly his saving influence, and to promote the spread of the church. Without doubt, the holy Spirit was at work in the world before Christ was glorified.[5] On the day of Pentecost, however, he came down on the disciples that he might remain with them forever (see Jn 14:16); on that day the church was openly displayed to the crowds and the spread of the gospel among the nations, through preaching, was begun. Finally, on that day was foreshadowed the union of all peoples in the catholicity of the faith by means of the church of the New Alliance, a church which speaks every language, understands and embraces all tongues in charity, and thus overcomes the dispersion of Babel.[6] The "acts of the apostles" began with Pentecost, just as Christ was conceived in the Virgin Mary with the coming of the holy Spirit and was moved to begin his ministry by the descent of the same holy Spirit, who came upon him while he was praying.[7] Before freely laying down his life for the world, the Lord Jesus organized the apostolic ministry and promised to send the holy

Spirit, in such a way that both would be always and everywhere associated in the fulfilment of the work of salvation.[8] Throughout the ages the holy Spirit makes the entire church "one in communion and ministry; and provides her with different hierarchical and charismatic gifts,"[9] giving life to ecclesiastical structures, being as it were their soul,[10] and inspiring in the hearts of the faithful that same spirit of mission which impelled Christ himself. He even at times visibly anticipates apostolic action,[11] just as in various ways he unceasingly accompanies and directs it.[12]

5. From the beginning of his ministry the Lord Jesus "called to himself those whom he wished and he caused twelve of them to be with him and to be sent out preaching" (Mk 3:13; see Mt 10:1-42). Thus the apostles were both the seeds of the new Israel and the beginning of the sacred hierarchy. Later, before he was assumed into heaven (see Acts 1:11), after he had fulfilled in himself the mysteries of our salvation and the renewal of all things by his death and resurrection, the Lord, who had received all power in heaven and on earth (see Mt 28:18), founded his church as the sacrament of salvation; and just as he had been sent by the Father (see Jn 20: 21), so he sent the apostles into the whole world, commanding them: "Go, therefore, and make disciples of all nations, baptizing them in the name of the Father and of the Son and of the holy Spirit; teaching them to observe all that I have commanded you" (Mt 28:19-20.); "Go into the whole world, preach the gospel to every creature. He who believes and is baptized will be saved; but he who does not believe, will be condemned" (Mk 16:15 ff.). Hence the church has an obligation to proclaim the faith and salvation which comes from Christ, both by reason of the express command which the order of bishops inherited from the apostles, an obligation in the discharge of which they are assisted by priests,

and one which they share with the successor of St. Peter, the supreme pastor of the church, and also by reason of the life which Christ infuses into his members: "From him the whole body, being closely joined and knit together through every joint of the system, according to the functioning in due measure of each single part, derives its increase to the building up of itself in love" (Eph 4:16). The mission of the church is carried out by means of that activity through which, in obedience to Christ's command and moved by the grace and love of the holy Spirit, the church makes itself fully present to all individuals and peoples in order to lead them to the faith, freedom and peace of Christ by the example of its life and teaching, by the sacraments and other means of grace. Its aim is to open up for all men and women a free and sure path to full participation in the mystery of Christ.

Since this mission continues and, in the course of history, unfolds the mission of Christ, who was sent to evangelize the poor, the church, urged on by the Spirit of Christ, must walk the road Christ himself walked, a way of poverty and obedience, of service and self-sacrifice even to death, a death from which he emerged victorious by his resurrection. So it was that the apostles walked in hope and by much trouble and suffering filled up what was lacking in the sufferings of Christ for his body, which is the church. Often, too, the seed was the blood of Christians.[13]

6. This task which must be carried out by the order of bishops, under the leadership of Peter's successor and with the prayers and cooperation of the whole church, is one and the same everywhere and in all situations, although, because of circumstances, it may not always be exercised in the same way. The differences which must be recognized in this activity of the church, do not flow from the inner nature of the mission itself, but from the circumstances in which it is

exercised.

These circumstances depend either on the church itself or on the peoples, groups or individuals to whom its mission is directed. Although the church possesses in itself the totality and fullness of the means of salvation, it does not always, in fact cannot, use every one of them immediately, but it has to make beginnings and work by slow stages to give effect to God's plan. Sometimes after a successful start it has cause to mourn a setback, or it may linger in a state of semi-fulfilment and insufficiency. With regard to peoples, groups and individuals it is only by degrees that it touches and penetrates them and so raises them to a catholic perfection. In each situation and circumstance a proper line of action and effective means should be adopted.

The special undertakings in which preachers of the gospel, sent by the church, and going into the whole world, carry out the work of preaching the gospel and implanting the church among people who do not yet believe in Christ, are generally called "missions". Such undertakings are accomplished by missionary activity and are, for the most part, carried out in defined territories recognized by the holy See. The special end of this missionary activity is the evangelization and the implanting of the church among peoples or groups in which it has not yet taken root.[14] All over the world indigenous particular churches ought to grow from the seed of the word of God, churches which would be adequately organized and would possess their own proper strength and maturity. With their own hierarchy and faithful, and sufficiently endowed with means adapted to the living of a full Christian life, they should contribute to the good of the whole church. The principal instrument in this work of implanting the church is the preaching of the gospel of Jesus Christ. It was to announce this gospel that the

Lord sent his disciples into the whole world, that men and women, having been reborn by the word of God (see 1 Pet 1:23), might through baptism, be joined to the church which, as the Body of the Word incarnate, lives and is nourished by the word of God and the Eucharist (see Acts 4:23).

Various stages, which are sometimes intermingled, are to be found in this missionary activity of the church; first there is the beginning or planting and then a time of freshness and youthfulness. Nor does the church's missionary activity cease once this point has been passed; the obligation to carry on the work devolves on the particular churches already constituted, an obligation to preach the gospel to all who are still outside. Moreover, it often happens that, for various reasons, the groups among whom the church operates are utterly changed so that an entirely new situation arises. Then the church must consider whether these new circumstances require that she should once again exercise her missionary activity.

The situation, however, is often such that for the time being there is no possibility of directly and immediately preaching the gospel. In that case missionaries, patiently, prudently, and with great faith, can and ought at least bear witness to the love and kindness of Christ and thus prepare a way for the Lord, and in some way make him present.

It is clear, therefore, that missionary activity flows immediately from the very nature of the church. Missionary activity extends the saving faith of the church, it expands and perfects its catholic unity, it is sustained by its apostolicity, it activates the collegiate sense of its hierarchy, and bears witness to its sanctity which it both extends and promotes. Missionary work among the nations differs from the pastoral care of the faithful and likewise from efforts aimed at restoring Christian unity. Nevertheless, these two latter are very closely connected with the church's missionary endeavor[15] because the division between Christians is injurious to the holy work of preaching the gospel to every creature,[16] and deprives many people of access to the faith. Because of the church's mission, all baptized people are called upon to come together in one flock that they might bear unanimous witness before the nations to Christ their Lord. And if they cannot yet fully bear witness to one faith, they should at least be imbued with mutual respect and love.

7. The reason for missionary activity lies in the will of God, "who wishes everyone to be saved and to come to the knowledge of the truth. For there is one God and one Mediator between God and humanity, himself a man, Jesus Christ, who gave himself as a ransom for all" (1 Tim 2:4-5), "neither is their salvation in any other" (Acts 4:12). Everyone, therefore, ought to be converted to Christ, who is known through the preaching of the church, and they ought, by baptism, become incorporated into him and into the church which is his body. Christ himself explicitly asserted the necessity of faith and baptism (see Mk 16:16; Jn 3:5) and thereby affirmed at the same time the necessity of the church, which people enter through baptism as through a door. Hence they cannot be saved who, knowing that the Catholic church was founded by God through Jesus Christ as necessary, still refuse to enter it, or to remain in it.[17] So, although in ways known to himself God can lead those who, through no fault of their own are ignorant of the gospel, to that faith without which it is impossible to please him (Heb 11:6), the church, nevertheless, still has the obligation and also the sacred right to evangelize. And so, today as always, missionary activity retains its full force and necessity.

By means of this activity the mystical Body of

Christ unceasingly gathers and directs its energies towards its own increase (Eph 4:11-16). The members of the church are impelled to engage in this activity because of the charity with which they love God and by which they desire to share with all people the spiritual goods of this life and the life to come.

Finally, by this missionary activity God is fully glorified, when men and women fully and consciously accept the work of salvation which he accomplished in Christ. By means of it God's plan is realized, a plan to which Christ lovingly and obediently submitted for the glory of the Father who sent him[18] in order that the whole human race might become one people of God, form one body of Christ, and be built up into one temple of the holy Spirit; all of which, as an expression of sisterly and brotherly concord, answers to a profound longing in all people. And thus, finally, the intention of the creator in creating men and women in his own image and likeness will be truly realized, when all who possess human nature, and have been regenerated in Christ through the holy Spirit, gazing together on the glory of God, will be able to say "Our Father."[19]

8. Missionary activity is intimately bound up with human nature and its aspirations. In manifesting Christ, the church reveals to men and women their true situation and calling, since Christ is the head and exemplar of that renewed humanity, imbued with that familial love, sincerity and spirit of peace, to which all women and men aspire. Both Christ and the church which bears witness to him transcend the distinctions of race and nationality, and so cannot be considered strangers to anyone or in any place.[20] Christ is the truth and the way which the preaching of the gospel lays open to all men and women when it speaks those words of Christ in their ear: "Repent, and believe the gospel" (Mk 1:15). Since they who

who do not believe are already judged (see Jn 3:18), the words of Christ are at once words of judgment and grace, of life and death. For it is only by putting to death that which is old that we can come to newness of life. Now although this refers primarily to people, it is also true of various worldly goods which bear the mark both of human sin and the blessing of God:"For all have sinned and have need of the glory of God" (Rom 3:23). No people are freed from sin by themselves or by their own efforts, nor are they raised above themselves or completely delivered from their own weakness, solitude or slavery; all have need of Christ who is the model, master, liberator, saviour, and giver of life.[21] Even in the secular history of humanity the gospel has acted as a leaven in the interests of liberty and progress, and it always offers itself as a leaven with regard to fellowship, unity and peace. So it is not without reason that Christ is hailed by the faithful as "the hope of the nations and their saviour."[22]

9. The period, therefore, between the first and second coming of the Lord is the time of missionary activity, when, like the harvest, the church will be gathered from the four winds into the kingdom of God.[23] For the gospel must be preached to all everyone before the Lord comes (see Mk 13:10).

Missionary activity is nothing else, and nothing less, than the manifestation of God's plan, its epiphany and realization in the world and in history; that by which God, through mission, clearly brings to its conclusion the history of salvation. Through preaching and the celebration of the sacraments, of which the holy Eucharist is the center and summit, missionary activity makes Christ present, who is the author of salvation. It purges of evil associations those elements of truth and grace which are found among peoples, and which are, as it were, a secret presence of God; and it restores them to Christ their source who overthrows the rule of the devil and limits the manifold malice of evil. So whatever goodness is found in people's minds and hearts, or in the particular customs and cultures of peoples, far from being lost is purified, raised to a higher level and reaches its perfection, for the glory of God, the confusion of the demon, and the happiness of humankind.[24] Thus missionary activity tends towards eschatological fullness;[25] by it the people of God is expanded to the degree and until the time that the Father has filled by his own authority (see Acts 1:7); of it was it said in prophecy:"Enlarge the space for your tent and spread out your tent clothes unsparingly" (Is 54:2).[26] By missionary activity the mystical Body is enlarged until it reached the mature fullness of Christ (see Eph 4:13); the spiritual temple where God is adored in spirit and truth (see Jn 4:23) grows and is built up on the foundation of the apostles and prophets, Jesus Christ himself being the chief cornerstone (Eph 2:20).

1. See Vatican Council II, Dogmatic Constitution on the Church, *Lumen gentium,* 1

2. See St Irenaeus, *Adv. Haer.* III, 18, 1:"The Word existing with God, through whom everything was made and who was always present to the human race . . ." (PG 7, 932); id. IV, 6, 7:"From the beginning, the Son, being present in his creation, reveals the Father to all whom the Father desires, at the time and in the manner desired by the Father" (id. 990); see IV, 20, 6 and 7 (id. 1037); Demonstratio n. 34 (Patr. Or. XII, 773; *Sources Chret.* 62, Paris 1958, p. 87); Clement of Alex., *Protrept.* 112, 1 (G.C.S. Clement 1, 79) *Strom.* Vl, 6, 44, 1 (G.C.S. Clement II, 453); 13, 106, 3 and 4 (id. 485). For the same doctrine see Pius XII, Radio Message, 31 Dec. 1952; Vatican Council II, Dogmatic Constitution on the Church, *Lumen gentium,* 16.

3. See Heb 1:2; Jn 1:3 and 10;1 Cor 8:6; Col 1:16.

4. See St. Athanasius, *Ep. ad Epictetum,* I (PG 26,1060); St Cyril of Jerusalem, *Catech.* 4, 9 (PG 33, 465); Marius Victorinus, *Adv. Arium,* 3, 3 (PL 8,1101); St Basil, *Epist.* 261, 2 (PG 32, 969); St Gregory Naz. Epist. 101 (PG 37, 181); St Gregory of Nyssa, *Antirrheticus, Adv. Apollin.,* 17 (PG 45, 1156); St Ambrose, *Epist.* 48, 5 (PL 16, 1153); St Augustine, *In Joann.* Ev., tr. XXIII, 6 (PL 35, 1585;

CChr. 36. 236); besides in this way, he shows, that the holy Spirit did not redeem us because he was not made flesh: *De Agone Christ.* 22, 24 (PL 40, 302); St Cyril of Alex, *Adv. Nestor.* I 1 (PG 76, 20); St Fulgentius, *Epist.* 17, 3, 5(PL 65, 284); *Ad Trasimundum,* III, 21 (PL 65, 284:de *tristitia et timore).*

5. It is the Spirit who spoke through the prophets: *Symb. Constantinople.* Denz.-Schoenmetzer, 150): St Leo the Great, *Sermon 76* (PL 54, 405-406):"When the holy Spirit filled the Lord's disciples on the day of pentecost, this was not the first exercise of his role but an extension of his bounty, because the patriarchs, prophets, priests, and all the holy people of the previous ages were nourished by the same sanctifying Spirit ... although the measure of the gifts was not the same."Also *Sermon* 77, 1 (PL 54, 412); Leo XIII,, Encyc. *Divinum illud* (AAS 1897, 650-651). Also St John Chrysostom, although he insisted on the newness of the mission of the holy Spirit on the day of Pentecost: In *Eph c.* 4, Hom. 10, 1 (PG 62,75).

6. The fathers of the church often speak of Babel and Pentecost: Origen, *In Genesim,* c. 1 (PG 12, 112); St Gregory Naz. *Oratio* 41, 16 (PG 36, 449); St John Chrysostom, *Hom. in Pentec.,* 2 (PG 50, 467); St Augustine, *Enn. in Ps.* 54, 11 (PL 36, 636; CChr. 39, 664 ff.); *Sermon* 271 (PL 38, 1245); St Cyril of Alex., *Glaphyra Genesim* II (PG 69, 79); St Gregory the Great, *Hom. in Evang.,* Lib. II, Hom. 30, 4 (PL 76, 1222); St Bede, in *Hexaem.,* lib. III (PL 91, 125). See also the image in the porch of the Basilica of St Mark, Venice.

The church speaks all languages and so gathers people into the catholicity of the faith: St Augustine, Sermons 266, 267, 268, 269 (PL 38,1225-1237), Sermon 165, 3 (PL 38, 946); St John Chrysost, In *Ep. I ad Cor.,* Hom. 35 (PG 74, 758); St Fulgentius, Sermon 8, 2-3 (PL 65, 743-744).

On Pentecost at the consecration of the apostles for their mission see J. A. Cramer, *Catena in Acta SS. Apostolorum,* Oxford 1838, p. 24ff.

7. See Lk 3:22; 4:1; Acts 10:38.

8. See Jn ch 14-17; Paul VI, Allocution delivered in the council on 14 September 1964: AAS (1964), 807.

9. See Dogm Const. *Lumen gentium,* 4.

10. St Augustine, Sermon 267, 4 (PL 38, 1231):"The holy Spirit does for the whole church what the soul does for all the members of one body."See Vatican Council II, Dogmatic Constitution on the Church, *Lumen gentium,* 7 (also note 8).

11. See Acts 10:44-47; 11:15; 15:8.

12. See Acts 4:8; 5:32; 8:26, 29, 39; 9:31; 10; 11:24, 28; 13:2, 4, 9; 16:6-7; 20:22-23; 21:11 etc.

13. Tertullian, *Apologeticum,* 50, 13 (PL 1, 534); (CChr. 1, 171).

14. St Thomas Aquinas already speaks of the apostolic duty to plant the church: see Sent. Lib. I, dist. 16, q.l, a2 ad 2 et ad 4; a.3 sol.; *Summa Theol.* Ia, q.43, a.7, ad 6; Ia IIae q.106, a.4 ad 4. See Benedict

XV, *Maximum illud,* 30 Nov. 1919 (AAS 1919, 445 and 453), Pius XI, *Rerum Ecclesiae,* 28 Feb. 1926 (AAS 1926, 74); Pius XII, 30 April 1939 to the Directors OO.PP.MM.; id., 24 June 1944, to the Directors OO.PP.MM. (AAS 1944, 210; also in AAS 1950, 727 and 1951, 508); id., 29 June 1948 to the indigenous clergy (AAS 1948, 374); id., *Evangelii Praecones,* 2 June 1951 (AAS 1951, 507); id., *Fidei Donum,* 15 Jan. 1957 (AAS 1957, 236); John XXIII, *Princeps Pastorum,* 28 Nov. 1959 (AAS 1959, 835); Paul VI, Hom. 18 Oct. 1964 (AAS 1964, 911).

The popes, fathers and scholastics often speak of the "spreading" *(dilatio)* of the church: St Thomas Aquinas, *Comm. in Matth.* 16, 28; Leo XIII, Encyc. *Sancta Dei Civitas* (AAS 1880, 241); Benedict XV, Encyc. *Maximum illud* (AAS 1919, 442); Pius XL Encyc. *Rerum Ecclesiae* (AAS 1926, 65).

15. Obviously included in this concept of missionary activity are in fact those parts of Latin America where there is no proper hierarchy, nor maturity of christian life, nor sufficient preaching of the gospel. Whether these territories are in fact recognized by the holy See as missionary is not a matter for the council. This is why with regard to the connection between the concept of missionary activity and definite areas, it is rightly said that such activity is "for the most part" exercised in definite geographical areas recognized by the holy See.

16. Decree *Unitatis Redintegratio,* 1.

17. See Vatican Council II, Dogmatic Constitution on the Church, *Lumen gentium* 14.

18. See Jn 7:18; 8:30 and 44; 8:50; 17:1.

19. As regards this synthetic idea see the doctrine of St Irenaeus on the Recapitulation. See also Hippolytus, *De Antichristo,* 3: "Loving all and desiring to save all, wishing to make of them daughters and sons of God and calling all the saints to form one perfect man . . ." (PG 10, 732; G.C.S. Hippolyt. I, 2 p. 6); *Benedictiones Jacob,* 7 (T.U., 38-1 p. 18, lin. 4 ff.); Origen, *In Ioann.* tom. 1, n. 16: "For those who have come to God, led by the Word who is with God, there is only one act of knowing God, that as sons they might be carefully formed in the knowledge of God, as at present the Son alone knows the Father" (PG 14, 49; G.C.S. Origen IV, 20); St Augustine, *De Sermone* Domini in monte, I, 41: "Let us love that which can lead us to those kingdoms where no one says: my Father, but all say to the one God: our Father" (PL 34, 1250); St Cyril of Alex., *In Ioann.:* "We are all in Christ, and our common human nature is revitalized in him. This is why he is called the new Adam . . . He who is by nature both Son and God, dwells in us and so in his Spirit we call Abba Father! The Word dwells in all, in one temple, that is to say in that temple which he has taken for us and from us in order that having all women and men in himself, he might, as St. Paul says, reconcile all women and men to the Father in one body" (PG 73, 161-165).

20. Benedict XV, *Maximum illud* (AAS 1919, 445):"As the church of God is Catholic, it is never a stranger to any race or nation" See John XXIII, Encyclical *Mater et Magistra:* "by divine right the church extends to all peoples ... since it injects its power into the veins, as it were, of a people, it is not, therefore, nor does it consider itself as just an institution which is imposed on this people from without .. . So all that appears to it as good and honest it strengthens and brings to perfection" (i.e. those who are reborn in Christ) (AAS 1961, 444).

21. See Irenaeus, *Adv. Haer* III, 15, n. 3 (PG 7, 919): 'They were preachers of truth and apostles of liberty."

22. Ant. O diei 23 December.

23. See Mt 24:31; *Didache* 10, 5 (Funk I, p. 32).

24. Vatican Council II, Dogmatic Constitution on the Church, *Lumen gentium,* 17. St Augustine, *Dc Civitate Dei* 19, 17 (PL 41, 646). Instr. S.C.P.F. *(Collectanea* I, n. 135, p.43).

25. According to Origen the gospel ought to be preached before tho consummation of this world: *Hom. in Lc.* XX1 (G.C.S. Orig. IX 136, 21 ff.); In *Matth. comm.* ser. 39 (XI, 75, 25, FF; 76, 4 ff); St Thomas Aquinas *Summa Theol.* Ia Ilae, q. 106, a.4 ad 4.

26. Hilary of Poitiers, In Ps. 14 (PL 9, 301); Eusebius of Caes., *In Isaiam* 54, 2-3 (PG 24, 462-463); Cyril of Alex, *In Isaiam V,* ch 54 1-3 (PG 70, 1193).

Chapter II

MISSIONARY WORK

10. The church, which has been sent by Christ to reveal and communicate the love of God to all individuals and to all peoples, is aware that for her a tremendous missionary work still remains to be done. There are two billion people — and their number is increasing day by day — who have never, or barely, heard the gospel message; they constitute large and distinct groups united by enduring cultural ties, ancient religious traditions, and strong social relationships. Of these, some belong to one or other of the

great religions, others have no knowledge of God, while others expressly deny the existence of God and sometimes even attack it. If the church is to be in a position to offer all women and men the mystery of salvation and the life brought by God, then it must implant itself among all these groups in the same way that Christ by his incarnation committed himself to the particular social and cultural circumstances of the women and men among who he lived.

Article 1: Christian Witness

11. The church must be present to these groups through those of its members who live among them or have been sent to them. All Christians by the example of their lives and the witness of the word, wherever they live, have an obligation to manifest the new person which they put on in baptism, and to reveal the power of the holy Spirit by whom they were strengthened at confirmation, so that others, seeing their good works, might glorify the Father (see Matt 5:16) and more perfectly perceive the true meaning of human life and the universal solidarity of humankind. In order to bear fruitful witness to Christ, they should establish relationships of respect and love towards those people, they should acknowledge themselves members of the group in which they live, and through the various undertakings and affairs of human life they should share in their social and cultural life. They should be familiar with their national and religious traditions and uncover with gladness and respect those seeds of the word which lie hidden among them. They must look to the profound transformation which is taking place among nations and work hard so that modern humanity is not turned away from the things of God by an excessive preoccupation with modern science and technology, but

rather aroused to desire, even more intensely, that love and truth which have been revealed by God. Just as Christ penetrated to people's hearts and by a truly human dialogue led them to the divine light, so too his disciples, profoundly pervaded by the Spirit of Christ, should know and converse with those among whom they live, that through sincere and patient dialogue they themselves might learn of the riches which a generous God has distributed among the nations. They must at the same time endeavor to illuminate these riches with the light of the gospel, set them free, and bring them once more under the dominion of God the saviour.

12. The presence of Christians among these human groups should be one that is animated by that love with which we are loved by God, who desires that we should love each other with that self-same love (see 1 Jn 4:11).

Christian charity is extended to all without distinction of race, social condition, or religion, and seeks neither gain nor gratitude. Just as God loves us with a gratuitous love, so too the faithful, in their charity, should be concerned for people, loving them with that same love with which God sought out humanity. As Christ went about all the towns and villages healing every sickness and infirmity, as a sign that the kingdom of God had come (see Mt 9:35 ff.; Acts 10:38), so the church, through its children, joins itself with people of every condition, but especially with the poor and afflicted, and willingly spends itself for them (see 2 Cor 12:15). It shares their joys and sorrows, it is familiar with the hopes and problems of life, it suffers with them in the anguish of death. It wishes to enter into fraternal dialogue with those who are working for peace, and to bring them the peace and light of the gospel.

Christians ought to interest themselves, and col-

laborate with others, in the right ordering of social
and economic affairs. They should apply themselves
with special care to the education of children and
young people through various types of schools, and
these are not to be considered solely as an outstanding means for forming and developing a christian
youth, but as a service of great value to people, especially in the developing countries, one that is ordered
to raising human dignity and promoting more human
conditions. They should, furthermore, share in the efforts of those people who, in fighting against famine,
ignorance and disease, are striving to bring about better living conditions and bring about peace in the
world. In this work the faithful, after due consideration, should be eager to collaborate in projects initiated by private, public, state, or international bodies,
or by other christian or even non-christian communities.

The church, nevertheless, has no desire to become
involved in the government of the temporal order. It
claims no other competence than that of faithfully
serving people in charity with the help of God (see Mt
20:26; 23:11).[1]

The disciples of Christ, being in close contact with
women and men through their life and work, hope to
offer them an authentic Christian witness and work
for their salvation, even in those places where they
cannot fully proclaim Christ. They are not working for
people's merely material progress or prosperity; in
teaching the religious and moral truths, which Christ
illumined with his light, they seek to enhance the dignity of women and men and promote community,
and, in this way, are gradually opening a wider approach to God. So people are helped to attain salvation by love of God and love of humanity; the mystery
of Christ begins to shine out, that mystery in which
has appeared the new people created in the likeness

of God (see Eph 4:24) and in whom the charity of God is revealed.

Article 2: Preaching the Gospel and Assembling the People of God

13. Wherever God opens a door for the word in order to declare the mystery of Christ (see Col 4:3) then the living God, and he whom he has sent for the salvation of all, Jesus Christ (see 1 Th 1:9-10; 1 Cor 1:18-21; Gal 1:31; Acts 14:15-17; 17:22-31), are confidently and perseveringly (see Acts 4:13, 29, 31; 9:27, 28;13:40;14:3; 19:8; 26:26; 28:31;1 Th 2:2; 2 Cor 3:12; 7:4; Phil 1:20; Eph 3:12; 6:19-20) proclaimed (see 1 Cor 9:15; Rom 10:14) to all women and men (see Mk 16:15). And this is in order that non-Christians, whose heart is being opened by the holy Spirit (see Acts 16:4), might, while believing, freely turn to the Lord who, since he is the "way, the truth and the life" (Jn 14:6), will satisfy all their inner hopes, or rather infinitely surpass them.

This conversion is, indeed, only initial; sufficient however to make a people realize that they have been snatched from sin, and are being led into the mystery of God's love, who invites them to establish a personal relationship with him in Christ. Under the movement of divine grace the new convert sets out on a spiritual journey by means of which, while already sharing through faith in the mystery of the death and resurrection, he passes from the old person to the new who has been made perfect in Christ (see Col 3:5-10; Eph 4:20-24). This transition, which involves a progressive change of outlook and morals, should be manifested in its social implications and effected gradually during the period of catechumenate. Since the Lord in whom he believes is a sign of contradiction (see Lk 2:34; Mt 10:34-39) the convert often has to suffer misunderstanding and separation, but he also experiences those joys which are generously granted by God.

The church strictly forbids that anyone should be forced to accept the faith, or be induced or enticed by unworthy devices; as it likewise strongly defends the principle that no one should be frightened away from the faith by unjust harassment.[2]

In accordance with the very ancient practice of the church, the motives for conversion should be examined and, if necessary, purified.

14. Those who have received from God the gift of faith in Christ, through the church,[3] should be admitted with liturgical rites to the catechumenate which is not merely an exposition of dogmatic truths and norms of morality, but a period of formation in the entire christian life, an apprenticeship of suitable duration, during which the disciples will be joined to Christ their teacher. The catechumens should be properly initiated into the mystery of salvation and the practice of the evangelical virtues, and they should be introduced into the life of faith, liturgy and charity of the people of God by successive sacred rites.[4]

Then, having been delivered from the powers of darkness through the sacraments of christian initiation (see Col 1:13),[5] and having died, been buried, and risen with Christ (see Rom 6:4-11; Col 2:12-13; 1 Pet 3:21-22; Mk 16:16), they receive the Spirit of adoption of children (see 1 Th 3:5-7; Acts 8:14-17) and celebrate with the whole people of God the memorial of the Lord's death and resurrection.

It is desirable that the liturgy of Lent and Paschal time should be restored in such a way that it will serve to prepare the hearts of the catechumens for the celebration of the Paschal Mystery, at whose solemn ceremonies they are reborn to Christ in baptism.

This christian initiation, which takes place during the catechumenate, should not be left entirely to the priests and catechists, but should be the concern of the whole christian community, especially of the sponsors, so that from the beginning the catechumens will feel that they belong to the people of God. Since the life of the church is apostolic, the catechumens must learn to cooperate actively in the building up of the church and in its work of evangelization, both by the example of their lives and the profession of their faith.

The juridical status of catechumens should be clearly defined in the new Code of Canon Law. Since they are already joined to the church[6] they are already of the household of Christ[7] and are quite frequently already living a life of faith, hope and charity.

Article 3: Forming the Christian Community

15. When the holy Spirit, who calls all women and men to Christ and arouses in their hearts the submission of faith by the seed of the word and the preaching of the gospel, brings those who believe in Christ to a new life through the womb of the baptismal font, he gathers them into one people of God which is a "chosen race, a royal priesthood, a holy nation, a purchased people" (1 Pet 2:9).[8]

Therefore, missionaries, the fellow workers of God (see 1 Cor 3:9), should raise up communities of the faithful, so that walking worthy of the calling to which they have been called (see Eph 4:1) they might carry out the priestly, prophetic and royal offices entrusted to them by God. In this way the christian community will become a sign of God's presence in the world. Through the eucharistic sacrifice it goes continually to the Father with Christ,[9] carefully nourished with the word of God[10] it bears witness to Christ,[11] it walks in charity and is enlivened by an apostolic spirit [12]

From the start the christian community should be so organized that it is able to provide for its own needs as far as possible.

This community of the faithful, endowed with the cultural riches of its own nation, should be deeply rooted in the people; families imbued with the spirit of the gospel should flourish[13] and be helped with suitable schools; groups and associations should be set up so that the spirit of the lay apostolate might pervade the whole of society. Finally, let charity shine out between Catholics of different rites.[14]

The ecumenical spirit should be nourished among neophytes; they must appreciate that their brothers and sisters who believe in Christ are disciples of Christ and, having been reborn in baptism, share in many of the blessings of the people of God. Insofar as religious conditions permit, ecumenical activity should be encouraged, so that, while avoiding every form of indifferentism or confusion and also senseless rivalry, Catholics might collaborate with their separated brethren, insofar as it is possible, by a common profession before the nations of faith in God and in Jesus Christ, and by a common, familial effort in social, cultural, technical and religious matters, in accordance with the Decree on Ecumenism. Let them cooperate, especially, because of Christ their common Lord. May his name unite them! There should be collaboration of this type not only between private persons, but also, subject to the judgment of the local ordinary, between churches or ecclesiastical communities in their undertakings.

The christian faithful who have been gathered into the church from every nation and "are not marked off from the rest of humanity either by country, by language, or by political institutions,"[15] should live for God and Christ according to the honorable usages of their race. As good citizens they should sincerely and actively foster love of country and, while utterly rejecting racial hatred or exaggerated nationalism, work for universal love among people.

In achieving all this, the laity, that is Christians who have been incorporated into Christ and live in the world, are of primary importance and worthy of special care. It is for them, imbued with the Spirit of Christ, to be a leaven animating and directing the temporal order from within, so that everything is always carried out in accordance with the will of Christ.[16]

However, it is not sufficient for the Christian people to be present or established in a particular nation, nor sufficient that it should merely exercise the apostolate of good example; it has been established and it is present so that it might by word and deed proclaim Christ to non-christian fellow countrymen and help them towards a full reception of Christ.

Various types of ministry are necessary for the implanting and growth of the christian community, and once these forms of service have been called forth from the body of the faithful, by the divine call, they are to be carefully fostered and nurtured by all. Among these functions are those of priests, deacons and catechists, and also that of Catholic Action. Religious brothers and sisters, likewise, play an indispensable role in planting and strengthening the kingdom of Christ in souls, and in the work of further extending it, both by their prayers and active work.

16. The church, with great joy, gives thanks for the priceless gift of the priestly vocation which God has given to so many young men from among those peoples recently converted to Christ. For the church is more firmly rooted in a people when the different communities of the faithful have ministers of salvation who are drawn from their own members —

bishops, priests and deacons, serving their own brothers and sisters — so that these young churches gradually acquire a diocesan structure with their own clergy.

What has been decreed by this council concerning the priestly vocation and priestly formation are to be religiously observed wherever the church is being planted for the first time and also by the young churches. Special importance is to be attached to what has been said about closely combining spiritual, doctrinal and pastoral formation; about living a life in accordance with the gospel without any thought of personal or family advantage; about fostering a deep appreciation of the mystery of the church. In this way they will learn, marvellously, to give themselves fully to the service of Christ's Body, and to the work of the gospel; they will learn to adhere to their bishop as loyal fellow workers, and to collaborate with their brothers.[17]

To attain this general end, the whole of the students' formation is to be organized in the light of the mystery of salvation, as it is revealed in the scriptures. They must discover and live the mystery of Christ and of human salvation as it is present in the liturgy.[18]

These general requirements for priestly training, both pastoral and practical, which have been laid down by the council,[19] must be accompanied with a willingness to come to grips with the particular nation's own way of thinking and acting. Therefore, the minds of the students must be opened and refined so that they will better understand and appreciate the culture of their own people; in philosophy and theology they should examine the relationship between the traditions and religion of their homeland and Christianity.[20] In the same way, priestly formation must take account of the pastoral needs of the region; the students must learn the history, goal and method of missionary activity, as well as the particular social, economic and cultural conditions of their own people. They should be formed in the spirit of ecumenism and properly prepared for friendly dialogue with non-Christians.[21] All this demands that, as far as possible, their studies for the priesthood should be undertaken in close contact with the way of life of their own people.[22] Finally, care must be taken to train them in proper ecclesiastical and financial administration.

Suitable priests should be selected, who, after a period of pastoral work, would pursue higher studies even at foreign universities, especially at Rome, or at other institutes of learning. As members of the local clergy, with their learning and experience, they should be a great asset to these young churches in discharging the more difficult ecclesiastical duties.

Wherever it appears opportune to episcopal conferences, the diaconate should be restored as a permanent state of life, in accordance with the norms of the constitution on the church.[23] It would help those men who carry out the ministry of the diaconate — preaching the word of God as catechists, governing scattered christian communities in the name of the bishop or parish priest, or exercising charity in the performances of social or charitable works — if they were to be strengthened by the imposition of hands which has come down from the apostles. They would be more closely bound to the altar and their ministry would be made more fruitful through the sacramental grace of the diaconate.

17. Also worthy of praise is that army of catechists. both men and women, to whom missionary work among the nations is so indebted, who imbued with an apostolic spirit make an outstanding and absolutely necessary contribution to the spread of the faith and the church by their great work.

In our days, when there are so few clerics to evangelize such great multitudes and to carry out the pastoral ministry, the role of catechists is of the highest importance. Therefore, their training must be in keeping with cultural progress and such that, as true co-workers of the priestly order, they will be able to perform their task as well as possible, a task which involves new and greater burdens.

The number of diocesan and regional schools should be increased where future catechists, while studying Catholic doctrine with special empnasis on the Bible and the liturgy, and also catechetical method and pastoral practice, would at the same time model themselves on the lives of christian women and men,[24] and tirelessly strive for piety and holiness of life. There should be conventions and courses where at certain times catechists would be brought up to date in those sciences and skills which are useful for their ministry, and where their spiritual life would be nourished and strengthened. In addition, those who give themselves fully to this work should be assured, by being paid a just wage, of a decent standard of living and social security.[25]

It is desirable that the sacred Congregation for the Propagation of the Faith should, in some suitable manner, provide special aids for the training and upkeep of catechists. If it seems necessary and right an institute for catechists should be founded.

The churches should also gratefully acknowledge the generous work of auxiliary catechists of whose help they have such need. These preside at prayers in their communities and also teach sacred doctrine. Proper care should be taken regarding their doctrinal and spiritual formation. It would be desirable too, wherever it seems opportune, to confer the canonical mission on properly trained catechists in the course of a public liturgical celebration, so that in the eyes of the people they might serve the cause of the faith with greater authority.

18. Right from the planting of the church the religious life should be carefully fostered, because not only does it provide valuable and absolutely necessary help for missionary activity, but through the deeper consecration made to God in the church it clearly shows and signifies the intimate nature of the christian vocation.[26]

Religious institutes which are working for the implanting of the church and which are deeply imbued with those mystical graces which are part of the church's religious tradition, should strive to give them expression and to hand them on in a manner in keeping with the character and outlook of each nation. They should carefully consider how traditions of asceticism and contemplation, whose seeds have been sown by God in certain ancient cultures before the preaching of the gospel, might be incorporated into the christian religious life.

Different forms of religious life should be promoted in the new churches, so that they might manifest different aspects of Christ's mission and the life of the church, devote themselves to various pastoral works, and prepare their members to exercises them properly. However, episcopal conferences should take care that congregations pursuing the same apostolic end are not multiplied, with consequent damage to the religious life and the apostolate.

The various undertakings aimed at establishing the contemplative life are worthy of special mention; some aim at implanting the rich tradition of their own order and retaining the essential elements of the monastic life, others are returning to the more simple forms of early monasticism. All, however, are eagerly seeking a real adaptation to local conditions. The contemplative life should be restored everywhere, because it belongs to the fullness of the church's presence.

1. See the allocution given by Paul VI in the council, 21 Nov. 1964: AAS 1964, 1013.

2. See Decl. on Religious Freedom 2, 4, 10; Const. on the Church in the Modern World, *Gaudium et spes.*

3. See Vatican Council II, Dogmatic Constitution on the Church, *Lumen gentium* 17.

4. See Vatican Council II, Constitution on the Sacred Liturgy, *Sacrosanctum Concilium,* 64-65.

5. On this deliverance from the slavery of the devil and of darkness in the gospel, see Mt 12:28; Jn 8:44; 12:31 (see Jn 3:8; Eph 2:1-2). On the liturgy of Baptism see Roman Ritual.

6. See Vatican Council II, Dogmatic Constitution on the Church, *Lumen gentium,* 14.

7. See St Augustine, *Tract. in Ioann.* ll, 4 (PL 35, 1476).

8. See Vatican Council II, Dogmatic Constitution on the Church, *Lumen gentium,* 9.

9. See Vatican Council II, Dogmatic Constitution on the Church, *Lumen gentium,* l0, ll, 34.

10. See Vatican Council II, Dogmatic Const. on Divine Revelation, *Dei verbum,* 21.

11. See Vatican Council II, Dogmatic Constitution on the Church, *Lumen gentium,* 12, 35.

12. See ibid., 23, 26.

13. See ibid. 11, 35, 41.

14. See Vatican Council II, Decree on the Catholic Eastern Churches, *Orientalium Ecclesiarum,* 30.

15. *Epist. ad Diognetum,* 5 (PG 2, 1173); see Vatican Council II, Dogmatic Constitution on the Church, *Lumen gentium,* 38.

16. See Vatican Council II, Dogmatic Constitution on the Church, *Lumen gentium,* 32; Decree on the Lay Apostolate, 3-7.

17. See Vatican Council II, Decree on the Training of Priests, *Optatam totius,* 4, 8, 9.

18. See Vatican Council II, Constitution on the Sacred Liturgy, *Sacrosanctum Concilium,* 17.

19. See Vatican Council II, Decree on the Training of Priests, *Optatam totius,* 1.

20. See John XXIII, Encyclical, *Princeps Pastorum* (AAS 1959, 843-844).

21. See Vatican Council II, Decree on Ecumenism, *Unitatis redintegratio,* 4.

22. See John XXIII, Encyclical, *Princeps Pastorum* (AAS 1959, 842).

23. See Vatican Council II, Dogmatic Constitution on the Church, *Lumen gentium,* 29.

24. See John XXIII, *Princeps Pastorum* (AAS 1959, 855).

25. It is a question of so called "full-time catechists."

26. See Vatican Council II, Dogmatic Constitution on the Church, *Lumen Gentium,* 31, 44.

Chapter III

PARTICULAR CHURCHES

19. This work of implanting the church in a particular human community reaches a definite point when the assembly of the faithful, already rooted in the social life of the people and to some extent conformed to its culture, enjoys a certain stability and permanence; when it has its own priests, although insufficient, its own religious and laity and possesses those ministries and institutions which are required for leading and spreading the life of the people of God under the leadership of their own bishop.

In these young churches the life of the people of God ought to mature in all those spheres of the christian life which are to be renewed in accordance with the norms of this council. Assemblies of the faithful must daily become more conscious of themselves as living communities of faith, liturgy and charity; lay people should strive to establish in the state an order of love and justice by means of civil and apostolic action; by living a true christian life families should become seed-beds of the lay apostolate and indeed of priestly and religious vocations. The faith should be imparted by means of a well adapted catechesis and celebrated in a liturgy that is in harmony with the character of the people; it should also be embodied in suitable canonical legislation and in the healthy institutions and customs of the locality.

Bishops and their priests must think and live with the universal church, becoming more and more imbued with a sense of Christ and the church. The communion of the young churches with the whole church should remain intimate, they should graft elements of its tradition on to their own culture and thus, by a mutual outpouring of energy, increase the life of the mystical body.[1] To this end, those theological, psychological and human elements which would contribute to this sense of communion with the whole church should be fostered.

These churches which are situated in the poorer parts of the world still suffer from a serious shortage of priests and a lack of material resources. Therefore, they depend very much on the continued missionary activity of the whole church to supply that assistance which is necessary for the growth of the church and the full development of christian life. This missionary activity should also help those churches which, although long established, are in a state of decline or weakness.

However, these churches should renew their common pastoral zeal and set up suitable joint projects so that vocations to both the diocesan clergy and religious institutes might be increased, assessed with greater certainty, and more effectively fostered,[2] that gradually these churches might be able to provide for themselves and help others.

20. As the local church must represent the universal church as perfectly as possible, it must remember that it has been sent to those who live in the same territory as itself, but do not believe in Christ so that it might be for them, by the example of the lives of the faithful and of the whole community, a sign indicating Christ.

The ministry of the word is also necessary so that the gospel might reach all people. The bishop should be, above all, a preacher of the faith who brings new disciples to Christ.[3] To fulfil this noble task as he ought he must be fully acquainted with conditions among his flock and also with those notions about God which are current among his countrymen. He must take special account of those changes which have been brought about through urbanization, migration and religious indifferentism.

In the young churches the local priests should give themselves generously to the work of evangelization. They should work with the foreign missionaries, with whom they form one priestly body.under the authority of the bishop, not only in ministering to the faithful and in celebrating divine worship, but also in preaching the gospel to those who are outside. They should show themselves ready and should eagerly offer themselves to their bishop to undertake missionary work in distant and abandoned areas of their own or other dioceses when the occasion arises.

Religious brothers and sisters should be aflame with this same zeal as should also lay people with regard to the people of their own country, especially those who are poorer.

Episcopal conferences should ensure that periodically there are refresher courses on the Bible and in spiritual and pastoral theology, so that amid all the change and flux the clergy will acquire a deeper knowledge of theology and of pastoral methods.

For the rest, everything that the council has enacted, especially in the Decree on the Life and Ministry of Priests, should be religiously observed.

Qualified ministers are needed to carry out the missionary program of a particular church; they must be prepared in good time and in a manner that is in keeping with the needs of each church. Since people, increasingly, are forming associations, it would be useful for episcopal conferences to draw up a common plan for dialogue with such groups. If it happens that in certain regions there is a group of people which is impeded from accepting the Catholic faith because they cannot adapt themselves to the particular guise in which the church presents itself in that place, then it is desirable that this situation should be specially[4] provided for, until all Christians can gather together in one community. If the holy See is able to provide missionaries, then bishops should invite them to their dioceses, they should welcome them and actively assist them in their undertakings.

In order that this missionary zeal might flourish among their compatriots it would help greatly if the young churches took part in the universal mission of the church as soon as possible and sent missionaries to preach the gospel throughout the whole world, even though they are themselves short of clergy. In a sense, their communion with the universal church will be perfect when they themselves take an active part in missionary work on behalf of other nations.

21. The church is not truly established and does not fully live, nor is a perfect sign of Christ unless there is a genuine laity existing and working alongside the hierarchy. For the gospel cannot become deeply rooted in the mentality, life and work of a people without the active presence of lay people. Therefore, from the foundation of a church very special care must be taken to form a mature christian laity.

The lay faithful belong fully both to the people of God and civil society. They belong to the nation into which they were born, they begin to share in its cultural riches by their education, they are linked to its life by many social ties, they contribute to its progress by personal effort in their professions, they feel its problems to be their own and they try to solve them. They belong also to Christ because by faith and baptism they have been reborn in the church, so that by newness of life and work they might belong to Christ (see 1 Cor 15:23), in order that all things might be subjected to God in Christ and that God might be all in all (see 1 Cor 15:28).

The principal duty of both men and women is to bear witness to Christ, and this they are obliged to do by their life and their words, in the family, in their social group, and in the sphere of their profession. In them must be seen the new person who has been created according to God in justice and holiness of truth (see Eph 4:24). They must give expression to this newness of life in their own society and culture and in a manner that is in keeping with the traditions of their own land. They must be familiar with this culture, they must purify and guard it, they must develop it in accordance with present-day conditions, they must perfect it in Christ so that the faith of Christ and the life of the church will not be something foreign to the society in which they live, but will begin to transform and permeate it. They should be linked with their compatriots by ties of sincere charity so that their manner of life reveals the new bond of unity and universal solidarity which derives from the mystery of Christ. They should spread the faith of Christ among those with whom they are connected by social and professional ties, and this obligation is all the more urgent since so many people can only come to hear the gospel and recognize Christ through lay people who are their neighbours. Indeed wherever possible lay people should be ready to carry out the special mission of preaching the gospel and teaching christian doctrine so that they might strengthen the young church by a more immediate cooperation with the hierarchy.

Ministers of the church should greatly value this arduous apostolate of the laity. They should so train them as members of Christ that they would become conscious of their responsibility for all. They should instruct them deeply in the mystery of Christ, teach them practical techniques, and help them in their difficulties, all according to the spirit of the constitution on the church and the decree on the lay apostolate.

And so while both pastors and laity each retain their own special functions and obligations, the whole of the young church will bear a simple, living, strong witness to Christ, that it might become a bright token of that salvation which comes to us in Christ.

22. The seed which is the word of God grows out of good soil watered by the divine dew, it absorbs moisture, transforms it, and makes it part of itself, so that eventually it bears much fruit. So too indeed, just as happened in the economy of the incarnation, the young churches, which are rooted in Christ and built on the foundations of the apostles, take over all the riches of the nations which have been given to Christ as an inheritance (see Ps 2:8). They borrow from the customs, traditions, wisdom, teaching, arts and sciences of their people everything which could be used to praise the glory of the Creator, manifest the grace of the saviour, or contribute to the right ordering of christian life.[5]

To achieve this, it is necessary that in each of the great socio-cultural regions, as they are called, theological investigation should be encouraged and the facts and words revealed by God, contained in sacred scripture, and explained by the fathers and magisterium of the church, submitted to a new examination in the light of the tradition of the universal church. In this way it will be more clearly understood by what means the faith can be explained in terms of the philosophy and wisdom of the people, and how their customs, attitude to life and social structures can be reconciled with the standard proposed by divine revelation. Thus a way will be opened for a more profound adaptation in the whole sphere of christian life. This manner of acting will avoid every appearance of syncretism and false exclusiveness; the christian life will be adapted to the mentality and character of each culture,[6] and local traditions together with the special qualities of each national family, illumined by the light of the gospel, will be taken up into a Catholic unity. So new particular churches, each with its own traditions, have their place in the community of the church, the primacy of Peter which presides over this universal assembly of charity[7] all the while remaining intact.

And so it is to be hoped, and indeed it would be a very good thing, that episcopal conferences should come together within the boundaries of each great socio-cultural region and by a united and coordinated effort pursue this proposal of adaptation.

1. See John XXIII, Encyclical, *Princeps Pastorum* (AAS 1959, 838).

2. See Vatican Council II, Decree on the Life and Ministry of Priests, *Presbyterorum ordinis*, 11; Decree on the Training of Priests, *Optatam totius*, 2.

3. See Vatican Council II, Dogmatic Constitution on the Church, *Lumen gentium*, 25.

4. See Vatican Council II, Decree on the Life and Ministry of Priests, *Presbyterorum ordinis*, 10, where the institution of personal "prelatures" is foreseen to facilitate special pastoral projects aimed at particular social categories insofar as it is demanded for the better exercise of the apostolate.

5. See Vatican Council II, Dogmatic Constitution on the Church, *Lumen gentium*, 13.

6. See The allocution of Paul VI at the canonization of the Ugandan Martyrs (AAS 1964, 908).

7. See Vatican Council II, Dogmatic Constitution on the Church, *Lumen gentium*, 13.

Chapter IV

MISSIONARIES

23. Although the obligation of spreading the faith falls individually on every disciple of Christ,[1] still the Lord Christ has always called from the number of his disciples those whom he has chosen, that they might be with him, so that he might send them to preach to

the nations (see Mk 3:13 ff.). So the holy Spirit, who shares his gifts as he wills for the common good (see 1 Cor 12:11), implants in the hearts of individuals a missionary vocation and at the same time raises up institutes in the church[2] which take on the duty of evangelization, which is the responsibility the whole church, and make it as it were their own special task.

Those people who are endowed with the proper natural temperament, have the necessary qualities and outlook, and are ready to undertake missionary work, have a special vocation,[3] whether they are natives of the place or foreigners, priests, religious or lay people. Having been sent by legitimate authority they go forth in faith and obedience to those who are far from Christ, as ministers of the gospel, set aside for the work to which they have been called (see Acts 13:2) "that the offering up of the Gentiles may become acceptable, being sanctified by the holy Spirit" (Rom 16:16).

24. When God calls, people must reply without taking counsel with flesh and blood (see Gal 1:16) and give themselves fully to the work of the gospel. However, such an answer can only be given with the encouragement and help of the holy Spirit. Those who are sent enter upon the life and mission of him "who emptied himself, taking the form of a slave" (Phil 2:7). Therefore, they must be prepared to remain faithful to their vocation for life, to renounce themselves and everything that up to this they possessed as their own, and to make themselves "all things to all" (1 Cor 9:22).

In preaching the gospel to the nations they will proclaim with confidence the mystery of Christ whose legates they are, so that in him they will dare to speak as they ought (see Eph 6:19 ff.; Acts 4:31), not being ashamed of the scandal of the cross. Meek and humble, following in the footsteps of their master, they will show that his yoke is sweet and his burden light (Mt 11:29 ff.). By a truly evangelical life,[4] with great patience and longanimity, in kindness and unfeigned love (see 2 Cor 6:4 ff.) they will bear witness to their Lord, if necessary to the shedding of his blood. They will ask God for strength and courage and in the midst of great affliction and abject poverty they will know abundance of joy (see 2 Cor 8:2). Let them be convinced that obedience is the special virtue of a minister of Christ who by his obedience redeemed the human race.

Preachers of the gospel should be renewed in spirit day by day, lest they should neglect the grace that is in them (see 1 Tim 4:14; Eph 4:23; 2 Cor 4:16). Ordinaries and superiors should gather the missionaries together from time to time, so that they might be strengthened in the hope of their calling and renewed in the apostolic ministry. Special houses should be provided for this purpose.

25. The future missionaries must be prepared for such an important task by a special spiritual and moral formation.[5] They must be prompt to take the initiative, constant in carrying out an undertaking, persevering in difficulties, patient and strong of heart in bearing loneliness, exhaustion, and fruitless labor. They must approach people with an open mind and heart, must willingly accept the duties entrusted to them; and generously accommodate themselves to the different customs and the changing circumstances of other peoples. In harmony and mutual love they will cooperate with their brethren and with all who dedicate themselves to this work, so that together with the faithful, and imitating the apostolic community, they might be of one heart and soul (see Acts 2:42; 4:32).

These interior dispositions should be diligently developed and fostered during the time of formation;

they should be elevated and nourished by the spiritual life. With a living faith and an inexhaustible hope, missionaries should be people of prayer; they should burn with a spirit of power, of love and of self control (see 2 Tim 1:7). Let them learn to be content with the circumstances in which they find himselves (Phil 4:11); let them carry about with them the death of Jesus, in a spirit of sacrifice, that the life of Jesus might work on those to whom they have been sent (see 2 Cor 4:10 ff.); let them willingly give all out of zeal for others; let them spend themselves for souls (see 2 Cor 12:15 ff.) so that "by the daily exercise of their duty they might grow in the love of God and of their neighbor."[6] Thus united with Christ in obedience to the will of the Father they will continue their mission under the authority of the hierarchy of the church and collaborate in the mystery of salvation.

26. Those who are sent to the different nations should, as worthy ministers of Christ, be nourished by the "words of faith and with good doctrine" (1 Tim 4:6) which they will draw mainly from sacred scripture while they are studying the mystery of Christ, whose preachers and witnesses they will be.

So all missionaries — priests, brothers, sisters and lay people — should be trained and formed according to their individual states, lest they be found unequal to the demands of their future tasks.[7] From the very beginning their doctrinal training should be such that they understand both the universality of the church and the diversity of peoples. This holds for all the studies which prepare them for their future ministry, and indeed for other sciences in which they might usefully be instructed so that they might have a general knowledge of peoples, cultures and religions, not only with regard to the past but also with respect to the present time. Whoever is to go among another people must hold their inheritance, language and way of life in high esteem. It is very necessary for future missionaries that they undertake missiological studies, that they know, that is, the teaching and the laws of the church regarding missionary activity, that they be aware of the paths which have been followed by the messengers of the gospel down through the centuries, and that they be familiar with the present state of the missions and with the methods considered most effective in the present time.[8]

If this full training is to be pervaded by a sense of pastoral solicitude, then a special and ordered apostolic formation should be imparted, both by means of instruction and practical exercises.[9]

The greatest possible number of brothers and sisters should be well instructed and prepared in the art of catechetics, so that they might be of even greater assistance in the work of the apostolate.

It is necessary that those who engage in missionary activity, even for a time, should receive a training suited to their condition.

These different forms of training should be undertaken in the countries to which they are to be sent, so that the missionaries might more fully understand the history, social structures and customs of the people, that they might have an insight into their moral outlook, their religious precepts, and the intimate ideas which they form of God, the world and humanity, according to their own sacred traditions.[10] They should learn their language so that they can speak it easily and correctly and so be able to enter more easily into the minds and hearts of the people.[11] They should, besides, be properly instructed as regards special pastoral needs.

Some should be more thoroughly prepared in missiological institutes, and other faculties and universities, that they might perform certain special duties more effectively,[12] and by their learning be a help to other missionaries in carrying out missionary work which, in our time especially, presents so many difficulties and opportunities. It is also extremely desirable that regional conferences of bishops should have available a good number of such experts and that they should make fruitful use of their knowledge and experience in the problems which attach to their office. Experts in the use of technical instruments and in social communication, whose importance all should greatly appreciate, should not be lacking.

27. All these requirements are really necessary for each person sent to the nations, yet in fact, they can scarcely be acquired by individuals. Since, however, it is clear from experience that the missionary task cannot be accompanied by lone individuals, a common vocation has gathered these individuals into institutes where, having combined their strength, they are properly trained and will carry out this work in the name of the church and under the direction of the hierarchy. These institutes have borne the burden and heat of the day for many centuries, devoting themselves fully or in part to this missionary work. Often vast territories to be evangelized were committed to them by the holy See in which they assembled a new people of God, and established a local church around its own pastors. By their zeal and experience, and in friendly collaboration, they will serve those churches which were established by their sweat and even in their blood, either by undertaking the care of souls, or by fulfilling certain special tasks for the common good.

Sometimes they undertake more urgent tasks all through a particular region, for example the evangelization of groups or peoples who for some special reason have not yet, perhaps, accepted the gospel message or have so far resisted it.[13]

If necessary, let them from their experience be

ready to train and help those who engage in missionary activity for a limited time.

For these reasons, and since there are still many nations to be brought to Christ, these institutes are still extremely necessary.

1. Vatican Council II, Dogmatic Constitution on the Church, *Lumcn gentium,* 17.

2. By "institutes" are meant the orders, congregations, institutes and associations which work in the missions.

3. See . Pius XI, Encyclical *Rerum Ecclesiae* (AAS 1926, 69-71); Pius XII, Encyclical *Saeculo exeunte* (AAS 1940, 256); Encyclical *Evangelii Praecones* (AAS 1951,506)

4. See Benedict XV, Encyclical *Maximum illud* (AAS 1919, 449-450).

5. See Benedict XV, Encyclical *Maximum illud* (AAS 1919, 448-449); Pius XII, Encyclical *Evangelii Praecones* (AAS 1951, 507). In the formation of missionary priests account must also be taken of what has been said in the Decree on the Training of Priests.

6. Vatican Council II, Dogmatic Constitution on the Church, *Lumen gentium,* 41.

7. See Benedict XV, Encyclical *Maximum illud* (ASS 1919, 440); Pius XII, Encyclical *Evangelii Praecones* (AAS 1951, 507).

8. Benedict XV, Encyclical *Maximum illud* (AAS 1919, 448); Decr. S.C.P.F., 20 May 1923 (AAS 1923, 369-370); Pius XII, Encyclical *Saeculo exeunte* (AAS 1940, 256); Vatican Council II,*Evangelii Praecones* (AAS 1951, 507); John XXIII, Encyclical *Princeps Pastorum* (AAS 1959, 843-844).

9. Vatican Council II, Decree on the Training of Priests, *Optatam totius,* 19-21; Apost. Constitution *Sedes Sapientiae* with the general statutes.

10. Pius XII, Encyclical *Evangelii Praecones* (AAS 1951, 523-524).

11. Benedict XV, Encyclical *Maximum illud* (AAS 1919, 448); Pius XII, *Evangelii Praecones* (AAS 1951, 507).

12. See Pius XII, *Fidei Donum* (AAS 1957, 234).

13. See Vatican Council II, Decree on the Life and Ministry of Priests, *Presbyterorum ordinis,* 10, where it speaks of dioceses, personal prelatures and such matters.

Chapter V

THE ORGANIZATION OF MISSIONARY ACTIVITY

28. Since Christians have different gifts (see Rom 12:6) they should collaborate in the work of the gospel, according to opportunity, ability, charism and ministry (see 1 Cor 3:10); all who sow and reap (see Jn 4:37), plant and water, should be united (see 1 Cor 3:8), so that "working together for the same end in a free and orderly manner"[1] they might together devote their powers to the building up of the church.

For this reason, the labors of those who preach the gospel, and the assistance given by other Christians, should be so organized and coordinated that "all may be done in order" (1 Cor 14:40) in every sphere of missionary activity and cooperation.

29. Since the responsibility of preaching the gospel throughout the whole world falls primarily on the body of bishops,[2] then the synod of bishops, or the "permanent commission of bishops for the universal church,"[3] among matters of general importance[4] should pay special attention to missionary activity which is the greatest and holiest duty of the church.[5]

There should be only one competent congregation for all missions and missionary activity, namely that of the "Propagation of the Faith," which would direct and coordinate missionary work and missionary cooperation throughout the world. The rights of the Eastern churches must, however, be safeguarded.[6]

Although the holy Spirit arouses a missionary spirit in the church in many ways, and indeed often anticipates the work of those whose task it is to guide the life of the church, nevertheless, this congregation should itself promote missionary vocations and spirituality, as also zeal and prayer for the missions, and it should furnish genuine and adequate information about them. It should raise up missionaries and distribute them according to the more urgent needs of certain regions. It should draw up an organized plan of action, issue directives and principles adapted to the work of evangelization and encourage the work. It is its job to encourage and coordinate the effective collection of funds which will be distributed according to need and utility, the size of the area, the numbers of believers and non-believers, undertakings and institutes, ministers and missionaries.

In collaboration with the Secretariat for the Promotion of Christian Unity it will seek ways and means for attaining and organizing familial cooperation and harmonious relations with the missionary undertakings of other christian communities, so that as far as possible the scandal of division might be removed.

It is therefore necessary that this congregation should be both an instrument of administration and an organ of dynamic direction, that it should use scientific methods and instruments adapted to modern conditions, that it be guided by present-day research in theology, methodology and pastoral missionary work.

In a manner and according to norms which should be laid down by the pope, selected representatives of all those who are engaged in missionary work should have an active part in the direction of this congregation and also a deliberative vote: that is, bishops from all over the world, after consultation with episcopal conferences, and also the heads of institutes and pontifical agencies. These should all be called together at set times and, subject to the authority of the pope, should exercise supreme control over all missionary work.

There should be a permanent body of consultors

and experts, noted for their learning and experience, attached to this congregation, whose task it will be to gather useful information as to the actual situation in various regions and as to the mental outlook of different groups, and so make scientifically-based proposals for missionary work and cooperation.

Institutes of religious sisters, regional missionary undertakings and lay organizations, especially those which are international, should also be suitably represented.

30. In order that the goal might be attained and results obtained in working for the missions, all missionary workers must be of "one heart and one soul" (Acts 4:32).

It is the responsibility of the bishop, as the head of the diocesan apostolate and its center of unity, to promote missionary activity, guide and coordinate it, so that the spontaneous zeal of those who engage in this work may be safeguarded and fostered. All missionaries, even exempt religious, are subject to this authority in all the various activities which have to do with the exercise of the sacred apostolate.[7] For better coordination, the bishop should, as far as possible, establish a pastoral council in which clergy, religious and lay people would have a part through elected delegates. He should also take care that apostolic action is not entirely restricted to those who have already been converted, but that a fair proportion of workers and funds is directed to the evangelization of non-Christians.

31. Graver questions and more urgent problems should be considered by episcopal conferences in common, without however, neglecting local differences.[8] In order that the insufficient supply of personnel and funds might not be wasted, and in order that undertakings might not be unnecessarily multiplied, it is recommended that resources should be pooled

and projects initiated which would serve the common good of all as, for example, seminaries, higher and technical schools, pastoral, catechetical and liturgical centers, and centers devoted to the means of social communication.

Similar cooperation should even be established between different episcopal conferences, wherever it is considered opportune.

32. It would also be useful to coordinate the work being done by institutes and ecclesiastical associations. They should all, of whatever type, submit to the local ordinary in everything that concerns missionary activity. Therefore, it would be very helpful to draw up contracts which would regulate relations between the local ordinary and the head of the institute.

When a territory is committed to the care of a particular institute, it should be the one concern of the ecclesiastical superior and the institute to organize everything to this end: that the new christian community might grow into a local church which will, in due course, be ruled by its own pastor and have its own clergy.

A new situation arises when the mandate to care for a particular territory expires. Then the conferences of bishops and the institutes will come together and draw up norms which will regulate relations between the local ordinaries and the institutes. It will be the responsibility of the holy See to outline the general principles in accordance with which regional or even local contracts will be drawn up.

Although the institutes will be prepared to continue the work which they have begun, collaborating in the ordinary care of souls, yet as the number of local clergy increases, it should be arranged that the institutes, insofar as it is in keeping with their end, would remain faithful to the diocese and generously undertake special work in it, or the care of some particular area of it.

33. Institutes which are engaged in missionary activity in the same territory should find ways and means of coordinating their work. So conferences of religious and unions of religious sisters, in which all the institutes of a particular nation or region would have a part, would be extremely helpful. These conferences would investigate what could be done by a common effort and would be closely linked with the conferences of bishops.

With equal reason, all these points could be usefully extended to collaboration between missionary institutes at home, so that common difficulties and projects might be more easily resolved and with less cost: the doctrinal formation of future missionaries, for example, courses for missionaries, relations with the civil authorities and with international or supranational organizations.

34. Since the proper and methodical exercise of missionary activity demands that those who work for the gospel should be scientifically prepared for their tasks, especially for dialogue with non-christian religions and cultures, and should be effectively assisted in carrying them out, it is desirable that for the good of the missions there should be collaboration among certain scientific institutes which specialize in missiology and in other sciences and arts useful for the missions, such as ethnology, linguistics, the history and science of religions, sociology, pastoral techniques and the like.

1. See Vatican Council II, Dogmatic Constitution on the Church, *Lumen gentium*, 18.

2. See Vatican Council II, Dogmatic Constitution on the Church, *Lumen gentium*, 23.

3. See Motu Proprio *Apostolica Sollicitudo*, 15 September 1965.

4. See Paul VI allocution given in the council, 21 Nov. 1964 (AAS 1964).

5. See Benedict XV, Encyclical *Maximum illud* (AAS 1919, 39-40).

6. If for special reasons some missions are for the time being under the control of other congregations, it is desirable that those congregations should be in contact with the sacred Congregation for the Propagation of the Faith so that it will be possible to maintain a completely constant and uniform rule and purpose in organizing and governing all missions.

7. See Vatican Council II, Decree on the Pastoral Office of Bishops in the church, *Christus Dominus,* 36-38.

8. See Vatican Council II, Decree on the Pastoral Office of Bishops in the church, *Christus Dominus,* 35, 5-6.

Chapter VI

COOPERATION

35. Since the whole church is missionary, and the work of evangelization the fundamental task of the people of God, this sacred synod invites all to undertake a profound interior renewal so that being vividly conscious of their responsibility for the spread of the gospel they might play their part in missionary work among the nations.

36. As members of the living Christ, incorporated into him and made like him by baptism, confirmation and the Eucharist, all the faithful have an obligation to collaborate in the expansion and spread of his body, so that they might bring it to fullness as soon as possible (see Eph 4:13).

So all the children of the church should have a lively consciousness of their own responsibility for the world, they should foster within themselves a truly catholic spirit, they should spend themselves in the work of the gospel. However, let everyone be aware that the primary and most important contribution they can make to the spread of the faith is to lead a profound christian life. Their fervor in the service of God and their love for others will be like a new spiritual breeze throughout the whole church, which will appear as the sign raised up among the nations (see Is 11:12), "the light of the world" (Mt 5:14) and "the salt of the earth" (Mt 5:13). This witness of their life will achieve its effect more easily if it is borne in union with other christian bodies, according to the norms of the Decree on Ecumenism, 12.[1]

From this renewed spirit, prayers and works of penance will be spontaneously offered to God that by his grace he might make fruitful the work of missionaries, that there might be missionary vocations, and the support of which the missions stand in need might be forthcoming.

So that each and every one of the christian faithful might be well acquainted with the present state of the church in the world and might hear the voice of the multitudes crying "help us" (see Acts 16:9), information regarding the missions should be published so as to make them feel they have a part to play in missionary activity, and make them open their hearts to people's immense and deep-seated needs, and come to their assistance.

Coordination of information and cooperation with national and international bodies is also necessary.

37. Since the people of God live in communities especially in dioceses and parishes by means of which, in a certain sense, they become manifest, it belongs to such communities to bear witness to Christ before the nations.

The grace of renewal cannot grow in communities unless each of them expands the range of its charity to the ends of the earth, and has the same concern for those who are far away as it has for its own members.

Through those of its daughters and sons, whom God has chosen for this very special work, the whole community prays, collaborates and works among the nations.

It would be advantageous, provided the worldwide missionary effort is not neglected, to keep contact with missionaries from the community, or with some diocese or parish in the missions, so that the union between the communities might be visible and contribute to their mutual development.

38. All bishops, as members of the body of bishops which succeeds the college of the apostles, are consecrated not for one diocese alone, but for the salvation of the whole world. The command of Christ to preach the gospel to every creature (Mk 16:15) applies primarily and immediately to them — with Peter, and subject to Peter. From this arises that communion and cooperation of the church which is so necessary today for the work of evangelization. Because of this communion, each church cares for all the others, they make known their needs to each other, they share their possessions, because the spread of the body of Christ is the responsibility of the whole college of bishops.[2]

By arousing, fostering and directing missionary work in his own diocese, with which he is one, the bishop makes present and, as it were, visible the missionary spirit and zeal of the people of God, so that the whole diocese becomes missionary.

It is the task of the bishop to raise up among his people, especially among those who are sick or afflicted, souls who with a generous heart will offer prayers and works of penance to God for the evangelization of the world. He should gladly foster vocations to missionary institutes among young people and clerics, and be grateful if God should choose some of them to play a part in the missionary activity of the church. He should exhort and assist diocesan congregations to undertake their own work in the missions; he should promote the works of missionary institutes among his people, especially the pontifical works for the missions. It is right that these works should be given first place, because they are a means by which Catholics are imbued from infancy with a truly universal and missionary outlook and also a means for instituting an effective collecting of funds for all the missions, each according to its needs.[3]

Since the need for workers in the vineyard of the Lord grows from day to day; and since diocesan priests themselves wish to play a greater part in the evangelization of the world, this sacred synod desires that bishops, being conscious of the very grave shortage of priests which impedes the evangelization of many regions, would, after a proper training, send to those dioceses which lack clergy some of their best priests who offer themselves for mission work, where at least for a time they would exercise the missionary ministry in a spirit of service.[4]

In order that the missionary activity of bishops might be more effectively exercised for the good of the whole church, it is desirable that episcopal conferences should regulate all those matters which concern organized cooperation in their own regions.

In their conferences the bishops should consider the question of sending diocesan priests for the evangelization of the nations; the particular contribution, in proportion to its income, which each diocese will be obliged to make every year for the work of the missions;[5] the direction and organization of ways and means for directly helping or, if need be, founding missionary institutes and seminaries of diocesan clergy for the missions; the fostering of closer links between such institutes and the dioceses.

It likewise pertains to episcopal conferences to found and promote agencies which will in a spirit of friendsip receive immigrants from missionary territories who have come for reasons of work or study, and which will aid them by suitable pastoral attention. By means of these immigrants people who are distant become, in a sense, neighbors, while a wonderful opportunity is offered to communities which have long been christian to speak with nations which have not yet heard the gospel, and of showing them the true face of Christ by their own acts of kindness and assistance.[6]

39. Priests represent Christ and are the collaborators of the order of bishops in that threefold sacred duty which, of its nature, pertains to the mission of the church.[7] They must be profoundly aware of the fact that their very life is consecrated to the service of the missions. Since by their own ministry — which consists mainly in the Eucharist, which gives the church its perfection — they are in communion with Christ the head, and are leading others to this communion, they cannot but be aware of how much is still lacking to the fullness of the body, and of how much must therefore be done that it might grow from day to day. They will therefore so organize their pastoral care that it will contribute to the spread of the gospel among non-Christians.

In their pastoral work priests will stimulate and maintain among the faithful a zeal for the evangelization of the world by teaching them through preaching and religious instruction about the church's duty to proclaim Christ to the nations; by impressing on christian families the honor and the need for fostering missionary vocations among their own sons and daughters: by promoting missionary fervor among young people from Catholic schools and associations so that future preachers of the gospel might come from them. They should teach them to pray for the missions and should not be ashamed to ask them for alms, being made beggars for Christ and the salvation of souls.[8]

University and seminary professors will instruct

the young as to the true condition of the world and the church, so that the need for a more intense evangelization of non-Christians will be clear to them and feed their zeal. In teaching dogmatic, biblical, moral and historical subjects, they should focus attention on their missionary aspects, so that in this way a missionary awareness will be formed in future priests.

40. Religious institutes of the contemplative and active life have up to this time played, and still play, the greatest part in the evangelization of the world. This sacred synod willingly acknowledges their merits and thanks God for all that has been done for the glory of God and the service of souls; it exhorts them to continue untiringly in the work they have begun, since they know that the virtue of charity which they are obliged to practice more perfectly because of their vocation, impels and obliges them to a spirit and a work that is truly Catholic.[9]

Institutes of the contemplative life, by their prayers, penances and trials, are of the greatest importance in the conversion of souls since it is in answer to prayer that God sends workers into his harvest (see Mt 9:38), opens the minds of non-Christians to hear the gospel (see Acts 16:14), and makes fruitful the word of salvation in their hearts (see 1 Cor 3:7). Indeed these institutes are requested to establish houses in missionary territories, as quite a few have already done, so that by living their life there in a manner adapted to the genuinely religious traditions of the people, they might bear an outstanding witness among non-Christians to the majesty and love of God, and to union in Christ.

Institutes of the active life, whether or not they pursue a strictly missionary ideal, should sincerely examine themselves before God as to whether they might be able to extend their work for the expansion of the kingdom of God among the nations; whether they might be able to leave certain ministries to others so as to spend their strength for the missions; whether they might be able to begin work in the missions, adapting their constitutions if necessary, in accordance, however, with the mind of the founder; whether their members engage in missionary work to the full extent of their possibilities; whether their form of life bears witness to the gospel in a manner adapted to the mentality and circumstances of the people.

Since, under the inspiration of the holy Spirit, secular institutes are growing daily in the church, their work, under the authority of the bishop, can be fruitful in many ways for the missions especially as an example of total dedication to the evangelization of the world.

41. Lay people should cooperate in the church's work of evangelization and share in its saving mission both as witnesses and living instruments,[10] especially if having been called by God they are accepted by the bishop for this work.

In lands which are already christian, lay people can cooperate in the work of evangelization by fostering knowledge and love of the missions in themselves and others, by encouraging vocations among their own families and in Catholic associations and schools, by offering aid of any description, so that the gift of faith which they have received freely might be bestowed on others.

In missionary lands, however, lay people, whether they are foreigners or inhabitants of the country, should teach in the schools, administer temporal affairs, collaborate in parochial and diocesan activity, establish and promote various forms of the lay apostolate, so that the faithful of the new churches might, as soon as possible, be able to play their own part in the life of the church.[11]

Finally, lay people should willingly give socio-economic assistance to peoples in the process of development; such cooperation is the more praiseworthy according as it is more closely connected with establishing institutions which affect the fundamental structures of social life, or are directed to the training of those who will have charge of public affairs.

Those lay people who promote the knowledge of peoples and religions, by their historical or scientific-religious investigations in universities and scientific institutes, and so help the preachers of the gospel and prepare for dialogue with non-Christians, are worthy of special praise.

In a spirit of brotherhood they should collaborate with other Christians, with non-Christians and especially with members of international associations, always bearing in mind that"the structure of the earthly city should be founded on the Lord and directed to him."[12]

To carry out all these tasks, lay people require the necessary technical and spiritual preparation which should be given in institutes designed for this purpose, so that their life might bear witness to Christ, among non-Christians, according to the words of the apostle: "Do not be a stumbling block to Jews and Greeks and to the church of God, even as I myself in all things please all people, not seeking what is profitable to myself but to the many, that they may be saved" (1 Cor 10:32-33).

Conclusion

42. The fathers of the council together with the Roman Pontiff, being deeply conscious of their duty to spread everywhere the kingdom of God, affectionately salute all preachers of the gospel, and making themselves sharers in their sufferings, they especially salute those who suffer persecution for the name of

Christ.[13]

They are filled with the same love that filled the heart of Christ for humanity. Aware that it is God who makes his kingdom to come on earth, they pour out their prayers, together with the christian faithful, that through the intercession of the Virgin Mary, Queen of the Apostles, the nations might soon be led to the knowledge of the truth (1 Tim 2:4) and that the glory of God, which shines in the face of Jesus Christ, might shed its light on all women and men through the holy Spirit (2 Cor 4:6).

1. See Vatican Council II, Decree on Ecumenism, *Unitatis redintegratio*, 12.

2. See Vatican Council II, Dogmatic Constitution on the Church, *Lumen gentium*, 23-24.

3. See Benedict XV, Encyclical *Maximum Illud* (AAS 1919, 453-454); Pius XI, Encyclical *Rerum Ecclesiae* (AAS 1926, 71-73); Pius XII Encyclical *Evangelii Praecones* (AAS 1951, 525-526); id., Encyclical *Fidei Donum* (AAS 1957, 241).

4. See Pius XII, Encyclical *Fidei Donum* (AAS 1957, pp. 245-246).

5. Vatican Council II, Decree on the Pastoral Office of Bishops in the Church, *Christus Dominus*, 6.

6. See Pius XII, Encyclical *Fidei Donum* (AAS 1957, 245).

7. See Vatican Council II, Dogmatic Constitution on the Church, *Lumen gentium*, 28.

8. See Pius XI, Encyclical *Rerum Ecclesiae* (AAS 1926, 72).

9. See Vatican Council II, Dogmatic Constitution on the Church, *Lumen gentium*, 44.

10. See ibid., 33, 35.

11. See Pius XII, Encyclical *Evangelii Praecones* (AAS 510-514), John XXIII, *Princeps Pastorum* (AAS 1959, 851-852).

12. See Vatican Council II, Dogmatic Constitution on the Church, *Lumen gentium*, 46.

13. See Pius XII, Encyclical *Evangelii Praecones* (AAS 1951, 527); John XXIII, Encyclical *Princeps Pastorum* (AAS 1959, 864).

DECREE ON ECUMENISM[a]

Unitatis Redintegratio
21 November, 1964

Introduction

1. The restoration of unity among all Christians is one of the principal concerns of the Second Vatican Council. Christ the Lord founded one church and one church only. However, many christian communions present themselves to people as the true inheritance of Jesus Christ; all indeed profess to be followers of the Lord but they differ in outlook and go their different ways, as if Christ himself were divided.[1] Certainly, such division openly contradicts the will of Christ, scandalizes the world, and damages the sacred cause of preaching the Gospel to every creature.

The Lord of the ages, nevertheless, wisely and patiently follows out the plan of his grace on our behalf, sinners that we are. In recent times, God has begun to bestow more generously upon divided Christians remorse over their divisions and longing for unity. Everywhere, large numbers have felt the impulse of this grace, and among the members of the separated christian communities also there increases from day to day a movement, fostered by the grace of the holy Spirit, for the restoration of unity among all Christians. Taking part in this movement, which is called ecumenical, are those who invoke the Triune God and confess Jesus as Lord and Saviour. They do this not merely as individuals but also as members of the corporate groups in which they have heard the Gospel, and which each regards as his or her church and indeed, God's. And yet, almost everyone, though in different ways, longs for the one visible church of God, a church truly universal and sent forth to the whole world that the world may be converted to the Gospel and so be saved, to the glory of God.

This sacred Council gladly notes all this. It has already declared its teaching on the church, and now, moved by a desire for the restoration of unity among all the followers of Christ, it wishes to set before all Catholics guidelines, helps and methods, by which they too can respond to the grace of this divine call.

Chapter I

CATHOLIC PRINCIPLES ON ECUMENISM

2. What has revealed the love of God among us is that the only-begotten Son of God has been sent by the Father into the world, so that, becoming human, he might by his redemption of the entire human race give new life to it and unify it.[2] Before offering himself up as a spotless victim upon the altar of the cross, he prayed to his Father for those who believe: "that all may be one, as you, Father, are in me, and I in you; I pray that they may be one in us, that the world may believe that you sent me" (Jn 17:21). In his church he instituted the wonderful sacrament of the Eucharist by which the unity of the church is both signified and brought about. He gave his followers a new commandment to love one another,[3] and promised the Spirit, their Advocate,[4] who, as Lord and life-giver, should remain with them forever. After being lifted up on the cross and glorified, the Lord Jesus poured forth the Spirit whom he had promised, and through whom he has called and gathered together the people of the New Covenant, which is the church, into a

unity of faith, hope and charity, as the Apostle teaches us:"There is one body and one Spirit, just as you were called to the one hope of your calling; one Lord, one faith, one baptism" (Eph 4:4-5). For "all you who have been baptized into Christ have put on Christ . . . for you are all one in Christ Jesus" (Gal 3:27-28). It is the holy Spirit, dwelling in those who believe and pervading and ruling over the entire church, who brings about that wonderful communion of the faithful and joins them together so intimately in Christ that he is the principle of the church's unity. By distributing various kinds of spiritual gifts and ministries,[5] the Spirit enriches the church of Jesus Christ with different functions "in order to equip the saints for the work of service, so as to build up the body of Christ" (Eph 4: 12).

In order to establish this his holy church everywhere in the world till the end of time, Christ entrusted to the College of the Twelve the task of teaching, ruling and sanctifying.[6] Among their number he chose Peter. And after Peter's confession of faith, he determined that on him he would build his church; to him he promised the keys of the kingdom of heaven,[7] and after his profession of love, entrusted all his sheep to him to be confirmed in faith[8] and shepherded in perfect unity,[9] with himself, Christ Jesus, forever remaining the chief corner-stone[10] and shepherd of our souls.[11]

It is through the faithful preaching of the Gospel by the Apostles and their successors — he bishops with Peter's successor at their head — through their administering the sacraments, and through their governing in love, that Jesus Christ wishes his people to increase, under the action of the holy Spirit; and he perfects among his people their sense of togetherness in unity: in the confession of one faith, in the common celebration of divine worship, and in maintaining the harmony of the family of God.

The church, then, God's only flock, like a standard lifted on high for the nations to see,[12] ministers the Gospel of peace to all humankind,[13] as it makes its pilgrim way in hope toward its goal, the homeland above.[14]

This is the sacred mystery of the unity of the church, in Christ and through Christ, with the holy Spirit energizing its various functions. The highest exemplar and source of this mystery is the unity, in the Trinity of Persons, of one God, the Father and the Son in the holy Spirit.

3. In this one and only church of God from its very beginnings there arose certain rifts,[15] which the Apostle strongly censures as damnable.[16] But in subsequent centuries much more serious dissensions appeared and large communities became separated from full communion with the Catholic Church — for which, often enough, people on both sides were to blame. However, one cannot charge with the sin of separation those who at present are born into these communities and in them are brought up in the faith of Christ, and the Catholic Church accepts them with respect and affection as brothers and sisters. For those who believe in Christ and have been properly baptized are put in some, though imperfect, communion with the Catholic Church. Without doubt, the differences that exist in varying degrees between them and the Catholic Church — whether in doctrine and sometimes in discipline, or concerning the structure of the church — do indeed create many obstacles, sometimes serious ones, to full ecclesiastical communion. The ecumenical movement is striving to overcome these obstacles. But even in spite of them it remains true that all who have been justified by faith in baptism are incorporated into Christ;[17] they therefore have a right to be called Christians, and with

good reason are accepted as sisters and brothers in the Lord by the children of the Catholic Church.[18]

Moreover, some, even very many, of the most significant elements and endowments which together go to build up and give life to the church itself, can exist outside the visible boundaries of the Catholic Church: the written Word of God; the life of grace; faith, hope and charity, with the other interior gifts of the holy Spirit, as well as visible elements. All of these, which come from Christ and lead back to Christ, belong by right to the one Church of Christ.

Our separated brothers and sisters also carry out many liturgical actions of the christian religion. In ways that vary according to the condition of each church or community, these liturgical actions most certainly can truly engender a life of grace, and, one must say, are capable of giving access to that communion in which is salvation.

It follows that the separated churches[19] and communities as such, though we believe they suffer from the defects already mentioned, have been by no means deprived of significance and importance in the mystery of salvation. For the Spirit of Christ has not refrained from using them as means of salvation which derive their efficacy from the very fullness of grace and truth entrusted to the Catholic Church.

Nevertheless, our separated sisters and brothers, whether considered as individuals or as communities and Churches, are not blessed with that unity which Jesus Christ wished to bestow on all those to whom he has given new birth into one body, and whom he has quickened to newness of life — that unity which the holy scriptures and the ancient Tradition of the church proclaim. For it is through Christ's Catholic church alone, which is the universal help toward salvation, that the fullness of the means of salvation can be obtained. It was to the apostolic college alone, of which Peter is the head, that we believe our Lord entrusted all the blessings of the New Covenant, in order to establish on earth the one Body of Christ into which all those should be fully incorporated who belong in any way to the people of God. During its pilgrimage on earth, this people, though still in its members liable to sin, is growing in Christ and is guided by God's gentle wisdom, according to God's hidden designs, until it shall happily arrive at the fullness of eternal glory in the heavenly Jerusalem.

4. Today, in many parts of the world, under the influence of the grace of the holy Spirit, many efforts are being made in prayer, word and action to attain that fullness of unity which Jesus Christ desires. This sacred council, therefore, exhorts all the catholic faithful to recognize the signs of the times and to take an active and intelligent part in the work of ecumenism.

The term "ecumenical movement" indicates the initiatives and activities encouraged and organized, according to the various needs of the church and as opportunities offer, to promote christian unity. These are: first, every effort to avoid expressions, judgments and actions which are not truthful and fair in representing the situation of the members of the separated christian communities, and so make mutual relations with them more difficult. Then, "dialogue" between competent experts from different Churches and communities; in their meetings, which are organized in a religious spirit, each explains the teaching of their communion in greater depth and brings out clearly its distinctive features. Through such dialogue everyone gains a truer knowledge and more just appreciation of the teaching and religious life of both communions. In addition, these communions engage more intensively and more cooperatively in fulfilling those duties toward the common good of humanity which are demanded by every christian conscience. They also come together for common prayer, where this is permitted. Finally, all are led to examine their own faithfulness to Christ's will for the church and, wherever necessary, undertake with vigor the task of renewal and reform.

Such actions, when they are carried out by the catholic faithful prudently patiently and under the attentive guidance of their bishops, promote justice and truth, concord and collaboration, as well as the spirit of love and unity. In this way, little by little, as the obstacles to perfect ecclesiastical communion are overcome, all Christians will be gathered, in a common celebration of the Eucharist, into the unity of the one and only church, which Christ bestowed on his church from the beginning. This unity, we believe, subsists in the Catholic Church as something she can never lose, and we hope that it will continue to increase until the end of time. However, it is evident that the work of preparing and reconciling those individuals who wish for full catholic communion is of its nature distinct from ecumenical action. But there is no opposition between the two, since both proceed from the marvellous plans of God.

In ecumenical work, Catholics must assuredly be concerned for the members of separated christian communities, praying for them, keeping them informed about the church, making the first approaches toward them. But their primary duty is to make a careful and honest appraisal of whatever needs to be renewed and done in the catholic household itself, in order that its life may bear witness more clearly and more faithfully to the teachings and institutions which have been handed down from Christ through the apostles.

For although the Catholic church has been endowed with all divinely revealed truth and with all means of grace, yet its members fail to live by them with all the fervor that they should. As a result, the radiance of the church's face shines less brightly in the eyes of our separated sisters and brothers and of the world at large, and the growth of God's kingdom is retarded. All Catholics must therefore aim at christian perfection[20] and, according to their various stations, all play their part, that the church, which bears in her own body the humility and dying of Jesus,[21] may daily be more purified and renewed, against the day when Christ will present her to himself in all her glory without spot or wrinkle.[22]

While preserving unity in essentials, let all in the church, according to the office entrusted to them, preserve a proper freedom in the various forms of spiritual life and discipline, in the variety of liturgical rites, and even in the theological elaborating of revealed truth. In all things let charity prevail. If they are true to this course of action, they will be giving ever richer expression to the authentic catholicity and apostolicity of the church.

On the other hand, Catholics must gladly acknowledge and esteem the truly christian endowments from our common heritage which are to be found among those separated from us. It is right and salutary to recognize the riches of Christ and virtuous works in the lives of others who are bearing witness to Christ, sometimes even to the shedding of their blood. For God is always wonderful in his works and worthy of all praise.

Nor should we forget that anything wrought by the grace of the holy Spirit in the hearts of our separated brothers and sisters can contribute to our own edification. Whatever is truly christian is never contrary to what genuinely belongs to the faith; indeed, it can always bring a more perfect realization of the very mystery of Christ and the church.

Nevertheless, the divisions among Christians prevent the church from realizing the fullness of catholicity proper to her in those of her children who, though joined to her by baptism, are yet separated from full communion with her. Furthermore, the church herself finds it more difficult to express in actual life her full catholicity in all its aspects.

This sacred council is gratified to note that participation by the catholic faithful in ecumenical work is growing daily. It commends this work to the bishops everywhere in the world that it may be advanced skilfully and guided wisely.

Chapter II

THE PRACTICE OF ECUMENISM

5. Concern for restoring unity involves the whole church, faithful and clergy alike. It extends to everyone, according to the talent of each, whether it be exercised in daily christian living or in theological and historical studies. This concern itself already reveals to some extent the bond of community existing between all Christians, and it leads toward full and perfect unity, in accordance with what God in his kindness wills.

6. Every renewal of the church[23] essentially consists in an increase of fidelity to her own calling. Undoubtedly this explains the dynamism of the movement toward unity. Christ summons the church, as she goes her pilgrim way, to that continual reformation of which she always has need, insofar as she is a human institution here on earth. Consequently, if, in various times and circumstances, there have been deficiencies in moral conduct or in church discipline, or even in

the way that church teaching has been formulated —
to be carefully distinguished from the deposit of faith
itself — these should be set right at the opportune
moment and in the proper way.

Church renewal therefore has notable ecumenical
importance. Already this renewal is taking place in
various spheres of the church's life: the biblical and
liturgical movements, the preaching of the Word of
God and catechetics, the apostolate of the laity, new
forms of religious life and the spirituality of married
life, and the Church's social teaching and activity. All
these should be considered as promises and guarantees for the future progress of ecumenism.

7. There can be no ecumenism worthy of the name
without interior conversion. For it is from newness of
attitudes of mind,[24] from self-denial and unstinted
love, that desires of unity take their rise and develop
in a mature way. We should therefore pray to the holy
Spirit for the grace to be genuinely self-denying,
humble, gentle in the service of others and to have an
attitude of generosity toward them. The Apostle of the
Gentiles says: "I, therefore, a prisoner for the Lord,
beg you to lead a life worthy of the calling to which
you have been called, with all humility and meekness,
with patience, forbearing one another in love, eager
to maintain the unity of the spirit in the bond of
peace" (Eph 4:1-3). This exhortation is directed especially to those raised to sacred orders in order that the
mission of Christ may be continued. He came among
us "not to be served but to serve" (Mt 20:28).

St John has testified: "If we say we have not sinned,
we make him a liar, and his word is not in us" (1 Jn
1:10). This holds good for sins against unity. Thus, in
humble prayer we beg pardon of God and of our separated sisters and brothers, just as we forgive those
who trespass against us.

The faithful should remember that they promote

union among Christians better, that indeed they live it better, when they try to live holier lives according to the Gospel. For the closer their union with the Father, the Word, and the Spirit, the more deeply and easily will they be able to grow in mutual love.

8. This change of heart and holiness of life, along with public and private prayer for the unity of Christians, should be regarded as the soul of the whole ecumenical movement, and merits the name, "spiritual ecumenism."

It is a recognized custom for Catholics to meet for frequent recourse to that prayer for the unity of the church with which the Saviour himself on the eve of his death so fervently appealed to his Father: "That they may all be one" (Jn 17:20).

In certain circumstances, such as in prayer services "for unity" and during ecumenical gatherings, it is allowable, indeed desirable, that Catholics should join in prayer with members of other christian churches and communities. Such prayers in common are certainly a very effective means of petitioning for the grace of unity, and they are a genuine expression of the ties which still bind Catholics to their separated sisters and brothers."For where two or three are gathered together in my name, there am I in the midst of them" (Mt 18:20).

Yet worship in common (*communicatio in sacris*) is not to be considered as a means to be used indiscriminately for the restoration of unity among Christians. There are two main principles upon which the practice of such common worship depends: first, that of the unity of the church which ought to be expressed; and second, that of the sharing in the means of grace. The expression of unity generally forbids common worship. Grace to be obtained sometimes commends it. The concrete course to be adopted, when all the circumstances of time, place and persons have been duly considered, is left to the prudent decision of the local episcopal authority, unless the bishops' conference according to its own statutes, or the holy See, has determined otherwise.

9. We must become familiar with the outlook of the separated churches and communities. Study is absolutely required for this, and it should be pursued in fidelity to the truth and with a spirit of good will. Catholics who already have a proper grounding need to acquire a more adequate understanding of the respective doctrines of the separated communities, their history, their spiritual and liturgical life, their religious psychology and cultural background. Most valuable for this purpose are meetings of the two sides — especially for discussion of theological problems — where each can treat with the other on an equal footing, provided that those who take part in them under the guidance of their authorities are truly competent. From such dialogue will emerge still more clearly what the situation of the Catholic church really is. In this way, too, we will better understand the outlook of our separated sisters and brothers and more aptly present our own belief.

10. Theology and other branches of knowledge, especially those of a historical nature, must be taught with due regard for the ecumenical point of view, so that they may correspond more exactly with the facts.

It is important that future pastors and priests should have mastered a theology that has been carefully elaborated in this way and not polemically, especially in what concerns the relations of separated brothers and sisters with the Catholic church. For it is upon the formation which priests receive that largely depends the instruction and spiritual formation the faithful and religious need.

Moreover, Catholics engaged in missionary work in the same territories as other Christians ought to know, particularly in these times, the problems and the benefits which affect their apostolate because of the ecumenical movement.

11. The manner and order in which catholic belief is expressed should in no way become an obstacle to dialogue with other Christians. It is, of course, essential that the doctrine be clearly presented in its entirety. Nothing is so foreign to the spirit of ecumenism as a false irenicism which harms the purity of catholic doctrine and obscures its genuine and certain meaning.

At the same time, catholic belief must be explained more profoundly and more precisely, in such a way and in such terms as our separated brothers and sisters can also really understand.

Furthermore, in ecumenical dialogue, catholic theologians, standing fast by the teaching of the church yet searching together with separated brothers and sisters into the divine mysteries, should do so with love for the truth, with charity, and with humility. When comparing doctrines with one another, they should remember that in catholic doctrine there exists an order or "hierarchy" of truths, since they vary in their relation to the foundation of the christian faith. Thus the way will be opened whereby this kind of friendly rivalry will incite all to a deeper realization and a clearer expression of the unfathomable riches of Christ.[25]

12. Before the whole world let all Christians confess their faith in God, one and three, in the incarnate Son of God, our Redeemer and Lord. United in their efforts, and with mutual respect, let them bear witness to our common hope which does not play us false. Since cooperation in social matters is so widespread today, all people without exception are called to work together; with much greater reason is this true of all who believe in God, but most of all, it is

specially true of all Christians, since they bear the seal of Christ's name. Cooperation among Christians vividly expresses that bond which already unites them, and it sets in clearer relief the features of Christ the Servant. Such cooperation, which has already begun in many countries, should be developed more and more, particularly in regions where social and technological evolution is taking place. It should contribute to a just appreciation of the dignity of the human person, to the promotion of the blessings of peace, the application of Gospel principles to social life, and the advancement of the arts and sciences in a truly christian spirit. It should use every possible means to relieve the afflictions of our times, such as famine and natural disasters, illiteracy and poverty, lack of housing, and the unequal distribution of wealth. Through such cooperation, all believers in Christ are able to learn easily how they can understand each other better and esteem each other more, and how the road to the unity of Christians may be made smooth.

Chapter III

CHURCHES AND ECCLESIAL COMMUNITIES SEPARATED FROM THE ROMAN APOSTOLIC SEE

13. We now turn our attention to the two principal types of division which affect the seamless robe of Christ.

The first divisions occurred in the East, either because of the dispute over the dogmatic formulae of the Councils of Ephesus and Chalcedon, or later by the dissolving of ecclesiastical communion between the Eastern Patriarchates and the Roman See.

Still other divisions arose in the West more than four centuries later. These stemmed from the events which are commonly referred to as the Reformation. As a result, many communions, national or confessional, were separated from the Roman See. Among those in which catholic traditions and institutions in part continue to exist, the Anglican communion occupies a special place.

These various divisions, however, differ greatly from one another not only by reason of their origin, place and time, but still more by reason of the nature and seriousness of questions concerning faith and church order. Therefore, without minimizing the differences between the various christian bodies, and without overlooking the bonds which continue to exist among them in spite of these differences, the Council has decided to propose the following considerations for prudent ecumenical action.

I. The Special Position of the Eastern Churches

14. For many centuries the churches of the east and of the west went their own ways, though a communion of faith and sacramental life bound them together. If disagreements in faith and discipline arose among them, the Roman See acted by common consent as moderator.

This council gladly reminds everyone of one highly significant fact among others: in the east there flourish many particular local churches; among them the patriarchal churches hold first place, and of them many glory in taking their origins from the apostles themselves. Hence, it has been, and still is, a matter of primary concern and care among the Orientals to preserve in a communion of faith and charity those family ties which ought to exist between local churches, as between sisters.

It must be remembered that, from their very origins, the churches of the east have had a treasury from which the church of the west has drawn largely for its liturgy, spiritual tradition and jurisprudence. Nor must we underestimate the fact that the basic dogmas of the christian faith concerning the Trinity and the Word of God made flesh from the Virgin Mary were defined in ecumenical councils held in the east. To preserve this faith, these churches have suffered, and still suffer much.

However, the heritage handed down by the apostles was received differently and in different forms, so that from the very beginnings of the church its development varied from region to region and also because of differing mentalities and ways of life. These reasons, plus external causes, as well as the lack of charity and mutual understanding, left the way open to divisions.

For this reason the council urges all, but especially those who commit themselves to the work of restoring the full communion that is desired between the eastern churches and the Catholic Church, to give due consideration to this special feature of the origin and growth of the churches of the east, and to the character of the relations which obtained between them and the Roman See before the separation, and to form for themselves a correct evaluation of these facts. Where this is done carefully it will greatly contribute to the dialogue in view.

15. Everyone knows with what great love the eastern Christians celebrate the sacred liturgy, especially the eucharistic mystery, source of the church's life and pledge of future glory. In this mystery the faithful, united with their bishops, have access to God the

Father through the Son, the Word made flesh who suffered and was glorified, in the outpouring of the holy Spirit. And so, made "sharers of the divine nature" (2 Pet 1:4), they enter into communion with the most Holy Trinity. Hence, through the celebration of the Eucharist of the Lord in each of these churches, the Church of God is built up and grows in stature,[26] and through concelebration, their communion with one another is made manifest.

In their liturgical worship, eastern Christians pay high tribute, in beautiful hymns of praise, to Mary ever Virgin, whom the ecumenical Synod of Ephesus solemnly proclaimed to be the holy Mother of God in order that Christ might be truly and properly acknowledged as Son of God and Son of Man, according to the scriptures. They also give homage to the saints, among them the Fathers of the universal church.

These churches, although separated from us, yet possess true sacraments, above all — by apostolic succession — the priesthood and the Eucharist, whereby they are still joined to us in closest intimacy. Therefore some worship in common (*communicatio in sacris*), given suitable circumstances and the approval of church authority, is not merely possible but is encouraged.

Moreover, in the east are to be found the riches of those spiritual traditions which are given expression in monastic life especially. From the glorious times of the holy Fathers, that monastic spirituality flourished in the east which later flowed over into the western world, and there provided a source from which Latin monastic life took its rise and has often drawn fresh vigor ever since. Therefore, it is earnestly recommended that Catholics avail themselves more often of the spiritual riches of the eastern Fathers which lift up all that is human to the contemplation of divine mysteries.

Everyone should realize that it is of supreme importance to understand, venerate, preserve and foster the rich liturgical and spiritual heritage of the eastern churches in order faithfully to preserve the fullness of christian tradition, and to bring about reconciliation between eastern and western Christians.

16. From the earliest times the churches of the east followed their own disciplines, sanctioned by the holy Fathers, by synods, and even by ecumenical councils. Far from being an obstacle to the church's unity, such diversity of customs and observances only adds to the beauty of the church and contributes greatly to carrying out her mission, as has already been stated. To remove all shadow of doubt, then, this holy synod solemnly declares that the churches of the east, while keeping in mind the necessary unity of the whole church, have the power to govern themselves according to their own disciplines, since these are better suited to the character of their faithful and better adapted to foster the good of souls. The perfect observance of this traditional principle — which however has not always been observed — is a prerequisite for any restoration of union.

17. What has already been said about legitimate variety we are pleased to apply to differences in theological expression of doctrine. In the study of revealed truth east and west have used different methods and approaches in understanding and confessing divine things. It is hardly surprising, then, if sometimes one tradition has come nearer to a full appreciation of some aspects of a mystery of revelation than the other, or has expressed them better. In such cases, these various theological formulations are often to be considered complementary rather than conflicting. With regard to the authentic theological traditions of the Orientals, we must recognize that they are ad-

mirably rooted in holy scripture, are fostered and given expression in liturgical life, are nourished by the living tradition of the apostles and by the works of the Fathers and spiritual writers of the east; they are directed toward a right ordering of life, indeed, toward a full contemplation of christian truth.

This sacred council thanks God that many eastern rite children of the Catholic Church preserve this heritage and wish to express it more faithfully and completely in their lives, and are already living in full communion with their brothers and sisters who follow the tradition of the West. It declares that this entire heritage of spirituality and liturgy, of discipline and theology, in the various traditions, belongs to the full catholic and apostolic character of the church.

18. After taking all these factors into consideration, this sacred council confirms what previous councils and Roman pontiffs have proclaimed: in order to restore communion and unity or preserve them, one must "impose no burden beyond what is indispensable" (Acts 15:28). It is the Council's urgent desire that every effort should be made toward the gradual realization of this unity in the various organizations and living activities of the church, especially by prayer and by trusting dialogue on points of doctrine and the more pressing pastoral problems of our time. Similarly, to the pastors and faithful of the Catholic Church, it commends the growth of close relations with those no longer living in the east but far from their homeland, so that friendly collaboration with them may increase in a spirit of love, without bickering or rivalry. If this task is carried on wholeheartedly, the council hopes that with the removal of the wall dividing the eastern and western church at last there may be but one dwelling, firmly established on the cornerstone, Christ Jesus, who will make both one.[27]

II. The Separated Churches and
Ecclesial Communities in the West

19. The churches and ecclesial communities which were separated from the Apostolic See of Rome during the grave crisis that began in the west at the end of the middle ages or in later times, are bound to the Catholic Church by a specially close relationship as a result of the long span of earlier centuries when the christian people had lived in ecclesiastical communion.

But since these churches and ecclesial communities differ considerably not only from us, but also among themselves, due to their different origins and convictions in doctrine and spiritual life, the task of describing them adequately is extremely difficult; we do not propose to do it here.

Although the ecumenical movement and the desire for peace with the Catholic Church have not yet taken hold everywhere, it is nevertheless our hope that an ecumenical spirit and mutual esteem will gradually increase among all Christians.

At the same time, however, one should recognize that between these churches and ecclesial communities, on the one hand, and the Catholic church on the other, there are very weighty differences not only of a historical, sociological, psychological and cultural character, but especially in the interpretation of revealed truth. To facilitate entering into ecumenical dialogue in spite of those differences, we wish to set down in what follows some considerations which can, and indeed should serve as a basis and encouragement for such dialogue.

20. Our thoughts are concerned first of all with those Christians who openly confess Jesus Christ as God and Lord and as the only Mediator between God and humanity for the glory of the one God, the

Father, the Son and the holy Spirit. We are indeed aware that there exist considerable divergences from the doctrine of the Catholic Church even concerning Christ the Word of God made flesh and the work of redemption, and thus concerning the mystery and ministry of the church and the role of Mary in the work of salvation. But we rejoice that our separated sisters and brothers look to Christ as the source and center of ecclesiastical communion. Their longing for union with Christ impels them ever more to seek unity, and also to bear witness to their faith among the peoples of the earth.

21. A love and reverence — almost a cult — of holy scripture leads our brothers and sisters to a constant and diligent study of the sacred text. For the Gospel "is the power of God for salvation to everyone who has faith, to the Jew first and then to the Greek" (Rom 1:16).

Invoking the holy Spirit, they seek God in these very scriptures as he speaks to them in Christ, the one whom the prophets foretold, the Word of God made flesh for us. In the scriptures they contemplate the life of Christ, as well as the teachings and the actions of the divine Master for our salvation, in particular the mysteries of his death and resurrection.

But when Christians separated from us affirm the divine authority of the sacred books, they think differently from us — some in one way, some in another — about the relationship between the scriptures and the church. For in the church, according to catholic belief, its authentic teaching office has a special place in expounding and preaching the written word of God.

Nevertheless, in the dialogue itself, the sacred word is a precious instrument in the mighty hand of God for attaining to that unity which the Saviour holds out to all.

22. By the sacrament of Baptism, whenever it is properly conferred in the way the Lord determined and is received with the proper dispositions of soul, people become truly incorporated into the crucified and glorified Christ and are reborn to a sharing of the divine life, as the Apostle says: "For you were buried together with him in baptism, and in him also rose again through faith in the working of God who raised him from the dead" (Col 2:12).[28]

Baptism, therefore, establishes a sacramental bond of unity among all who through it are reborn. But baptism, of itself, is only a beginning, a point of departure, for it is wholly directed toward the acquiring of fullness of life in Christ. Baptism is thus ordained toward a complete profession of faith, a complete incorporation into the system of salvation such as Christ himself willed it to be, and finally, toward a complete integration into eucharistic communion.

Although the ecclesial communities separated from us lack the fullness of unity with us which flows from baptism, and although we believe they have not preserved the proper reality of the eucharistic mystery in its fullness, especially because of the absence of the sacrament of Orders, nevertheless when they commemorate the Lord's death and resurrection in the holy supper, they profess that it signifies life in communion with Christ and await his coming in glory. For these reasons, doctrine about the Lord's supper, about the other sacraments, worship, and ministry in the church, should figue among subjects of dialogue.

23. The christian way of life of these our sisters and brothers is nourished by faith in Christ. It is strengthened by the grace of baptism and by hearing the word of God. This way of life expresses itself in private prayer, in meditation on the scriptures, in the life of a christian family, and in the worship of the community gathered together to praise God. Furthermore,

their worship sometimes displays notable features of a liturgy once shared in common. The faith by which they believe in Christ bears fruit in praise and thanksgiving for the benefits received from the hands of God. Joined to it is a lively sense of justice and a true charity toward others. This active faith has been responsible for many organizations for the relief of spiritual and material distress, the advancement of the education of youth, the improvement of social conditions of life, and the promotion of peace throughout the world.

And if in moral matters there are many Christians who do not always understand the Gospel in the same way as Catholics, and do not admit the same solutions for the more difficult problems of modern society, they nevertheless want to cling to Christ's word as the source of christian virtue and to obey the command of the Apostle: "Whatever you do in word or in work, do all in the name of the Lord Jesus, giving thanks to God the Father through him" (Col 3:17). Hence, ecumenical dialogue could start with the moral application of the Gospel.

24. Now, after this brief exposition of the conditions under which ecumenical activity may be practised, and of the principles by which it is to be guided, we confidently look to the future. This sacred Council urges the faithful to abstain from any frivolous or imprudent zeal, such as can cause harm to true progress toward unity. Their ecumenical activity cannot be other than fully and sincerely catholic, that is, loyal to the truth we have received from the Apostles and the Fathers, and in harmony with the faith which the Catholic Church has always professed, and at the same time tending toward that fullness in which our Lord wants his Body to grow in the course of time.

This holy council firmly hopes that the initiatives of the sons and daughters of the Catholic Church, joined with those of their separated brothers and sisters, will go forward, without obstructing the ways of divine Providence, and without prejudging the future inspirations of the holy Spirit. Further, this council declares that it realizes that this holy objective — the reconciliation of all Christians in the unity of the one and only church of Christ — transcends human powers and gifts. It therefore places its hope entirely in the prayer of Christ for the church, in the love of the Father for us, and in the power of the holy Spirit. "And hope does not disappoint, because God's love has been poured forth in our hearts through the holy Spirit who has been given to us" (Rom 5:5).

a. Revised for this edition by Bernard Treacy, OP, editor, *Doctrine and Life*, Dublin.

1. See 1 Cor 1:13.
2. See 1 Jn 4:9; Col 1:18-20; Jn 11:52.
3. See Jn 13:34.
4. See Jn 16:7.
5. See 1 Cor 12::4-11.
6. See Mt 28:18-20, in conjunction with Jn 20:21-23.
7. See Mt 16:19, in conjunction with Mt 18:18.
8. See Lk 22:32.
9. See Jn 21:15-18.
10. See Eph 2:20.
11. See 1 Pet 2:25; Vatican Council I, Session 4 (1870), the Constitution *Pastor Aeternus:* Coll. Lac. 7, 482a.
12. See Is 11:10-12.
13. See Eph 2:17-18, in conjunction with Mk 16:15.
14. See 1 Pet 1:3-9.
15. See 1 Cor 11-18-19; Gal 1:6-9; 1 Jn 2:18-19.
16. See 1 Cor 1 11 ff.; 11-22.
17. See Council of Florence, Session 8 (1439), the Decree *Exultate Deo:* Mansi 31, 1055 A.
18. See St Augustine, In Ps. 32, Enarr. II, 29: PL 36, 299.
19. See Lateran Council IV (1215), Constitution IV: Mansi 22, 990; Council of Lyons II (1274), Profession of faith of Michael Palaeologus: Mansi 24, 71 E; Council of Florence, Session 6 (1439), Definition *Laetentur caeli:* Mansi 31,1026 E.
20. See Jas 1:4; Rom 12:1-2.
21. See 2 Cor 4:10; Phil 2:5-8.
22. See Eph 5:27.
23. See Lateran Council V, Session 12 (1517), Constitution

Constituti: Mansi 32, 988 B-C.

24. See Eph 4:23.

25. See Eph 3:8.

26. See St John Chrysostom, *In Ioannem Homelia* XLVI, PG 59, 260-262.

27. See Council of Florence, Sess. VI (1439), Definition *Laetentur caeli:* Mansi 31, 1026 E.

28. See Rom 6:4.

DECREE ON THE CATHOLIC EASTERN CHURCHES[a]

Orientalium Ecclesiarum

21 November, 1964

Introduction

1. The Catholic Church values highly the institutions of the eastern churches, their liturgical rites, ecclesiastical traditions and their ordering of christian life. For in those churches, which are distinguished by their venerable antiquity, there is clearly evident the tradition which has come from the apostles through the Fathers[1] and which is part of the divinely revealed, undivided heritage of the universal church. This holy, ecumenical synod, therefore, has a special care for the eastern churches, which are living witnesses of this tradition, and wishes them to flourish and to fulfill with new apostolic strength the task entrusted to them. Accordingly it has decided to set down some guiding principles for these churches, in addition to those which refer to the church universal, leaving all else to be cared for by the eastern synods and the Apostolic See.

The Particular Churches or Rites

2. The holy Catholic Church, which is the Mystical Body of Christ, is made up of the faithful who are organically united in the holy Spirit by the same faith,

the same sacraments and the same government, and who, coming together in various hierarchically linked different groups, thus form particular churches or rites. Between those churches there is such a wonderful communion that this variety, so far from diminishing the Church's unity, rather serves to emphasize it. For the Catholic Church wishes the traditions of each particular church or rite to remain whole and entire, and it likewise wishes to adapt its own way of life to the various needs of time and place.[2]

3. These individual churches, both eastern and western, while they differ somewhat among themselves in what is called "rite," namely in liturgy, in ecclesiastical discipline and in spiritual tradition, are none the less all equally entrusted to the pastoral guidance of the Roman Pontiff, who by God's appointment is successor to Blessed Peter in primacy over the universal church. Therefore these churches are of equal rank, so that none of them is superior to the others because of its rite. They have the same rights and obligations, even with regard to preaching the Gospel in the whole world (see Mk 16:15), under the direction of the Roman Pontiff.

4. Provision must be made therefore everywhere in the world to protect and advance all these individual churches. For this purpose, each should organize its own parishes and hierarchy, where the spiritual good of the faithful requires it. The hierachies of the various individual churches who have jurisdiction in the same territory should meet at regular intervals for consultation, and thus foster unity of action. They should make united efforts to promote common activities, the better to further the good of religion and to safeguard more effectively the discipline of their clergy.[3] All clerics and those who are to receive sacred orders should be well instructed concerning rites and particularly in practical rules for inter-ritual questions. Lay

people also should receive instruction concerning rites and their rules in their catechetical formation.

Finally, each and every Catholic, as also the baptized members of any non-catholic church or community who come to the fullness of catholic communion, must retain their own rite everywhere in the world, and follow it to the best of their ability,[4] without prejudice to the right of appealing to the Apostolic See in special cases affecting persons, communities or districts. The Apostolic See which is the supreme arbiter of inter-church relations will provide for all such needs in an ecumenical spirit, acting directly or through other authorities, giving suitable rules, decrees or rescripts.

Preservation of the Spiritual Heritage of the Eastern Churches

5. History, tradition and very many ecclesiastical institutions give clear evidence of the great debt owed to the eastern churches by the church universal.[5] Therefore this holy council not merely praises and appreciates as is due this ecclesiastical and spiritual heritage, but also insists on viewing it as the heritage of the whole church of Christ. For that reason this council solemnly declares that the churches of the east like those of the west have the right and duty to govern themselves according to their own special disciplines. For these are guaranteed by ancient tradition, and seem to be better suited to the customs of their faithful and better fitted for bringing about the good of their souls.

6. All members of the eastern churches should be firmly convinced that they can and ought always preserve their own legitimate liturgical rites and ways of life, and that changes are to be introduced only to forward their own organic development. They themselves are to carry out all these prescriptions with the

greatest fidelity. They are to aim always at a more perfect knowledge and practice of their rites, and if they have fallen away due to circumstances of times or persons, they are to strive to return to their ancestral traditions.

Those who by reason of their office or apostolic ministry have frequent dealings with the eastern churches or their faithful should be instructed as their office demands in theoretical and practical knowledge of the rites, discipline, doctrine, history and character of the members of the eastern churches.[6] It is recommended strongly to religious orders and associations of the Latin rite, which are working in eastern countries or among the eastern faithful, that they should set up, so far as is possible, houses or even provinces of the eastern rite to make their apostolic work more effective.[7]

The Eastern Patriarchs

7. The patriarchate as an institution has existed in the church from the earliest times, and was already recognized by the first ecumenical councils.[8]

By the term "eastern patriarch" is meant the bishop who has jurisdiction over all the bishops, metropolitans not excepted, clergy and people of his own territory or rite, according to the rules of canon law and without prejudice to the primacy of the Roman Pontiff.[9]

Wherever a prelate of any rite is appointed outside the territory of his patriarchate, he remains attached to the hierarchy of his rite, in accordance with canon law.[9a]

8. The patriarchs of the eastern churches, although some are of later date than others, are all equal in patriarchal rank, without prejudice to their legitimately established precedence of honor.[10]

9. Following the most ancient tradition of the

church, special honor is to be given to the patriarchs of the eastern churches, since each is set over his patriarchate as father and head. Therefore this holy council enacts that their rights and privileges be restored in accordance with the ancient traditions of each church and the decrees of the ecumenical councils.[11]

These rights and privileges are those which existed in the time of union between east and west, although they may have to be adapted somewhat to present-day conditions.

The patriarchs with their synods are the highest authority for all business of the patriarchate, not excepting the right of setting up new eparchies (dioceses) and appointing bishops of their rite within the patriarchal territory, without prejudice to the inalienable right of the Roman Pontiff to intervene in any particular case.

10. What is laid down concerning patriarchs applies also, in accordance with canon law, to major archbishops who rule the whole of some individual church or rite.[12]

11. Since the patriarchal system is the traditional form of government in the eastern churches, the holy ecumenical council wishes, where there is need, that new patriarchates to be set up. This is reserved to an ecumenical council or to the Roman Pontiff.[13]

Sacramental Discipline

12. The holy ecumenical council confirms and approves the ancient discipline concerning the sacraments which exist in the eastern churches, and also the ritual observed in their celebration and administration, and wishes this to be restored where such a need arises.

13. The established practice with regard to the minister of Confirmation, which has existed among east-

ern churches from ancient times, is to be fully restored. Accordingly priests are empowered to confer
this sacrament, using chrism blessed by their patriarch or bishop.[14]

14. All priests of an eastern rite can confer this
sacrament validly, either in conjunction with baptism
or separately, on all the faithful of any rite, including
the Latin rite.[15] For liceity, however, they must follow
what is laid down by both common and particular
canon law. Priests of the Latin rite, in accordance with
the faculties which they hold regarding the administration of this sacrament, may administer it also to the
faithful of the eastern churches, without prejudice to
the rite. For liceity they must follow the prescriptions
of common and particular canon law.[16]

15. The faithful are obliged to take part in the
Divine Liturgy on Sundays and feast days or, according to the regulations or custom of their own rite, in
the celebration of the Divine Office.[17] To enable the
faithful more easily to fulfill this obligation, it is laid
down that the time for fulfilling this precept extends
from Vespers of the vigil to the end of the Sunday or
feast day.[18] The faithful are strongly recommended to
receive the Sacred Eucharist on these days, and to do
so more frequently, even every day.[19]

16. In view of the fact that the faithful of the different individual churches are constantly intermingled
in the same district or eastern territory, the faculties
for hearing confessions given to priests of any rite by
their own ordinaries[19a] duly and without any restriction extend to the whole territory of the ordinary who
grants them, and also to the places and faithful of any
rite in the same territory, unless an ordinary of the
place explicity refuses this for places of his own rite.[20]

17. In order that the ancient discipline of the sacrament of Orders may flourish once more in the eastern
churches, the holy council wishes the institution of

the permanent diaconate to be restored where it has fallen into disuse.[21] For the subdiaconate and the lesser orders, their rights and obligations, the legislative authority of each individual church should make provision.[22]

18. In order to provide against invalid marriages, and also in order to promote the permanence and sanctity of marriage as well as peace in the home, this holy council lays down that when eastern Catholics marry baptized eastern non-Catholics the canonical form of celebration for these marriages is of obligation only for liceity. For their validity, the presence of a sacred minister is sufficient, provided that the other prescriptions of canon law are observed.[23]

Divine Worship

19. For the future, the setting up, transference or suppression of feast days common to all the eastern churches is reserved solely to an ecumenical council or the Apostolic See. On the other hand, the setting up, transference or suppression of feast days for any of the individual churches is within the competence not only of the Apostolic See but also of patriarchal or archiepiscopal synods, due regard being had for the whole area affected as also for the other individual churches.[24]

20. Until all Christians agree, as is hoped, on one day for the celebration of Easter by all, in the meantime as a means of fostering unity among Christians who live in the same area or country, it is left to the patriarchs or to the supreme ecclesiastical authorities of the place to consult all parties involved and so come to unanimous agreement to celebrate the feast of Easter on the same Sunday.[25]

21. Regarding the law of the seasons of the Church's year, individual faithful who live outside the area or territory of their own rite may follow in all

points the discipline in force in the place where they are living. In families of mixed rite this law may be observed according to one and the same rite.[26]

22. Eastern clerics and religious should celebrate the Divine Office which from ancient times has been greatly held in honour among the eastern churches, according to the prescriptions and traditions of their own particular discipline.[27] The faithful also, following the example of their ancestors, should take part devoutly and as much as they can in the Divine Office.

23. The patriarch with his synod, or the supreme authority of each church with advice of prelates, has the right to regulate the languages to be used in the sacred liturgical functions, and also, after reference to the Apostolic See, to approve translations of texts into the vernacular.[28]

Relations With Members of the Separated Churches

24. The eastern churches in communion with the Apostolic See of Rome have the special duty of fostering the unity of all Christians, in particular of eastern Christians, according to the principles laid down in the decree of this holy council, "On Ecumenism," by prayer above all, by their example, by their scrupulous fidelity to the ancient traditions of the east, by better knowledge of each other, by working together, and by an understanding attitude towards persons and things.[29]

25. Nothing more should be demanded of separated eastern Christians who come to catholic unity under the influence of the grace of the holy Spirit than what the simple profession of the catholic faith requires. And since a valid priesthood has been preserved among them, eastern clerics who come to catholic unity may exercise their Orders, in accordance with the regulations laid down by the compe-

tent authority.[30]

26. Any worship in common which runs counter to the unity of the church, or which involves formal adherence to error or the danger of aberration in the faith, of scandal and of indifferentism, is forbidden by the law of God.[31] However, with regard to our eastern brothers and sisters, pastoral experience shows that various circumstances affecting individuals can and ought to be taken into account, where the unity of the church is not harmed and there are no dangers to be guarded against, but where the need of salvation and the spiritual good of souls are prime considerations. Therefore, the Catholic Church, by reason of circumstances of time, place and persons, has often followed and still follows a less rigorous course of action, offering to all the means of salvation and a witness to charity among Christians, through a common sharing in the sacraments and in other sacred functions and things.

In view of this, "lest, through the harshness of our judgement, we be an obstacle to those who are being saved,"[32] and in order to further union with the eastern churches separated from us, the holy council has laid down the following lines of action:

27. In view of the principles just noted, eastern Christians who are separated in good faith from the Catholic Church, if they are rightly disposed and make such request of their own accord, may be given the sacraments of Penance, the Eucharist and the Anointing of the Sick. Moreover, Catholics also may ask for those same sacraments from non-catholic ministers in whose church there are valid sacraments, as often as necessity or true spiritual benefit recommends such action, and access to a catholic priest is physically or morally impossible.[33]

28. Further, given the same principles, a common sharing in sacred functions, things and places, is per-

mitted for a just cause between Catholics and their eastern separated sisters and brothers.[34]

29. This more relaxed regulation concerning common sharing in sacred things (*communicatio in sacris*) with our brothers and sisters of the separated eastern churches is entrusted to the watchfulness and control of local ordinaries. They should consult together, and if it seems good also consult the ordinaries of the separated churches, and so direct relations among Christians by timely and effective precepts and regulations.

Conclusion

30. The holy council finds great joy in the earnest and fruitful collaboration of the eastern and western catholic churches, and at the same time makes the following declaration: All these legal arrangements are made in view of present conditions, until such time as the Catholic Church and the separated eastern churches unite together in the fullness of communion.

In the meantime, however, all Christians, eastern and western, are strongly urged to pray to God daily with fervor and constancy in order that, by the help of God's most holy Mother, all may be one. They should pray also that the fullness of the strength and consolation of the holy Spirit the Paraclete may be given to those many Christians, whatever church they belong to, who for their courageous profession of the name of Christ endure suffering and privation. "Let us all love one another with the affection of brothers and sisters, outdoing one another in showing honor" (Rom 12:10).

Each and all of these matters which are laid down in the decree have been approved by the Fathers. And we, by the apostolic power given by Christ to us, and in union with the venerable Fathers, approve, decree and prescribe them in the holy Spirit, and we order that what has been laid down by the council is to be promulgated to the glory of God.

a. Translated by P. A. O'Connell, SJ. Revised for this edition by Bernard Treacy, OP, editor, *Doctrine and Life*, Dublin.

1. Leo XIII, Apostolic Letter, *Orientalium dignitas*, 30 Nov. 1894: in Acta Leonis XIII, vol. XIV, pp. 201-202.

2. St. Leo IX, Letter *In terra pax*, 1053, "Ut enim"; Innocent III, Fourth Lateran Council, 1215, ch. IV, "Licet Graecos"; Letter *Inter quattuor*, 2 Aug. 1206, "Postulasti Postmodum"; Innocent IV, Letter *Cum de cetero*, 27 Aug. 1247; Letter *Sub catholicae*, 6 March 1254, introd.; Nicholas III, Instruction *Istud est memoriale*, 9 Oct. 1278; Leo X, Apostolic Letter *Accepimus nuper*, 18 May 1521; Paul III, Apostolic Letter *Dudum*, 23 Dec. 1534; Pius IV, Constitution *Romanus Pontifex*, 16 Feb. 1564, sec. 5; Clement VIII, Constitution *Magnus Dominus*, 23 Dec. 1595, sec. 10; Paul V, Constitution *Solet circumspecta*, 10 Dec. 1615, sec. 3; Benedict XIV, Encyclical *Demandatam*, 24 Dec. 1743, sec. 3; *Allatae sunt*, 26 June 1755, sec. 3, 6-19, 32; Pius VI, Encyclical *Catholicae communionis*, 24 May 1787; Pius IX, Letter *In suprema*, 6 Jan. 1848, sec. 3; Apostolic Letter *Ecclesiam Christi*, 26 Nov. 1853; Constitution *Romani Pontificis*, 6 Jan. 1862; Leo XIII, Apostolic Letter *Praeclara*, 20 June 1894, n. 7; *Orientalium dignitas*, 30 Nov. 1894, introd.; etc.

3. Pius XII, Motu proprio *Cleri sanctitati*, 2 June 1957, Can. 4.

4. Ibid. Can. 8: "without the permission of the Apostolic See", following the practice of preceding centuries. Similarly, with regard to baptized non-Catholics, Can. 11 states: "They may adopt the rite they prefer." In the text as proposed there is a positive ruling on the observance of rite for all persons and places.

5. See Leo XIII, Apostolic Letters *Orientalium dignitas*, 30 Nov. 1894; *Praeclara gratulationis*, 20 June 1894; and the documents cited in note 2, above.

6. Benedict XV, Motu proprio *Orientis catholici*, 15 Oct. 1917; Pius XI, Encyclical *Rerum orientalium*, 8 Sept. 1928, etc.

7. The practice of the Catholic Church in the time of Pius XI, Pius XII, John XXIII abundantly shows this tendency.

8. See First Council of Nicea, Can. 6; First Council of Constantinople, Can. 2 and 3; Chalcedon, Can. 28 and 9; Fourth Council of Constantinople, Can 17 and 21; Fourth Lateran Council, Can 5 and 30; Florence, decree *Pro Graecis*, etc.

9. First Council of Nicea, Can. 6; First Council of Constantinople, Can. 3; Fourth Council of Constantinople, Can. 17; Pius XII, Motu proprio *Cleri sanctitati*, Can. 216, Sec. 2, n. 1.

9a. "Prelate" in the Latin Code means "ordinary," strictly speaking (see Codex Juris Canonici, Can. 110), and has been used twice to translate *hierarcha*, where "Ordinary" would have sufficed. — Translator.

10. In the Ecumenical Councils: First Council of Nicea, Can. 6; First Council of Constantinople, Can. 3; Fourth Council of Constantinople, Can. 21; Fourth Lateran Council, Can. 5; Florence, decree *Pro Graecis*, 6 July 1439, sec. 9. See Pius XII, Motu proprio *Cleri sanctitati*, 2 June 1957, Can. 219, etc.

11. See above, note 8.

12. See Council of Ephesus, Can. 8; Clement VIII, *Decet Romanum Pontificem*, 23 Feb. 1596; Pius VII, Apostolic Letter *In universalis Ecclesiae*, 22 Feb. 1807; Pius XII, Motu proprio *Cleri sanctitati*, 2 June 1957, Can. 324-339; Council of Carthage, 419, Can. 17.

13. See Council of Carthage, 419, Can. 17, 57; Chalcedon, 451, Can. 12; Innocent I, Letter *Et onus et honor*, about 415:"Nam quid sciscitaris"; Nicholas I, Letter *Ad consulta vestra*, 13 Nov. 866:"A quo autem"; Innocent III, Letter *Rex regum*, 25 Feb. 1204; Leo XII, Apostolic Constitution *Petrus apostolorum princeps*, 15 Aug. 1824; Leo XIII, Apostolic Letter *Christi Domini*, 1895; Pius XII, Motu proprio *Cleri sanctitati*, 2 June 1957, Can 159.

14. See Innocent IV, Letter *Sub catholicae*, 6 March 1254, sec. 3, n. 4; Second Council of Lyons, 1274 (Profession of Faith presented by Michael Palaeologus to Gregory X); Eugene IV, in Council of Florence, Constitution *Exultate Deo*, 22 Nov. 1439, sec. 11; Clement VIII, Instruction *Sanctissimus*, 31 Aug. 1595; Benedict XIV, Constitution *Etsi pastoralis*, 26 May 1742, sec. II, n. 1, sec. III, n. 1, etc.; Council of Laodicea, 347-381, Can. 48; Council of Sis. of the Armenians, 1342; Council of Lebanon of the Maronites, 1736, Pt. II. ch. III, n. 2, and other particular Councils.

15. See Instruction of the holy Office to the Bishop of Spis, 1783; the Sacred Congregation of Propaganda, for the Copts, 15 March 1790, n. XIII; Decree of 6 Oct. 1863, C, a; the Sacred Congregation for the eastern church, 1 May 1948; the Reply of the holy Office, 22 April 1896, with the letter of 19 May 1896.

16. Code of Canon Law, Can. 782, sec. 4; Decree of the Sacred Congregation for the eastern church, *On the Administration of the Sacrament of Confirmation to Faithful of the eastern churches by Latin Priests Who Have This Faculty for Faithful of Their Own Rite*, 1 May 1948.

17. See Council of Laodicae, 347-381, Can. 29; St Nicephorus of Constantinople, ch. 14; Council of Duin of the Armenians, 719, Can. 31; St Theodore Studites, serm. 21; St Nicholas I, *Letter Ad consulta vestra*, 13 Nov. 866:"In quorum Apostolorum","Nosse cupitis","Quod interrogatis","Praeterea consulitis","Si die Dominico"; and particular Councils.

18. This is something new, at least where there is an obligation of assisting at the Sacred Liturgy. However, it does correspond to the liturgical day among the Orientals.

19. See Canons of the Apostles, 8 and 9; Council of Antioch, 341, Can. 2; Timothy of Alexandria, interr. 3; Innocent III, Consti-

tution *Quia divinae,* 4 Jan. 1215; and very many more recent particular Councils of tho eastern churches.

19a. *Hierarcha* in eastern terminology means "Ordinary"; loci has to be added to indicate "local ordinary" — Translator.

20. While safeguarding the principle of territorial jurisdiction, the intention in this canon, for the good of souls, is to make provision for the situation which arises from plurality of jurisdiction over the same territory.

21. See First Council of Nicea, Can. 18; Council of Neocaesarea, 314-325, Can. 12; Council of Sardica, 343, Can. 8; St Leo the Great, Letter *Omnium quidem,* 13 Jan. 444; Chalcedon, Can. 6; Fourth Council of Constantinople, Can. 23, 26; etc.

22. The subdiaconate is considered a minor order by many of the eastern churches, but by the Motu proprio *Cleri sanctitati* of Pius XII there are prescribed in its regard the obligations of major orders. The canon here proposes a return to the ancient discipline of each of the churches regarding the obligations of subdeacons, thus derogating from the common law laid down in *Cleri sanctitati.*

23. See Pius XII, Motu proprio *Crebrae allatae,* 22 Feb. 1949, Can. 32, sec. 2, n. 5 (power of the patriarchs to dispense from the form); *Cleri sanctitati,* 2 June 1957, Can. 267 (power of the patriarchs regarding *sanatio in radice);* the Holy Office and the Sacred Congregation for the eastern church granted in 1957 the power of dispensing from the form and of applying *sanatio* because of defect of form for five years: "Outside the patriarchates, to metropolitans and to other local ordinaries É who have no superior under the holy See."

24. See St. Leo tho Great, Letter *Quod saepissime,* 15 April 454: "Petitionem quem"; St Nicephorus of Constantinople, ch. 13; Council of Patriarch Sergius, 18 Sept. 1596, Can 17; Pius VI, Apostolic Letter Assueto paterne, 8 April 1775; etc.

25. Constitution on the Sacred Liturgy (D.l).

26. See Clement VIII, Instruction Sanctissimus, 31 Aug. 1595, sec. 6: "Si ipsi Graeci"; the holy Office, 7 June 1673, ad 1, 3; 13 March 1727, ad l; the Sacred Congregation of Propaganda, Decree, 18 Aug. 1913, Art. 33; Decree, 14 Aug. 1914, Art. 27; Decree, 27 March 1916, Art. 14; Sacred Congregation for the eastern church, Decree, 1 March 1929, Art. 36; Decree, 4 May 1930, Art. 41.

27. See Council of Laodicea, 347-381, Can. 18; Council of Mar Isaac of the Chaldeans, 410, Can. 15; St Nerses Glaien of the Armenians, 1166; Innocent IV, Letter Sub *catholicae,* 6 March 1254, sec. 8; Benedict XIV, Constitution *Etsi pastoralis,* 26 May 1742, sec. 7, n. 5; Instruction *Eo quamvis tempore,* 4 May 1745 sec. 42 ff.; and more recent particular Councils: Armenians (1911), Copts (1898), Maronites (1736), Rumanians (1872), Ruthenians (1891), Syrians (1888).

28. From eastern tradition.

29. From the sense of the Bulls of Union of the different Catholic eastern churches.

30. An obligation established by the Council regarding the members of the separated eastern churches and all orders of whatever degree, whether of divine or ecclesiastical right.

31. This doctrine is also held in the separated churches.

32. St Basil the Great, Canonical Letter to Amphilochius, PG 32, 669 B.

33. As foundation for this moderation of the law are considered the following: (a) validity of the sacraments; (b) good faith and good disposition; (c) the necessity of eternal salvation; (d) the absence of one's own priest; (e) the exclusion both of the dangers to be avoided and of formal adhesion to error.

34. There is question here of so-called "extra-sacramental sharing in worship." It is the council which grants this mitigation, while all necessary conditions are observed.

35. See Rom 12:10.

DECREE ON THE MASS MEDIA[a]

Inter Mirifica
4 December, 1963

1. The genius of humankind, especially in our times, has produced marvellous technical inventions from creation, with God's help. Mother church is particularly interested in those which directly touch the human spirit and which have opened up new avenues of easy communication of all kinds of news, ideas and directives. Chief among them are those means of communication which of their nature can reach and influence not just single individuals but the very masses and even the whole of human society. These are the press, the cinema, radio, television and others of like nature. These can rightly be called the means of social communication.

2. Mother church knows that if these means are properly used they can be of considerable benefit to humanity. They contribute greatly to relaxation, the enrichment of people's minds and the spread and consolidation of the kingdom of God. But the church also knows that they can be used in ways which are damaging and contrary to the Creator's design. Indeed, she grieves with a mother's sorrow at the harm all too often inflicted on society by their misuse.

The holy synod shares the solicitude of popes and bishops in a matter of such importance and feels that it is its duty to treat of the main problems connected with the mass media. It is confident that the teaching and directives set out here will contribute not only to the salvation of Christians but also to the progress of all of humanity.

Chapter I

3. The Catholic Church was founded by Christ our Lord to bring salvation to everybody and consequently is duty bound to preach the gospel. It believes that its task involves using the media to proclaim the good news of salvation as well as teaching people how to use them properly.

The church has an innate right to use and own any of these media which are necessary or useful for the formation of Christians and for all of its pastoral work. It is the duty of pastors of souls to instruct and direct the faithful in their use, so that they will contribute to their own salvation and perfection and that of all of humanity.

For the rest, it will be principally for lay people to animate the media with a christian and human spirit and to ensure that they fulfill humanity's hopes for them, in accordance with God's design.

4. If the media are to be handled properly, it is imperative that all who use them know and apply faithfully the principles of the moral order. They should take into account, first of all, the content, which each medium conveys in its own way. They should also take account of the circumstances in which the communication takes place — its aim, that is to say, and the people, the place, the time, etc. — for these can modify and even totally alter its morality. In this regard, particular importance may attach to the manner in which any given medium achieves its effect. A particular medium may have very considerable impact, so much so that, especially if inexperienced, people will only with difficulty advert to it, control it or, if need be, reject it.[b]

5. It is essential that the consciences of all those involved be properly formed on the use of the media, especially with regard to certain matters which are particularly controversial today.

The first of these is information, or the gathering of news and its dissemination. Because of the progress of modern society and the increasing mutual interdependence of its members, it is clear that information is most useful and, very often, indispensable. If news of facts and happenings is made public without delay, everyone will have constant access to sufficient information and thus will be able to contribute effectively to the common good. Further, it will be easier for everyone to contribute to the prosperity and the progress of society as a whole.

There exists therefore in human society a right to information on matters which are of concern to people either as individuals or as members of society, according to each one's circumstances. The proper exercise of this right demands that the content of the communication be true and — within the limits set by justice and charity — complete, and that it be presented decently and appropriately. This means that in the gathering and in the publication of news the moral law and people's legitimate rights and dignity should be upheld. Not all knowledge is profitable, but on the other hand "love builds up" (1 Cor 8 :1).

6. The second question bears on the relation between moral standards and what people term the rights of art. The controversies to which this problem increasingly gives rise frequently trace their origin to a false understanding of ethics and aesthetics, and the council consequently asserts that all must accept the absolute primacy of the objective moral order. It alone is superior to and is capable of harmonizing all forms of human activity, even the most admirable, not excepting art. Only the moral order touches people in

the totality of their being as God's rational creatures, called to a supernatural destiny. If the moral order is fully and faithfully observed, it leads them to perfection and happiness.

7. Lastly, the reporting, description or representation of moral evil by the media can lead to a deeper knowledge and exploration of humanity and, by employing suitable dramatic effects, to a portrayal of the true and the good in all their splendor. If, however, this is to be more profitable than harmful to souls, the moral law must be faithfully observed, especially when dealing with matters best treated with reserve or with matters which easily arouse people's base desires, wounded as they are by original sin.

8. Public opinion exercises enormous influence nowadays over the lives, private or public, of all citizens, of whatever class. It is therefore necessary that all members of society meet the demands of justice and charity in this domain and that they try, through the media, to form and expand sound public opinion.

9. Recourse to the media is a matter of free choice and carries special responsibilities for readers, viewers and listeners. They should choose wisely, in a manner calculated to encourage whatever is of value morally, culturally and artistically; they should avoid whatever might be a cause or occasion of spiritual harm to themselves or a source of danger to others through bad example, and should avoid whatever stands in the way of good, and facilitates harmful, communications. This happens most frequently when financial support is given to media which are run on a commercial basis.[c]

If they are to obey the moral law, those who use the media ought to ascertain in time what opinions are held by competent authorities in such matters and ought to conform to them as a right conscience would dictate. They should take the proper steps to guide and form their consciences so that they may more readily resist less wholesome influences and fully support the good.

10. Those who receive the media, and especially the young, should learn moderation and discipline in their use of them. They should aim to understand fully what they see, hear and read. They should discuss them with their teachers and with experts in such matters and should learn to judge them properly. Parents on their part should remember that it is their duty to see that entertainments, publications and such like which might endanger faith and morals do not enter their homes and that their children are not exposed to them elsewhere.

11. A special responsibility for the proper use of the media rests on journalists, writers, actors, designers, producers, programmers, distributors, operators, sellers, critics — all those, in a word, who are in any way involved in making and transmitting communications. It is clear that a very great responsibility rests on all of these people in today's world: they have power to direct humankind along a good or along an evil path by the information they impart and the influence they exert.

It will be for them to regulate economic, political and artistic matters in their own sphere in a way that will not conflict with the common good. To achieve this result more surely, they will do well to form professional organizations capable of imposing on their members — if necessary by a formal pledge to observe a moral code — a respect for the moral law in the problems they encounter and in their activities.

They should always be mindful of the fact that a very large proportion of their readership and audience are young people who are in need of a press and entertainment which will provide wholesome diversion and will raise their minds to higher things. They should ensure that religious features are entrusted to serious and competent persons and are handled with due reverence.

12. Civil authorities have particular responsibilities in this field because of the common good, toward which the media are directed. It is the responsibility of the civil authority to defend and safeguard — especially for the press — a true and just freedom of information, for the progress of modern society demands it, and to foster religious, cultural and artistic values. It should guarantee to those who use the media the free exercise of their lawful rights. It is, further, the duty of the civil authorities to assist those projects which, despite their usefulness especially for the young, could not otherwise be attempted.

Finally, the civil authorities, who by law are committed to ensuring the well-being of the citizens, are also bound to ensure — by promulgating laws and rigorously enforcing them, thus combining justice with vigilance — that public morality and social progress are not gravely endangered by the misuse of the media. The liberty of individuals and groups is not in the least compromised by such vigilance, especially where serious guarantees cannot be given by those who are professionally engaged in the media.

Special measures should be taken to protect young people from publications and entertainments harmful to them.

Chapter II

13. All the members of the church should make a concerted effort to ensure that the media are utilized in the service of the many works of the apostolate without delay and as energetically as possible, where and when they are needed. They should forestall projects likely to prove harmful, especially in those re-

gions where moral and religious progress would require their intervention more urgently.

Pastors of souls should act especially promptly in this matter, since it is closely linked with their task of preaching the Gospel. Lay people who work professionally in the media should endeavor to bear witness to Christ: first of all, by doing their work competently and in an apostolic spirit, secondly by collaborating directly, each one according to her or his ability, in the pastoral activity of the church, making a technical, economic, cultural or artistic contribution.

14. First of all, a wholesome press should be encouraged. However, with a view to forming readers imbued with a truly christian spirit, an authentically catholic press ought to be established and supported. Such a press, whether it be established and directed by the ecclesiastical authorities or by individual Catholics, would have for its explicit purpose to form, to consolidate and to promote a public opinion in conformity with the natural law and with catholic teaching and directives. It would also publish news of the church's life and informed comment on it. The faithful should be reminded of the need to read and circulate the catholic press if they are to judge all events from a christian standpoint.

The production and screening of films which provide wholesome entertainment and are worthwhile culturally and artistically should be promoted and effectively guaranteed, especially films destined for the young. This is best achieved by supporting and co-ordinating productions and projects by reputable producers and distributors, by marking the launching of worthwhile films with favorable criticism or the awarding of prizes, by supporting and co-ordinating cinemas managed by Catholics and people of integrity.

Likewise, decent radio and television programs

should be effectively supported, especially those suited to the family. Ample encouragement should be given to catholic transmissions which invite listeners and viewers to share in the life of the church and which convey religious truths. Where opportune, catholic stations should be established and their transmissions should be marked by high quality and effectiveness.

The noble and ancient art of the theatre has been widely popularized by the media. One should take steps to ensure that it contributes to the human and moral formation of its audiences.

15. Priests, religious and laity should be trained at once to meet the needs described above. They should acquire the competence needed to use the media for the apostolate.

First, lay people must be given the necessary technical, doctrinal and moral formation. To this end, schools, institutes or faculties must be provided in sufficient number, where journalists, writers for films, radio and television, and anyone else concerned, may receive a complete formation, imbued with the christian spirit, especially with regard to the church's social teaching. Actors should also be instructed and helped so that their gifts too can benefit society. Lastly, literary critics and critics of films, radio, television and the rest should be carefully prepared so that they will be fully competent in their respective spheres and will be trained and encouraged to give due consideration to morality in their critiques.

16. Since people of different ages and cultural backgrounds have access to the media, they need theoretical and practical formation in their proper use, a formation tailored not merely to the character of each medium but to the needs of each group. Projects designed to effect this, especially among the young, should be encouraged and multiplied in catholic

schools at all levels, in seminaries and lay apostolate associations and should be directed in accordance with the principles of christian morality. For quicker results, catholic teaching and discipline in this matter should be given and explained in the catechism.

17. It would be shameful if by their inactivity Catholics allowed the word of God to be silenced or obstructed by the technical difficulties which these media present and by their admittedly enormous cost. For this reason this holy synod reminds them that they have the obligation to maintain and assist catholic newspapers, periodicals, film-projects, radio and television stations and programs. For the main aim of all these is to propagate and defend the truth and to secure the permeation of society by christian values. At the same time the synod appeals strongly to groups or individuals who wield influence in technology or the economic field to give generously of their resources and of their knowledge for the support of the media, in so far as they are at the service of authentic culture and of the apostolate.

18. To make the church's multiple apostolate in the field of social communication more effective, a day is to be set aside each year in every diocese, at the bishop's discretion, on which the faithful will be reminded of their duties in this domain. They should be asked to pray for the success of the church's apostolate in this field and to contribute toward it, their contributions to be scrupulously employed for the support and the further development of the projects which the church has initiated in view of the needs of the catholic world.

19. A special office of the Holy See is at the disposal of the sovereign pontiff in the exercise of his supreme pastoral responsibility for the media.[1]

20. It is for bishops to oversee activities and projects of this sort in their own dioceses, to promote and,

where they touch the public apostolate, to regulate them, including those under the control of exempt religious.

21. An effective national apostolate requires acceptance of a common objective and combination of effort. This synod therefore decides and ordains that national offices for the press, the cinema, radio and television be established everywhere and be properly supported. The main task of these offices will be the formation of a right conscience in the faithful in their use of the media and to encourage and regulate everything done by Catholics in this domain.

In each country, the direction of these offices is to be entrusted to episcopal commissions or bishops appointed to do the task. The offices should also have on their staffs lay people who are technically qualified and instructed in catholic teaching.

22. The influence of the media extends beyond national frontiers, making individuals citizens of the world, as it were. National projects should, consequently, cooperate with each other at international level. The offices mentioned in paragraph 21 should each collaborate closely with its corresponding international catholic organization. These international organizations are approved by the Holy See alone and are responsible to it.

Conclusions

32. The council expressly directs the commission of the Holy See referred to in par. 19 to publish a pastoral instruction, with the help of experts from various countries, to ensure that all the principles and rules of the council on the media be put into effect.

24. For the rest, the council is confident that all the daughters and sons of the church will welcome the principles and regulations contained in this decree and will observe them faithfully. Thus, they will not

suffer damage as they use the media. Rather will the media, like salt and light, add savor to the earth and light to the world. Further, it invites all people of good will, especially those who control the media, to use them solely for the good of humanity, for its fate becomes more and more dependent on their right use. The name of the Lord will thus be glorified by these modern inventions as it was in former times by the masterpieces of art; as the apostle said: "Jesus Christ is the same yesterday, today, and forever" (Heb 13:8).

a. Translated and revised for this edition by AF. The full title is the *Decree on the Means of Social Communication*. In this decree the word 'media' is given a wider meaning than it has in current usage. It covers theatre, cinema, all of radio and television, and not merely newspapers or news transmissions by radio and television.

b. There is reference here to subliminal and subaudial messages in television, radio, cinema, etc. Article 4 is very condensed — 'distilled from three different passages of the original schema' (Karlheiz Schmidthüs, in his commentary on the decree, Vorgrimler, vol. 1, p. 96). Shmidthüs explained what it is about as follows : 'There are communications and communications, we are told: it depends whether what is conveyed accords with the nature of the medium used, whether it is conveyed with proper intentions, who conveys it, whether its source is a private or an official one, what audience it is addressed to, and therefore how far the audience is able to form a critical judgment about it, how far the reader, listener, or viewer is likely to be able to evaluate it, at what time and place it is conveyed, and therefore who has access to it. And finally the passage points out the special effect each medium has on the senses, and the overpowering influence all may exert on the inexperienced. ... A series of pictures may be so dramatic as to overwhelm people's judgment, leaving them defenceless against the impressions to which they are exposed' (op. cit., pp. 96-97).

c. Karlbeinz Schmidthüs explained: 'First readers, listeners and viewers are reminded that they can and must use their freedom to make a selection among the material offered by the media of communication, and that their selection — at least where the media are run on a commercial basis — can influence that material itself, since its commercial success depends on satisfactory sales and attendance.' (commentary on the decree, Vorgrimler, op. cit., vol. 1, p 100).

1. The council fathers, however, willingly grant the wish of the Secretariat for the Press and Entertainments and respectfully request the Supreme Pontiff to extend the duties and competence

of this office to all the media, including the press and to appoint experts to it, including lay people, from various countries. (This secretariat is the "office" referred to in the text. Pope Paul VI extended the competence of the secretariat on 2 April 1964, by the Motu Proprio, In *Fructibus Multis*. The secretariat was renamed The Pontifical Commission for the Means of Social Communication. It was this body which published *The Pastoral Instruction on the Means of Social Communication*, whose publication was requested in the decree (no 32) and which is to be found in F1, pp. 293-249. Editor.

DECLARATION ON RELIGIOUS LIBERTY[a]

Dignitatis Humanae
7 December, 1965

**On the Right of the Person and Communities
to Social and Civil Liberty in Religious Matters**

1. People nowadays are becoming increasingly conscious of the dignity of the human person;[1] a growing number demand that people should exercise fully their own judgment and a responsible freedom in their actions and should not be subject to external pressure or coercion but inspired by a sense of duty. At the same time, to prevent excessive restriction of the rightful freedom of individuals and associations, they demand constitutional limitation of the powers of government. This demand for freedom in human society is concerned chiefly with the affairs of the human spirit, and especially with what concerns the free practice of religion in society. This Vatican council pays careful attention to these spiritual aspirations and, with a view to declaring to what extent they are in accord with truth and justice, searches the sacred tradition and teaching of the church, from which it draws forth new insights in harmony with the old.

The sacred council begins by proclaiming that God himself has made known to the human race how people by serving him can be saved and reach happiness in Christ. We believe that this one true religion exists in the Catholic and Apostolic church, to which the Lord Jesus entrusted the task of spreading it among all peoples when he said to the apostles:"Go therefore and make disciples of all nations baptizing them in the name of the Father and of the Son and of the Holy Spirit, teaching them to observe all that I have commanded you" (Mt 18:19-20). All are bound to seek the truth, especially in what concerns God and the church, and to embrace it and hold on to it as they come to know it.

The sacred council likewise proclaims that these obligations bind people's consciences. Truth can impose itself on the human mind by the force of its own truth, which wins over the mind with both gentleness and power. So, while the religious freedom which human beings demand in fulfilling their obligation to worship God has to do with freedom from coercion in civil society, it leaves intact the traditional catholic teaching on the moral obligation of individuals and societies towards the true religion and the one church of Christ. Furthermore, in dealing with the question of liberty the sacred council intends to develop the teaching of recent popes on the inviolable rights of the human person and on the constitutional order of society.

Chapter I

THE GENERAL PRINCIPLE OF RELIGIOUS FREEDOM

2. The Vatican council declares that the human person has a right to religious freedom. Freedom of this kind means that everyone should be immune from coercion by individuals, social groups and every human power so that, within due limits, no men or women are forced to act against their convictions nor are any persons to be restrained from acting in accordance with their convictions in religious matters in

private or in public, alone or in association with others. The council further declares that the right to religious freedom is based on the very dignity of the human person as known through the revealed word of God and by reason itself.[2] This right of the human person to religious freedom must be given such recognition in the constitutional order of society as will make it a civil right.

It is in accordance with their dignity that all human beings, because they are persons, that is, beings endowed with reason and free will and therefore bearing personal responsibility, are both impelled by their nature and bound by a moral obligation to seek the truth, especially religious truth. They are also bound to adhere to the truth once they come to know it and to direct their whole lives in accordance with the demands of truth. But human beings cannot satisfy this obligation in a way that is in keeping with their own nature unless they enjoy both psychological freedom and immunity from external coercion. Therefore, the right to religious freedom is based not on subjective attitude but on the very nature of the individual person. For this reason, the right to such immunity continues to exist even in those who do not live up to their obligation of seeking the truth and adhering to it. The exercise of this right cannot be interfered with as long as the just requirements of public order are observed.

3. This becomes even clearer if one considers that the highest norm of human life is the divine law itself — eternal, objective and universal, by which God orders, directs and governs the whole world and the ways of the human community according to a plan conceived in his wisdom and love. God has enabled the human person to share in this law so that, under the gentle disposition of divine providence, many may be able to arrive at an ever deeper knowledge of

unchangeable truth.[3] For this reason everybody has the duty and consequently the right to seek the truth in religious matters so that, through the use of appropriate means, they may form prudent judgments of conscience which are sincere and true.

The search for truth, however, must be carried out in a manner that is appropriate to the dignity and social nature of the human person: that is, by free enquiry with the help of teaching or instruction, communication and dialogue. It is by these means that people share with each other the truth they have discovered, or think they have discovered, in such a way that they help one another in the search for truth. Moreover, it is by personal assent that they must adhere to the truth they have discovered.

The human person sees and recognizes the demands of the divine law through conscience. All are bound to follow their conscience faithfully in every sphere of activity so that they may come to God, who is their last end. Therefore, the individual must not be forced to act against conscience nor be prevented from acting according to conscience, especially in religious matters. The reason is because the practice of religion of its very nature consists primarily of those voluntary and free internal acts by which human beings direct themselves to God. Acts of this kind cannot be commanded or forbidden by any merely human authority.[4] But the social nature of the human person requires that individuals give external expression to these internal acts of religion, that they communicate with others on religious matters, and profess religion in community. Consequently, to deny the free exercise of religion in society, when the just requirements of public order are observed, is to do an injustice to the human person and to the very order established by God for human beings.

Furthermore, the private and public acts of religion,

by which people direct themselves to God, according to their convictions, transcend of their very nature the earthly and temporal order of things. Therefore, the civil authority, to which is committed the care of the common good in the temporal order, must recognize and look with favor on the religious life of the citizens. But, if it presumes to control or restrict religious activity it must be judged to have exceeded the limits of its power.

4. The freedom or immunity from coercion in religious matters which is the right of individuals must also be accorded to people when they act in community. Religious communities are a requirement of the social character of human nature and of religion itself.

Therefore, provided the just requirements of public order are not violated, these groups have a right to immunity, so that they may organize themselves according to their own principles. They must be allowed to honor the supreme Godhead in public worship, help their members to practise their religion and strengthen them with religious instruction, and promote institutions in which members may work together to organize their own lives according to their religious principles.

Religious communities also have the right not to be hindered by legislation or administrative action by the civil authority in the selection, training, appointment and transfer of their own ministers, in communicating with religious authorities and communities in other parts of the world, in erecting buildings for religious purposes, and in the acquisition and use of the property they need.

Religious communities have the further right not to be prevented from publicly teaching and bearing witness to their beliefs by the spoken or written word. However, in spreading religious belief and in introducing religious practices everybody must, at all times, avoid any action which seems to suggest coercion or dishonest or unworthy persuasion, especially when dealing with the uneducated or the poor. Such a manner of acting must be considered an abuse of one's own right and an infringement of the rights of others.

Also included in the right to religious freedom is the right of religious groups not to be prevented from freely demonstrating the special value of their teaching for the organization of society and the inspiration of human activity in general. Finally, the right of people, prompted by their own religious sense, to be free to hold meetings or establish educational, cultural, charitable and social organizations is based on their nature as social beings and on the nature of religion.

5. Every family, in that it is a society with its own basic rights, has the right freely to organize its own religious life in the home under the control of the parents. These have the right to decide in accordance with their own religious beliefs the form of religious upbringing which is to be given to their children. The civil authority must therefore recognize the right of parents to choose in genuine freedom schools or other systems of education. Parents should not be subjected directly or indirectly to unjust burdens because of this freedom of choice. Furthermore, the rights of parents are violated if their children are compelled to attend classes which are not in agreement with the religious beliefs of the parents or if there is but a single compulsory system of education from which all religious instruction is excluded.

6. The common good of society consists in the sum total of those conditions of social life which enable people to achieve a fuller measure of perfection with greater ease. It consists especially in safeguarding the rights and duties of the human person.[5] For this reason, the protection of the right to religious freedom is

the common responsibility of individual citizens, social groups, civil authorities, the church and other religious communities. Each of these has its own special responsibility in the matter according to its particular duty to promote the common good.

The protection and promotion of the inviolable rights of the human person is an essential duty of every civil authority.[6] The civil authority must therefore undertake effectively to safeguard the religious freedom of all the citizens by just legislation and other appropriate means. It must help to create conditions favorable to the fostering of religious life so that the citizens will be really in a position to exercise their religious rights and fulfill their religious duties and so that society itself may enjoy the benefits of justice and peace, which result from people's faithfulness to God and his holy will.[7]

If because of the circumstances of a particular people special civil recognition is given to one religious community in the constitutional organization of a State, the right of all citizens and religious communities to religious freedom must be recognized and respected as well.

Finally, the civil authority must see to it that equality of the citizens before the law, which is itself an element of the common good of society, is never violated either openly or covertly for religious reasons and that there is no discrimination between citizens.

From this it follows that it is wrong for a public authority to compel its citizens by force or fear or any other means to profess or repudiate any religion or to prevent anyone from joining or leaving a religious body. There is even more serious transgression of God's will and of the sacred rights of the individual person and the family of nations when force is applied to destroy or repress religion either throughout the whole world or in a single region or in a particular community.

7. The right to freedom in matters of religion is exercised in human society. For this reason, its use is subject to certain regulatory norms.

In availing of any freedom people must respect the moral principle of personal and social responsibility: in exercising their rights individuals and social groups are bound by the moral law to have regard for the rights of others, their own duties to others and the common good of all. Everybody must be treated with justice and humanity.

Furthermore, since civil society has the right to protect itself against possible abuses committed in the name of religious freedom, the responsibility of providing such protection rests especially with the civil authority. However, this must not be done in an arbitrary manner or by the unfair practice of favoritism but in accordance with legal principles which are in conformity with the objective moral order. These principles are necessary for the effective protection of the rights of all citizens and for the peaceful settlement of conflicts of rights. They are also necessary for an adequate protection of that just public peace which is to be found where people live together in good order and true justice. They are required too for the necessary protection of public morality. All these matters are basic to the common good and belong to what is called public order. For the rest, the principle of the integrity of freedom in society should continue to be upheld. According to this principle, people's freedom should be given the fullest possible recognition and should not be curtailed except when and in so far as is necessary

8. People nowadays are subjected to a variety of pressures and run the risk of being prevented from acting in accordance with their own free judgment. On the other hand, there are many who, under the

pretext of freedom, seem inclined to reject all submission to authority and to make light of the duty of
obedience.

For this reason this Vatican council urges everyone,
especially those responsible for educating others, to
form people who will respect the moral order, will
obey lawful authority and be lovers of true freedom
— people, that is, who will form their own judgments
in the light of truth, direct their activities with a sense
of responsibility, and strive for what is true and just in
willing cooperation with others.

Religious liberty therefore should have this further
purpose and aim of enabling people to act with
greater responsibility in fulfilling their own obligations in society.

Chapter II

RELIGIOUS FREEDOM IN
THE LIGHT OF REVELATION

9. What this Vatican council has to say about the
individual's right to religious freedom is based on the
dignity of the person, the demands of which have
become more fully known to human reason through
centuries of experience. Furthermore, this teaching on
freedom is rooted in divine revelation, and for this
reason, Christians are bound to respect it all the more
conscientiously. Although revelation does not affirm,
in so many words, the right to immunity from external coercion in religious matters, it nevertheless
makes known the dignity of the human person in all
its fullness. It shows us Christ's respect for the freedom with which people are to fulfill their duty of

believing the word of God, and it teaches us the spirit which disciples of such a Master must acknowledge and follow in all things. All this throws light on the general principles on which the teaching of this declaration on religious freedom is based. Above all, religious freedom in society is in complete harmony with the act of christian faith.

10. One of the key truths in catholic teaching, a truth that is contained in the word of God and is constantly preached by the Fathers,[8] is that human beings should respond to the word of God freely, and that therefore nobody is to be forced to embrace the faith against their will.[9] The act of faith of its very nature is a free act. The human person, redeemed by Christ the Saviour and called through Jesus Christ to be an adopted child of God,[10] can assent to God's self-revelation only through being drawn by the Father[11] and through submitting to God with a faith that is reasonable and free. It is therefore, fully in accordance with the nature of faith that in religious matters every form of human coercion should be excluded. Consequently, the principle of religious liberty contributes in no small way to the development of a situation in which human beings can without hindrance be invited to the christian faith, embrace it of their own free will and give it practical expression in every sphere of their lives.

11. God calls people to serve him in spirit and in truth. Consequently, they are bound to him in conscience, but not coerced. God has regard for the dignity of the human person which he himself created; human persons are to be guided by their own judgment and to enjoy freedom. This fact received its fullest manifestation in Christ Jesus in whom God perfectly revealed himself and his ways. For Christ, who is our master and Lord[12] and at the same time is meek and humble of heart,[13] acted patiently in attract-

ing and inviting his disciples.[14] He supported and confirmed his preaching by miracles to invite the faith of his hearers and give them assurance, but not to coerce them.[15] He did indeed denounce the unbelief of his listeners but he left vengeance in God's hands until the day of judgement.[16] When he sent his apostles into the world he said to them: "The one who believes and is baptized will be saved; the one who does not believe will be condemned" (Mk 16:16). He himself recognized that weeds had been sown through the wheat but ordered that both be allowed to grow until the harvest, which will come at the end of the world.[17]

He did not wish to be a political Messiah who would dominate by force[18] but preferred to call himself the Son of Man who came to serve, and "to give his life as a ransom for many" (Mk 10:45). He showed himself as the perfect Servant of God[19] who "will not break a bruised reed or quench a smouldering wick" (Mt 12:20). He recognized civil authority and its rights when he ordered tribute to be paid to Caesar, but he gave clear warning that the greater rights of God must be respected: "Render therefore to Caesar the things that are Caesar's, and to God, the things that are God's" (Mt 22:21). Finally, he brought his revelation to perfection when he accomplished on the cross the work of redemption by which he achieved salvation and true freedom for the human race. For he bore witness to the truth[20] but refused to use force to impose it on those who spoke out against it. His kingdom does not establish its claims by force,[21] but is established by bearing witness to and hearing the truth and it grows by the love with which Christ, lifted up on the cross, draws people to himself.[22]

Taught by Christ's word and example the apostles followed the same path. From the very beginnings of the church, the disciples of Christ strove to persuade people to confess Christ as Lord, not however, by applying coercion or with the use of techniques unworthy of the Gospel but, above all, by the power of the word of God.[23] They vigorously proclaimed to all the plan of God the Saviour, "who desires that everybody be saved and come to the knowledge of the truth"(1 Tim 2:4). At the same time, however, they showed respect for the weak, even when these were in error, and in this way made it clear how"each of us shall give account of ourselves to God" (Rom 14:12)[24] and for that reason we are all bound to obey our conscience. Like Christ, the apostles were constantly bent on bearing witness to the truth of God and they showed the greatest courage in speaking"the word of God with boldness" (Acts 4:31)[25] before people and rulers. With a firm faith they upheld the truth that the Gospel itself is indeed the power of God for the salvation of all who believe.[26] They therefore despised"all worldly weapons"[27] and followed the example of Christ's meekness and gentleness as they preached the word of God with full confidence in the divine power of that word to destroy those forces hostile to God[28] and lead people to believe in and serve Christ.[29] Like their Master, the apostles too recognized legitimate civil authority: "Let every person be subject to the governing authorities . . . the one who resists the authorities resists what God has appointed" (Rom 13:1-2).[30] At the same time, they were not afraid to speak out against public authority when it opposed God's holy will:"We must obey God rather than men and women" (Acts 5:29).[31] This is the path which innumerable martyrs and faithful have followed through the centuries all over the world.

12. The church, therefore, faithful to the truth of the Gospel, follows in the path of Christ and the apostles when it recognizes the principle that religious liberty is in keeping with human dignity and divine revela-

tion and gives it its support. Through the ages it has preserved and handed on the doctrine which it has received from its Master and the apostles. Although, in the life of the people of God in its pilgrimage, through the vicissitudes of human history, there have at times appeared patterns of behavior which was not in keeping with the spirit of the Gospel and were even opposed to it, it has always remained the teaching of the church that no one is to be coerced into believing.

Thus, the leaven of the Gospel has long been at work in people's minds and has contributed greatly to a wider recognition by them in the course of time of their dignity as persons. It has contributed too to the growth of the conviction that in religious matters the human person should be kept free from all manner of coercion in civil society.

13. Among those things which pertain to the good of the church and indeed to the good of society here on earth, things which must everywhere and at all times be safeguarded and kept free from all harm, the most outstanding surely is that the church enjoy that freedom of action which its responsibility for human salvation requires.[32] This is a sacred liberty with which the only-begotten Son of God endowed the church which he purchased with his blood. Indeed, it belongs so intimately to the church that to attack it is to oppose the will of God. The freedom of the church is the fundamental principle governing relations between the church and public authorities and the entire civil order.

As the spiritual authority appointed by Christ the Lord with the duty, imposed by divine command, of going into the whole world and preaching the Gospel to every creature,[33] the church claims freedom for itself in human society and before every public authority. The church also claims freedom for itself as a society of people who have the right to live in civil society in accordance with the demands of the christian faith.[34]

When the principle of religious freedom is not just proclaimed in words or incorporated in law but is implemented sincerely in practice, only then does the church enjoy in law and in fact those stable conditions which give it the independence necessary for fulfilling its divine mission. Ecclesiastical authorities have been insistent in claiming this independence in society.[35] At the same time the christian faithful, in common with everybody else, have the civil right of freedom from interference, the right to lead their lives according to their conscience. A harmony exists therefore, between the freedom of the church and that religious freedom which must be recognized as the right of every individual and every community and must be sanctioned by constitutional law.

14. In order to satisfy the divine command: "Make disciples of all nations" (Mt 28:19), the Catholic church must spare no effort to ensure "that the word of the Lord may speed on and triumph" (2 Th 3:1).

The church therefore insistently urges its children, in the first place, to see to it that "supplications, prayers, intercessions and thanksgivings be made for all of humanity.... This is good and is acceptable in the sight of God our Savior, who desires all humanity to be saved and to come to the knowledge of the truth" (1 Tim 2:1-4).

However, in forming their consciences the faithful must pay careful attention to the holy and certain teaching of the church.[36] For the Catholic Church is by the will of Christ the teacher of truth. It is its duty to proclaim and teach with authority the truth which is Christ and, at the same time, to declare and confirm by her authority the principles of the moral order which spring from human nature itself. In addition, towards those who are not of the faith, Christians should behave properly, "in the holy Spirit, genuine love, truthful speech" (2 Cor 6:6-7), and should try, even if it involves shedding their blood, to spread the light of life with all confidence[37] and apostolic courage.

Disciples owe it to Christ, their Master, to grow daily in his knowledge of the truth they have received from him, to be faithful in announcing it and vigorous in defending it without having recourse to methods which are contrary to the spirit of the Gospel. At the same time, the love of Christ urges them to treat with love, prudence and patience[38] those who are in error or ignorance with regard to the faith. They must take into account their duties towards Christ, the life-giving Word whom they must proclaim, the rights of the human person and the measure of grace which God has given to everybody through Christ in calling them freely to accept and profess the faith.

15. It is certain, therefore, that the people of today want to profess their religion freely in private and in public. Indeed, it is a fact that religious freedom has already been declared a civil right in most constitutions and has been given solemn recognition in international documents.[39]

But there are forms of government under which, despite constitutional recognition of the freedom of religious worship, the public authorities themselves try to deter the citizens from professing their religion and make life particularly difficult and dangerous for religious bodies.

This sacred council gladly welcomes the first of these two facts as a happy sign of the times. In sorrow however, it denounces the second as deplorable. It urges Catholics and appeals to all peoples to consider very carefully how necessary religious liberty is, especially in the present condition of the human family.

It is clear that with the passage of time all nations are coming into a closer unity, people of different cultures and religions are being bound together by closer links, and there is a growing awareness of individual responsibility. Consequently, to establish and strengthen peaceful relations and harmony in the human race, religious freedom must be given effective constitutional protection everywhere and people's supreme right and duty to be free to lead a religious life in society must be respected.

May God, the Father of all, grant that the human family, by carefully observing the principle of religious liberty in society, may be brought by the grace of Christ and the power of the holy Spirit to that "glorious freedom of the children of God" (Rom 8: 21) which is sublime and everlasting.

a. Translated by Laurence Ryan, Bishop of Kildare and Leighlin, who also revised it for this edition.

1. See John XXIII, Encyclical *Pacem In Terris,* 11 April 1963: AAS 55 (1963), p. 279; ibid., p. 265; Pius XII, Radio Message, 24 Dec. 1944: AAS 37 (1945), 14.

2. See John XXIII, Encyclical *Pacem in Terris,* 11 April 1963: AAS 55 (1963), pp. 260-261; Pius XII, Radio Message, 24 Dec. 1942: AAS 35 (1943), p. 19; Pius XI Encyclical *Mit brennender Sorge,* 14 March 1937: AAS 29 (1937), p. 160; Leo XIII, Encyclical *Libertas praestantissimum,* 20 June 1888: *Acta Leonis XIII,* 8, 1888, pp. 237-238.

3. See St Thomas Aquinas, *Summa Theologiae,* I-II, q. 91, a. 1-2.

4. See John XXIII, Encyclical *Pacem in Terris,* 11 April 1963: AAS 55 (1963), p. 270; Paul VI, Radio Message 22 Dec. 1964: AAS 57 (1965), pp. 181-182; St Thomas Aquinas, *Summa Theologiae,* I-II, q. 91, a. 4.

5. See John XXIII, Encyclical *Mater et Magistra,* 15 May 1961: AAS 53 (1961), p. 417; Idem, Encyclical *Pacem in Terris,* 11 April 1963: AAS 55 (1963), p. 273.

6. See John XXIII, Encyclical *Pacem in Terris,* 11 April 1963: AAS 55 (1963), pp. 273-274; Pius XII, Radio Message, 1 June 1941. AAS 33 (1941), p. 200.

7. See Leo XIII, Encyclical *Immortale Dei,* 1 Nov. 1885: AAS 18 (1885), p. 161.

8. See Lactantius, *Divinarum Institutionum,* 5, 19: CSEL 19, pp. 463-464, 465; PL 6, 614 and 616 (ch. 20); St Ambrose, *Epistola ad Valentinianum Imp.,* Letter 21: PL 16, 1005; St Augustine, *Contra*

Litteras Petiliani, II, 83: CSEL 52 p. 112; PL 43, 315; see C. 3, q. 5, c. 33 (ed. Friedberg, col. 939); Idem, Letter 23: PL 33, 98; Idem, Letter 34: PL 33, 132, Idem, Letter 35: PL 33, 135; St. Gregory the Great, *Epistola ad Virgilium et Theodorum Episcopos Massiliae Galliarum*, Registrum Epistolarum I, 45: MGH Letter 1, p. 72: PL 77, 510-511 (bk. 1, ep. 47); Idem, *Epistola ad Iohannem Episcopum Constantinopolitanum*, Registrum Epistolarum III, 52; MGH Letter 1, p. 210; PL 77, 649 (bk. III, letter 53); CChr 140, 199. see D. 45, c. 1 (ed. Friedberg, col. 160); council. of Toledo, IV, c. 57: Mansi 10, 633; see D. 45, c. 5 (ed. Friedberg, col. 161-162); Clement III: Decretals, V, 6, 9 (ed. Friedberg, col. 774); Innocent III, *Epistola ad Arelatensem Archiepiscopum*, Decretals, III, 42, 3 (ed. Friedberg, col. 646).

9. See ClC, c. 1351; Pius XII, Allocution to the prelates, Auditors and other Ministers of the Tribunal of the Sacred Roman Rota, 6 Oct. 1946, p. 394; Idem, Encyclical *Mystici Corporis*, 29 June 1943, AAS 1943 p.243.

10. See Eph I:5.

11. See Jn 6:44.

12. See Jn 13:13.

13. See Mt 11:29.

14. See Mt 11:28-30; Jn 6:67-68.

15. See Mt 9:28-29; Mk 9:23-24; 6:5-6; Paul V, Encyclical *Ecclesiam Suam,* 6 Aug. 1964: AAS 56 (1964), pp. 642-643.

16. See Mt 11:20-24; Rom 12:19-20; 2 Th 1:8.

17. See Mt 13:30 and 40-42.

18. See Mt 4:8-10; Jn 6:15.

19. See Is 42:1-4.

20. See Jn 18:37.

21. See Mt 26 51-53; Jn 18:36.

22. See Jn 12:32.

23. See 1 Cor 2:3-5; 1 Th 2:3-5.

24. See Rom 14:1-23; 1 Cor 8:9-13; 10:23-33.

25. See Eph 6 :19-20.

26. See Rom 1:16.

27. See 2 Cor 10:4; 1 Th, 5:8-9.

28. See Eph 6:11-17.

29. See 2 Cor 10:3-5.

30. See 1 Pet 2:13-17.

31. See Acts 4:19-20.

32. See Leo XIII, Letter *Officio Sanctissimo,* 22 Dec. 1887: AAS 20 (1887), p. 269; Idem, Letter Ex *Litteris,* 7 April 1887: AAS 19 (1886), p. 465.

33. See Mk 16:15; Mt 28:18-20; Pius XII, Encyclical *Summi pontificatus,* 20 Oct. 1939: AAS 31 (1939), pp. 445-446.

34. See Pius XI, Letter *Firmissimam Constantiam,* 28 Mar. 1937: AAS 29 (1937), p. 196.

35. See Pius XII, Allocution *Ci riesce,* 6 Dec. 1953: AAS 45 (1953), p. 802.

36. See Pius XII, Radio message, 23 Mar. 1952: AAS 44 (1952), pp. 270-278.

37. See Acts 4:29.

38. See John XXIII Encyclical *Pacem in Terris,* 11 April 1963: AAS 55 (1963), pp. 299-300.

39. See John XXIII, Encyclical *Pacem in Terris,* 11 April 1963: AAS 55 (1963), pp. 295-296.

DECLARATION ON THE RELATION OF THE CHURCH TO NON-CHRISTIAN RELIGIONS[a]

Nostra Aetate
28 October, 1965

1. In our day, when people are drawing more closely together and the bonds of friendship between different peoples are being strengthened, the church examines more carefully its relations with non-christian religions. Ever aware of its duty to foster unity and charity among individuals, and even among nations, it reflects at the outset on what people have in common and what tends to bring them together.

Humanity forms but one community. This is so because all stem from the one stock which God created to people the entire earth (see Acts 17:26), and also because all share a common destiny, namely God. His providence, evident goodness, and saving designs extend to all humankind (see Wis 8:1; Acts 14:17; Rom 2:6-7; 1 Tim 2:4) against the day when the elect are gathered together in the holy city which is illumined by the glory of God, and in whose splendor all peoples will walk (see Apoc 21:23 ff.).

People look to their different religions for an answer to the unsolved riddles of human existence. The problems that weigh heavily on people's hearts are the same today as in past ages. What is humanity? What is the meaning and purpose of life? What is upright behavior, and what is sinful? Where does suffering originate, and what end does it serve? How can genuine happiness be found? What happens at death? What is judgment? What reward follows death? And finally, what is the ultimate mystery, beyond human explanation, which embraces our entire existence, from which we take our origin and towards which we tend?

2. Throughout history, to the present day, there is found among different peoples a certain awareness of a hidden power, which lies behind the course of nature and the events of human life. At times, there is present even a recognition of a supreme being, or still more of a Father. This awareness and recognition results in a way of life that is imbued with a deep religious sense. The religions which are found in more advanced civilizations endeavor by way of well-defined concepts and exact language to answer these questions. Thus, in Hinduism people explore the divine mystery and express it both in the limitless riches of myth and the accurately defined insights of philosophy. They seek release from the trials of the present life by ascetical practices, profound meditation and recourse to God in confidence and love. Buddhism in its various forms testifies to the essential inadequacy of this changing world. It proposes a way of life by which people can, with confidence and trust, attain a state of perfect liberation and reach supreme illumination either through their own efforts or with divine help. So, too, other religions which are found throughout the world attempt in different ways to overcome the restlessness of people's hearts by outlining a program of life covering doctrine, moral precepts and sacred rites.

The Catholic Church rejects nothing of what is true

and holy in these religions. It has a
manner of life and conduct, the p₁
trines which, although differing in man
own teaching, nevertheless often reflec.
truth which enlightens all men and wome
claims and is in duty bound to proclaim w.
Christ who is the way, the truth and the life
In him, in whom God reconciled all things to ₁
(see 2 Cor 5:18-19), people find the fullness of
religious life.

The church, therefore, urges its sons and daughte
to enter with prudence and charity into discussion
and collaboration with members of other religions.
Let Christians, while witnessing to their own faith
and way of life, acknowledge, preserve and encourage
the spiritual and moral truths found among non-
Christians, together with their social life and culture.

3. The church has also a high regard for the Muslims. They worship God, who is one, living and sub-
sistent, merciful and almighty, the Creator of heaven
and earth,[1] who has also spoken to humanity. They
endeavor to submit themselves without reserve to the
hidden decrees of God, just as Abraham submitted
himself to God's plan, to whose faith Muslims eagerly link their own. Although not acknowledging him as
God, they venerate Jesus as a prophet; his virgin
Mother they also honor, and even at times devoutly
invoke. Further, they await the day of judgment and
the reward of God following the resurrection of the
dead. For this reason they highly esteem an upright
life and worship God, especially by way of prayer,
alms-deeds and fasting.

Over the centuries many quarrels and dissensions
have arisen between Christians and Muslims. The
sacred council now pleads with all to forget the past,
and urges that a sincere effort be made to achieve
mutual understanding; for the benefit of all, let them

gether preserve and promote peace, liberty, social
justice and moral values.

4. Sounding the depths of the mystery which is the
church, this sacred council remembers the spiritual
ties which link the people of the new covenant to the
stock of Abraham.

The church of Christ acknowledges that in God's
plan of salvation the beginnings of its faith and election are to be found in the patriarchs, Moses and the
prophets. It professes that all Christ's faithful, who as
people of faith are daughters and sons of Abraham
(see Gal 3 :7), are included in the same patriarch's call
and that the salvation of the church is mystically prefigured in the exodus of God's chosen people from
the land of bondage. On this account the church cannot forget that it received the revelation of the Old
Testament by way of that people with whom God in
his inexpressible mercy established the ancient covenant. Nor can it forget that it draws nourishment from
that good olive tree onto which the wild olive branches of the Gentiles have been grafted (see Rom 11:17-
24). The church believes that Christ who is our peace
has through his cross reconciled Jews and Gentiles
and made them one in himself (see Eph 2:14-16).

Likewise, the church keeps ever before its mind the
words of the apostle Paul about his kin: "they are
Israelites, and it is for them to be sons and daughters,
to them belong the glory, the covenants, the giving of
the law, the worship, and the promises; to them belong the patriarchs, and of their race according to the
flesh, is the Christ" (Rom 9:4-5), the Son of the Virgin
Mary. It is mindful, moreover, that the apostles, the
pillars on which the church stands, are of Jewish
descent, as are many of those early disciples who proclaimed the Gospel of Christ to the world.

As holy scripture testifies, Jerusalem did not recognize God's moment when it came (see Lk 19:42). Jews

for the most part did not accept the Gospel; on the contrary, many opposed its spread (see Rom 11:28). Even so, the apostle Paul maintains that the Jews remain very dear to God, for the sake of the patriarchs, since God does not take back the gifts he bestowed or the choice he made.[2] Together with the prophets and that same apostle, the church awaits the day, known to God alone, when all peoples will call on God with one voice and "serve him shoulder to shoulder" (Soph 3:9; see Is 66:23; Ps 65:4; Rom 11:11-32).

Since Christians and Jews have such a common spiritual heritage, this sacred council wishes to encourage and further mutual understanding and appreciation. This can be achieved, especially, by way of biblical and theological enquiry and through friendly discussions.

Even though the Jewish authorities and those who followed their lead pressed for the death of Christ (see Jn 19:6), neither all Jews indiscriminately at that time, nor Jews today, can be charged with the crimes committed during his passion. It is true that the church is the new people of God, yet the Jews should not be spoken of as rejected or accursed as if this followed from holy scripture. Consequently, all must take care, lest in catechizing or in preaching the word of God, they teach anything which is not in accord with the truth of the Gospel message or the spirit of Christ.

Indeed, the church reproves every form of persecution against whomsoever it may be directed. Remembering, then, its common heritage with the Jews and moved not by any political consideration, but solely by the religious motivation of christian charity, it deplores all hatreds, persecutions, displays of anti-semitism levelled at any time or from any source against the Jews.

The church always held and continues to hold that

Christ out of infinite love freely underwent suffering and death because of the sins of all, so that all might attain salvation. It is the duty of the church, therefore, in its preaching to proclaim the cross of Christ as the sign of God's universal love and the source of all grace.

5. We cannot truly pray to God the Father of all if we treat any people as other than sisters and brothers, for all are created in God's image. People's relation to God the Father and their relation to other women and men are so dependent on each other that the Scripture says "they who do not love, do not know God" (1 Jn 4:8).

There is no basis therefore, either in theory or in practice for any discrimination between individual and individual, or between people and people arising either from human dignity or from the rights which flow from it.

Therefore, the church reproves, as foreign to the mind of Christ, any discrimination against people or any harassment of them on the basis of their race, color, condition in life or religion. Accordingly, following the footsteps of the holy apostles Peter and Paul, the sacred council earnestly begs the christian faithful to "conduct themselves well among the Gentiles" (1 Pet 2:12) and if possible, as far as depends on them, to be at peace with all people (see Rom 12:18) and in that way to be true daughters and sons of the Father who is in heaven (see Mt 5:45).

a.. Translated by Father Killian, OCSO. Revised for this edition by AF.

1. See St Gregory VII, Letter 21 to Anzir (Nacir), King of a. Mauretania: PL 148, col. 450 ff.

2. See Rom 11:28-29; see Vatican Council II, Dogmatic Constitution on the Church, *Lumen gentium.*

DECLARATION ON CHRISTIAN EDUCATION[a]

Gravissimum Educationis
28 October, 1965

Preface

The paramount importance of education in people's lives and its ever-growing influence on the social progress of the age are matters to which the holy ecumenical council has given careful consideration.[1] In fact, the education of youth, and indeed a certain ongoing education of adults, have been rendered both easier and more necessary by the circumstances of our times. As they become more conscious of their own dignity and responsibility, people are keen to take an increasingly active role in social life and especially in the economic and political spheres.[2] The wonderful progress in technical skill and scientific enquiry and the new means of social communication give people the opportunity of enjoying more leisure — and many of them take advantage of it — and of availing themselves of their birthright of culture of mind and spirit and of finding fulfillment in closer relations with other groups and nations. Accordingly, efforts are being made everywhere to ensure a continuing development of education. The fundamental rights which people, and especially children and parents, have in regard to education are being affirmed and made a matter of public record.[3] As the number of pupils is rapidly increasing, schools are being established far and wide, and other scholastic institutions are being opened. Methods of education and instruction are being developed by new experiments, and great efforts are being made to provide these services for all, although many children and young people are still without even elementary education, and many others are deprived of a suitable education — one inculcating simultaneously truth and charity.

For her part, holy mother church, in order to fulfil the mandate she received from her divine founder to announce the mystery of salvation to all and to renew all things in Christ, is committed to promoting people's welfare through their entire lives, including their life on earth insofar as it is related to their heavenly vocation;[4] she has therefore a part to play in the development and extension of education. Accordingly, the holy synod hereby promulgates some fundamental principles concerning christian education, especially in regard to schools. These principles should be more fully developed by a special postconciliar commission and should be adapted to the different local circumstances by episcopal conferences.

1. All people of whatever race, condition or age, in virtue of their dignity as human persons, have an inalienable right to education.[5] This education should be suitable to the particular destiny of the individuals,[6] adapted to their ability, sex and national cultural traditions, and should be conducive to amicable relations with other nations in order to promote true unity and peace in the world. True education aims to give people a formation which is directed towards their final end and the good of that society to which they belong and in which, as adults, they will have their share of duties to perform.

Due weight being given to the advances in psychological, pedagogical and intellectual sciences, children and young people should be helped to develop har-

moniously their physical, moral and intellectual qualities. They should be trained to acquire gradually a
more perfect sense of responsibility in the proper
development of their own lives by constant effort and
in the pursuit of liberty, overcoming obstacles with
unwavering courage and perseverance. As they grow
older, they should receive a positive and prudent sex
education. Moreover, they should be so prepared to
take their part in the life of society that, having been
duly trained in essential and useful skills, they may be
able to participate actively in the life of society in its
various aspects. They should be open to dialogue with
others and should willingly devote themselves to the
promotion of the common good.

Similarly, the sacred synod affirms that children
and young people have the right to be stimulated to
make sound moral judgments based on a well-
formed conscience and to put them into practice with
a sense of personal commitment, and to know and
love God more perfectly. Accordingly, it asks all those
who are involved in civil administration or in education to ensure that young people are never deprived
of this sacred right. It therefore urges the church's
daughters and sons to give their services generously
in the whole field of education, especially with the
aim of extending more rapidly the benefits of suitable
education and instruction throughout the world.[7]

2. All Christians — that is, all those who having
been reborn in water and the Holy Spirit[8] are called
and in fact are children of God — have a right to a
christian education. Such an education not only develops the maturity of the human person in the way
we have described, but is especially directed towards
ensuring that those who have been baptized, as they
are gradually introduced to a knowledge of the mystery of salvation, become daily more appreciative of
the gift of faith which they have received. They should

learn to adore God the Father in spirit and in truth (Jn 4:23), especially through the liturgy. They should be trained to live their own lives in the new self, justified and sanctified through the truth (Eph 4 22-24). Thus, they should truly develop as persons, proportioned to the completed growth of Christ (see Eph 4:13), and make their contribution to the growth of the Mystical Body. Moreover, conscious of their vocation they should learn to give witness to the hope that is in them (see 1 Pet 3:15) and to promote the christian concept of the world whereby the natural values, assimilated into the full understanding of humanity redeemed by Christ, may contribute to the good of society as a whole.[9] Accordingly the sacred synod directs the attention of pastors of souls to their very grave obligation to do all in their power to ensure that this christian education is enjoyed by all the faithful and especially by the young who are the hope of the church.[10]

3. Since it is the parents who have given life to their children, on them lies the gravest obligation of educating their family.[11] They must therefore be accepted as primarily and principally responsible for their education. The role of parents in education is of such importance that it is almost impossible to provide an adequate substitute. It is therefore the duty of parents to create a family atmosphere inspired by love and devotion to God and humanity which will promote an integrated, personal and social education of their children. The family is therefore the principal school of the social virtues which are necessary to every society. It is therefore, above all, in the christian family, inspired by the grace and the responsibility of the sacrament of Matrimony, that children should be taught to know and worship God and to love their neighbor, in accordance with the faith which they have received in earliest infancy in the sacrament of

Baptism. In it, also, they will have their first experience of a well-balanced human society and of the church. Finally it is through the family that they are gradually initiated into membership of civil society and of the people of God. Parents should, therefore, appreciate how important a role the truly christian family plays in the life and progress of the whole people of God.[12]

The task of imparting education belongs primarily to the family, but it requires the help of society as a whole. As well as the rights of parents, and of those others to whom the parents entrust some share in their duty to educate, there are certain duties and rights vested in civil society inasmuch as it is its function to provide for the common good in temporal matters. It is its duty to promote the education of youth in various ways. It should recognize the duties and rights of parents, and of those others who play a part in education, and provide them with the requisite assistance. In accordance with the principle of subsidiarity, when the efforts of the parents and of other organizations are inadequate it should itself undertake the duty of education, with due consideration, however, for the wishes of the parents. Finally, insofar as the common good requires it, it should establish its own schools and institutes.[13]

Education is, in a very special way, the concern of the church, not only because the church must be recognized as a human society capable of imparting education, but especially because it has the duty of proclaiming the way of salvation to all, of revealing the life of Christ to those who believe, and of assisting them with unremitting care so that they may be able to attain to the fullness of that life.[14]

The church as a mother is under an obligation, therefore, to provide for its children an education by virtue of which their whole lives may be inspired by the spirit of Christ. At the same time it will offer its assistance to all peoples for the promotion of a well-balanced perfection of the human personality, for the good of society in this world and for the development of a world worthy of humanity.[15]

4. In the exercise of its functions in education, the church is appreciative of every means that may be of service, but it relies especially on those which are essentially its own. Chief among these is catechetical instruction,[16] which illumines and strengthens the faith, develops a life in harmony with the spirit of Christ, stimulates a conscious and fervent participation in the liturgical mystery [17] and encourages people to take an active part in the apostolate. The church values highly those other educational media which belong to our common inheritance and which make a valuable contribution to the development of character and to people's formation. These it seeks to ennoble by imbuing them with its own spirit. Such are the media of social communication,[18] different groups devoted to the training of mind and body, youth associations and especially schools.

5. Among the various organs of education the school is of outstanding importance.[19] In nurturing the intellectual faculties which is its special mission, it develops a capacity for sound judgement and introduces the pupils to the cultural heritage bequeathed to them by former generations. It fosters a sense of values and prepares them for professional life. By providing for friendly contacts between pupils of different characters and backgrounds it encourages mutual understanding. Furthermore it constitutes a center in whose activity and growth not only the families and teachers but also the various associations for the promotion of cultural, civil and religious life, civic society, and the entire community should take part.

Splendid, therefore, and of the highest importance

is the vocation of those who help parents in carrying out their duties and act in the name of the community by undertaking a teaching career. This vocation requires special qualities of mind and heart, most careful preparation and a constant readiness to accept new ideas and to adapt the old.

6. Parents, who have a primary and inalienable duty and right in regard to the education of their children, should enjoy the fullest liberty in their choice of school. The public authority, therefore, whose duty it is to protect and defend the liberty of the citizens, is bound according to the principles of distributive justice to ensure that public subsidies to schools are so allocated that parents are truly free to select schools for their children in accordance with their conscience.[20]

But it is the duty of the state to ensure that all its citizens have access to an adequate education and are prepared for the proper exercise of their civic rights and duties. The state itself, therefore, should safeguard the rights of children to an adequate education in schools. It should be vigilant about the ability of the teachers and the standard of teaching. It should watch over the health of the pupils and in general promote the work of the schools in its entirety. In this, however, the principle of subsidiarity must be borne in mind, and therefore there must be no monopoly of schools which would be prejudicial to the natural rights of the human person and would militate against the progress and extension of education, and the peaceful coexistence of citizens. It would, moreover, be inconsistent with the pluralism which exists today in many societies.[21]

Accordingly the sacred synod urges the faithful to cooperate readily in the development of suitable methods of education and systems of study and in the training of teachers competent to give a good education to their pupils. They are urged also to further by their efforts, and especially by associations of parents, the entire range of the schools' activities and in particular the moral education given in them.[22]

7. Acknowledging its grave obligation to see to the moral and religious education of all its children, the church should give special attention and help to the great number of them who are being taught in non-catholic schools. This will be done by the living example of those who teach and have charge of these children and by the apostolic action of their fellow-students,[23] but especially by the efforts of those priests and lay people who teach them christian doctrine in a manner suited to their age and background and who provide them with spiritual help by means of various activities adapted to the requirements of time and circumstance.

Parents are reminded of their grave obligation to make all necessary arrangements and even to insist that their children may be able to take advantage of these services and thus enjoy a balanced progress in their christian formation and their preparation for life in the world. For this reason the church is deeply grateful to those public authorities and associations which, taking into consideration the pluralism of contemporary society, and showing due respect for religious liberty, assist families to ensure that the education of their children in all schools is given in accordance with the moral and religious principles of the family.[24]

8. The church's role is especially evident in catholic schools. These are no less zealous than other schools in the promotion of culture and in the human formation of young people. It is, however, the special function of the catholic school to develop in the school community an atmosphere animated by a spirit of liberty and charity based on the Gospel. It enables

young people, while developing their own personalities to grow at the same time in that new life which has been given them in Baptism. Finally it so directs the whole of human culture to the message of salvation that the knowledge which the pupils acquire of the world, of life and of humanity is illumined by faith.[25] Thus the catholic school, open, as it should be, to modern developments, prepares its pupils to contribute effectively to the welfare of humanity and to work for the extension of the kingdom of God, so that by living an exemplary and apostolic life they may be, as it were, a saving leaven in the community.

Accordingly, since the catholic school can be of such service in developing the mission of the people of God and in promoting dialogue between the church and the community at large to the advantage of both, it is still of vital importance even in our times. The sacred synod therefore affirms once more the right of the church freely to establish and conduct schools of all kinds and grades, a right which has already been asserted time and again in many documents of the magisterium.[26] It emphasizes that the exercise of this right is of the utmost importance for the preservation of liberty of conscience, for the protection of the rights of parents, and for the advancement of culture itself.

Teachers must remember that it depends chiefly on them whether the catholic school achieves its purpose.[27] They should therefore be properly prepared for their work, having the appropriate qualifications and adequate learning both religious and secular. They should also be skilled in the art of education in accordance with the discoveries of modern times. Possessed by charity both towards each other and towards their pupils, and inspired by an apostolic spirit, they should bear testimony by their lives and their teaching to the one teacher, who is Christ.

Above all, they should work in close cooperation with the parents. In the entire educational program they should, together with the parents, make full allowance for the difference of sex and for the particular role which providence has appointed to each sex in the family and in society. They should endeavor to awaken in their pupils a spirit of personal initiative and, even after they have left school, they should continue to help them with their advice and friendship and by the organization of special groups imbued with the true spirit of the church. The sacred synod declares that the services of such teachers constitute an active apostolate, one which is admirably suited to our times and indeed is very necessary. At the same time, they render a valuable service to society. Catholic parents are reminded of their duty to send their children to catholic schools wherever this is possible, to give catholic schools all the support in their power, and to cooperate with them in their work for the good of their children.[28]

9. Although catholic schools may vary in kind from place to place, all schools which are in any way dependent on the church should conform as far as possible to this prototype.[29] Furthermore the church attaches particular importance to schools, especially in the territories of newly founded churches, which include non-catholics among their pupils.

Moreover, in establishing and conducting catholic schools one must keep modern developments in mind. Accordingly, while one may not neglect primary and intermediate schools, which provide basic education, one should attach considerable importance to those establishments which are especially necessary nowadays, such as: professional[30] and technical colleges, institutes for adult education and for the promotion of social work, institutions for the handicapped, and training colleges for teachers of religion and of other branches of education.

The sacred synod earnestly exhorts the pastors of the church and all the faithful to spare no sacrifice in helping catholic schools to become increasingly effective, especially in caring for the poor, for those who are without family ties, and for non-believers.

10. The church likewise devotes considerable care to higher-level education, especially in universities and faculties. Indeed, in the institutions under its control the church endeavors systematically to ensure that the treatment of the individual disciplines is consonant with their own principles, their own methods, and with a true liberty, of scientific enquiry. Its object is that a progressively deeper understanding of them may be achieved, and by a careful attention to the current problems of these changing times and to the research being undertaken, the convergence of faith and reason in the one truth may be seen more clearly. This method follows the tradition of the doctors of the church and especially St Thomas Aquinas.[31] Thus, the christian outlook should acquire, as it were, a public, stable and universal influence in the whole process of the promotion of higher culture. The graduates of these institutes should be outstanding in learning, ready to undertake the more responsible duties of society, and to be witnesses in the world to the true faith.[32]

In catholic universities in which there is no faculty of theology there should be an institute or course of theology in which lectures may be given suited also to the needs of lay students. Since the advance of knowledge is secured especially by research into matters of major scientific importance, every effort should be made in catholic universities and faculties to develop departments for the advancement of scientific research.

The sacred synod earnestly recommends the establishment of catholic universities and faculties strategically distributed throughout the world, but they should be noteworthy not so much for their numbers as for their high standards. Entry to them should be made easy for students of great promise but of modest resources, and especially for those from newly developed countries.

There is a close correlation between the progress made by students doing higher studies and the well-being of society and of the church itself.[33] For this reason, not only should pastors of the church see to the spiritual life of students attending catholic universities, they should also, in their solicitude for the spiritual formation of all their flock, establish by joint episcopal action catholic residences and centers even in the non-catholic universities. In these, priests, religious and lay people, carefully chosen and prepared for the task, should provide permanent centers of guidance, spiritual and intellectual, for the students. Special interest should be taken in young people of outstanding ability, whether they be students of catholic or other universities, who seem to be suited to teaching or research, and they should be encouraged to adopt an academic career.

11. The church anticipates great benefits from the activities of the faculties of the sacred sciences.[34] For to them she confides the very grave responsibility of preparing her own students, not only for the priestly ministry, but especially either for teaching in the institutes of higher ecclesiastical study, or for the advancement of learning by their own investigations, or finally by undertaking the even more exacting duties of the intellectual apostolate. It is the function also of these faculties to promote research in the different fields of sacred learning. Their object will be to ensure that an ever-growing understanding of sacred revelation be achieved, that the inheritance of christian wis-

dom handed down by former generations be more
fully appreciated, that dialogue with our separated
brothers and sisters and with non-Christians be promoted, and that problems posed by advances in
knowledge be addressed.[35]

Therefore the ecclesiastical faculties, having made
such revision of their own statutes as seems opportune, should do all in their power to promote the
sacred sciences and related branches of learning, and
by the employment of modern methods and aids they
should train their students for higher research.

12. As cooperation, which is becoming daily more
important and more effective at diocesan, national
and international levels, is very necessary also in the
educational sphere, every care should be taken to encourage suitable coordination between catholic
schools. Such collaboration between these and other
schools as the welfare of the whole community requires should also be developed.[36]

A greater measure of coordination and the undertaking of joint activities will be especially fruitful in
academic institutes. In every university, therefore, the
various faculties should assist each other insofar as
their particular provinces permit. The universities also
should combine in joint enterprises, such as organizing international congresses and allotting scientific
research among themselves. They should also communicate the results of their research to each other,
interchange professors on a temporary basis, and in
general promote all measures which may be mutually helpful.

Conclusion

The sacred synod appeals to the students themselves to appreciate the excellence of the teaching vocation and to show a readiness to undertake it generously, especially in those countries where the educa-

tion of young people is at risk because of a shortage of teachers.

The sacred synod furthermore affirms its deep gratitude to those priests, men and women religious, and laity who in a spirit of evangelical dedication have devoted themselves to the all important work of education and schools of all kinds and grades. It urges them to persevere generously in the work they have undertaken, and to strive so to excel in inspiring their pupils with the spirit of Christ, in their mastery of the art of teaching, and in their zeal for learning that they may not only promote the internal renewal of the church but also maintain and augment its beneficial presence in the world today and especially in the intellectual sphere.

a. Translated by Matthew Dillon, OSB Revised for this edition by AF.

1. Among many documents, see especially: Benedict XV, Apostolic Letter *Communes Litteras*, 10 April 1919: AAS 11 (1919) p. 172; Pius XI, Encyclical *Divini Illius Magistri*, 31 Dec. 1929: AAS 22 (1930) pp. 49-86; Pius XII, Allocution to youths of Ital. Cath. Action, 20 April 1946: See *Discorsi e Radiomessaggi*, vol. 8, pp. 53-57; Pius XII, Allocution to fathers of Families of France, 18 Sept. 1951: *Discorsi e Radiomessaggi*, vol. 13, pp. 241-245; John XXIII, message on 30th anniv. of *Divini Illius Magistri*, 30 Dec. 1959: AAS 52 (1960) pp. 57-59; Paul VI, Allocution to Fed. Instits., 30 Dec. 1963: *Encicliche e Discorsi di Paulo VI*, vol. I, Rome 1964, pp. 601-603; there may be consulted also *Acta et Documenta Conc. Oecum. Vat. II apparando*, series I, *Antepraeparatoria*, vol. 3, pp. 363-364, 370-371, 373, 374.

2. See John XXIII, Encyclical *Mater et Magistra*, 15 May 1961: AAS 53 (1961) p. 402, 413, 415-417, 424; and Encyclical *Pacem in terris*, 11 April 1963: AAS 55 (1963) pp. 278 ff.

3. See *United Nations' Universal Profession of the Rights of Man*, 10 Dec. 1948; and, in conjunction, John XXIII, Encyclical *Pacem in Terris*, 11 April 1963: AAS 55 (1963) pp. 295 ff.; also UN *Declaration on the Right of the Child*, 20 Nov. 1959; also *Protocole additionnel, à la convention de sauvegarde des droits de l'homme et des libertés fondamentales*, Paris, 20 March 1952.

4. See John XXIII, Encyclical *Mater et Magistra*, 15 May 1961: AAS 53 (1961) p. 402; also Vatican Council II, Dogmatic Constitution on the Church, *Lumen gentium*, n. 17: AAS 57 (1965) p. 21.

5. See Pius XII, Radio message 24 Dec. 1924: AAS 35 (1943) pp. 12, 19; John XXIII, Encyclical *Pacem in Terris*, 11 Apr. 1963: AAS 55

(1963) p. 259 ff.; also see declarations in note (3) above.

6. See Pius XI, Encyclical *Divini Illius s Magistri,* 31 Dec. 1929: AAS 22 (1930) p. 50 ff.

7. See John XXIII, Encyclical *Mater et Magistra,* 15 May 1961; AAS 53 (1961) p. 441 ff.

8. See Pius XI, Encyclical *Divini Illius Magistri,* loc. cit., p 83.

9. See Vatican Council II, Dogmatic Constitution on the Church, *Lumen gentium* n. 36: ,AAS 57 (1965) p.41 ff.

10. See Vatican Council II, Decree on the Pastoral Function of Bishops, *Christus Dominus,* n. 12-14. 11. See Pius XI, Encyclical *Divini Illius Magistri,* loc. cit., p. 50 ff.; Encyclical. *Mit brennender Sorge,* 14 March 1937: AAS 29 (1937) p. 164 ff., also Pius XII, Allocution to Ital. Cath. Teachers, 8 Sept. 1946: *Discorsi e Radio- messaggi,* vol. 8, p. 218.

12. See Vatican Council II, Dogmatic Constitution on the Church, *Lumen gentium* n. 11, 35: AAS 57 (1965) pp. 16, 40 ff.

13. See Pius XI, Encyclical *Divini Illius Magistri,* loc. cit. p. 63 ff.; Pius XII, Radio Message, 1 June 1941: AAS 33 (1941) p. 200; Allocution to Cath. Teachers, 8 Sept. 1946: *Discorsi e Radiomessaggi,* vol. 8, p. 218; re principle of subsidiarity, see John XXIII, Encyclical *Pacem in Terris,* 11 April 1963: AAS 44 (1963) p. 294.

14. See Pius XI, Encyclical *Divini Illius Magistri,* loc. cit. p. 53 ff. and 56 ff., also Encyclical *Non abbiamo bisogno,* 29 June 1931: AAS 23 (1931) p. 311 ff.; Pills XII, Letter to Italian Social Week 20 Sept. 1955: *L'Osservatore Romano,* 29 Sept. 1955.

15. The church praises civil authorities — local, national and international — who through an awareness of the urgent needs of the present age, work indefatigably so that all people may enjoy a fuller education and human culture. See Paul VI, Allocution to U.N. Assembly, 4 Oct. 1965: AAS (1965) pp. 877-885.

16. See Pius XI, Motu Proprio *Orbem Catholicum,* 29 June 1923: AAS 15 (1923) pp. 327-329; Decree *Provido sane* 12 An 1935: AAS 27 (1935) pp. 145-152; Vat. 11 Decree on the Pastoral Function of Bishops in the Church, nn 13-14

17. See Vatican Council II, Constitution on the Sacred Liturgy, *Sacrosanctum Concilium,* n. 14: AAS 56 (1964) p.104

18. See Vatican Council II, Decree on the Mass Media, *Inter mir- ifica,* nn. 13-14: AAS 56 (1964) pp. 149 ff.

19. See Pius XI Encyclical *Divini Illius Magistri,* loc cit. p. 76; Pius XII, Allocution to Assoc. of Cath. Teachers of Bavaria, 31 Dec 1956; *Discorsi e Radiomessaggi,* vol 18. p 746

20. See III Prov. Council of Cincinnati (1861); Pius XI, Encyclical *Divini Illius Magistri,* loc. cit., p. 60, 63 ff.

21. See Pius XI, Encyclical *Divini Illius Magistri,* loc. cit. p. 63; also Encyclical *Non abbiamo bisogno,* 29 June 1931: AAS 23 (1931) p. 305; also Pius XII, Letter to 28th Ital. Social Week, 20 Sept. 1955 *L'Osservatore Romano,* 29 Sept. 1955; also Paul VI Allocution to Christian Assoc. of Ital. Workers, 6 Oct. 1963: *Encicliche e Discorsi di*

Paolo VI, vol. 1, Rome, 1964, p. 230.

22. See John XXIII, Message for 30th Anniv. of *Div. Illius Magistri,* 30 Dec. 1959: AAS 52 (1960) p. 57.

23. The church places a high value upon the apostolic action which catholic teachers and those associated with them are able to perform even in these schools.

24. See Pius XII, Allocution to Assoc. of Cath. Teachers of Bavaria, 31 Dec. 1956: *Discorsi e Radiomessaggi,* vol 18, pp. 745 ff.

25. See First Prov. Council of Westminster (1852, *Collectio Lacensis,* vol. 3, col. 1334, a/b; also Pius XI, Encyclical Div. *Illius Magistri,* loc. cit., pp. 77 ff.; also Pius XII, Allocution to Assoc. of Cath Teachers of Bavaria, loc. cit. p. 746; also Paul VI, Allocution to federated Institutes, 30 Dec. 1963: *Encicliche e Discorsi di Paolo* VI, vol. 1, Rome, 1964, pp. 602 ff.

26. See most importantly the documents recommended in (l); in addition, this right of the church is proclaimed by many provincial councils and in the most recent declarations of many episcopal conferences.

27. See Pius XI, Encyclical *Div. Illius Magistri, loc. cit.,* pp. 80 ff.; also Pius XII, Allocution to Ital. Secondary Teachers, 5 Jan. 1954: *Discorsi e Radiomessaggi, vol. 15,* pp. 551-556, also John XXIII, Allocution to Ital. Assoc. of Cath. Teachers, 5 Sept. 1959: *Discorsi, Messaggi, Colloqui,* vol. 1, Rome, 1960, pp. 427-431.

28. See Pius, *Allocution to* Ital. Secondary Teachers, 5 Jan. 1954 *loc.* cit. p. 555.

29. See Paul VI, *Allocution* to Internat. Office of Cath. Education, 25 Feb. 1964: *Encicliche e Discorsi* di Paolo VI, vol. 2, Rome, 1964, p. 232.

30. See Paul VI, *Allocution* to Ital. Workers, 6 Oct. 1963: loc. cit. vol. 1, Rome, 1964, p. 229.

31. See Paul VI, *Allocution* to 6th Internat. Thomistic Congr. 10 Sept. 1965: AAS 57 (1965) pp. 788-792.

32. See Pius XII, *Allocution to* Higher Institutes of France, 21 Sept. 1950: *Discorsi e Radiomessaggi,* vol. 12, pp. 219-221; Letter to 22nd Congr. of *Pax Romana,* 12 Aug. 1952: *loc. cit.,* vol. 14 pp. 567-569; John XXIII, Allocution *to* Fed. of Cath. Universities, 1 April 1959: *Discorsi, Messaggi, Colloqui, vol. 1,* Roma, 1960, pp. 226-229; Paul VI, *Allocution* to Acad. Senate of University of Milan, 5 April 1964 *Encicliche e Discorsi di Paolo VI,* vol. 2, Rome, 1964, pp. 438-443.

33. See Pius XII, *Allocution* to Acad. Senate of Univ. of Rome, 15 June 1952, *Discorsi e Radiomessaggi,* vol. 14, p. 208: "The direction which society will take tomorrow will be largely decided by the mind and heart of university students of today."

34. See Pius XI, Apost. Constit. *Deus Scientiarum Dominus,* 24 May, 1931: AAS 23 (1931) pp. 245-247.

35. See Pius XII, Encyclical *Humani Generis,* 12 Aug. 1950: AAS 42 (1950) pp. 568 ff., 578; also Paul VI, Encyclical *Ecclesiam suam,* Part 3, 6 Aug. 1964: AAS 56 (1964) pp. 637-659; also Vatican Council

II, Decree on Ecumenism, *Unitatis redintegratio.*

36. See John XXIII, Encyclical *Pacem in Terris*, 11 April 1963: AAS 55 (1963) p. 284 and *passim.*

Index

Language of the liturgy, 130, 131, 132, 133, 136, 137, 139, 140, 141, 142, 150, 152, 153, 154, 158-159. *See also* Liturgy
  Eastern Churches, 532
  Latin, 130, 148
Last Supper
  institution of the Eucharist, 134, 135
Latin language, 130, 148
  translation from, 130
Lauds, 145
Law, Divine
  religious freedom and, 554
Lay apostolate. *See* Apsotolate
Lay Brothers, 392, 397. *See also* Religious persons
Lent, 151-152
Liberty of religion. *See* Religious liberty
Life, Conduct of. *See* Conduct of life
Little Offices. *See* Divine Office
Liturgical books
  revision of, 126-130, 131, 158
Liturgical celebrations. *See* Liturgy; Rites and ceremonies
Liturgical commissions, 133, 134
Liturgical education, 125
  music, 152-155
  of the clergy, 150
Liturgical laws
  authority, 126-127
  clergy and, 125
  reform of the liturgy, 129-131
  Sacred art and furnishings, 156-159
Liturgical life
  clergy, 133
  diocesan, 132-133
  laity, 125
  parish, 132-133
  promotion of, 132-133
  sacrifice and sacraments, 120
Liturgical movement, 133

Liturgical reform. *See* Reform of the liturgy
Liturgical services. *See* Liturgy; Rites and ceremonies. *See also* Particular rites, e.g., Marriage rite
Liturgical year, 149-152
  martyrs and saints, 152
  Mary in, 149
  Proper of the Time, 151
  revision, 150-151
  sacred music, 152-155
Liturgy, 117-161. *See also* Language of the liturgy; Mystical Body; Rites and ceremonies
  Bible in, 127
  devotions, popular, 123
  foretaste of heavenly liturgy, 121
  grace and, 122
  importance of, 117-124
  in adjacent regions, 131
  in Latin, 130
  laity and, 125
  Lenten, 151
  local adaptation of, 131, 139, 150, 154
  nature of, 119-124
  pastors and the, 123
  priestly office of Christ, 121
  reform of, 117, 126-134
  regulation of by bishops, 127, 132-133
  restoration and promotion of, 117-134
  translations from Latin, 131
Lord's day. *See* Sunday
Love. *See also* Charity
  agape, 414
  in marriage, 218-228
  of enemies, 193-194
  of God, 203-205
  of neighbors, 188
Lumen Gentium, 385
Luxury
  renunciation of, 395